HOLLYWOOD**TV**

THE STUDIO SYSTEM IN THE FIFTIES

HOLLY

Texas Film Studies Series
Thomas Schatz, Editor

WOODTV

The Studio System in the Fifties

by **Christopher Anderson**

UNIVERSITY OF TEXAS PRESS   AUSTIN

First edition, 1994

Requests for permission to reproduce material
from this work should be sent to
Permissions, **University of Texas Press,**
Box 7819, Austin, TX 78713-7819.

⊗ The paper used in this publication
meets the minimum requirements of
American National Standard for Information Sciences—
Permanence of Paper for Printed Library Materials,
ANSI Z39.48-1984.

Library of Congress Cataloging-in-Publication Data

Anderson, Christopher, 1960–
Hollywood TV : the studio system in the fifties / by Christopher
Anderson.
        p.   cm. — (Texas film studies series)
Includes bibliographical references and index.
ISBN 0-292-73059-4. — ISBN 0-292-70457-7 (PBK.)
1. Television—United States—Production and direction.
2. Motion picture studios—California—Los Angeles—His-
tory.   3. Motion pictures and television—United States.
                                        I. Title.   II. Series.
                                        PN1992.75.A49   1994
        384.55'4'097309045—dc20   93-37276

To
Sharon
and
Calvin Anderson

Contents

Acknowledgments

By guiding me through the Warner Bros. and David O. Selznick archives, several people made it possible to conceive of a book about television production in 1950s Hollywood. I would like to thank Charles Bell, Prentiss Moore, and Steve Wilson of the Harry Ransom Humanities Research Center, University of Texas, Mary Anne Jensen of the Firestone Library, Princeton University, and particularly Leith Adams of the Department of Special Collections, University of Southern California, who shared his knowledge of the Warner Bros. collection and provided many valuable ideas about TV production at the studio. I would like to thank Madeline F. Matz at the Library of Congress. I also would like to thank those who worked at Warner Bros. Television and who graciously agreed to take time to talk with me about their experiences: William T. Orr, Roy Huggins, Hugh Benson, Harry Tatleman, Richard Bare.

I am indebted to friends and teachers from the University of Texas for providing the inspiration to begin writing this book. I would like to thank Joli Jensen, Janet Staiger, and Douglas Kellner for their comments on early versions of the manuscript. Horace Newcomb first encouraged me to write about television; his advice and support over the years have been invaluable. I am grateful also to many friends who have continued to share ideas and moral support, though we are now scattered across the country: Jeff Sconce, Mark Alvey, Hilary Radner, John Gibson, Jim Wehmeyer, Barbara Wehmeyer, Mark Fenster, Steve Lee, Steve Fore, and James Hay.

I am also indebted to friends, students, and colleagues at Indiana University, where I completed the book. I have received valuable support from my colleagues in the Department of Telecommunications, especially Don Agostino and Kathy Krendl, who as successive departmental chairs encouraged this project in countless ways. Through their patience and generosity, Beverly Stoeltje, Richard Bauman, James

Naremore, and Barbara Klinger have provided the supportive environment that is essential to the writing process. Michael Curtin has spent endless hours discussing this project with me and has read the manuscript at several stages in its development. His thoughtful criticism and enthusiasm for the project have made my task easier.

I have benefited from the patience and support of Frankie Westbrook, my editor at the University of Texas Press. I am most deeply indebted to series editor Tom Schatz, who literally has been involved in this project since its first moment of existence—when he introduced me to the Warner Bros. archives. Since that time this manuscript, in one form or another, has accompanied him across the globe, from the floor of the Grand Canyon to the shores of the Baltic. We have covered many miles during our ongoing conversation about Hollywood and television—never more literally than during an exhausting all-night transatlantic flight—yet his commitment to the project has never wavered. I could not have written this book without him.

Finally, I'd like to thank Rachael Stoeltje. While others read the finished product, she lived through the process. Only a strong person would prefer the latter.

HOLLYWOOD**TV**

THE STUDIO SYSTEM IN THE FIFTIES

·|·
Introduction:
Hollywood
in the Home

The transformation of the American motion picture industry following World War II has been viewed as a rupture, a crisis so grave that it forced the major studios to abandon or adulterate many of the practices that had virtually defined the Hollywood studio system since the 1920s. For those who worked within the film industry, the decade of the 1950s has been depicted as the decline and fall of an empire, a time of bewilderment in New York boardrooms and panic on Hollywood backlots. Screenwriter Robert Ardrey has described a scene in the exclusive Green Room at the Warner Bros. commissary during this era. Fresh from examining the latest sagging box office figures, Jack Warner burst into the dining hall, jabbing at contract producers and writers as they ate their lunches. "I can do without you! And you! And you! I can do without you!" he exclaimed as he strode defiantly among the tables. Suddenly face to face with Jerry Wald, by far the studio's most successful producer, Warner paused for an instant and then shouted, "I can *almost* do without you!"[1]

While such tales of temporary madness are probably apocryphal, they have fascinated fans, scholars, and even those who participated in the events, coloring memories of the era and shaping historical accounts. When once-powerful industry leaders such as Darryl Zanuck, Louis B. Mayer, and David O. Selznick fell from grace in the industrial reorganization of the 1950s, they perceived their enforced exile in epic terms, as a barbaric attack on Hollywood's glorious tradition. Selznick, in a letter to his friend and former partner John Hay Whitney, depicted the 1950s as the movie industry's Dark Ages: "Our old stomping ground, what is laughingly known as the motion picture industry, is very mixed up and unhappy. Whatever the weakness of the old and rugged pioneers, who are all disappearing from the scene almost simultaneously—what a hardy race they were!—their successors are pygmies by comparison. There is no leadership; all is chaos."[2]

Since stories of imperial decay draw their strength from nostalgia, it is no wonder that television, the era's new technology of mass entertainment, often played the antagonist in the mythic version of Hollywood's postwar crisis. And while television was not the sole cause of the changes that took place in Hollywood during the late 1940s and early 1950s, one can appreciate the movie industry's reported hostility toward a medium that threatened to displace the motion picture as the preeminent cultural commodity in twentieth-century America. Most hostile were the studio bosses; indeed, tales of Jack Warner's early animosity toward television are legendary. Studio personnel say that during the early 1950s Warner delivered an edict to producers at his studio, forbidding them to include television sets in the decor of Warner Bros. films. From our vantage point in a world saturated by television, it is hard to believe that a TV set could trigger such desperate measures from one of Hollywood's most venerable moguls, yet Warner was scarcely alone in voicing his animosity toward the industry's emergent competitor.

Throughout the early 1950s, the industry trade press debated whether television ultimately would reveal itself to be friend or foe of the movie studios. As television began its unprecedented expansion following World War II, revenues throughout the motion picture industry plunged dramatically. Warner Bros. suffered some of the worst losses, with net profits falling from a record $22 million in 1947 to $2.9 million in 1953—a decline of nearly 90 percent in just six years.[3] Under conditions that threatened the very existence of the studio system, television served many in the Hollywood community as a convenient stock villain.

Yet Hollywood did not view television from a single perspective, or from a consistently antagonistic posture. In spite of the movie industry's legendary antipathy, the aversion of the major studios to TV actually lasted only a few short years during the early 1950s, and it was provoked not by fear of competition or ignorance of a new technology but by government decisions that essentially surrendered control of the television industry to the radio networks and erased any hopes that the studios had of forming competitive networks.

Even during the period when executives at the major studios demonized television, many independent producers and smaller studios embraced the opportunity to produce films for the new medium.[4] Long excluded from the lucrative profits guaranteed the major studios by their restrictive system of distribution and exhibition, independent producers looked upon TV as an open market, a new exhibition outlet beyond the stifling grasp of the major studios. Although the future of the telefilm business was far from certain in 1950, the atmosphere of opportunity among Hollywood's independent producers was similar to that of the film industry's earliest days, before the major studios dominated the business.

In network TV's early days, independent telefilm production companies were formed by a varied cast of entrepreneurs: émigrés from the major studios (Jerry Fairbanks), former B-movie makers (Hal Roach, Jr.), radio syndicators (Frederick Ziv), talent agencies (Music Corporation of America, or MCA), real estate investors (Lou Snader), oilmen (Jack Wrather), and, most prominently, actors (Bing Crosby, Jack Webb, Lucille Ball, and Desi Arnaz). In 1951 these producers began to leave their mark on the medium. During the fall of that year, Ball and Arnaz premiered *I Love Lucy* (1951–1957), the first filmed situation comedy to have a national impact. Webb followed later that season with *Dragnet* (1952–1959), the first successful crime series shot on film. Within a year *I Love Lucy* and *Dragnet* stood atop the network ratings as the most popular series on TV.

By mid-decade, as the television audience expanded, even old guard Hollywood leaders discovered incentives to produce for television. The month of October 1954 stands out as a key transitional moment in the relations between Hollywood's major powers and the TV industry. Early in the month, Columbia Pictures became the first major studio to produce episodic TV series when its TV subsidiary, Screen Gems, premiered *The Adventures of Rin Tin Tin* on the American Broadcasting Company (ABC) (1954–1959) and *Father Knows Best* on the Columbia Broadcasting System (CBS) (1954–1963). Within three days in late October, two of the film industry's top independent producers, David O. Selznick and Walt Disney, joined the migration to prime time.

Selznick made Hollywood's most auspicious debut with a two-hour celebration of electricity and American enterprise titled *Light's Diamond Jubilee*. The movie industry's most famous independent producer, Selznick had achieved a reputation for glamour and craftsmanship with such epic movies as *Gone with the Wind* (1939) and *Duel in the Sun* (1946). His prime-time debut extended this reputation to television by introducing to the medium such renowned movie talents as directors King Vidor and William Wellman, writer Ben Hecht, and actors Joseph Cotten, Helen Hayes, Thomas Mitchell, Lauren Bacall, and David Niven—and by featuring an unlikely performer in a commercial broadcast, President Dwight D. Eisenhower. Sponsored by the electric industry, this program capped a yearlong celebration of Thomas Edison's invention of the incandescent light bulb seventy-five years earlier. Thanks to the financial support of the electric industry, Selznick's extravaganza monopolized the airwaves as few commercial broadcasts ever have, appearing on almost every existing TV station and capturing the largest viewing audience in the new medium's history. On that Sunday night in late October, loyal viewers of NBC's (National Broadcasting Company) *Colgate Comedy Hour*, CBS's *Toast of the Town*, ABC's *Flight #7*, and the beleaguered DuMont Television Network's *Rocky King, Detective*, found their prime-time routines disrupted by this inescapable broadcast. In a year during which television viewers were confronted with a number of so-called spectacular, one-of-a-kind events, *Light's Diamond Jubilee* was still unique, the most ambitious program that Hollywood had offered television to that point.

Selznick's program attracted considerable attention, but Disney's premiere of *Disneyland* three days later was just as eagerly anticipated by television viewers. Disney had forged a reputation as the cinema's maestro of family entertainment; now his TV series promised to deliver what *Time* described as "the true touch of enchantment" to American homes. In spite of the technological limitations of the black-and-white TV set, especially its inability to reproduce animation's color spectacle, Disney expected the home video receiver to replace the movie theater as the portal to the Disney universe. In fact, as the title of the series suggests, *Disneyland* offered television viewers a reward that moviegoers couldn't share—privileged witness to the embodiment of "Walt's dream," the Disneyland amusement park then under construction. During the weeks that followed the premiere of *Disneyland*, the nation awoke to Walt's dream of an innovative amusement park designed expressly for the country's baby-boom families.

In reviews of the week's TV fare, critics recognized that the Selznick and Disney productions were milestones in the budding relations between the two media. "The two best TV shows of last week—and perhaps of this year," *Time* magazine reported, "originated in Hollywood and were created by veteran moviemakers."[5] Thus, by October 1954 filmed television production was no longer solely the dominion of companies on the distant fringes of the studio system but had become a viable option for the most well-established Hollywood producers. The major studios—led by Warner Bros., Twentieth Century–Fox, and MGM—joined the field during the 1955 season. Over the next four years, Hollywood studios became the predominant suppliers of the networks' prime-time programming.[6]

The remarkable commitment by the major studios to television production can be illustrated with many examples, but the conversion at Warner Bros. was particularly telling. In January 1959, after decades in the movie business and only four years in TV, Warner Bros. found itself without a single theatrical motion picture in front of the cameras. The studio had not abandoned movie production, of course, but it had embraced series television, emerging as the single largest source of network series. Its eight different series—led by the hits *Cheyenne* (1955–1962), *Maverick* (1957–1962), and *77 Sunset Strip* (1958–1964)— filled over one-third of ABC-TV's prime-time schedule and generated $30 million in annual revenue from network license fees alone. In order to meet the network's demand for programming, the studio had geared up its operations to produce the equivalent of a full-length feature film *each working day*. Even during periods when feature production slumped, TV production kept the studio bursting with activity. As a result, Jack Warner's early animosity toward the medium soon gave way to a pragmatic enthusiasm. "Television," he asserted during a speech in June 1959, "has been a very healthy influence on the motion picture industry. It's the ninth wonder of the world."[7] Warner's decade-long passage from antipathy to enchantment suggests just how much the stakes of movie and TV production changed for the major studios during the 1950s.

Of course, Selznick and Disney were not the first independent film producers who turned to television, nor was Warner Bros. the first major studio to embrace the new medium. But their emergence as suppliers of TV programming during the 1950s represents one of the most significant moments in the transition from the "Old Hollywood" of the studio era to the "New Hollywood" in which movie studios have become subsidiaries of transnational media and leisure conglomerates. The shift to television production in Hollywood— particularly by those producers with the heaviest investment in the Old Hollywood—marked television's emergence as America's principal postwar culture industry, while it also signaled a growing trend toward the integration of media industries. Since the movie studios began producing television, the diversification of media corporations into related fields and the consolidation of capital through corporate mergers have produced an environment in which the media industries are increasingly interwoven. Although these tendencies existed before the 1950s, the impulse toward integration rose markedly during that tumultuous decade and has become more pronounced in subsequent years. To appreciate the implications of the decision by the major studios to produce television, therefore, it is useful to view their actions as characteristic of a larger trend. The motion picture industry during the 1950s was less an empire on the verge of ruin than one struggling, under unsettling conditions, to redefine its frontiers.

Although Hollywood experienced changes during the 1950s, these weren't necessarily the seismic shifts described in the epic accounts of the industry's demise. Certain impermanent conditions had enabled the major studios to dominate the movie industry for more than a quarter of a century, but these conditions dissolved in the fluid social, political, and economic environment of post–World War II America. A number of converging forces propelled the industry into its postwar economic slump: the Supreme Court's 1948 *Paramount* decision, which ordered the major studios to divest themselves of their lucrative theater chains; heightened competition for the public's leisure and entertainment spending; demographic shifts in postwar American society; restricted foreign markets; and increased production costs in the industry.[8]

By the mid-1950s, in response to these conditions, the studio system had largely given way to independent production. The studios gradually phased out the standardized production of the moderate- to low-budget, formulaic films that had sustained the industry by providing a dependable means for meeting the fixed expense of studio overhead and the screen-time demands of exhibitors. This change meant dropping term contracts with creative personnel and reducing production at the studios. Instead, the major studios encouraged independent producers (many of whom were former studio producers, directors, or actors) to create individual, highly differentiated films that the studios would finance, distribute, and market. Under this strategy, the major studios appeared to be headed toward a new role as packagers, financiers, and distributors of independently produced feature films.

With the growth of the television audience during the 1950s, however, the television networks soon began courting the studios, trying to convince them of their potential importance as product suppliers which could profit from the networks' efforts to consolidate and expand power over advertisers and local affiliates. Studio telefilm production represented an alternative to the dominant mode of television production in the early 1950s, a system that had been imported almost directly from network radio. As in radio, advertising agencies purchased broadcast time in the network schedule and then produced live, New York–based programs to fill the time slots. Sponsors owned the program and often controlled the programming slot as though it were a franchise held at the sponsor's discretion. By turning to Hollywood studios and their existing production operations, the networks could step up their efforts to wrest control of programming from the agencies without themselves having to risk the heavy financial burden of program production. In addition, by investing in

studio-produced telefilm series, the networks could guarantee themselves a portion of the residual profits that filmed series promised to
deliver as "reruns" once they had completed their network run and
passed into syndication.

The studios discovered that supplying television programs to the
networks offered a new rationale for standardized, studio-based production. By shifting their mass production efforts into series television, a number of the major Hollywood studios were able to capitalize
on *aspects* of the studio system even as the system itself changed.
Thanks to its telefilm operations, Warner Bros., for instance, maintained term contracts with actors, directors, producers, and technicians, continued regular studio operations, and guaranteed a steady
supply of product that was financed, produced, and owned by Warner Bros. until the entire studio was sold in the late 1960s. Thus commercial television, far from sounding the death knell of the Hollywood studios, offered a perfunctory salvation, an opportunity to
reorganize and sustain established production operations when other
social, economic, and political forces threatened to end the studios'
established hegemony in the movie industry.

The studios probably would have survived in some form solely
through a strategy of financing and distributing independently produced feature films, but television actually supported their continued
dominance of the movie industry. At the same time, the TV networks
embraced Hollywood-produced programming in order to consolidate
their own control over the television industry. By the end of the
1950s, with the fates of the networks and studios deeply entwined,
filmed television series emerged as the dominant product of the Hollywood studios and the dominant form of prime-time programming—
a pattern that has remained unchanged for more than thirty years.

The goal of this book is to make sense of this transitional period in
the history of the motion picture and television industries by focusing
on the transition into television production among Hollywood's most
powerful studios and independent producers, those whose stake in
the studio system had been the greatest. For both independent producers and major studios, the shift to TV was integrally bound up
with other corporate strategies developed during the 1950s, including
the studios' sponsorship of independent production, their commitment to big-budget blockbusters, and their diversification into other
related fields. Among these strategies, the shift to TV was shaped not
only by contemporary conditions but also by Hollywood's history of
relations with the broadcasting industry. As this book examines the
role of TV production in Hollywood's evolving corporate strategies,

therefore, it also must ask how Hollywood producers envisioned television's value to the movie industry, both as a market and as a medium for symbolic expression. With different stakes and different experiences during the studio era, independent producers and major studios developed distinctly different conceptions of television, and those conceptions shaped the programming they produced.

Hollywood's emergence in television was not simply a matter of powerful movie producers' invading the TV industry and imposing their values and traditions on an underdeveloped medium. Indeed, the television industry already possessed a well-defined economic structure built upon the networks' ability to deliver viewers to advertisers by broadcasting regularly scheduled programming to a national audience. Movie producers who had grown accustomed to the ways of the studio system discovered that it wasn't going to be easy to adapt to a culture industry defined and controlled by other companies. In almost every instance, the corporate commitment to change was soon followed by the realization that change in the culture industries is more easily anticipated than managed. Consequently, the transition involved an active process in which movie producers haggled with networks and sponsors over economic relations, creative control, and program forms, while also attempting to conceptualize the organization and execution of TV production within their own companies.

First, the Hollywood studios had to negotiate the shifting relations of power in the TV industry, particularly since the networks enlisted the studios partially as a tactic for toppling the sponsors' control over production. In contrast to their impact on the movie industry, therefore, the studios had little hope of dominating the TV industry. Caught in a struggle between networks and sponsors, they seldom were able to dictate the terms under which they produced and distributed their programs. Their participation in TV played out in ways they scarcely anticipated, because it occurred under conditions they couldn't control, or sometimes even understand.

Second, as networks and sponsors debated the question of how to maximize the TV audience and the impact of advertising during the medium's early years, they experimented with scheduling strategies, program formats, and genres, producing different types of programming that constituted the experience of TV in a variety of ways. The decision to enlist Hollywood producers was an example of this experimentation. During the 1950s, Hollywood produced various types of programs for television, but ultimately helped the networks to define episodic series as the medium's dominant form. Episodic series were not necessarily what many of the studios had imagined producing when they began, but their participation in the industry ultimately reoriented their efforts in that direction and in many ways solidified the networks' commitment to the episodic series as prime time's dominant programming form.

Finally, Hollywood producers had to reconceptualize the studio system's established mode of production within the context of the television industry. To make this adjustment, they had to develop a system of production that responded to new technology (the TV set), a new form of distribution (network broadcasting), a new site of exhibition (the home), a new means of measuring popularity (ratings), a new commercial purpose (delivering viewers to advertisers), and new sources of revenue (network broadcast and syndication). Production practices had to be redesigned to take into account the demands of networks and advertisers, the economic restrictions of the medium, and negotiations with labor unions that also were attempting to adapt to the new medium. Narrative strategies had to be adjusted to the rapid pace of TV production, the conventions of episodic series, and the conditions of home viewing. The type of text most appropriate for these conditions was the subject of intensive, ongoing debate.

Although this book will discuss all of the major studios and a number of independent production companies, it will focus primarily on case studies of three different organizations—David O. Selznick Productions and Walt Disney Productions, both major independent producers that functioned on the periphery of the studio system, and Warner Bros. Pictures, a fully integrated major studio during the studio era.

Each of these companies conducted its transition to television quite differently, and the variations capture the range of Hollywood's responses to the medium. Whereas independent producers like Selznick and Disney hoped to evade the restricted economic environment of the studio system via television, a major studio like Warner Bros. hoped somehow to sustain the status quo of the studio era. Dealing with networks and advertisers who endorsed distinctly different definitions of the medium, these Hollywood producers defined television in relation to the studio system, evaluating its potential in terms of whether it sustained or disrupted familiar notions of how to produce popular entertainment. They struggled to decide how to entertain, how to tell stories, and how to prosper in a medium they didn't control. At the same time, Hollywood producers also sought to define television in relation to the imagined outcome of the changes facing the movie industry. While each of these producers had participated for decades in the studio system, their widely varying forecasts for television's future led them along divergent paths. Why did each company choose its particular strategy for television production? How did it determine what kind of programs to produce? How did each define the relationship between television production and its ongoing film production? How did each company imagine television's role in the New Hollywood?

Because Selznick and Disney were independent producers, they had a degree of freedom in dealing with television that was unavailable to a major studio. Still, the transition to TV was more difficult for Selznick and Disney than for Warner Bros. because, as independent producers, they lacked the personnel and the financial resources demanded by television production. Selznick and Disney saw television as an opportunity for innovation, but even they had radically different experiences in TV. Selznick was hired by an advertising agency to deliver a particular program and, therefore, faced constant battles with his corporate patrons over conflicting ideas about how television should be produced. Disney signed his first contract with ABC, a network eager to be associated with Hollywood producers and one that initially shielded the producer from conflict.

For Selznick, years of negotiations with the major TV networks and elaborate plans to monopolize the field of television production ultimately generated a total of only two hours of prime-time entertainment, *Light's Diamond Jubilee*. While Disney was not interested in cornering the TV market, his first series, *Disneyland*, became the linchpin in a new strategy of diversification that ultimately vaulted his company into the ranks of major studios and launched the struggling ABC into competition with the other networks. Selznick produced the most heavily viewed entertainment program in the medium's early history but inspired few imitators in Hollywood. *Disneyland*, on the other hand, provided the catalyst for the major studios' involvement in TV, even as Disney distanced himself from the Old Hollywood by shifting into projects like his amusement park. Obvious questions arise: Why didn't Selznick's plans pay off? How did Disney prosper through TV even though his interests in television production were fairly limited?

The most firmly entrenched in the studio system of the three, Warner Bros. entered television inspired by the public relations success of the Disney program, which was invaluable in publicizing the studio's feature films and amusement park. Signing its first contract with ABC, Warner Bros. initially modeled its TV strategies after those of Disney, as did MGM and Twentieth Century–Fox that same year. But when it failed to duplicate Disney's ratings success, Warner Bros. responded to demands by the network and sponsors by shifting entirely to the production of episodic series. Within a few years, the majority of the studio's activities were oriented toward series production, leading many other Hollywood producers in the same direction. MGM and Twentieth Century–Fox were less successful in making the adjustment to series production; thus Warner Bros. became the leader in the major studios' shift into television. By the end of the 1950s, under conditions that it hadn't dictated, Warner Bros. provided an influential model for both the organization of TV production and the form of TV narrative. And yet during the early 1960s Warner Bros. was surpassed by a number of companies, as the studio failed to develop new series to replace its fading first generation. How and why did Warner Bros. become TV's largest producer only four years after creating its first series? What caused the studio's rapid decline at the very moment when television production elsewhere in Hollywood was booming?

The activities of these producers represent different strategies for Hollywood's interaction with television and for the TV industry's use of Hollywood during a period in which no single type of programming dominated prime time. Above all, this book attempts to explain why certain types of programs emerged under these conditions. Too few historians have acknowledged that broadcast programs are cultural texts produced within historically specific economic and social conditions to communicate some meanings to audiences. In most histories of television, the programs are fairly insignificant, envisioned less as symbolic forms than as the residue of economic relations or the reflection of social issues. But the rise of Hollywood-produced TV programming was motivated by more than economic decisions, and its consequences extended beyond the bottom line of network and studio profits.

The introduction into prime time of programming created by movie producers was one example of the experimentation in program forms taking place in television during the 1950s, as networks, sponsors, producers, policymakers, and audiences shaped television's role in American culture. Often identified as TV's "Golden Age" because of nostalgia for the prestigious anthology dramas and live comedies produced in New York during its early years, the decade of the 1950s was actually a period in which the TV industry entertained a wide range of program types as the medium extended from its original base in major cities and its relatively upscale initial viewership to an increasingly national audience.

The dramas and comedies of the Golden Age represented not so much the thwarted potential of network television as the dying gasps of a culture preserved from network radio, vaudeville, and the theater at a time when television was still only a metropolitan phenomenon. Selznick's extravaganza, on the other hand, represented one potential strategy in the networks' early efforts to construct the experience of television viewing for a *national* audience. His long-standing ambition to mount prestigious productions coincided with an early goal of networks and advertisers to define television viewing as "spectacular," an extraordinary national event delivered at once to homes across the country. By producing series television, Disney and Warner Bros. participated in an alternative programming strategy adapted from network radio, but one still oriented toward a national audience. In contrast with programming forms that traded on uniqueness, weekly episodic series encouraged an experience of television viewing as something ordinary, one component of the family's household routine.

The process by which Hollywood-produced programming came to dominate prime time can be seen as the consolidation of American television; the episodic series that emerged became the template for TV narrative. Not until the major studios entered television did the medium reach the stage at which a single type of text characterized prime time in the same way that the feature film had come to typify the cinema. No more did Warner Bros. invent series narrative than did Desilu Productions with *I Love Lucy*, Freeman Gosden and Charles Correll with radio's *Amos and Andy*, MGM with its series of Andy Hardy movies, or Charles Dickens with his serialized novels. But the appearance of a major movie studio like Warner Bros. as the leading producer in television signaled the emergence of the episodic TV series as the medium's central expressive form. The rise of telefilm series produced in Hollywood represented the consolidation of a particular type of text that has dominated prime-time television ever since. Because this happened in Hollywood during the 1950s, one cannot understand how American television developed without asking how the process was affected by changes in the movie industry during the postwar years. In many ways, the history of American TV is the history of Hollywood TV.

Considering that all of the major studios had shifted into television production by the late 1950s, it is surprising how little attention has been paid until recently to the relations between the film and broadcasting industries. The tendency to treat American cinema and television as discrete cultural institutions is one of the fundamental issues that needs to be addressed in an attempt to understand the rise of television production in Hollywood. Traditionally, histories of American cinema and broadcasting have been organized around a series of familiar narratives that form the framework for understanding the development of movies, radio, and television. One of the most well-rehearsed narratives depicts the broadcasting and motion picture industries as antagonists locked in a struggle over the hearts and minds of a fickle public. Accounts of the interactions between the motion picture industry and the broadcasting industry generally adopt a structure that traces the movie industry's initial disdain for radio and television, followed by its antagonism after the unexpected success of those two media, and finally its reluctant acquiescence to the new order of commercial entertainment forged by broadcasting's popular appeal. One early article succinctly represented this narrative structure, with its movement from conflict to resolution, as a tale of "complacency, competition, cooperation."[9]

The persistence of this historical narrative is evidenced in the writings of media scholars who see the rise of commercial television as the most apparent explanation for what they perceive to be the artistic decline of the American cinema since the studio era. Critic Todd Gitlin, for instance, has argued that the decay of the American cinema can be measured by the stages in the movie industry's capitulation to television. He bemoans the fact that "television, the bastard child of the movies and radio, has triumphed over its parents, leaving Hollywood to revel in revenues, publicity, passable product, and past glories." Suggesting that contemporary movies have become bleak, Gitlin describes the history of the American cinema since World War II as a gradual contamination in which "the thread—or sewage—of mainstream television runs through the whole process."[10]

During the past decade, however, a number of historians have demonstrated that this influential master narrative has obscured the symbiotic relationship that has existed between the motion picture and broadcasting industries since the founding of national radio networks during the 1920s. The publication of Michele Hilmes's *Hollywood and Broadcasting*, William Boddy's *Fifties Television*, and the anthology *Hollywood in the Age of Television*, edited by Tino Balio, signaled the full emergence of this revisionist movement in media history. This movement not only questions common assumptions about relations between the media by demonstrating their nearly continuous engagement over the years, but it also raises serious doubts about the usefulness of any media history that isolates cinema and broadcasting from one another or from the other cultural institutions in a particular era.[11]

While the boundaries that separate the media at first may appear natural and self-evident, their existence is not based on any inherent differences in the nature of media technology, the structure of media industries, or the attributes of media texts. Examined on any of these levels, distinctions between the media quickly blur. Instead, the boundaries that separate the media in our culture are the products of discourse, including both the discourse generated by the media industries and that produced by scholars and critics. As historian Carolyn Marvin notes, "Media are not fixed natural objects; they have no natural edges. They are constructed complexes of habits, beliefs, and procedures embedded in elaborate cultural codes of communication."[12] In other words, media are cultural constructs created, distinguished, and sustained by the social meanings ascribed to them. Traditional histories have drawn discrete boundaries around individual media by concentrating on a limited range of issues. Film history has tended to focus on the production and distribution of feature films; broadcasting history usually has emphasized technical innovation in electronics manufacturing, government regulation, and the economics of network broadcasting.[13] Above all, traditional histories have implied that the two media are distinctly separate, shaped by different historical forces while in pursuit of conflicting goals.

In practice, however, the motion picture and broadcasting industries seldom disguised their many alliances, and the general public seemed to have recognized the interpenetration of the media as soon as movies and radio began to share the stage as the country's most prominent forms of popular entertainment. During the late 1920s and early 1930s, every major studio attempted to form its own radio network, and both of the existing major radio networks sought entrance into the movie business. Will Rogers, the top-ranked box office star of the early 1930s, also was one of radio's most popular performers. Director Cecil B. De Mille's period of greatest box office success coincided with his appearance as the host of *Lux Radio Theatre* beginning in 1936. In his memoirs, De Mille recalled the radio show as "the experience which brought me closer to the American people than anything else I have ever done." By offering Hollywood's most popular stars in abridged audio adaptations of contemporary feature films, *Lux Radio Theatre* attracted thirty million movie-going listeners each week and brought Hollywood's glamorous aura across the threshold of the American home. During De Mille's decade-long tenure with the series, every film he directed appeared among the ten top-grossing films of its year.[14] Recognizing radio's promotional value, the studios also adapted successful radio programs for the silver screen—for example, the 1937 Warner Bros. feature *Hollywood Hotel,* a musical based loosely on the radio series hosted by newspaper columnist Louella Parsons.

In June 1936 Marlene Dietrich and Clark Gable joined host Cecil B. De Mille
for the first *Lux Radio Theatre* broadcast from Hollywood, an adaptation
of the 1930 movie *Morocco*.
(Courtesy of Photofest)

By the time both the movie industry and network radio reached the height of their popular and commercial success in the 1940s, Hollywood celebrities appeared regularly on their own programs or on those, like *Lux Radio Theatre*, designed to promote feature films. Performers like Bob Hope and Bing Crosby consistently dominated the era's rankings of top movie and radio stars, and it is no coincidence that Hope, Crosby, and De Mille were all under contract to Paramount, the studio most committed to economic investment in the broadcasting industry during the studio era. Together, the films of these three radio celebrities accounted for two-thirds of Paramount's top-grossing motion pictures during the 1940s, the studio's most profitable decade during the studio era.[15] It thus seems possible that the popular success of movies and radio during the 1930s and 1940s depended at least partially on the fact that the media were not isolated from one another but were perceived as complementary experiences in which stars and stories passed easily from one medium to another.

As these brief examples suggest, the tendency to depict the cinema and broadcasting as isolated cultural institutions obscures their long-standing interdependence. Nowhere is this tendency more evident than in relation to the issue of advertising and commercial sponsorship, a point at which the studios' interests seem most distinct from those of broadcasters and yet one at which their interests frequently coincide. Because the movie industry must justify a policy of paid admissions while the commercial sponsorship of radio and TV programs makes them appear to be available free of charge, the movie industry has a stake in differentiating the two media, in making it seem unquestionable that movies have greater intrinsic value than TV programs and thus warrant audience "investment" at the box office. This pervasive distinction—circulated throughout the culture by film industry marketing, the popular press, scholars, and critics—has been articulated along a number of familiar lines: the cinema's technological superiority (the movie industry's marketing of technical innovations such as CinemaScope, 3-D, and Dolby sound), its greater capacity for spectacle or verisimilitude (press reports about lavish budgets and special effects or about an actor or director's fanatical obsession with "accuracy"), its relative freedom in depicting sexuality and violence, or the creative license provided to some of its directors. These criteria and others have been used at one time or another to mark the cinema's difference from television.

The most conveniently mapped boundary between the cinema and television, however, has been drawn over the issue of commercial sponsorship. During the convergence of the movie and television industries in the 1950s, for instance, a number of Hollywood movies

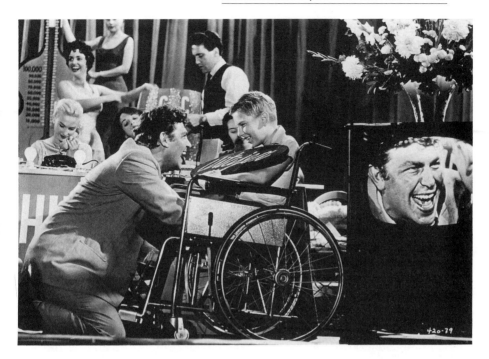

Andy Griffith stars as Lonesome Rhodes, a drifter turned down-home demagogue whose cynical ambitions are masked by the TV cameras that make possible his rise to fame, in the 1957 movie *A Face in the Crowd.*
(Courtesy of Wisconsin Center for Film and Theater Research © Warner Bros.)

expressed a distinction between the media by lobbing satirical bomb-shells at television's commercial motives. This critique of television appeared in satires like *Callaway Went Thataway* (1951), *It's Always Fair Weather* (1955), *A Face in the Crowd* (1957), and *Will Success Spoil Rock Hunter?* (1957). In its surprisingly elitist echoes of the contemporary "mass culture" debate, the relatively consistent representation of tele-vision in these movies seems more a product of the Frankfurt School than of Tinsel Town. Television, as depicted in these films about the TV and advertising industries, is a merchant of false consciousness, a medium irredeemably compromised by its devotion to advertising. The TV producers, celebrities, and advertising agency personnel who populate these stories are twisted by greed or flawed by cynicism, but their flaws are hidden from the TV viewers within the narrative. The TV audiences imagined by these movies are oblivious to the false ap-peals taking place on the TV screen and to the machinations taking place just offscreen.

As cinema spectators, however, moviegoers are able to recognize such dissimulations because the movie narratives provide privileged access to the characters' motives, revealing the hidden schemes that are masked by commercial television's obsession with surface detail. Indeed, these films construct a preeminent position for the cinema by representing the medium's epistemological superiority over television. Noticing this narrative motif in subsequent films depicting the institutions of television, Colin MacCabe has described it as "cinema's ability to make visible what is invisible to television." Through a variety of narrative strategies, films that represent television often stress "the opposition between the knowledgeable position we occupy as viewers in the cinema compared with the ignorance of the television audience."[16] This motif implicitly argues that the cinema is superior to television, not because of inherent technological advantages but because of television's commercialism, which inhibits its ability—or willingness—to depict social reality accurately.[17]

Movie industry discourse has often implied that the cinema exists in an autonomous sphere outside the corrupting influence of the marketplace, an idea best expressed by MGM's famous slogan, *ars gratia artis*. Along with the studio's unmistakable roaring lion, MGM's assertion of artistic autonomy served as the trademark for the particular cultural commodity that MGM marketed—feature films carrying the connotation of aesthetic quality. The irony of an entertainment corporation's advancing the doctrine of art for art's sake is obvious. As Theodor Adorno has noted, however, the disavowal of commercial impulses recurs throughout modern mass culture: "Vestiges of the aesthetic claiming to be something autonomous, a world unto itself, remain even within the most trivial product of mass culture. In fact, the present rigid division of art into autonomous and commercial aspects is itself largely a function of commercialization. It was hardly accidental that the slogan *l'art pour l'art* was coined in the Paris of the first half of the nineteenth century, when literature really became large-scale business for the first time."[18] Likewise, the studios' efforts to position their films within an autonomous aesthetic sphere developed from marketing strategies designed to differentiate their product from that of competitors. This practice continued even after the major studios themselves began to produce television films, and the separation of the media had become harder to define, because the studios still had to justify the distinction between the films they produced for television broadcast and those that could be viewed only in theaters.

In spite of the movie industry's attempts to separate itself from broadcasting's crass motives and obvious ploys, however, the American cinema has never strayed far from the call of advertising. "When the first movie cameraman shot the first street scene that included a shop sign," Charles Eckert has written, "all of the elements of a new advertising medium were implicit." [19] Even during the first decades of the industry, producers signed deals with corporate sponsors, agreeing to tout brand-name products in their films. Studios assigned personnel to facilitate interaction with advertisers and even created divisions to produce explicitly sponsored films. Although the studios were eager to generate revenue through advertising, exhibitors appreciated the need to distinguish the movie-going experience from commercial broadcasting (to justify paid admissions) and, therefore, resisted the presence of advertising in movie theaters. Fearing repercussions from angry exhibitors and alienated moviegoers, the major studios ultimately introduced a more sublimated type of advertising and forged a more discreet relationship with advertisers. Brand-name products entered movies through "product placements," agreements to showcase products subtly within the milieu of the narrative. More-obvious commercial tie-ins were shifted outside of the narrative, to marketing campaigns and celebrity product endorsements that accompanied a movie's release. The cinema never became an advertiser-supported medium, but its aims have been relatively consistent with those of commercial broadcasters. Although some critics see product placements as a recent phenomenon that demonstrates the contamination of the cinema by television's influence, Eckert suggests that the silver screen has always been a type of "living display window" for consumer culture. [20]

The motion picture industry's long-standing alliance with commercial sponsors, often obscured by common conceptions of the cinema's aesthetic autonomy, provides a pertinent example of the convergence of movies and related social institutions. This convergence blurs the boundaries between narrative and advertising in movies—an accusation traditionally leveled at commercial broadcasting. And like commercial broadcasting, the cinema promoted the values of consumer culture, including an ideology in which the consumption of commodities is centered primarily in the home and the institution of the family.

The impulse of manufacturers and advertisers to cultivate the home as the primary arena of consumption led advertisers to Hollywood, but it also led Hollywood into the American home—at first tentatively via the domestic medium of radio, then wholeheartedly upon the arrival of television. Indeed, Laura Mulvey argues that the cultural shift from the public exhibition of movies to the domestic reception of television during the 1950s coincides with "the triumph of the home as point of consumption in the capitalist circulation of commodities." Measuring the significance of this development for American culture, Nick Browne writes, "The commercial development of television in the post–World War II years as a mechanism for reaching into the household represents a singularly significant moment in the development of the American economy and culture. Through television, American business has represented, penetrated, and constructed the family with an eye to its aptitude for consumption."[21]

Hollywood recognized television's ability to reach into the household, the privileged site of consumer culture, and was as eager as any manufacturer to place its products in the American home. After deciding to enter television production, the motion picture industry even participated in the cultural discourse that helped to define television as a domestic medium, identified with the values of home and family.[22] In announcing the decision of Warner Bros. to produce television programming, for instance, Harry Warner took great pains to distinguish the studio's TV product from its theatrical features. In this instance, he didn't focus on the relative budgets, production values, narrative strategies, or stars; instead, he emphasized the divergent social functions of the two media. Warner Bros. TV, he proclaimed, would emphasize the educational aspects of television, which "can accomplish social good that sound films have failed to accomplish. . . . In my opinion, proper programs can unite families—father, mother, children—at home, rather than separate them as the search for amusement and 'a good time' has done in the past."[23] How ironic it seems that Harry Warner, a man who made his fortune with the motion picture, could implicate the movies and other public amusements as forces for corruption, while imagining television as the entertaining savior of the American family.

From Cecil B. De Mille's radio show to television production at Warner Bros., the movie industry has sought through the electronic media to convey traces of Hollywood to the American home—an impulse that continues today in cable TV and home video. Whether it meant displaying consumer goods in cinematic narratives, marketing ancillary products identified with movie stars and stories, promoting feature films through broadcasting, or exhibiting its own films and series on TV, the motion picture industry consistently demonstrated an interest in colonizing the domestic spaces of social life, a trend that Edward Buscombe describes as "the privatization of consumption in general and of entertainment in particular."[24] The studios collaborated with broadcasters and advertisers throughout the studio era and were eager to join them in cultivating the potentially lucrative market of the postwar American home. The rise of TV production among Hollywood's major studios may have seemed like a radical departure for companies traditionally devoted to theatrical exhibition, but, in fact, it realized ambitions that the industry had harbored for decades.

·II·
Thwarted Ambitions in the Studio Era

A search for the origins of television production among Hollywood's major studios might begin by asking why a studio like Warner Bros. chose to produce series television starting in 1955. On the other hand, it might be just as reasonable to ask why Warner Bros. waited so long. After all, the networks established regular prime-time programming in 1948, and the episodic series that filled many of the subsequent hours weren't so different from the B movies the studio had produced in its heyday.

One explanation for the studio's reticence is that network television in its early years simply wasn't a viable market. With a limited number of stations on the air and a correspondingly small audience who had access to TV sets, early advertising revenue couldn't provide an economic base sufficient to support Hollywood's production standards. License fees paid for original programming by networks and advertisers during the early 1950s were paltry by major studio standards; at a time when most feature films cost over $1 million, the TV industry paid only $25,000 per half-hour episode. Movie executives complained that studio overhead and union contracts alone made such tight budgets inconceivable for the major studios. Nevertheless, Warner Bros. signed its initial TV contract in 1955 for a fee of $65,000 for each one-hour episode—a figure only marginally greater than the TV industry standard throughout the early 1950s. Executives also expressed some fear that theater owners might boycott movies from studios that produced TV programming or licensed their film libraries for broadcast. But the Supreme Court's 1948 *Paramount* decision, which broke the studio system's vertical integration by forcing the studios to divorce their theater chains, disrupted the theatrical market, leaving many exhibitors without much leverage against the studios.[1] Neither restrictive budgets nor fear of exhibitors kept Warner

Bros. out of television. Why, then, didn't the studio launch into television production during the earliest stages of network TV?

The common explanation has centered on Jack Warner's hostility to television; his aversion has been seen as a sign of complacency or contempt for an unproven rival. But such apocryphal stories have only clouded our understanding of the major studios' long-term commitment to broadcasting, which dates back to the earliest days of radio. Warner Bros. founded its first radio station in 1925, produced radio programming during the 1930s, conducted TV research throughout the 1940s, and during the late 1940s planned to construct one of the country's first TV stations. In contrast with this enduring commitment, Jack Warner's animosity shaped studio policy for only a few years in the early 1950s. His attitude has been mistaken for outright opposition to television when, in fact, it was only a temporary consequence of the studio's failure to enter the emergent TV industry at the outset and on its own terms.

Like Warner Bros., all of the major studios forged close ties with the broadcasting industry beginning in the radio era. In its own way, each of the major studios—as well as prestige independent producers like David Selznick and Walt Disney—envisioned an integral role for broadcasting within the movie industry. But Hollywood producers weren't blindly optimistic; they proceeded cautiously because they were reluctant to take any action that would simply reinforce the dominance of the existing radio networks.

From the earliest days of radio to the era of network TV, the studios wanted not merely to participate in electronic communication but to *control* the radio and television industries. Consequently, two primary goals motivated their attempts to integrate broadcasting into the movie industry. First, studios or their parent companies invested directly in technology, stations, and networks, in keeping with general corporate strategies for diversification. Second, the studios sought a determinant role in the development of both radio and TV broadcasting in order to influence what they anticipated would become a revolutionary new mode of distribution and exhibition for their films.

Observed from this perspective, as Michele Hilmes argues, "a new picture emerges of Hollywood as an active experimenter with the new technology, presenting a serious challenge to the established broadcasting interests."[2] If the studios demonstrated any reservation about broadcasting, it was their reluctance to reinforce the networks' power by supplying them with programming. Otherwise, the major studios planned to make radio and television broadcasting an extension of the studio system.

• • •

With a pool of contract talent and a huge supply of story properties, a major studio like Warner Bros. could have produced programming for radio or television at any time before 1955. But in the studio system the ability to create a product was never sufficient justification for production. In a 1946 article, industry reporter Ernest Borneman described the peculiar complexity of this situation. "If you want to make cheese or furniture or mousetraps," he suggested, "you begin by making cheese or building furniture or manufacturing mousetraps, and then you sell them. But if you want to make movies, you do not begin with production; you begin with distribution."[3] To appreciate why Warner Bros. chose not to sign a contract for television production until 1955, one must understand why a major studio would hesitate to be simply a producer. In other words, one must understand the logic of the studio system.

From the 1920s through the 1950s the studio system was an industrial oligopoly in which eight companies produced and distributed three-quarters of the feature films made in the United States and raked in 90 percent of the industry's total revenue. During the 1920s, the five major companies—Paramount, Loew's (which owned MGM studios), Warner Bros., Twentieth Century–Fox, and Radio-Keith-Orpheum (RKO)—achieved vertical integration by controlling the production, distribution, and exhibition of their movies. The three minor companies—Columbia, Universal, and United Artists—distributed their own movies, but by the 1930s they no longer owned theater chains. Independent companies like those of David O. Selznick, Walt Disney, Samuel Goldwyn, and a host of less noted producers orbited the studio system; they produced movies but sought distribution through the major studios or other distribution exchanges.

During this period the major studios established the features that would characterize the movie industry in the studio era. Studio executives managed the production process by organizing a detailed division of labor that isolated the tasks required to conceive and execute feature films. Motion pictures were differentiated and marketed to the public principally according to stars and genres. The studios distributed films both nationally and internationally and dominated their exhibition by cornering the market on key first-run theaters in major cities. For the major studios, motion picture production was but one component in a vertically integrated system.[4]

While the popular conception of the movie industry centers on those who make movies—stars, directors, writers, producers—theatrical exhibition actually dominated the studio system. Theater ownership accounted for over 90 percent of the assets held by the major studios. The majors dominated the industry not by simply producing the most entertaining or acclaimed films but by controlling first-run theaters and the channels of distribution. As historian Douglas Gomery explains, "It was through the theatrical end of the industry . . . that the Big Five operated as a collusive unit, protecting each other, shutting out all potential competitors, and guaranteeing profits for even the worst performer."[5] Although the majors owned only 16 percent of the theaters in the United States, they dominated the market by establishing a restrictive distribution system that arbitrarily segmented the nation and determined when individual theaters would be allowed to exhibit a film after its initial release in major cities. Studio-owned first-run theaters in large cities charged the highest admission prices; subsequent-run theaters received the film later and charged theater patrons less. While the studios collected a percentage of the box office revenue from all theaters, their first-run venues accounted for 75 percent of the industry's theatrical revenue.

Distribution and exhibition shaped the studio system, providing the basis for the major studios' domination of the industry. "Anyone during the 1930s and 1940s could have invested the necessary millions in film production, but then any new corporation would somehow have had to get the films onto theater screens," Gomery argues. "In other words, it was the mundane worlds of movie wholesaling and retailing which provided the Big Five with the necessary muscle to erect and maintain barriers to entry to keep away all serious competitors for two decades."[6] A marketplace ruled by the major studios gave the movie industry a rigid economic structure in which a company's commercial potential was determined almost entirely by its position in the industry hierarchy.

Maximum power and profitability belonged to Paramount, Loew's, Warner Bros., Twentieth Century–Fox, and RKO, the five studios whose firm grip on the nation's first-run theaters gave them control over the most lucrative urban markets. Next in order came Columbia and Universal, two full-fledged studios that produced and distributed top features but did not own theater chains, and United Artists, which served as a distribution company for Hollywood's top independent producers. The most successful independent producers, like Samuel Goldwyn, David Selznick, and Walt Disney, made their own films but signed distribution agreements with the studios in order to gain access to first-run theaters. At the bottom of the industry's economic order were those independent producers and small studios without major studio distribution. These producers relied on other distribution exchanges, scrapping for limited and unpredictable profits in independent theaters.

This system had undeniable benefits for the major studios, as it

maximized profits, minimized risks, and virtually eliminated competition from outsiders. Yet it also enforced structural constraints, including an institutional inertia in which the need to maintain the system outweighed most other factors in studio decisions. Based on their
experiences in the movie industry, Hollywood executives recognized
that it would be impossible to consolidate control over broadcasting if
they entered solely as producers. The major studios were unwilling
to produce broadcast programming as long as other companies controlled the networks of distribution. Along with the other major studios, therefore, Warner Bros. spent the years leading up to its debut
in series television attempting to construct or to acquire a system of
broadcast distribution that would justify producing for the electronic
media. These efforts centered on attempts to build stations and to
form networks.

Initially, the studios attempted to gain a foothold in broadcasting as
part of the industrywide expansion during the 1920s. As an extension
of the move to sound-film technology, all of the studios at least explored the possibility of forming radio networks in order to diversify
their assets, to control outlets for promotion, and to place Hollywood
in a position to influence the specific deployment of television technology. Warner Bros. actually took the industry's pioneering steps
into broadcasting during 1925, a year before RCA founded NBC as the
first official broadcast network. Backed by Wall Street financing, the
relatively minor movie company during that year set out on a course
of unprecedented expansion designed to elevate it to a position
among the industry leaders. While the company was acquiring an
impressive chain of theaters and the production company, Vitagraph,
Sam Warner convinced his brothers, Abe, Harry, and Jack, to establish a Hollywood radio station that would be useful to the growing
Warner Bros. organization, both as an introduction to the field of
broadcasting and as an additional avenue for promoting feature films.

Warner Bros. inaugurated station KFWB in Los Angeles during
March 1925 and subsequently opened station WBPI from its flagship
Warner Bros. Theater in New York City in 1926. At the time, Harry
Warner actually proposed that the studios form a radio network to air
programs that would celebrate the movie industry. "Through these
sources," he imagined, "programs could be devised to be broadcast
before and after show hours, tending to create interest in all merito-
rious pictures being released. . . . Such programs would serve to
whet the appetites of the radio audience and make it want to see the
persons they have heard and the pictures they are appearing in."[7]
Although Warner Bros. did not expand beyond these two stations

A 1920s-era portrait of MGM producer Harry Rapf (*right*) and the Warner brothers
(*left to right*): Sam, Harry, Jack, and Albert (Abe).
(Courtesy of Wisconsin Center for Film and Theater Research)

during the 1920s, its purchase from Western Electric of electronic
equipment needed to run station KFWB initiated a relationship between the two companies that would lead to the various sound-on-
film innovations of the mid- to late 1920s. The profits that resulted
from the studio's innovation of sound boosted the company into the
ranks of Hollywood's major studios and enabled it later to diversify
into broadcasting and a number of interests outside filmmaking.[8]

While Warner Bros. was the first studio to enter the field of broadcasting, Paramount and RKO soon emerged as the industry leaders
in attempts to integrate radio into the movie industry. Paramount
failed during 1927 in its first effort to purchase a radio network,
United Independent Broadcasters; in 1929, however, after William
Paley had purchased the network and rechristened it the Columbia
Broadcasting System (CBS), Paramount acquired 49 percent of it
through an elaborate stock-swapping agreement. While the studio
grabbed a piece of the burgeoning broadcast industry, CBS gained
access to the movie industry's talent pool and received the infusion of

working capital needed to challenge NBC, the more powerful network. Another major studio, RKO, had direct ties to broadcasting, since it was founded in 1928 as a wholly owned subsidiary of NBC's parent company, RCA, which also had a stake in the recent shift to sound films. Other movie companies, such as Loew's and Fox, made less-ambitious efforts to establish radio networks, but at one point in the late 1920s it looked to many as though two powerful radio–motion picture combines—CBS-Paramount and RCA-RKO—were about to battle for total domination of the American entertainment industry.[9]

The expected battle, as well as the increased integration of the media industries, failed to materialize because of the Depression, which forced all of the major studios into a period of financial retrenchment. The CBS and Paramount alliance collapsed under the weight of studio debts. Their agreement had specified that Paramount would purchase its own stock from CBS by March 1932 for a flat fee of $5 million, provided CBS had earned $2 million in the intervening two years. By March 1932, however, the effects of the Depression had dramatically reversed the fortunes of the two companies. Fueled by advertising revenue generated during the phenomenal growth of radio, CBS had surpassed expected earnings. Meanwhile, Paramount had gone into debt financing the conversion to sound and the expansion of its theater chain. Following the terms of the contract, CBS and Paramount were disentangled in 1932 when each company purchased the share of its stock still owned by its partner. CBS emerged strengthened by the deal, both by the influx of cash at a crucial moment in 1929 and by its newfound autonomy in 1932; Paramount escaped barely intact, with the buyout proving to be a huge burden for the financially weakened studio.

RKO was in similar financial distress by the early 1930s as RCA withdrew from its role in financing the subsidiary. RKO suffered a net loss of $5.7 million in 1931, a loss that could not be absorbed by a parent company hit by the double blow of the Depression and the government-mandated divestiture that separated RCA from General Electric and Westinghouse. The cost of buying out General Electric and Westinghouse left RCA's cash reserves depleted, with nothing to keep RKO afloat. The studio survived, though only after financial restructuring and with less financial support from the parent company throughout the 1930s.

Although the broadcasting ambitions of Warner Bros. ultimately didn't match those of Paramount or RKO, the studio did stake out territory in the radio field. During 1930, for instance, Warner Bros. purchased its first music publishing company and acquired National

Radio Advertising, one of the leading organizations in the field of broadcast transcriptions, an early version of pre-recorded programming using acetate discs. With an infusion of capital from the studio, this became the first company able to plan, produce, and sell pre-recorded radio programming through one centralized organization. Other broadcast-related subsidiaries acquired or founded during this era included several music publishing companies, Warner Bros. Broadcasting Company (which owned and operated KFWB), Brunswick Radio Corporation (a manufacturer of radio equipment), and a 65 percent interest in Transamerica Broadcasting and Television Corporation, a company that produced radio programming and developed station properties.[10]

During May 1936, Harry Warner announced the studio's ambition to start a third radio network that would compete with NBC and CBS. Even though the most powerful motion picture companies had failed in their earlier attempts to establish radio networks, Warner Bros. offered $2 million for a 40 percent share of the Mutual Broadcasting System. The Mutual network would be able to expand, and its loosely organized affiliates, less dependent on the network than affiliates of CBS or NBC, would be persuaded to accept more network programming and to adhere to its schedule. The network would construct studios in New York and Los Angeles where Warner Bros. talent would produce programming. According to industry reports, the studio and William Randolph Hearst had reached an informal agreement by which the Hearst stations also would join this new network.

The studio's most immediate concern in trying to invest in a network was to create an outlet for promotion, particularly for the musical numbers performed in its features. Because Warner Bros. in January 1936 had refused to sign the latest radio agreement with the music composers' licensing organization, ASCAP, both of the major networks and more than half of the country's unaffiliated radio stations refused to perform the music and songs from studio features, which dealt its advertising a severe blow. This experience reinforced the recognition at Warner Bros. that real power in broadcasting rested in distribution; otherwise, producers were at the mercy of the companies that controlled access to the national audience. By establishing its own electronic distribution system, Warner Bros. hoped to air studio-produced radio programs and to prepare itself for what the trade journals at the time described as "the potentialities of visual broadcasting."

Following a brief period of negotiation, however, Mutual rejected the offer. Chastened, Warner Bros. signed the ASCAP agreement, and its songs were allowed back on the airwaves.[11]

Having failed to form radio networks during the 1930s, the studios increasingly learned to capitalize on the medium's promotional value by allowing performers, songs, and story properties to appear on radio. This trend originated early in the decade when Paramount and RKO were involved directly in radio, but it didn't take off until the 1934 success of two radio programs, *Hollywood Hotel,* hosted by gossip columnist Hedda Hopper, and *Forty-five Minutes in Hollywood.* Both programs publicized currently released movies using interviews with Hollywood personalities and restaged excerpts from feature films.[12] Exhibitors feared that the value of feature films would be eroded by radio exposure and threatened to boycott studio productions promoted over the air, but the studios themselves barely hesitated before rushing stars and story properties into broadcasting. Heralding movie stars and familiar genres, programs like *Lux Radio Theatre* and *Screen Guild Theater* reinforced Hollywood's established publicity schemes while increasing their range of exposure.

Hollywood soon rivaled New York and Chicago as a broadcasting center. At least thirty programs originated from the West Coast, featuring stars like Bing Crosby, Fred Astaire, Jack Benny, and Eddie Cantor. Warner Bros. stars Edward G. Robinson and Dick Powell appeared briefly in their own dramatic series. Soon the major studios began to develop their own promotional programs. In 1937 Warner Bros. premiered *Your Hollywood Parade,* with Powell as the host. Studio contract players Bette Davis and Olivia de Havilland appeared as guests on the inaugural broadcast. The following year Warner Bros. produced *Warner Bros. Academy Theater,* syndicating transcriptions of the program through its Transamerica Broadcasting subsidiary. Sponsored by the Gruen Watch Company, the program featured young contract performers by engaging them in informal chats and dramatizations of studio features soon to be released.[13]

At the same time that radio looked toward Hollywood for programming, the movie studios began to cultivate stars and story ideas from radio, hoping to capitalize on the publicity that accompanied exposure in the national medium. Warner Bros. tried unsuccessfully to make movie stars of three well-known radio singers: James Melton, Kenny Baker, and Rudy Vallee, one of radio's most popular entertainers. The radio industry also served as the setting for a number of Warner Bros. movies during the mid- to late 1930s, including *Stars over Broadway* (1935) and *Two against the World* (1936). During this period of enchantment with radio, the studio signed an obscure Midwestern radio announcer named Ronald Reagan and gave him a starring role—as a radio announcer—in *Love Is on the Air* (1937). Reagan also appeared briefly—again as a radio announcer—in the studio's most interesting example of media cross-promotion, the 1937 musical *Hollywood Hotel*. Although remembered today mainly for its director, Busby Berkeley, and its famous anthem, "Hooray for Hollywood," *Hollywood Hotel* was a topical exploitation film in the purest sense, produced to capitalize on the notoriety of Hedda Hopper's radio series. As a movie based on a radio program that served principally to advertise movies, *Hollywood Hotel* demonstrated the strange bond between Hollywood and radio during the 1930s. In the movie, radio's commercial reflection of the movie industry is reflected back again as fiction. In this peculiar hall of mirrors, the distinction between advertising and entertainment is not merely obscured, it is erased; *Hollywood Hotel* asserts that advertising is entertainment.

Faced with the problem of concocting a movie narrative based on a radio program that blended celebrity interviews and performances, *Hollywood Hotel*'s screenwriters, Jerry Wald, Maurice Leo, and Richard Macaulay, irreverently satirized the movie industry's courtship of broadcasting, particularly its cynical attempts to transform ill-prepared radio celebrities into movie stars. In the film, Dick Powell, the host of Warner Bros.'s own radio program, plays a musician and singer in Benny Goodman's orchestra who signs a movie contract and flies to Hollywood. An elaborately contrived farce, the story chronicles Powell's manipulation by studio bosses, his subsequent fall from grace and estrangement from his bandmates, and his surprise reemergence as a star during a climactic broadcast of the Hopper program. This familiar plot dissolves during the climax as the movie simulates a broadcast of *Hollywood Hotel*, taking greater care to display the program's announcer, orchestra, and star than to sustain Powell's saga. The broadcast concludes Powell's rise to stardom by displacing many of the other narrative threads developed during the movie. For instance, after having been central to the story, Benny Goodman's orchestra disappears without a trace, replaced during the final scene by the *Hollywood Hotel* orchestra familiar to fans of the radio program.

By the end of the movie, the narrative is driven less by the question of whether Powell will become a star than by the goal of appealing to curiosity about the visual appearance of the radio program's stars and sets. Indeed, the broadcast's prominence in the movie suggests that one of the studio's principal goals in producing the picture was to satisfy the desire of the radio audience to visualize Hopper's broadcast. In this case, the spectacle of the cinema was used to supplant the technical constraints of broadcasting.

The interplay between movies and radio in *Hollywood Hotel* epitomized the easy exchange between the media that existed by the end of the 1930s, leading to what Charles Eckert describes as "a kind of

By the late 1930s Hollywood's stars moved easily between movies and radio.
Laurence Olivier, Merle Oberon, James Stewart, Vivien Leigh, and others perform
in a radio adaptation of the 1939 movie *Wuthering Heights.*
(Photo by Coburn/Courtesy of Photofest)

symbiosis which blurred the outlines of both media."[14] Movie stars appeared on radio; radio celebrities emerged as movie stars. Radio producers learned to adapt feature films for broadcast; studios molded radio programs into Hollywood narratives. Even *Citizen Kane* (1941), the Hollywood cinema's most revered masterpiece, was a product of this era; Orson Welles and his Mercury Theater colleagues were lured to Hollywood by a motion picture industry eager to capitalize on their radio fame. But, though radio's promotional value was unmistakable, the symbiotic relationship between the media was circumscribed by the reluctance of studios to assume a subordinate role as program suppliers for the broadcast networks. These early interactions between the industries, therefore, did not signal an evolutionary stage in the integration of the media. On the contrary, the studios came to view radio as a dead end. Although major studio participation in radio programs demonstrated Hollywood's interest in broadcasting, these programs were an outgrowth of the movie industry's promotional practices, a set of activities subordinate within the studio system to the primary concern with the production and distribution of motion pictures.

Even as the movie studios failed to grasp power in the radio industry during the 1930s, the Hollywood community paid close attention to television, inspired by widely circulated accounts of technological research and by optimistic forecasts that promised a market for television by the end of the decade.[15] For years the industry as a whole had monitored television's technological development, with the Motion Picture Producers and Distributors of America (MPPDA), an industry trade organization, commissioning reports as early as the mid-1920s. During the mid-1930s, MPPDA president Will Hays commissioned A. Mortimer Prall, the son of Federal Communications Commission chairman Annis Prall, to prepare a study that would guide the movie industry during the transition to television. "The motion picture industry," Prall reported, "has its greatest opportunity for expansion knocking on its door. It must prepare now for this new industry which is certain to become an important part of our American life."[16] Prall's study suggested that an industry pool be established to produce programming for television and that motion picture interests either construct enough stations to form a national network or combine to purchase control of an existing radio network.

In spite of financial constraints imposed by the Depression, individual producers kept an attentive eye on television because they recognized that its potential implications for the movie industry were too important to ignore. During the wave of enthusiasm over television research in the 1930s, Warner Bros. carefully monitored television patents filed by Theodor Nakken, Ludwig Silberstein, and others. Rumors in the trade press even claimed that Warner Bros. attempted to lure television research pioneer Vladimir Zworykin away from RCA during the late 1930s.[17]

Contracts negotiated by studios and independent producers began to include clauses governing television rights. Indeed, television played a central role in Walt Disney's decision in 1936 not to renew his distribution contract with United Artists. Neither Disney nor United Artists knew what to expect from television at this early stage, but Disney had the foresight to request that he retain all television rights to his motion pictures. When United Artists refused to concede those rights during a series of harsh negotiations, Disney abandoned the company and signed with RKO.[18] Although this may have seemed like an arcane reason to end a business relationship—especially since broadcast television still existed almost solely in research laboratories—Disney's decision paid huge dividends for the producer in the years to come.

David Selznick, another independent producer during the studio era, had great ambitions for broadcasting, because he believed that television would enable him to achieve equal status with the major studios. Selznick had been a young production executive at the two studios that forged the strongest ties with the electronic media during the early years of network radio, first at Paramount during its merger with CBS in the late 1920s and then at RKO in the early 1930s. He hadn't participated in the negotiations, but he was an astute observer in search of alternatives to the studio system. During this period, he became acquainted with RCA chairman David Sarnoff and struck up a lifelong friendship with CBS president William Paley, who became his most trusted adviser in matters related to broadcasting.

When Selznick calculated the possibilities for his own production company during his final days as a major studio executive in 1934, the prospect of establishing a presence in radio or the nascent field of television represented one among many options for a company freed from the constraints of the studio system. Selznick clipped a November 1934 front-page article in the *Hollywood Reporter* stating that commercial receivers would hit the market by January 1935. "Television Is Ready," the headline brazenly proclaimed.[19] When Selznick founded his independent production company, Selznick International Pictures, in 1935, its early financial and creative resources were directed toward becoming a respected force in Hollywood film production, but the prospects for some sort of merger with television were never far from Selznick's mind.

Within months after forming Selznick International, Selznick and his board of directors began to look for investments in television. Selznick's personal enthusiasm for the new medium was matched by that of his company's major investor, John Hay "Jock" Whitney, who was already a partner in the new Technicolor corporation and an advocate of technological innovation in the film industry. He and Selznick perceived television investments "as a step toward the future and as a protection to our own pictures during the transition stage," after which television would rival the cinema as an entertainment medium.[20] Like the major studios, Selznick International planned initially to invest in television in order to control a new mode of distribution; the company first sought a financial interest in television technology—to control licensing as Whitney had with Technicolor.

Because it was inconceivable that Selznick would be able to gain any influence at RCA, the dominant electronics manufacturer, Selznick's general counsel, John Wharton, arranged a June 1936 meeting

John Hay "Jock" Whitney and David O. Selznick shortly after the founding of
Selznick International Pictures.
(Courtesy of Film Collection, Harry Ransom Humanities Research Center,
University of Texas at Austin © Selznick International Pictures)

with Farnsworth Television Corporation, for which he also served as
counsel. Founded by young television pioneer Philo T. Farnsworth
with limited financial support from Philco, Farnsworth Television
was chronically short of capital and, according to industry rumor, in-
filtrated by RCA spies, who passed along the company's vital research. Still, the Farnsworth company was RCA's only real competitor
in TV electronics.

When Farnsworth vice president Seymour Turner visited Selznick
International, he argued that neither company could become competitive in the nascent TV industry unless they collaborated. Farnsworth required capital; Selznick wanted to control a new mode of
distribution. Turner described the state of television research, advis-
ing that the medium was "much closer to practical consumer use than
most people believe and it behooves the picture companies to wake
up and pay attention." With his customary enthusiasm for new ven-

tures, Selznick pounced on the idea. "If and when television breaks," he speculated in 1936, "it is going to completely revolutionize the business. I cannot stress too strongly the feeling that we should do everything possible to get into TV at this point."[21]

Negotiations between the companies ran throughout 1936 and 1937, even as Selznick International produced its first feature films. Visiting Farnsworth's Philadelphia studio for a demonstration, John Wharton and Jock Whitney for the first time experienced TV, a hazy green image on a screen that measured just five by six inches. Farnsworth himself discussed television's future as he envisioned it, asserting that it would be a local phenomenon, limited to single cities because of the cost of transmission over AT&T-controlled long-distance lines. He described the potential for theater TV and suggested that Selznick construct an experimental station in Hollywood. Selznick's initial impulse was to slice through the confusion by tying up Farnsworth in a long-term commitment in which they would form a jointly owned company, with Farnsworth providing the technology and the broadcasting operations, and Selznick supplying the programming. Achieving this merger, Selznick International would participate in the television industry, regardless of its future direction. Farnsworth balked at the plan because his company needed a capital investment in order to finance further research.[22]

Since Wharton was on the boards of both companies (a situation that increasingly represented a conflict of interests), he later suggested that Selznick International attempt to take over Farnsworth's company. He claimed to be aware of an unnamed "curious internal situation" at Farnsworth that would enable Selznick to seize management control for an investment of only $75,000 to $150,000. As Wharton explained, such an investment might not pay off immediately, but "it would protect us from the possibility of RCA ever coming back into the motion picture field by virtue of a monopoly on television." By controlling Farnsworth Television, Selznick International might gain enough leverage to negotiate a "favored nation" status with RCA. In Wharton's words, "It might well enable us to work out a deal with RCA whereby they would supply the necessary financing to enable us to experiment and become the top of the field in television entertainment."[23]

Selznick himself witnessed a demonstration of television technology for the first time in late 1937. Afterward, he expressed both fascination and caution. "While it is absolutely startling," he remarked, "I don't feel we are in any position to make an investment at this time in anything so visionary, even though I most heartily agree that we should keep in touch with it. It is clear that the problems incident to it are many years from solution." For an independent production company struggling to assert itself among the major studios, belief in television's future was a far cry from risking its precious funds in speculation. Ultimately, Selznick summed up his attitude toward television at this stage of the medium's development: "I do not believe that television can be stopped. Some day, it will undoubtedly have a future so stupendous that we cannot even foresee its possibilities."[24]

During the movie industry's prosperous decade of the 1940s, the major studios shifted their attention to television and jockeyed for position in the new field even as they struggled to maintain the studio system in the face of external pressures. The major studios recognized that commercial television would be launched once the war ended. At the same time, however, they were aware that conditions in the movie industry—pending antitrust litigation, a tightened international market, and a rise in independent production—would require changes in the studio system. Eager to control the future of distribution and exhibition through television, each of the studios made substantial investments in two aspects of the medium: theater TV and station ownership (although many also explored subscription TV, a forerunner of cable TV).[25] As in the early radio era, Paramount clearly led the industry's efforts to diversify into television. The studio's investment in local TV stations like Los Angeles's KTLA, in the DuMont Network and its manufacturing division, and in theater TV through its alliance with Scophony Corporation of America made it the movie industry's dominant presence in television.[26]

As with radio, Warner Bros. never equaled Paramount's commitment to TV, but, again, it didn't lag far behind. In 1944 Warner Bros. made its first direct move into television when it filed an application with the FCC for a Hollywood television station to be operated by radio station KFWB. Six months later, the studio purchased seventeen acres with intentions of constructing the station. An application for a Chicago station followed in April 1948, and the studio prepared applications in five other cities. In July 1948 Warner Bros. took an ambitious step by asking the FCC to approve the $1.05 million transfer to Warner Bros. of two radio stations and Los Angeles TV station KLAC, which were owned by Dorothy Thackery, former publisher of the *New York Post*.[27]

Warner Bros. also joined in a partnership with Twentieth Century–Fox and RCA in 1947 to develop direct-projection theater TV that would compete with the Paramount-Scophony system. Begun in 1947, this collaborative research led to a public screening of the Joe Louis–"Jersey" Joe Walcott heavyweight prizefight at the Fox-Philadelphia

Theater in June 1948 and to demonstrations on the studio's Burbank lot in late 1948 and early 1949. Over the course of the year 1948,
the studio even conducted extensive, though unsuccessful, negotiations to purchase the American Broadcasting Company.[28] For Warner
Bros., these investments represented the first steps in organizing a
distribution network that would support the production of television
programming.

It is no coincidence that Warner Bros. stepped up its TV-related
activities in 1948, a year in which studio executives faced the worst
destabilization of the studio system since the Depression. After the
industry's peak year of 1946, nationwide box office attendance had
declined steadily, while foreign revenue also diminished as a result
of protectionist legislation enacted by European countries.[29] Warner
Bros. profits went into an immediate tailspin, falling from 1947's record $22 million to $11.8 million in 1948.[30] The Supreme Court's 1948
Paramount decision threatened to curtail another source of revenue by
eliminating the steady profits from studio-controlled theaters once
the studios divested themselves of their theater circuits. Although
Warner Bros. did not immediately sell its theaters, the studio faced
the entertainment industry's uncertain future with the prospect of
continually diminishing revenues and an accumulated backlog of
twenty-three unreleased features by the end of 1948. Under these
conditions, Warner Bros. virtually ceased studio operations from November 1948 to February 1949. When the trade press interpreted the
shutdown as a distress signal, Jack Warner rushed forward to deny
the rumors. The studio's temporary inactivity was not a shutdown
per se, he claimed, but an opportunity for "appraisal, analysis, and
planning for the future."[31]

This period of reflection initiated the studio's development of a new
conception of the movie industry, including a revised vision of the
market for motion pictures and of appropriate production strategies.
Steve Trilling, Jack Warner's executive assistant, expressed this new
philosophy in a memo to director Vincent Sherman:

> We . . . want to carefully analyze and estimate the values of our future
> properties before going into production, so that we are able to meet pres-
> ent world picture conditions, and as they will be in the future. We will
> not start a picture until the script, cast, and price are right. If we feel a
> picture will cost too much or present difficulties, we will fold it rather
> than hazard any extreme gamble. In short, we will be much more selec-
> tive and choosie, much the way we find the public is now in the picture
> buying. We cannot take any more chance now making a picture just for
> the mere sake of making a picture—without having some definite conclu-

sion as to the end result and cost. Further, we don't want to keep jam-
ming pictures through and find ourselves overloaded with an inventory
of expensive pictures which, when released, might prove to be on the
moldy, untimely side.[32]

From Trilling's account, it appears that the studio had recognized
that its factorylike mode of production had fallen out of step with
changing conditions at the box office. As historian Janet Staiger has
noted, since the early 1940s the studios increasingly had stressed
the production of separate and unique features by independent units
within the studio. Postwar economic conditions further encouraged
this turn toward independent production in which each film was
financed, conceived, and executed separately.[33] As the market for
unique, differentiated features surpassed that for routine productions, the studio's established production system had become a liability. Once the studios lost control of theaters, the ordinary pictures
that had always delivered small, steady profits could no longer be
guaranteed to earn money. Even with severe production cutbacks, the
studio system produced too many films for the dwindling post-1948
market, leaving a glut of undistributed films that became less timely
as they awaited release. According to Trilling, the studio planned to
solve these problems by shifting to the production of individual features that would be made in response to perceived market demands
and not merely to the need to keep the studio machinery operating.

As a result of their reflections during this period, Warner Bros. executives devised a new production strategy that promised to salvage
aspects of the studio system by integrating film and television production. Harry Warner declared in January 1949 that Warner Bros.
would launch itself into television production at its Burbank studios
as soon as the FCC approved the purchase of the Thackery stations.
Using its prospective owned-and-operated stations and its theater-TV
franchises as the cornerstone for expansion into further station ownership or the development of a network, the company would produce
programming both for broadcast television and for theater TV. Jack
Warner would continue to supervise the production of theatrical features, while Harry would assume responsibility for the television division.[34] Although no specific production plans were described, this
decision marked the origins at Warner Bros. of the policy that ultimately would lead the studio system into the television age. Increasingly, theatrical features would be produced individually by independent units, while the studio's traditional mode of production would
be dedicated to serving the television market. The studio would bal-

ance the shift toward unique, expensive films with a standardized product that would serve the same function that its more routine features had served during much of the studio era.

From the mid- to late 1940s, Harry and Jack Warner appreciated the potential value of television for the studio system—as long as the studios controlled TV stations and, ideally, a TV network. From all appearances, Warner Bros. intended to build its own television network by purchasing existing stations and by constructing its own. The studio's elaborate preparations during 1948 for an assault on the broadcasting industry, however, dissipated partially as a side effect of the *Paramount* decision. Its plans for station ownership were dashed when the FCC stepped in following the Supreme Court ruling to investigate whether the major studios legitimately had the right to own television stations. The Communications Act of 1934 had authorized the FCC to refuse station licenses to any individual or organization convicted of monopolistic practices. The commission was now prepared to decide whether this provision should be applied to the movie studios whose collusive practices had precipitated the *Paramount* decision. While no ruling was ever delivered, the Warner Bros. application process was abruptly suspended in 1948 when the FCC declared a "freeze" on TV station licensing, postponing decisions on all pending applications.

Historian William Boddy has argued that the FCC's station application freeze of 1948–1952, declared as an opportunity to evaluate federal policy toward television, actually gave an insurmountable advantage to CBS and NBC by enabling them to solidify their positions in local markets during a period of limited competition. Ultimately, the government's role in excluding the major studios from owning television stations during this period was of critical importance in determining the structure of the television industry. As Douglas Gomery has noted, the *Paramount* decision not only broke up the studio system but also "guaranteed that the majors would not secure a significant place in the ownership of U.S. television networks and stations. The radio industry was able to secure a hold which continues to the present day." Even as the government used the *Paramount* decision to thwart the studios' plan to establish their own networks and stations, the FCC's reluctance to support alternative technologies also made the studios' research in theater TV and subscription TV financially untenable. As Michele Hilmes explains, "Through a tendency to protect established interests against innovative competition . . . and what is surely one of the worst examples of regulatory foot-dragging in history, the FCC managed to delay, avert, and handicap testing and operation of these systems to the point that the companies involved could no longer support their efforts."[35]

With the tacit support of the FCC, the radio networks extended their power into the TV industry by establishing owned-and-operated stations in major cities and by signing a large number of stations as affiliates. Meanwhile, Warner Bros. and the other major studios watched helplessly during the freeze as their plans for television disintegrated. Warner Bros. dismissed its Chicago station application in May 1949, after a studio survey concluded that the first year of operation in Chicago—if that year ever came—would cost nearly $800,000. Ultimately, the Thackery TV interests in Los Angeles grew tired of waiting for the FCC to approve the Warner Bros. purchase of their stations and canceled the deal. The studio's theater-TV project fared no better; although Warner Bros. had planned an initial network of twenty-five theaters equipped to project video broadcasts, it would install television systems in only thirteen of its theaters in the coming years.[36] In spite of its clear designs on the television business, therefore, Warner Bros. found itself in the early 1950s with no substantial connections to the new medium.

The frustrations of television were merely one of the problems facing Warner Bros. in 1950, as the studio began an even more drastic retrenchment than that which followed its temporary shutdown in 1948. Production at the studio had diminished as a result of rising costs and a backlog of features awaiting release. Of the twenty films that Warner Bros. had planned to send into production during 1950, only six had gone before the cameras by July.[37] The studio's steadily declining profits and reduced productivity demanded major changes.

During the spring of 1951, Warner Bros. developed a strategy designed to solve these problems by dismantling components of the studio while shifting even more strongly toward independent production. First, the studio cut fixed costs by firing a number of its employees. While Warner Bros. already had trimmed its payroll by allowing many talent contracts to expire, the studio now eliminated office staff, nearly half of its publicity department, and the entire story department.[38] The story department had been essential during the studio era because it conducted continuous reconnaissance for the story material needed to fuel the production machinery; its dissolution, suggesting that Warner Bros. no longer planned to develop its own story properties, provided a strong indication of the studio's new policies.

These plans were made more explicit by the second maneuver in the new Warner Bros. strategy, the signing of a ten-picture distribution deal with an independent producer, Fidelity Pictures. Warner Bros. was merely one participant in the industrywide shift to independent production that began during the 1940s and escalated in the early 1950s, when it offered an obvious solution to the problem of declining profits.[39] Warner Bros. previously had distributed independent films, such as those of Milton Sperling's U.S. Pictures and the Cagney brothers' William Cagney Productions; it also had established "in-house" independent companies and released films made on a profit-participation basis with individuals like Bette Davis, Errol Flynn, and director Michael Curtiz. Yet these films all had been produced at the studio, using studio crews and facilities. The Fidelity deal marked a turning point because it was Warner Bros.'s first agreement to finance and distribute films produced by an entirely independent company. At the time of the deal, Jack Warner announced that it represented a new policy designed to cut the studio's financial risk on production and to decrease studio overhead.[40]

While Harry and Jack Warner attempted to stabilize the company, however, they also pursued a more drastic option. Throughout the early 1950s, industry rumors speculated that the brothers had decided to bail out of the film business, that they awaited only a suitable offer. One of the more insistent rumors claimed that RCA, eager to reestablish its presence in the motion picture industry in order to supply filmed programming for NBC, would purchase the company.[41] In early May 1951, during the same week that the studio signed the distribution deal with Fidelity, the brothers put an end to the rumors by announcing that they had sold the company to a syndicate headed by Louis Lurie, a San Francisco realtor and theater-chain owner.

When asked whether the sale had any relation to the Supreme Court decision that forced the dismantling of the studio system, Harry told the press that he would rather sell the company "than help tear down what my brothers and I have built up." Lurie had begun negotiating with the Warner brothers over the purchase of the company's theater chain alone, but he soon set his sights on the company as a whole. He offered the brothers $15 per share for the controlling 24 percent interest owned by the Warner families, bringing the deal to a total of $25 million. According to Lurie, the Warner brothers were so eager to sell that arranging the deal was "easier than getting into the Stork Club."[42]

Word of the potential sale sent the industry into an uproar over what *Newsweek* described as "the first abdication by a Hollywood dynasty."[43] In retrospect, the Warner brothers–Lurie discussions offered the first glimpse into the transformations that would mark the

studio system once conglomerates absorbed the studios. As an industry outsider, Lurie had allegiance neither to the studio system nor to
the traditions of Hollywood. For him, the Warner Bros. purchase was
solely a business venture, the studio itself merely an asset to be auc-
tioned off to the highest bidder. He planned to dismantle the studio
by liquidating all corporate assets. He would sell the 436 theaters,
which had an estimated market value of $75 million, as prime urban
real estate; the film library could be sold to television; and the studio
itself would be turned over to Louis B. Mayer, who had quarreled
with Loew's president Nicholas Schenck, and wanted to exit MGM
and form his own independent company.[44] By jumping the seemingly
sinking ship of the movie industry, the Warner brothers appeared to
be admitting what the other studios most feared—that the studio system had become outmoded and vulnerable to hostile takeover by outsiders, that the studios themselves might be more valuable when bro-
ken into pieces and liquidated than when maintained at productive
levels.

As quickly as the deal had come together, however, it crumbled.
Although Jack and Albert Warner strongly supported the sale, Harry
began to stall, demanding a series of concessions that finally para-
lyzed negotiations. In a statement made to the press less than two
weeks after the deal was announced, Harry displayed noble motives
for breaking off negotiations. "We felt that we could not withdraw
from the great undertaking which has been so vital a part of our
lives," he explained. While these feelings may have been partially
responsible for the deal's demise, the fact remains that Lurie pulled
out when Harry demanded that the brothers be personally indemni-
fied against all possible claims resulting from the *Paramount* decision—an untenable condition since no one could predict what litigation might result from the decision and the attempts by studios to
meet its requirements.[45]

Finding themselves still in the movie business, the Warner brothers
remained committed to their new policy of cutting fixed costs and
pursuing independent production deals. The company also enforced
strict limits on its feature film budgets. During the period from 1946
to 1950, Warner Bros. had released eighteen features produced on
budgets greater than $2 million. Between 1950 and 1954, only three of
the studio's features cost more than $2 million. After selling the com-
pany's theater chain to Fabian Enterprises in February 1953, the studio closed down in March for another three months, with executives
asked to take a 50 percent cut in salary. Industry reporters perceived
the studio's decision to cut operating expenses and to postpone production as a response to uncertainty over the direction that the in-

dustry might take once new technologies like CinemaScope and 3-D were implemented. In spite of this shutdown, however, Warner Bros. increased its reliance on independent production by advancing more than $8.5 million to independents during the first half of 1953. Of the thirty-eight Warner Bros. features either in production or completed by the end of 1953, seventeen were produced by independents like John Wayne, Howard Hawks, John Huston, Elia Kazan, and George Stevens. Although these co-production deals set a new direction for the company, they provided no immediate boost at the box office; the studio's annual profits continued to decline in 1953, falling to $2.9 million, the lowest figure in over a decade.[46]

As the looming disintegration of the studio system threatened the predictable profits that had enabled the studios to dominate the movie industry, Warner Bros. committed itself to a future that involved streamlined studio operations, tighter budgets, and a larger role in financing and distributing independent productions—a strategy shared by the other major studios. Although the studios struggled to restabilize the studio system and to generate additional revenue in a changing economic environment, they seldom considered the option of television production once the implications of the *Paramount* decision and the FCC's station application freeze became apparent. Only Paramount, with local stations in Chicago and Los Angeles that had been acquired before the freeze, had any immediate hope of influencing TV distribution. Lacking established distribution networks in television, the other majors weren't likely to produce TV programming.

At nearly every stage, the studios' schemes to dominate the airwaves had been frustrated by external events, the intervention of federal regulation, or the threat of antitrust litigation. Major studio expansion into radio was halted by the Depression and by the difficulty in competing with the established networks. The studios enlisted reluctantly as radio producers after they failed to form competitive networks, but only because they recognized that commercial broadcasting provided an unparalleled opportunity to expand the reach of feature-film advertising and promotion. At the dawn of network television in the late 1940s and early 1950s, the major studios again were denied a role in the broadcasting industry, in this case by the Federal Communications Commission. The FCC's inquiries into the studios' antitrust violations and its general reluctance to support technological or economic alternatives to the established networks blocked almost every plan originated in Hollywood. As at the other major studios, therefore, the history of broadcasting at Warner Bros. before 1955 is a chronicle of thwarted ambitions. Jack Warner's hostility toward television was a product of this frustrating history.

Blocked from owning individual stations and from building a network, Warner Bros. executives knew that they had lost the opportunity to compete with the established TV networks. Producing for television without controlling distribution was an unthinkable compromise for Harry and Jack Warner. Doubtless the studio system would have to adapt in order to survive, but the Warner brothers weren't yet prepared to create a product that the studio would neither distribute nor exhibit; distribution was still the key to a studio's power and self-determination. Based on their experience near the top of the studio system hierarchy, Warner Bros. executives recognized that television production by itself promised limited revenue and a subordinate status in the TV industry.

Significantly, the studio's legendary antagonism toward television did not begin until this moment—when it became clear that there was no hope of integration on any terms other than those dictated by the networks. Jack Warner's hostility to television has been depicted as the natural result of competition between the two media industries; in fact, it might never have existed had the FCC not taken actions that prevented the studios from competing directly as broadcasters. Judging by the studio's plans for television in the late 1940s, Warner Bros. executives conceived of television as a central component of the postwar studio system. Considering this long-term commitment to broadcasting, therefore, the real break with Warner Bros. tradition came when Jack Warner announced in the early 1950s that "the only screens which will carry Warner Bros. products will be the screens of motion picture theaters the world over." [47] Thwarted ambitions to form its own TV network kept the studio from producing TV programs during the medium's earliest days. But while Warner Bros. and the major studios other than Paramount retreated from television during the early 1950s, independent film producers brought television production to Hollywood.

·III·
Escape from the Studio System:
Independent Producers and Television

Once it became evident in the early 1950s that the radio networks would hold dominion over the airwaves in television also, the major studios were reluctant to produce television programming. But television production appealed immediately to those Hollywood producers who hadn't shared equally in the studio system's rewards. For any Hollywood producer that was not at the top of the industry hierarchy, the studio system was at best an inconvenience and at worst an instrument of oppression. To these producers, the TV screen appeared like a beacon to guide them toward an elusive goal—escape from the studio system. The television industry during the late 1940s and early 1950s wasn't an ideal alternative to the studio system, since the networks were beginning to monopolize the nation's TV stations as effectively as the studios had controlled theaters. By comparison, however, the market for TV programming was relatively open.

Though the majority of network programs were produced for live broadcast by New York–based advertising agencies, Hollywood producers discovered a welcome market; the successful ones were able to license filmed programming to networks and local stations or to national, regional, and local sponsors who would then purchase broadcast time. Early television offered meager financial rewards, but it opened new channels of distribution outside the influence of the major studios, providing refuge to producers whose movies traditionally had languished in tiny neighborhood or rural theaters. At the same time, TV also became a viable choice for second-rank studios like Columbia and Universal, and for such prestigious independents as Selznick and Disney. Because none of these producers owned theaters that needed to be supplied by a primary product—the feature film—each had grown accustomed to designing films that fit a market controlled by more powerful companies. With a smaller stake in a deteriorating studio system, these producers were more than willing to imagine alternatives to the movie industry.

In attempting to understand television's potential, however, Hollywood's independent producers and smaller studios shared with the major studios a tendency to conceive of television through the template of their experience with the studio system. Like the major studios, independent producers seemed less concerned with defining the unique qualities of an electronic medium than with measuring it against the medium they knew best. The important difference, however, was that the major studios conceived of television as an *extension* of the studio system, whereas Hollywood's less powerful producers saw it as a viable *alternative*—one potentially able to transform the movie industry by carving out a greater role for independent producers.

In two articles published in the *New York Times Magazine* during 1949 and 1950, Samuel Goldwyn (or, more likely, a ghostwriter) expressed the beliefs of many independent producers when he considered television's potential value for Hollywood. Goldwyn exhorted the movie industry to recognize that it had entered its third major era without even recognizing it. "First there was the silent period," he wrote. "Then the sound era. Now we are on the threshold of the television age. The thoroughgoing change which sound brought to picture-making will be fully matched by the revolutionary effects . . . of television upon motion pictures." Goldwyn perceived television as a magnificent opportunity but also as the scourge of producers too inflexible to imagine its rewards. "Once again it will be true, as it was in the early days of the motion-picture history, that it will take brains instead of just money to make pictures," he wrote. "This will be hard on a great many people who have been enjoying a free ride on the Hollywood carousel, but it will be a fine thing for motion pictures as a whole." Goldwyn's praise for television barely masked his ridicule of the major studios, whose oligopoly had thwarted competition for nearly three decades. A worthy opponent, television would challenge the complacency bred by the studios' monopolistic practices; it would benefit the movie industry as a whole but not all companies equally. Leaving "no room for the deadwood of the present or the faded glories of the past," television would serve as a ruthless instrument of social Darwinism, purifying the industry through competition. Ultimately, however, the medium offered new opportunities only as long as the major studios' influence could be contained. "Television will cause Hollywood to achieve new heights," he asserted, but only if the studios were forbidden from extending their monopolistic tendencies into the new medium, an event that would "blight" its development.[1]

Some independent producers, like Goldwyn, merely talked about television, but many others attempted to integrate television into their corporate strategies. By the late 1940s, studios like Columbia and Universal, prestigious independents like Selznick and Disney, and marginal independents like Hal Roach envisioned television as the catalyst for expanding their fortunes in the postwar entertainment industries. For companies outside the studio system's top flight, adoption of TV production occurred in stages. The earliest efforts involved attempts to conceive of television's role in the activities of independent producers. Once the television industry began to take shape in the late 1940s, Hollywood's most opportunistic independent producers actively negotiated with sponsors and networks to determine the initial programming forms and the economics of filmed TV production. By the early 1950s, many of these marginal producers were replaced by a second wave of independent producers who began to formalize the relations between Hollywood and the television industry, in the process making telefilm production a recognizable component of the movie industry. In an effort to understand how telefilm production took shape in Hollywood, one finds that the era's mistakes, misapprehensions, and deadlocked negotiations are as interesting as its success stories. The failures are reminders that there was nothing inevitable about the rise of television produced in Hollywood; under conditions dictated primarily by advertisers and the networks, Hollywood producers struggled to make sense of the new medium.

After failing to form an alliance with Philo T. Farnsworth during the 1930s, David Selznick continued to be fascinated by television, occasionally toying with the idea of establishing a TV production unit even before the networks organized regular prime-time schedules in 1948.[2] By 1948, twenty-one commercial television stations had gone on the air, the audience was growing, and the medium's long-promised rewards seemed close at hand. At the same time, Selznick's company needed a quick financial fix. Following the unprecedented commercial and critical success of *Gone with the Wind* (1939) and *Rebecca* (1940) Selznick had emerged as one of the most powerful producers in Hollywood, equal in influence to any of the major studio chiefs. Indeed, he had scored a major coup during 1940, when his independent production company surpassed all of the major studios in annual net profits. Selznick International didn't distribute its movies or own any theaters, but it earned $10 million from the release of three films: *Gone with the Wind, Rebecca,* and *Intermezzo* (1939). Only MGM approached Selznick's earnings, and half of its $8.7 million in profits actually came from distributing *Gone with the Wind.*[3] But a decade that promised still greater achievements ended abruptly with the disastrous failures of *The Paradine Case* (1947) and *Portrait of Jennie* (1948). Because Selznick distributed these two films through Selznick Releasing Organization, a distribution division founded in 1946 to distribute the hugely successful *Duel in the Sun* (1946), the entire Selznick corporation had to absorb the blow from these box office bombs. Debts accumulated by the distribution division made further production nearly unthinkable. In part because of volatility in the motion picture market in the late 1940s, Selznick postponed domestic production until the corporation repaid the largest portion of its debts.[4]

Since the studio still had contracts with actors and with production and distribution staffs, Selznick hoped that television production could provide an infusion of cash, employment for contract talent, and a little free advertising for his faltering features. In April 1948, he met with a number of NBC executives who encouraged him to consider developing a series to be titled *Selznick Theater of the Air.* Intrigued by the idea, Selznick approached the Liggett and Myers Tobacco Company, with which he had established contacts during negotiations over a possible radio series in the early 1940s.

In those days, Selznick had been eager to exploit the public relations value of a radio series that would feature appearances by him, his studio contract performers, and contract director Alfred Hitchcock, whom Selznick presciently described as "a tremendous asset around whom a program could be built."[5] Those negotiations collapsed, however, because Selznick presented the sponsors with a list of unyielding demands designed to ensure his authority as producer. "I have not had anybody tell me anything about what I could or couldn't do for about twelve years," he explained, "and I don't intend to start now taking orders or supervision or censorship from anyone."[6] The pattern for Selznick's relationship with sponsors was established during this initial engagement, when he made it clear that he would not adapt willingly to the power relations of commercial broadcasting, in which producers worked for advertisers and the agencies that represented them.

In spite of the previous ill-fated negotiations with Liggett and Myers, Selznick persuaded Dutch Ellis, the executive in charge of advertising for the company's Chesterfield account, to order an initial weekly series based upon screen tests made at the production company. Selznick reasoned that his studio's screen tests could pay for themselves, while at the same time promoting the studio's feature films and stars. "By having the tests actually made while they are being televised," he suggested, "we could not only make one test a week, thereby permitting us to test more people than we do now; we could save 100 percent of the cost; we could make a profit on them; and we could open up a tremendous advertising medium for ourselves." The budget for a normal test was $2,000; the TV version would cost $1,000 extra. Chesterfield agreed to the production of a pilot at a cost of no more than $3,000, which would be split evenly by the companies.[7]

Selznick Test Stage would return to one of Selznick's favorite promotional ploys—depicting Hollywood's star system as a narrative, the story of his Svengalian quest for the rare woman capable of becoming a star under his tutelage. The search for the ideal actress to portray Scarlett O'Hara had been one of the most widely publicized elements of *Gone with the Wind*, and studio publicity frequently emphasized the producer's discovery and "creation" of other female stars, most notably Ingrid Bergman, Joan Fontaine, and Jennifer Jones.[8] (Aside from Gregory Peck, Selznick had little success in developing male stars.) As recent critics have demonstrated, the "star system" was a central component of movie marketing in the studio system. By managing the star's image as it was developed through movie roles and promotion—press releases, interviews, personal appearances, portraits, and product endorsements—the studios actively attempted to produce unique, identifiable stars.[9] Television would allow Selznick to depict this process by offering TV viewers exclusive insight into casting procedures, an aspect of film production that is suppressed in movies themselves but widely discussed in the surrounding media. Yet Selznick planned to depict the star-making process not as the calculated creation and management of a star image but as an epiphany, the discovery of an individual whose essential identity radiates the enigmatic aura of stardom, one of Hollywood's most compelling myths.

Each episode of *Selznick Test Stage* would provide a context for a legitimate screen test by embedding it within a narrative that contained two major plots: Selznick's ongoing search for stars and the actress's or actor's hope of being discovered. The episode's early scenes would emphasize Selznick's quest and remind viewers of the role that screen tests had played in the history of Selznick Productions, perhaps displaying the tests of Vivien Leigh, Ingrid Bergman, and others. This historical segment would be followed by a shift to the second narrative thread—an account of the events leading up to the test, an interview with the anxious participant, and, finally, the test itself. Interspersed throughout the program would be "tasteful" commercials for Chesterfield and promotional excerpts from Selznick releases. To ensure that his contract performers would not explicitly promote the cigarettes, Selznick suggested that "Chesterfield plugs should be ample and subtle" within the scenes—with people on-screen casually handing each other packs of Chesterfields, or with Chesterfield posters in the background of scenes.[10] The management of a star image involved control over all discourses that shaped moviegoers' perception of the star, including product endorsements. Selznick diligently guarded against his sponsor's promotional goals' interfering with his own.

Once the cameras rolled, however, the relationship between Selznick and the sponsor deteriorated. Dutch Ellis, Chesterfield's representative, began to spend time at the studio, negotiating, offering suggestions, keeping an eye on his company's investment. This was standard behavior for a sponsor, but it irritated Selznick, who tolerated no interference. When Ellis suggested that Selznick actors actually endorse Chesterfield cigarettes during the program, Selznick became incensed. "I think Ellis has put one over on us," he cried. "In my dealings for television shows I have made clear to everyone . . . that we could not cheapen our stars by having them make any endorsements at this time." Selznick feared that such vulgar associations, "so completely antithetical to our dignified handling of our people," would rob his stars of their glamour. Selznick asked his staff to remind Ellis "how much more valuable it would be to have subtle plugs such as there being Chesterfields on the make-up table, on the set, the director smoking them, an assistant director offering someone a cigarette."[11]

As was characteristic of him, Selznick stood firm over his autonomy as a producer. "Dutch Ellis should not be made familiar with any of our activities on budgeting or plans," he ordered. "It is none of his concern. He is our customer and not our partner."[12] In Selznick's mind, he had redefined radio's tradition of sponsorship, stripping the patron of all power. As he had demonstrated with radio, Selznick was unwilling to adapt to the power relations in commercial broadcasting. With his usual obstinacy, he thought that there was room in broadcasting for him to play the role of prestigious independent producer just as he had in the movie industry—to produce his own programs at his own pace, accountable only to himself. In essence, he believed that he could *participate* in television without *becoming* television, that TV would adapt to Selznick and not vice versa. Not surprisingly, he eventually severed the relationship with Chesterfield without having delivered the pilot episode.

Undaunted by his encounter with TV sponsors, Selznick officially formed Selznick Television Corporation in July 1948, bankrolling the company with an initial investment of $25,000 from his own pocket. He released a statement to the press explaining that the new company would begin production of "experimental" TV programs within the next sixty days. *Selznick Test Stage* would be the company's premiere production, but the company would produce five to ten half-hour filmed series within the next two years. Selznick even felt confident enough to promise one NBC executive that the company immediately would institute a production program of more than five hundred episodes per year.[13]

By September 1948, however, Selznick's interest in television had waned as his enthusiasm ran up against the realization that, because of the size of the audience, television sponsors still were able to finance only the least-expensive productions. The final budget estimate for the *Selznick Test Stage* pilot ran to $6,880—a minimal sum by Selznick's feature film standards but more than four times what Chesterfield had offered to pay.[14] His initial enthusiasm for many other proposed projects diminished as he realized that they were either dull or, in the case of opera and ballet, too expensive for TV in 1948. Such highbrow programs represented the sort of entertainment that Selznick ultimately hoped to bring to television, and yet he was forced to admit that these programs, with budgets running at least $30,000 per half-hour, could not be financed by the medium's limited economic base. "Television," he lamented, "is very far from the point where it can absorb operatic films, ballet films, etc., for which there is still too small a market to pay the cost, with the likelihood that this market will not be sufficiently expanded for a long time to come."[15]

Like those executives of the major studios who had planned to integrate television into the studio system, Selznick had expressed great interest in broadcasting. He envisioned television as a potentially invaluable element of the movie industry and attempted to develop programming designed specifically for the medium. But like the major studios that had elected not to enter television under conditions dominated by networks, sponsors, and advertising agencies, Selznick balked at the prospect of adapting to the producer's circumscribed role in the new medium. Selznick's privileged status as one of the few independent producers to profit from the studio system made him nearly as inflexible as the studio chiefs in his encounters with the broadcasting industry. His inability to carry out plans for radio and TV production through the late 1940s was a result of this rigidity, a product of his refusal to acknowledge that the TV industry had developed its own standards, its own relations of power.

•   •   •

As a result of hesitation by major studios and prestigious independent producers, television production originated in Hollywood as the domain of producers with razor-thin profit margins and little stake in the studio system. As small-scale entrepreneurs, these producers experienced few of the reservations that deterred the movie industry's major powers. They had grown accustomed to squeezing themselves into the cracks and crevices of the studio system—operating on tiny budgets, surviving on minimal profits, designing products that earned money in the neglected areas of a market defined by larger companies. Independent producers and small studios typically filled the exhibitors' need for such products as B features, short subjects, serials, and travelogues, the less-prestigious and not-as-profitable entertainment that completed a theater's daily program, but that the major companies produced with less frequency after the early 1940s.

Adaptability was the key to survival in a market that discriminated against any small producer, and independent producers by necessity worked with a much broader definition of filmed entertainment, considering many formats that strayed from the major studios' dominant feature-length narratives. Unburdened by a commitment to any particular system of distribution or exhibition, to a certain conception of the producer's autonomy and authority, or to any particular definition of the cinematic text, these producers were less devoted to a single medium than to exploiting the potential of any market and any product that promised a return on their investment.

An entrepreneur like Jerry Fairbanks epitomized the spirit of the early telefilm pioneers. A producer of short subjects at Paramount for many years, Fairbanks chased the lure of television riches in 1946 when he opened his own telefilm production company in a small studio at the heart of Sunset Boulevard's Poverty Row studios. Inspired by the general corporate culture at Paramount, the studio most committed to television, and by the ingenuity of the studio's short-subject division, Fairbanks envisioned TV production as his opportunity to surmount the obstacles presented by the studio system. Although there were only a dozen TV stations broadcasting at the time, Fairbanks believed the most optimistic projections forecasting that more than a thousand stations would be bombarding the nation's airwaves by 1953. While many of these stations would be network affiliates broadcasting live programming from New York, Fairbanks and others speculated that these thousand stations quickly would exhaust the network's capabilities, leaving behind an insatiable appetite for filmed programming. Although TV production didn't promise to be immediately profitable, Fairbanks imagined this imminent demand and saw no ceiling on the potential value of filmed TV programs.

Jerry Fairbanks introduced three-camera shooting to telefilm production with his "Multicam" system. Using three 16-millimeter cameras, a cramped set, and carefully rehearsed choreography, Fairbanks could shoot a half-hour episode, such as this 1950 production of *Silver Theater*, in one day. (Courtesy of Bison Archives © Jerry Fairbanks Productions)

Fairbanks was a tinkerer and a cut-rate visionary; he relished the challenge of adapting studio system production techniques to the demanding economies of television during an era when a half-hour television program couldn't count on more than a $20,000 budget. In the trade journals and popular press, Fairbanks touted his "Multicam" production system, which adapted live TV's three-camera shooting technique to film production. While there were precedents for multi-camera shooting in the film industry, Fairbanks used 16-millimeter Mitchell cameras mounted on tripod dollies to approximate video's capacity for quick, continuous shooting while creating a product—a motion picture print—that was durable, reproducible, and transportable, with a visual quality that surpassed that of live TV's kinescopes.

Because of his budget, Fairbanks couldn't afford to duplicate video's practice of running all three cameras simultaneously. In order to economize on the use of film stock, much of the editing was completed "in-camera," with only one designated camera running at any given moment. This technique necessitated rigorous pre-production planning in which lighting, camera angles, editing decisions, and the movement of cameras and performers had to be precisely orchestrated before the cameras ever rolled. Cables and banks of 300-watt reflector lights were suspended from the ceiling so they wouldn't impede the movement of actors or cameras. Newly developed zoom lenses were fitted onto the cameras to facilitate rapid shifts in focus or changes in composition. Fairbanks registered a number of patents related to this process, including the tripod dollies, an electronic method for marking synchronization among all three cameras and the sound recorder, and a device for following focus on the Mitchell camera's parallax viewer. While other filmed half-hour episodes required production schedules of two or three days, Fairbanks could shoot an episode in a matter of hours. Production costs were kept so low that the single most expensive item in the budget was the cost of film stock and processing, which accounted for only 3 percent of a feature film budget but was 25 to 30 percent of the budget for any Fairbanks program.[16]

In 1948, NBC contracted Fairbanks to produce the first filmed series for network TV, *Public Prosecutor,* starring John Howard. The program, like most Fairbanks productions, looks primitive by the standards of its contemporary feature-film production. Narrated by Howard, a swarthy actor who addresses the camera throughout much of the story, the bare-bones mystery plots are condensed to fit into fifteen-minute segments modeled after the format of radio episodes. The verbal exposition is so insistent that the images begin to seem redundant; the episodes truly resemble radio with pictures. Sets are often undecorated. Actors appear distracted, if not anguished, as they try to hit their marks consistently on the first take. In spite of the opportunities for shot selection offered by the Multicam system, the camerawork consists mainly of single-take medium shots or simple over-the-shoulder dialogue sequences. In promoting his Multicam system, Fairbanks claimed that his minimum length of time per take was five minutes, with the average take lasting between seven and eight minutes. Although this may be true of other Fairbanks programs, an episode of *Public Prosecutor* contains frequent, seemingly unnecessary, editing within any given sequence. The network-financed budget for the series was $8,800 per episode. Still, the network couldn't find sponsors—not even after reducing the asking price to $5,000 per episode. With each episode's production costs exceeding $10,000, Fairbanks discontinued production before completing a season's worth of programs.[17] Although his company survived the setback, this effort was certainly not an impressive debut for filmed programming on the networks.

Fairbanks developed a close relationship with NBC and CBS during the early years of network TV. In order to broadcast live programs over affiliates that were not connected to the networks by coaxial cable, NBC and CBS often needed filmed copies that could be transported physically from station to station. The Fairbanks company filmed many of these programs, which originated on the West Coast, including *The Ed Wynn Show* (1949–1950), *Truth or Consequences* (1950–1958), and *The Alan Young Show* (1950–1953). Fairbanks also filmed a number of syndicated action-adventure series for other independent producers, such as *Front Page Detective* (1951–1953) with Edmund Lowe. Many other independent producers joined Fairbanks in this first speculative period of telefilm production, which extended from 1946 through the 1951–1952 TV season. "Everybody who could buy or borrow a little drugstore movie camera announced himself as a TV-film producer," Fairbanks said in describing these early days.[18]

News accounts during this period estimated that more than eight hundred producers sought telefilm riches in the years before 1952. As a result, more than two thousand unsold pilots languished on storage shelves or rotted in trash bins, having failed to attract sponsors for network broadcast or syndication. Neglected studios, empty warehouses, supermarkets, and family garages were transformed into temporary soundstages; 16-millimeter cameras disappeared from the stores; personal savings accounts were drained—all in the frantic gold rush years of the early telefilm industry.

The most visible producers to appear during this first stage of telefilm production were the B-movie cowboys, who quickly became icons of the early video age: William "Hopalong Cassidy" Boyd, Gene Autry, and Roy Rogers. Boyd provided the telefilm industry's first unabashed success story, fueling every independent producer's wildest fantasies about deliverance from the studio system. During the 1940s he had shrewdly invested $350,000 to acquire the television rights to the series of Hopalong Cassidy feature films in which he had starred since 1935; in addition, he acquired the rights to use the Hopalong Cassidy character in other media, including television, and in character merchandising. After marketing the features to local stations during the late 1940s, Boyd produced a new *Hopalong Cassidy* TV series for NBC beginning in 1949 and running to 1951.

By tapping into the growing postwar youth market and by taking advantage of television's emergent position at the center of an expanding popular culture marketplace, Boyd founded a Hopalong

Cassidy industry that within only a few years included a radio series, a comic strip, comic books, a popular fan club, and a dazzling array of licensed merchandise—with an estimated total value of $200 million.[19] Spurred by Boyd's canny reincarnation, Autry and Rogers also revived moribund careers and earned fantastic wealth by producing television Westerns on the same dusty backlots that had once provided the settings for their B Westerns.

From the frenzied pack of fly-by-night producers that surrounded these cowboy heroes in the early telefilm business, five significant production companies emerged: Fairbanks, Hal Roach Studios, Bing Crosby Enterprises, Ziv Television Programs, and Louis Snader Productions. The varied backgrounds of these producers—and the programs they produced—give some sense of the many career routes that delivered early entrepreneurs to the telefilm industry.[20]

The Hal Roach Studios arrived in television as an established Poverty Row movie studio. From its longtime position on the margins of the movie industry, the Roach studio was familiar with the many low-budget alternatives to standard narrative features. The studio itself was almost dormant in 1949 when Hal Roach, Jr., after years of kicking around the industry, joined the company and persuaded his father to rent space to telefilm producers and to form a TV production unit. During the early years, Roach produced situation comedies like *The Stu Erwin Show* (1950–1955) and *My Little Margie* (1952–1955) and crime dramas like *Racket Squad* (1950–1953). As the studio increased its output, Hal Junior became one of the early influential figures in the telefilm business, helping to found both the Television Film Producers Association and the National Academy of Television Arts and Sciences.

Bing Crosby was a performer and a shrewd businessman who had always moved easily among movies, radio, recordings, and live performances. Under the guidance of Basil Grillo and Crosby's brother Everett, Bing Crosby Enterprises had diversified successfully into a number of unrelated businesses, producing orange juice, ice cream, sport shirts, and a wide variety of endorsed merchandise. An early proponent of the shift from live radio broadcast to transcribed performances, Crosby also was a chief investor in Ampex's development of videotape. As a result of these interests, Crosby was probably the most reputable and highly capitalized of the early telefilm producers. Crosby's company during its early years focused primarily on anthology series, including *Fireside Theater* (1950–1958) and *Rebound* (1952).

Frederick Ziv, a syndicator of radio transcriptions to local stations, viewed telefilm production as an obvious extension of his existing business—an alternative to live broadcasting that provided local radio

Department heads at Hal Roach Studios in 1952 coordinate the production of five television series: *The Stu Erwin Show, Racket Squad, Amos and Andy, Abbott and Costello,* and *Mystery Theatre.* After being practically dormant in 1949, television production raised the studio's output to the equivalent of two feature films a week.
(Courtesy of Bison Archives © Hal Roach Studios)

stations with some autonomy from the networks. Ziv Television Programs packaged fifteen-minute sports and news programs for TV beginning in 1948. In 1949 the company began production on *The Cisco Kid* (1950–1956), its first dramatic TV series. By shooting the series in color when all other producers were using black-and-white film, Ziv ensured the residual value of the series for decades. Ziv's subsequent work consisted primarily of action series with male heroes, such as *Boston Blackie* (1951–1953) and *Dangerous Assignment* (1951–1952).

Louis Snader, an ex-musician and real estate tycoon, was probably the least likely member of this group of producers, and his success was the shortest-lived. Louis Snader Productions produced the television version of *Dick Tracy* in 1950, but Snader hoped to make his real mark through his introduction in 1949 of "Telescriptions," three-minute filmed musical performances featuring stars like Peggy Lee, Mel Torme, and the Jordanaires. Producing twelve per day at a cost of $2,500 each, Snader imagined that his short films could be programmed flexibly into the daily schedule of local stations. Snader anticipated that these Telescriptions would be hosted by TV jockeys, who would become as influential as radio's newly celebrated disc jockeys.[21] Snader's peculiar contribution to the early telefilm, in which he imagined TV mimicking radio's new recorded-music format and unwittingly anticipated the form of music videos, gives some idea of the flexibility of these producers, of their willingness to explore the options made possible by TV.

By 1950, the financial risks of telefilm production had erected barriers to entry that quickly reduced the number of producers. Since the traditional radio model of sponsorship still dominated the television industry, these early telefilm producers dreamed of attracting a sponsor who would give them access to a slot in the network prime-time schedule or one that would finance first-run syndication. The cost of achieving this goal was steeper than one might imagine. While a single half-hour episode cost $12,000 to $15,000 to produce in 1951, most sponsors were unwilling to commit to a series based solely on viewing a pilot episode. Sponsors had become skeptical after being burned by producers who had thrown extraordinary effort and expense into a pilot and then failed to duplicate its quality in the regular episodes. With sponsors wary of using a single episode to judge the potential of an entire series, independent producers often had to produce anywhere from thirteen to a full season of thirty-nine episodes in order to pitch a series to sponsors. Few independent producers had the resources to manage an initial investment in the neighborhood of $200,000 when there were few guarantees of success and even fewer bankers willing to loan money to telefilm producers.[22]

The fortunate producers signed distribution deals that generally gave sponsors the rights to the first national broadcast of the series, whether it aired on the networks or in first-run syndication. Producers usually retained the subsequent distribution rights for domestic and foreign syndication. Yet even those producers able to line up a sponsor didn't succeed immediately, since the first-run license fee for programs generally equaled only 50 to 75 percent of the production costs. Most telefilm series didn't break even until their second or third run in local markets. As historian William Lafferty has shown, this version of financing originated with the first successful telefilm series, Procter and Gamble's *Fireside Theater*.[23]

Because of the limited TV audience in the late 1940s and the relatively low-cost alternative of live TV, Procter and Gamble chose not to finance the entire cost of telefilm production. When the sponsor contracted Gordon LeVoy to produce the first season of *Fireside Theater* in

1949, it paid only 60 percent of production costs, but agreed that rights to the series would revert to LeVoy thirty days after the last episode was broadcast. LeVoy made a nice profit in spring 1950 when CBS paid him $225,000 for the rights to syndicate the series for four years. When Bing Crosby Productions took over production of *Fireside Theater* in 1950, Procter and Gamble continued its licensing pattern, paying $10,000 of the $14,000 production costs for each episode. Because of its widespread adoption, this precedent for deficit financing was known originally in the TV industry as the "Procter and Gamble formula."[24]

This method of financing quickly established two economic principles of telefilm production. First, television series generally are produced at a deficit, with the production company absorbing costs that exceed first-run license fees paid by sponsors or networks. Second, profits for television series lie in residual rights to the program—its value in subsequent-run syndication, international distribution, and merchandising of related products.[25] This financial arrangement had many implications for telefilm production. It raised the stakes for telefilm producers by lifting the budget restrictions imposed by fixed license fees. The promise of riches in subsequent markets encouraged producers to gamble by increasing their production budgets—and their deficits—in order to distinguish their programs from those of competitors. This development not only encouraged inflationary tendencies in the telefilm industry but benefited companies that had the financial security to withstand the burden of large production deficits. In addition, deficit financing inspired producers to keep in mind the secondary markets beyond network broadcast, since these markets were the source of profits. This introduced a tension into the creative process, since programs had to be shaped with an eye on both the primary market of network broadcast and the various secondary markets that could follow. Surprisingly, these implications of deficit financing—which are still a factor in the TV industry—emerged during the earliest years of telefilm production in Hollywood.

Most of these developments in the telefilm business occurred outside the interests of the Hollywood studios that were trying to cope with the shifting fortunes of the postwar motion picture industry. Despite the major studios' announcements since the mid-1930s of their intentions to establish a presence in television, only two studios from the studio system actually attempted to make the transition to television production during the late 1940s and early 1950s: Universal-International and Columbia. It is ironic that Universal and Columbia

were the first studio system pioneers in TV production—they traditionally had demonstrated the least interest in expanding into broadcasting. While the five largest studios jockeyed for position—buying
radio stations, investing in television research, applying for TV station licenses—Universal and Columbia never had the investment
capital to pursue diversification. Along with United Artists, Universal
and Columbia did not own the revenue-generating theater chains that
provided the major studios with financial security. The major studios
planned to impose themselves on the broadcasting industry through
direct investment and ownership of the technology and facilities, but
lesser studios like Universal and Columbia saw their relationship to
the TV industry as an extension of their subordinate status in the
studio system. Because they were willing to supply product to a market beyond their control, Universal and Columbia probably were best
equipped to adapt to the programming demands and economic relationships of television.

Universal first began television production in 1947 as one measure
in a desperate attempt to put the brakes on runaway financial losses
that had piled up following the box office failure of a number of prestige independent productions that the studio had financed and distributed starting in 1946. While these deals with producers such as
Fritz Lang, Walter Wanger, Mark Hellinger, and Alexander Korda led
to a number of exceptional films, such as *Scarlet Street* (1946), *The
Killers* (1946), and *The Naked City* (1948), they also ultimately helped
send the studio from a record profit of $4.6 million in 1946 to a record
loss of $3.2 million just two years later.[26]

Universal turned to the production of TV commercials as a side
venture of its New York–based subsidiary, United World Films, the
world's largest distributor of 8- and 16-millimeter film. The company
immediately established itself by producing for clients such as Lever's
Lux Soap, General Electric, and Gulf Oil. By 1949 the company had
moved its TV operations to Los Angeles in hopes of expanding into
the production of documentaries and other types of programming.
Since net profits of the TV division for the first year were less than
$40,000, the studio probably intended less for TV production to boost
its profits than for it to buy time by paying for facilities and labor at a
moment when lack of funds even forced the studio to shut its doors
temporarily.[27]

In the early 1950s, after Decca Records purchased a majority interest in Universal and installed its president, Milton Rackmil, as the
head of the studio, Universal solved its financial problems by returning to the production of moderate- to low-budget features designed
to service subsequent-run theaters.[28] Universal staked its comeback at

the box office during the 1950s on a series of proto–situation comedies featuring Ma and Pa Kettle and Francis the Talking Mule (whose producer, Arthur Lubin, eventually created the TV series *Mr. Ed* [1961–1965]), but the studio couldn't crack the market for TV series. After its relocation to Los Angeles, United World had the misfortune of joining the deluge of other independent telefilm producers trying to sell series to networks and sponsors. In 1951, the company produced a thirteen-episode television series titled *Fighting Man,* but found no takers. In spite of the fact that Rackmil channeled funds into the production of TV pilots throughout 1952, United World's telefilms could not break through the independent production glut; sponsors showed no interest in its series. In December 1952, Universal's TV operation announced that it would forget series production and focus strictly on commercials,[29] a policy that remained unchanged for the rest of the decade.

Although Columbia initially entered television under much the same strategy as Universal, its rapid diversification beyond commercials made it more successful. In spring 1949, Columbia president Harry Cohn hired his nephew, Ralph, the son of studio cofounder Jack Cohn, to conduct a preliminary study of Columbia's immediate and long-range prospects in the field of television. For the previous two years Ralph Cohn had acquired a firsthand knowledge of television while running a two-man organization, Pioneer Television, which produced TV commercials in New York. Cohn presented his boss with a fifty-page analysis in which he predicted that it would be many years before television would be a profitable market for Columbia's library of motion pictures. While anticipating the growth of this market, he suggested, Columbia should immediately assemble an organization to produce TV commercials and, ultimately, filmed programs for both network and local broadcast.[30]

In June 1949 Columbia formed a television production subsidiary through Screen Gems, the former animation company that had produced the studio's short subjects since the Cohns purchased it from Charles Mintz in 1934. During the first two years of its existence, Screen Gems produced only TV commercials, delivering more than two hundred for such clients as American Tobacco, Hamilton Watch, and BVD.[31] Through this contact with the advertising industry, Cohn and his staff became acquainted with many of the most prominent agencies at a time when sponsors and agencies still exercised direct control over much of prime time.

In 1951, Screen Gems signed a deal with DuPont to create seven half-hour episodes for the company's historical anthology series, *Cavalcade of America* (1952–1955). The deal between Screen Gems and

DuPont differed from other telefilm production deals because it resembled the model of production financing developed by the advertising agencies during the radio era and carried over into New York–based live TV production. Under the terms of this contract, the studio produced the episode for DuPont, and the sponsor received outright ownership of the negatives.

Clearly, Screen Gems could not profit from television production under such an arrangement. Unless the studio retained all residual rights to its product and was able to distribute it in markets other than network TV, the studio would never be anything but a minor subcontractor in the field of TV production. This realization was driven home when each episode produced by the studio cost at least $7,000 more than DuPont had agreed to pay. Although the sponsor covered the difference—a practice which could have occurred only at this early stage of the industry's development—Screen Gems realized that simple production of episodes was not the way to become a major force in the field of television.[32]

In the spring of 1952, fully aware of the mistakes made in the previous deal, Ralph Cohn and Columbia production chief Irving Briskin negotiated with the J. Walter Thompson advertising agency and its client, Ford Motor Company, to produce a half-hour anthology series that would star new studio contract players. Although Columbia had created the television subsidiary as a way to deflect pressure from theatrical exhibitors and ultimately chose not to use its own talent in the series because of concern about potential hostility from exhibitors, Briskin's presence at the negotiations demonstrated the extent of Columbia's commitment to TV production. Screen Gems agreed to produce a thirty-nine-episode anthology series, *Ford Theater*, which the sponsor would place in its existing 9:30 P.M. Thursday time slot on NBC. Ford paid $22,000 per episode in exchange for the right to broadcast each episode twice on the network. Although the episodes would cost at least $25,000 to produce, Screen Gems this time would retain all subsequent rights to the series, hoping to recover its costs and earn profits from syndication.[33]

With the Ford deal, Screen Gems no longer served as a mere supplier of programming to a sponsor. By adopting the established practice of deficit financing and by retaining the subsequent rights to the episode, the studio opened itself to the potentially limitless profits of syndication. Once Screen Gems had established *Ford Theater* in prime time, it formed its own syndication division and distributed the series to local markets under the title *All-Star Theater*. With nearly two hundred episodes ultimately distributed in syndication, the series reinforced the studio's belief that the cost of an expensive series could be recovered through secondary markets. According to Ralph Cohn, the anthology series also offered another important benefit; like B-movie production in the studio system, it served as a training ground, allowing young writers, directors, and producers to experiment in a variety of genres, including comedy, romance, and action-adventure.[34]

The turning point for telefilm production came during 1951 and 1952. In spite of the FCC's station application freeze, which didn't end until 1952, the national television audience had grown rapidly, with the percentage of households having a TV set expanding from 9 percent in 1950 to 34 percent by 1952. In addition, a number of successful filmed programs broadcast during prime time convinced sponsors, the networks, and influential film industry figures that filmed series had both immediate and long-term value. The economic formula of deficit financing coupled with rising production costs and the uncertain market for syndication drove away the most speculative producers. As better-capitalized producers like Screen Gems became more ambitious, the average cost of a half-hour episode jumped from $12,000 in 1949 to $20,000 by 1952. At the same time, however, the syndication market promised a slow and unpredictable return on the investment. The FCC freeze had limited the market for syndicated programming, and the existing market hadn't yet developed a stable pricing system. Stretched between higher immediate costs and profits that might be endlessly deferred, speculative telefilm production collapsed. One trade publication stated that in 1951 there were seventy-five independent companies with forty series in production, only twenty-five of which were of suitable quality for prime time. By 1952, the number of independents had fallen to fewer than thirty. On the other hand, demand for filmed series by the networks increased as the number of filmed series in prime time jumped from fourteen in 1951 to twenty-seven in 1952.[35]

The success of telefilm series like *Fireside Theater*, which finished the 1950–1951 season as the nation's second-rated series, convinced talent agencies that their radio and movie performers should enter telefilm production. The long-term value of filmed properties seemed clear, especially as more stations came on-line; now the networks and major sponsors began to demonstrate an increased willingness to program telefilm series in prime time. Ziv TV and the Roach studio still thrived after the early years, but the next wave of telefilm production was led primarily by second- or third-rank movie stars and radio performers like Lucille Ball and Desi Arnaz, Dick Powell, and Jack Webb. Supported by their talent agencies, these performers formed production companies in order to produce their own series.

Just as actors and actresses in the movie industry were accelerating the shift to independent production by taking advantage of capital gains tax breaks, aspiring TV stars in search of investments, freedom from the major studios, or a career revival populated the second wave of telefilm entrepreneurs. The years 1951–1952 witnessed the debut of a number of network telefilm series—most notably *Amos and Andy*, *I Love Lucy*, and *Dragnet*—whose popularity fueled the growth in filmed television production. Unlike the first wave of telefilm producers, these producers were financially secure. Because of their reputations in radio or movies and the backing of established talent agencies, they often were able to get series commitments from sponsors and networks based on a single pilot episode. And as a result of these commitments, they found it much easier to arrange bank financing to cover production deficits and company expenses.

Talent agencies played a crucial role in this stage of the industry's development. To find work for actors as motion picture production declined, they began to package clients in series designed to take advantage of the long-term profit potential of filmed TV programming. Often the line between agent and producer was blurred by those who served both functions simultaneously. In 1952 the largest talent agency in the business, MCA, formed its own TV production company, Revue Productions, which ultimately produced series for such clients as Alfred Hitchcock and Ronald Reagan. Another agent, Don Sharpe, was probably the most influential, if the most neglected, participant in this stage of telefilm's development. Described as the industry's "Mr. Big" by *Television* magazine in 1953, Sharpe had a significant impact on many of the filmed series of the early 1950s.[36] During 1950, Sharpe advised his client Brian Donleavy to transfer his radio series, *Dangerous Assignment*, to television in a first-run syndication series produced by Ziv. Donleavy received 50 percent profit participation in the series, and Sharpe collected his first TV credit as executive producer. He negotiated a series deal for client Robert Cummings to star in *My Hero* (1952–1953) and helped another client, Douglas Fairbanks, Jr., to found his own production company, Dougfair, which produced *Terry and the Pirates* (1952) and *Douglas Fairbanks, Jr. Presents* (1952–1957).

Sharpe assisted a number of his clients in forming two of the fastest-growing independent production companies that emerged during the 1950s—Desilu Productions and Four Star Productions. In 1951 Sharpe negotiated with Phillip Morris and CBS for *I Love Lucy*, a TV series starring his clients Lucille Ball and Desi Arnaz and produced by their own production company, Desilu. In spite of the demands by Phillip Morris and the network that the show be broadcast live from New

In 1951, Lucille Ball and Desi Arnaz founded Desilu, the telefilm industry's
fastest-rising independent production company.
(Courtesy of Wisconsin Center for Film and Theater Research
© Desilu Productions)

York, Sharpe, Ball, and Arnaz insisted that the series be filmed in Hollywood—in order to take advantage of production facilities and to ensure the value of the series by capturing it on film. As a concession, Desilu agreed to pay for the additional expense of production but also retained all rights to the episodes. The deal paid off handsomely following the show's huge success, when CBS ultimately purchased the rights to the series from Desilu for $5 million.[37] In 1952, Sharpe persuaded Singer Sewing Machine to spend $1.25 million financing twenty-six episodes of *Four Star Playhouse* (1952–1956), an anthology series produced by and starring three Sharpe clients—Dick Powell, David Niven, and Charles Boyer.[38] The fourth star, Ida Lupino, appeared in episodes but never owned stock in the company. Like Desilu, Four Star expanded from its initial production of a single series to become one of the largest suppliers of filmed TV programming by the end of the decade.

The budgets for this second wave of telefilm series—averaging $20,000 per episode in 1952—still demanded ingenuity from producers who had no choice but to economize whenever possible. Often able to spend less than $800 on script development costs, the series couldn't afford to hire screenwriters from the film industry.[39] Instead, many employed radio writers or Hollywood newcomers who adapted public domain stories or, if the series had come from radio, recast previously produced radio scripts. The most successful early telefilm series, such as *Amos and Andy, Dragnet,* and *I Love Lucy,* began by recycling scripts used during their radio incarnations (the *I Love Lucy* scripts came from Ball's radio series, *My Favorite Husband*).

Stylistic choices also were shaped by budgetary restrictions. Although *Dragnet* was widely acclaimed at the time for its uncanny sense of verisimilitude, the 1950s version of the Jack Webb–produced series today seems surreal thanks to the somnambulistic performances and talking-head shooting style necessitated by Webb's cost-cutting device—using TelePrompTers to eliminate the need for rehearsal. Based on his experience in radio, Webb decided that *Dragnet*'s actors should read directly from TelePrompTers placed beneath the camera lens, rather than waste valuable time memorizing lines. Since the series ran simultaneously on radio and television, Webb often used the same scripts for both versions, making only minimal concessions to the opportunities provided by a visual medium. These decisions led to *Dragnet*'s monotonous conversational scenes and its unintentionally Brechtian performances, often-parodied elements of a narrative world populated by seemingly emotionless automatons.[40]

Of course, not all of the financial constraints from this era produced effects that became dated so quickly. Recognizing the residual value of a telefilm series, Desi Arnaz and Don Sharpe wanted to shoot *I Love Lucy* on film, but they also wanted to capture the spontaneity of Lucille Ball's comic performances, particularly her rapport with audiences. Desi Arnaz and famed cinematographer Karl Freund found a solution by using a three-camera shooting style similar to that adopted by Jerry Fairbanks. Contrary to their claims, Arnaz and Freund did not originate this shooting strategy, but, unlike Fairbanks, they could afford to run all three cameras simultaneously while filming before a studio audience.[41] Consequently, they were able to combine the vital performances made possible by live, three-camera shooting with the visual quality of film. The same technique is still very much in evidence in contemporary situation comedies.

Built on radical economic constraints, Hollywood's earliest television triumphs scarcely affected the major powers in the movie industry. During the first stage of television production in Hollywood, from roughly 1946 until 1951, telefilm production took place on the distant fringes of the studio system. Telefilm's underfinanced, uncoordinated early ventures, the province of Hollywood outsiders and castoffs, merited little attention from industry leaders. In dormant studios and improvised locations throughout the Los Angeles area, would-be telefilm moguls cranked out speculative pilots and full-blown series, shooting on shoestring budgets and scheming to corner a market that promised an elusive bounty. Rarely did these productions find their way onto network schedules.

Gradually, however, the market for telefilm production solidified as sponsors and the networks looked to Hollywood for programming and as more established independent producers turned to television in hopes of reaping profits through syndication and merchandising. The second stage of telefilm production began in 1951 and 1952 as minor studios like Screen Gems and independent producers with the backing of established talent agencies produced half-hour filmed series for national sponsors who offered access to the networks' primetime schedules. Live programs still dominated prime time, but the unprecedented popularity of filmed series like *I Love Lucy* and *Dragnet* demonstrated the appeal of Hollywood series.

In spite of their success in the ratings, however, it is worth remembering that these filmed series stood little chance of passing muster among the era's arbiters of taste. Restricted by the meager budgets that advertising revenue could support during the first decade of national broadcasting, the series were bargain-basement knockoffs of the movie industry's cheapest productions. Series like *Hopalong Cassidy* and *Racket Squad* copied the most common and least-esteemed action genres—Westerns, crime, science fiction, exotic adventures; others adopted radio-series formats like the situation comedy.

Jack Gould of the *New York Times* expressed the critical response to these series when he declared in 1952 that "the decision of television to put many of its programs on film has turned out to be the colossal boner of the year. On every count—technically and qualitatively—the films cannot compare with 'live' shows, and they are hurting video, not helping it. . . . To regard the medium as merely a variation on the neighborhood picture house is to misunderstand the medium." [42] From the perspective of a New York critic who dreaded the apparently inevitable disappearance of prestigious live programming, television may have seemed to possess an essential identity as a medium for live broadcast. But the independent producers who participated in the early stages of telefilm production also were in the process of defining the medium; they perceived it precisely as a welcome variation on the neighborhood movie theaters that had been their domain throughout the studio era.

In concert with sponsors and the networks, therefore, opportunistic independent producers who were marginal to the studio system institutionalized television production in Hollywood. Some of these producers—particularly Screen Gems, Desilu, and Four Star—prospered throughout the 1950s, building major corporations on the profits from television series. But the telefilm industry's second stage was as brief as its first, its end signaled by a pair of Hollywood-produced TV programs broadcast during a single week in October 1954: the David Selznick–produced spectacular *Light's Diamond Jubilee* and the premiere of Walt Disney's *Disneyland*. Although Selznick and Disney shared with early telefilm producers the belief that television offered an alternative to the studio system, they were by far the most prominent Hollywood producers to enter television. The programs that they produced defined television as something more than an electronic version of the neighborhood movie theater. Their ambitious plans for integrating television into the future of the movie industry ultimately provided the catalyst for the telefilm industry's third stage—the rise to power of Hollywood's major studios.

·IV·
The Sponsor's Medium: *Light's Diamond Jubilee* and the Campaign for the Peaceful Atom

During the early years of network television, most Hollywood producers made the transition from movies to television without fanfare, since there was little glory to be found in the meager budgets and relentless pace of TV series production. In striking contrast, David Selznick debuted as the producer of *Light's Diamond Jubilee,* the most heralded entertainment program in the brief history of television, a two-hour tribute to Thomas Edison that aired Sunday evening, 24 October 1954, on all four existing TV networks and more than three hundred stations. Sponsored at a record cost of $1 million by the nation's electrical utilities and manufacturers, including industry giants General Electric and Westinghouse, *Light's Diamond Jubilee* took exclusive possession of the airwaves on that evening, reaching more than 75 million people—by most estimates the largest audience in entertainment history up to that time.

To produce the program, Selznick recruited a number of his most respected colleagues in the movie industry, including writer Ben Hecht, directors William Wellman and King Vidor, and cinematographer James Wong Howe. Whether measured by its budget, its audience, or the stature of its movie industry participants, *Light's Diamond Jubilee* towered over any TV program previously produced in Hollywood. For Selznick, the magnitude of his debut justified nearly two decades of frustrated negotiations with the broadcasting industry and allowed him to stake a claim as the movie industry's most visionary producer.

In return for the opportunity to produce Hollywood's most ambitious TV program, however, Selznick ultimately had to confront what for him was an unpleasant reality of the television industry: Advertisers, the medium's financial patrons, controlled every stage of the production process. Following the pattern established in radio, advertisers dominated early television production because they purchased broadcast time from the networks and treated certain time slots as virtual corporate franchises; their agents, the advertising agencies, produced the programs that filled these slots. Since TV networks served mainly as conduits for programs produced by advertisers, the networks exercised surprisingly little influence over the structure and content of prime-time programs. Producers hired by the advertising agencies held even less power because they generally worked under close agency supervision. As Michele Hilmes has noted, the networks may have been responsible for determining the economic structure of the television industry, but the "true originators of most of the broadcast forms still with us" were the major advertising agencies.[1] Because of Selznick's reputation in the movie industry, his prime-time debut attracted attention to the role of the TV producer, but television in 1954 was unmistakably a sponsor's medium. Advertisers played the preeminent role in creating television programs.

The impulse to produce *Light's Diamond Jubilee* originated neither with Selznick nor with the networks, but with the electric industry's trade organization, the Edison Electric Institute, and with its advertising agency, N. W. Ayer and Son. For these organizations, the Selznick-produced program was an integrated component in one of the most ambitious public relations campaigns attempted since the rise of network television. By staging publicity events to elicit media coverage, distributing an endless stream of press releases, and placing advertisements in the national media, the Ayer agency and the Edison Electric Institute inspired a national celebration leading to the seventy-fifth anniversary of Edison's invention of the incandescent light.

This campaign, also titled Light's Diamond Jubilee, was motivated by more than devotion to an American hero; its implicit purpose was to polish the industry's image during a time of political debate over whether atomic energy should be entrusted to private industry. With an ambition born of the bottomless coffers at General Electric and Westinghouse, the electric industry exploited all forms of mass communication to transform its promotional campaign into an apparently spontaneous national celebration. The event gathered momentum not only because it was backed by the clout of the electric industry but also because it received the support of the Eisenhower administration, which had launched its own promotional campaign, Atoms for Peace, in an effort to win public approval for an atomic energy policy that favored commercial production.

While it would be difficult to prove that Light's Diamond Jubilee or Atoms for Peace exerted a tangible influence on public attitudes and government policy, the effort to promote the peaceful atom was clearly intended to influence the era's political process. In crafting these campaigns, representatives of industry and the state revealed a concern with cultural politics, an awareness that popular culture is a primary arena of political contest, not merely the reflection of struggles taking place elsewhere in society.[2] Two of the most interesting public events in the campaign for the peaceful atom were staged specifically for television. In addition to the October 1954 broadcast of *Light's Diamond Jubilee*, television viewers also witnessed the September 1954 ground-breaking ceremony for the first commercial nuclear reactor, in which President Eisenhower triggered an automated bulldozer at the power plant's Pennsylvania construction site while standing in a TV studio in Denver.

These broadcasts had characteristics of traditional public ceremonies, but there were no ceremonial sites and no participants beyond the primary actors. The experience of being present at either broadcast location would have paled in comparison to viewing the ceremonies on television. In other words, these broadcasts represented a new and quintessentially modern cultural form—a public event that existed solely to be televised.

The broadcast of *Light's Diamond Jubilee*, therefore, stands as much more than an intriguing detour in the career of David Selznick. Judged by its ambition of intervening in the social and political life of the era, *Light's Diamond Jubilee* represented an attempt to define television's role as the central form of mass communication in post–World War II America. For Selznick, the TV networks, and especially the sponsors, the program embodied one potential form of television, an extravagant vision of the new medium's technical capabilities and economic relations, its expressive forms and persuasive appeals.

For the networks, such blockbuster programs, known within the industry as "spectaculars," transformed television viewing from a mundane household activity into an irresistible national event. As network service extended beyond its early metropolitan audiences, event programming represented a potential strategy for creating programs with nationwide appeal and for delivering viewers to advertisers at a time when no single programming format dominated prime time. For the movie industry, Selznick's role as Hollywood impresario, orchestrating the film industry's top talents in the service of huge corporate sponsors, offered a new model for integrating the motion picture and TV industries, one infinitely preferable to the low-budget operations of previous telefilm producers.

Finally, as the electric industry's monument to a founding father, *Light's Diamond Jubilee* was a testament to the prominence of sponsors in early television. Since the nineteenth century the electric industry had used many forms of advertising and promotion to sell the ineffable commodity of electricity. Demonstrations of electric lighting and displays of technical ingenuity had become the industry's stock-in-trade, but television, the era's ultimate electronic achievement, offered the industry a chance to create its most sublime spectacle—the transformation of atomic energy into a beneficent source of power and profit. To achieve this goal required a plan not only for depicting atomic energy's utopian promise but also for assuaging fears of its apocalyptic menace. Even David Selznick himself came to recognize that he was a modest participant in this grand project.

The yearlong Light's Diamond Jubilee celebration was conceived by the Edison Electric Institute and the N. W. Ayer and Son advertising agency as a response to specific conditions that the electric industry faced during the early 1950s. Its most obvious goal was to promote the consumer use of electricity and the purchase of electrical goods during the national economic recession which had existed since the end of the Korean War in June 1953. The electric industry, burdened by overproduction of electrical appliances since World War II, hoped that Diamond Jubilee advertising would boost sluggish sales and spur increased consumption of electricity, electrical appliances, and other manufactured goods.[3]

In this aspect of the campaign, Edison's light bulb was identified as the first modern consumer good; its shifting social status, from luxury item to household necessity, set the pattern for the social integration of all subsequent goods. One Diamond Jubilee magazine advertisement drew the relationship between Edison and the modern culture of consumption fairly explicitly. At the lower left of the ad, Edison is depicted in a dramatic tableau, staring pensively at his primal light bulb and illuminated by its glow. Pictured above Edison's epiphany are twenty-eight modern domestic appliances, such items as a griddle, an air conditioner, a sewing machine, and a TV set. "How far ahead of Edison are you?" the advertisement asks, inviting the reader to place a check beside each household acquisition.[4] Using Edison's light bulb as the genesis, this advertisement makes modernity comprehensible, finding its origin in Edison's invention and measuring its progress through each new electrical appliance added to the household repertoire. Edison made the resource of electricity accessible to the home and triggered the surge of modernization that had produced a cornucopia of goods. Household use of electricity, the ad implied, offered ordinary citizens a chance to participate in the wave of progress that Edison started.

The Diamond Jubilee was designed also as a public relations cam-

This advertisement for *Light's Diamond Jubilee* appeared in *American Magazine* in October 1954.

paign to intervene in the latest round of debates over ownership in the electric industry. While most industrialized nations defined electricity as a publicly owned resource, the United States had allowed private corporations to dominate its production and distribution. According to historians Richard Randolph and Scott Ridley, the legitimacy of the electric industry's structure and conduct had always rested on an ideological struggle over meaning—a question of whether electricity should be defined as "a 'service' like water, guided by social policies, or a magical 'commodity' whose growth and use would depend on corporate strategies." This debate had swirled around the electric industry since the early twentieth century, when it emerged as "the most capital-intensive industry in the world."[5] As a result, the electric industry recognized that symbolic acts designed to influence public perception and to encourage consumerism were as important to its existence as the production of electricity and manufactured goods.

The industry attempted to limit government intervention by defining electricity as a privately controlled commodity and by identifying its commercial interests with the public good in a democratic society. Advertisements frequently depicted the consumption of electricity and the industry's newest electrical appliances as an essential requirement for full citizenship. Industry-sponsored publicity also identified the resource of electricity solely as a product of the electric *industry*, attributing the social benefits of electricity to its commercial producers.[6] Meanwhile, those who opposed the industry and supported publicly produced electricity tried to curtail the industry's monopolistic practices by defining electricity as a public resource—like the electromagnetic spectrum in broadcasting policy. Liberal politicians, and the federal government during the Roosevelt administration, fought the electric industry with investigations into industry practice, stricter regulations, and publicly funded electrification projects.[7]

The public's acceptance of privately produced electricity declined during the 1930s and 1940s, diminished by the impact of the Depression and the influence of the regulatory reforms and industry criticism instigated by the Roosevelt administration. Support for commercial electrical production eroded to such an extent that an opinion poll conducted by the Edison Electric Institute in 1949 found that 63 percent of Americans favored a complete shift to publicly funded electrification projects such as the Tennessee Valley Authority.[8] A survey of electric industry trade journals during the 1950s reveals that the electric industry was concerned that public support for commercial electricity had grown more capricious than ever. These anxieties frequently were expressed through the rhetoric of Cold War–era anticommunism, which was used to cast suspicion on the impulse behind publicly funded electrification projects. Writing in the industry bulletin published by the Edison Electric Institute, public relations expert Edwin Vennard recommended ceaseless investment in public relations because, without it, American citizens exhibited a dangerous tendency toward "the same social, economic, and political principles espoused by Socialists and Communists." Public opinion polls, he reported, "showed that when people are informed as to the facts about our American economy, they tend to believe in the free enterprise system; but when people are uninformed as to the facts about the capitalistic system, they tend to believe in collectivism."[9]

Vennard's surprising argument that Americans aren't natural capitalists demonstrated to electric industry leaders the need for constant instruction that implicated American citizens in capitalism's rewards, particularly as these rewards were articulated by the industry. When Charles E. Wilson, committee chairman for Light's Diamond Jubilee, described the celebration's goals to an Edison Electric Institute convention, he reminded his audience that the commemoration of Edison's achievement was merely the campaign's first and least ambitious step. More important was the need to strike against the growing skepticism that called into question the industry's very existence. "The bitterly ironic aspect of this situation," he explained, "is that the sinister force of international communism bases its outward appeal on the promise of better things for the masses of the people. It is up to us to keep working to prove that the way to achieve this goal is by the methods that have come into our lives during the seventy-five years of the electrical industry." Ideally, he argued, the Diamond Jubilee should identify the values expressed by the commercial electric industry as indispensable values of American society: "Light's Diamond Jubilee should give the American people a new concept of the contributions made by a great industry to a great nation, to our high standard of living, comfort, and well-being."[10]

Efforts to define electricity as a privately controlled commodity gained momentum on another front following Eisenhower's election as president in 1952. The business-oriented Eisenhower administration was determined to dismantle most of the New Deal–era regulations governing the electric industry at a time when politicians, scientists, and industry leaders questioned who should control the most recent and potentially lucrative innovation in electrical production— atomic energy. According to journalist Daniel Ford, "President Truman had considered atomic energy 'too important a development to be made the subject of profit-seeking.'" Consequently, the Atomic Energy Act of 1946, passed during the Truman administration, "had expressly forbidden private ownership of nuclear materials and had established an absolute government monopoly over nuclear energy." As Randolph and Ridley note, however, "Wall Street executives calculated that atomic energy would eventually permeate every aspect of industry. Whoever controlled its development and use would hold the same cornerstone that the early electric power moguls had staked out at the center of the nation's economy."[11] The electric industry longed to control atomic energy production, but existing laws hampered its ambitions.

In spite of early popular enthusiasm for atomic energy after the war, many influential scientists and politicians believed that nuclear technology was potentially too lethal to be turned over to private industry. Peter Lilienthal, chairman of the Atomic Energy Commission (AEC) and an otherwise enthusiastic booster of atomic energy, warned in 1948, "As things now stand, an atomic furnace or an atomic power plant is virtually an atomic bomb arsenal. . . . This undertaking is so close to issues of life and death for our country that the kind of development—the amount of manpower and funds, the direction and the pace of development—these must of necessity be determined not by private considerations but considerations of public safety."[12] The detonation of the first Soviet atomic weapon in 1949, the United States' decision in 1950 to produce a hydrogen bomb, and the outbreak of the Korean War in the same year further undermined electric industry arguments that nuclear fission could be harnessed by commercial interests to serve a benign marketplace. By the early 1950s surveys indicated that public enthusiasm for nuclear power—whether produced by government or private industry—had waned considerably since the early postwar years.[13]

The Eisenhower administration was determined to shift the tone of the atomic energy debates in order to convince Congress to rewrite the Atomic Energy Act of 1946, which many conservatives believed had slowed the pace of atomic energy development by excluding what Eisenhower's AEC chairman, Lewis L. Strauss, described as "the genius and enterprise of American business." At the United Nations in December 1953 Eisenhower delivered a speech introducing his administration's Atoms for Peace initiative. "The greatest of destructive forces can be developed into a great boon for the benefit of all mankind," he declared before the U.N. General Assembly. "The United States knows that peaceful power from atomic energy is no dream of the future. That capability, already proved, is here—now, today." Strauss echoed this rhetoric when he promised a convention of science journalists that the "peaceful" atom would end famine and disease while providing the world with "electric energy too cheap to meter."[14]

Eisenhower's speech launched a cultural campaign for atomic energy, designed and coordinated by the AEC, which was in a paradoxical position as both regulator and promoter of atomic energy. The campaign unleashed a flurry of information and inspired public ceremonies created to cultivate consensus support for the administration's energy agenda. Eisenhower's speech was translated immediately into ten languages, published in pamphlet form, and distributed internationally by the United States Information Agency. The AEC, in association with an electric industry lobbying group, Atomic Industrial Forum, produced and distributed dozens of short films that depicted atomic energy's imminent benefits for American social life. Distributed to churches, schools, and civic groups, these films had titles like *Atoms for the Doctor, Atomic Greenhouse, Atomic Zoo, Nuclear Energy Goes Rural,* and *Power and Promise.*[15]

The electric industry's tribute to Edison, and to the wealth of consumer goods that it claimed as his legacy, dovetailed so completely with the AEC's Atoms for Peace campaign that it would have been difficult for most Americans to distinguish the government initiative from its counterpart in private industry, or to perceive that the flurry of optimistic information about atomic energy actually emanated from specific sources. Both public relations campaigns debuted in late 1953 and aimed at a similar political goal: convincing legislators and the American public that the production of electrical power through nuclear fission could be managed most effectively by the commercial electric industry.

The two campaigns differed only in the personality around which each revolved. The Diamond Jubilee's explicit goal was to commemorate Edison's invention of the incandescent light, which industry promotion pinpointed as the breakthrough that led to the practical application of electricity. Because Edison's work was built on the research of many predecessors who already had developed electric lamps, his contribution was distinguished primarily by its adaptability to practical, or conveniently marketable, uses. By explicitly celebrating Edison, therefore, the electric industry implicitly represented its origins in the research that developed a practical commodity form for the resource of electricity. Edison's biography had served as the foundation myth of the electric industry for years, but the Diamond Jubilee promised to reinvigorate the Edison story for the atomic age by enacting it as a national spectacle. Edison was the human face of a vast industry, its virtuous embodiment amid controversy over the industry's past abuses and its role in the future of atomic energy.[16]

While the figure of Edison at the center of the Diamond Jubilee recalled the origins of commercial electricity, President Eisenhower in the Atoms for Peace campaign pointed toward a transcendent future. The intertwined publicity campaigns told the story of electricity as the steady march of progress from Edison's rudimentary light bulb to the boundless promise of atomic energy. As the campaigns blended, the line connecting Edison and Eisenhower as the story's central subjects expressed a continuity between the electric industry's past, present, and future, creating a narrative logic that reinforced the political agenda shared by the industry and the Eisenhower administration.

Through the coordinated, collective action of these campaigns, reminiscent of the effort behind a world's fair or a wartime mobilization, representatives of the electric industry and the federal government hoped to influence the experience of social reality in postwar America, making the era's rapid changes comprehensible and meaningful by placing them within a symbolic framework, a narrative of technological and social progress leading to a utopian future. "There is certainly no need to dwell at length on the correlation between the development of our electrical industry and this nation's progress," Charles Wilson told his electric industry colleagues. "This is a story that is as familiar to us as the palms of our hands. Our problem is to make it equally familiar to our fellow citizens." [17]

The Diamond Jubilee was conceived as a massive project of public edification, both a history lesson and a blueprint for the future. In planning the celebration, the Edison Electric Institute and the N. W. Ayer and Son advertising agency seem to have been inspired by the most prominent model for such an ambitious cultural project—the industrial exposition. As a specific cultural form that blended education and entertainment in the service of industry, the industrial exposition had originated with the Crystal Palace exhibition in England during 1851, continued through the great American and European world's fairs of the late nineteenth century, and had been exemplified most recently by the 1939 New York World's Fair. These industrial expositions were modern festivals created to glorify a world of manufactured goods, to celebrate a vague future of democratic consumerism, and to represent the social power of exposition organizers and patrons. It may seem incongruous to compare the Diamond Jubilee with industrial expositions, but the electric industry had been a prominent participant in many of them, and its celebration of Edison shared with them a particular ideological agenda and certain strategies for expressing industry's ability to transform society. Indeed, it is possible to see the Diamond Jubilee as an attempt to create a contemporary form for the industrial exposition, to transform an essentially nineteenth-century public event into one better suited to twentieth-century forms of mass communication.

London's Crystal Palace exhibition of 1851 established the general form for all future expositions. According to historian Tom Richards, the Crystal Palace "assembled the dominant institutions and vested interests of mid-Victorian England to pay homage to the way commodities were produced. . . . The Crystal Palace was a monument to consumption, the first of its kind, a place where the combined mythologies of consumerism appeared in concentrated form. . . . At one and the same time, the Crystal Palace was a museum and a market: it brought together a host of rare and exclusive things and promised, in a way that is very hard to pin down, that each and every one of them would one day be democratically available to anyone and everyone." By creating an environment where the public encountered goods arranged in spectacular display, the exhibition introduced a new form for representing commodities, enhancing their value by distinguishing them in this setting from their routine existence in the marketplace and their use in everyday life. The Crystal Palace succeeded, according to Richards, "precisely because it elevated the commodity above the mundane act of exchange." [18]

Late-nineteenth-century expositions connected the vast array of displayed goods with demonstrations of scientific and technological ingenuity to affirm an ideology of progress and the promise of a future technological utopia. In his description of nineteenth-century American fairs, historian Robert Rydell claims, "At a time when the American economy was becoming increasingly consolidated and when the wealth generated by the country's expansion was concentrated in fewer and fewer hands, the exposition builders promised that continued growth would result in eventual utopia. Therein lay the mythopoeic grandeur of the fairs: an ideology of economic development, labeled 'progress,' was translated into a utopian statement about the future." [19]

During these expositions, the emerging electric industry learned valuable lessons about how to represent the mysterious commodity of electricity, because electric-light spectacles, at a time when few homes had electric service, were a popular and dramatic manifestation of technology's ability to transcend everyday existence. In fact, as historian Carolyn Marvin has noted, "the electric light was a public spectacle before it was anything else, certainly before it was a common furnishing in private residences." [20] The Chicago World's Fair and Columbian Exposition of 1893 used electric lighting to transform the nighttime fairgrounds into a sparkling city of wonder. The fair exhibited the latest electrical inventions, displayed 90,000 electric lights on buildings and monuments, and featured magnificent illuminated fountains that left spectators awestruck. One of the most popular attractions was the Edison Tower of Light, an 82-foot-tall pedestal covered with multicolored incandescent bulbs. [21] With its buildings aglow, the entire fair served as a brilliant advertisement for electricity even before electricity had any practical value to consumers.

Although most world's fairs embodied this technocratic fantasy of society transformed by the most advanced technology that capitalism could muster, the 1939 New York World's Fair expressed the theme most completely with its promise to provide a glimpse into "The World of Tomorrow." Visitors to the fair, according to historian

Television debuted at the 1939 New York World's Fair, broadcasting such events as
David Sarnoff's dedication of the RCA pavilion.
(Courtesy of Photofest © NBC)

Folke T. Kihlstedt, "saw a vision of the future in which democracy,
capitalism, and consumerism were affirmed by science and technology."[22] Again, the electric industry was well represented at this
fair. Alongside many other electrical displays, General Electric and
Westinghouse demonstrated "Homes of Tomorrow," model homes
filled with electrical gadgets and push-button controls that revealed a
futuristic vision of domestic life.[23] The New York World's Fair also
introduced a technology with the potential to transform industrial
expositions and other public events that relied on the physical presence of participant-spectators. The innovation was television, which
RCA debuted in a broadcast of the fair's opening ceremony.

Writing before the fair opened, critic Eugene Raskin suggested that
expositions already had become outmoded thanks to the development of motion pictures. The problem facing an exposition, he said,
was "to create what is basically a spectacle, which people all over the
world will pay to see, and in which commercial organizations will pay

for the privilege of participating." Consequently, he suggested, "the best way to build a World's Fair is not to build it at all, but to make a motion picture of it."[24] Movies could offer a similar sense of spectacle, while also situating manufactured goods within a narrative of progress. It is no coincidence, therefore, that the New York World's Fair featured films so prominently, with more than five hundred shown in the various exhibits.[25]

Obviously, if movies offered an alternative to the exposition, television promised to be an even more enticing option. Even with the limited technical capabilities of early broadcasts, television had a unique ability to transmit live images of the exposition's technocratic utopia directly into the home—with the "world of tomorrow" embodied in each new TV set. No longer would manufacturers have to depend on visitors' making a pilgrimage to their artfully constructed environment of goods; in the near future, virtually the same experience would be available to consumers without their ever having to leave home.

Diamond Jubilee organizers shared the values of earlier industrial exposition organizers, but they also seemed convinced that the exposition as a cultural form was outmoded and inefficient. Light's Diamond Jubilee would take the exposition to the people, using television as its vehicle. The climactic *Light's Diamond Jubilee* broadcast, Charles Wilson explained, "will bring the electrical progress story right into the living rooms of millions of homes throughout the land—appropriately enough through one of our industry's modern miracles."[26]

Should Wilson's appropriation of television as one of the electric industry's "modern miracles" seem dubious, Carolyn Marvin suggests that there is a profound link between Edison's electric light and television, one that points to the kind of transformation of public events that the Diamond Jubilee hoped to exploit. "Television's inheritance from the electric light is both technological and social," she states. "The original electronic effect, the so-called Edison effect, though poorly understood at the time of its discovery, was created in an electric lamp. The development of electronic tubes and transistors out of this puzzle in a light bulb eventually helped make many face-to-face public gatherings superfluous as families retreated indoors to well-lighted living rooms to watch on television the descendants of public spectacles that had once entertained communities in the town square."[27]

Just as the industrial exposition once had demonstrated the foremost accomplishments of industry, television, by its very presence, now seemed to confirm the relationship between technological advances and social progress that echoed through the Diamond Jubilee.

While the technology offered a tangible metaphor for the campaign's utopianism, the medium provided the means for inserting this spectacle into both the public sphere of government policy-making and the private sphere of domestic consumption. In order to take advantage of the social changes which the introduction of the electric light had helped to promote, the organizers of the Diamond Jubilee needed to transform the industrial exposition into a media event—a public event designed to showcase contemporary communication technology, one created specifically to be televised.

The term "media event" circulates widely through our culture and has acquired many negative connotations. It commonly defines the ways in which the media legitimizes "inauthentic" or artificially contrived public events by treating them as though they are "authentic" or natural forms of social interaction. This usage generally implies that, before the introduction of the mass media, events in the public sphere were somehow more authentic because they were untainted by the media's presence. Subsequently, media coverage has distorted preexisting, autonomous events or, as in Daniel Boorstin's notion of the "pseudo-event," has produced a realm of simulated events that exist only because they have been fabricated by and for the media.[28]

In their reflection on the structure and performance of media events, however, critics Daniel Dayan and Elihu Katz offer a different definition of the term, one which will be useful in making sense of *Light's Diamond Jubilee*. They define a media event as an extraordinary television program that disrupts the medium's routine flow of programming in order to draw the attention of a large portion of the viewing audience to some sort of national ceremony or spectacle. "Television's power lies not only in the way in which it structures the flow of daily life, but with its consequent ability of deciding to interrupt this flow," they argue. Media events disrupt the everyday experience of television and transform the normal role of television programming: "They cancel all other programs, bringing television's clock to a stop, and while they are on the air, they cannot themselves be interrupted. Their performance belongs to 'sacred' time. It brings social activity to a standstill. For a while, it occupies society's 'center.'"[29]

Media events of this type often involve television coverage of traditional national ceremonies, such as a royal wedding or a presidential inauguration. Explaining the function of such broadcasts during the early years of BBC radio, historians David Cardiff and Paddy Scannell characterize such large-scale events as "programs of national identity." As broadcasters struggled to establish the legitimacy of early radio, they sometimes aired national ceremonies that emphasized the "wonder" of radio technology and employed the medium "to forge a link between the dispersed and disparate listeners and the symbolic heartland of national life." Like Dayan and Katz, Cardiff and Scannell describe these programs through an analogy with sacred rituals. Often completely monopolizing the airwaves, such programs were set apart from radio's normal daily output; they diffused symbols of collective identity and were designed to be listened to en masse. "Just on these special occasions," the authors explain, "each family of listeners was encouraged to desist from the profane pursuit of its individual tastes and habits to experience a tribal unity as radio paraded the sacred emblems of church or state or empire."[30] Radio technology made it feasible to broadcast to a national audience, but media events actually defined radio as the nation's central cultural form by uniting the various segments of the audience in ways that normal programming could not.

In addition to traditional ceremonies covered by television, Dayan and Katz also take into account the growing number of original ceremonies and spectacles staged expressly for television. Dayan and Katz aren't concerned with questions about the authenticity of these media events, because they believe that television's presence has transformed the very nature of public events. "It is conceptually distracting to ask if a broadcast offers a 'true' rendition of the corresponding event," they argue. "Given the openly performative nature of television's role, the problematics of 'truth' and 'falsehood' become almost irrelevant."[31] In their view, media events have redefined the structure and meaning of public events in contemporary society. Whereas some critics might dismiss television spectacles for distorting the traditional structure of public events, or for diminishing their significance, Dayan and Katz caution us to recognize that public events have no authentic form that remains unchanged through time; public events are the products of specific historical conditions. As they explain:

> Public events are not fixed in a given form once and forever. Throughout history they have tended to adapt themselves to the prevailing modes of making an event public: "publicness" is our neologism. The dominant mode of publicness is now changing. We are witnessing the gradual replacement of what could be called a "theatrical" mode of publicness—an actual meeting of performers and audiences . . . by a new mode of publicness based on the separation of performers and audiences, and on the rhetoric of narrative rather than the virtue of contact. . . . Separated from the large majority of their public, ceremonies now display the texture, internal coherence, narrative beat, and visual gloss which used to characterize Hollywood spectaculars.[32]

Dayan and Katz describe the media event as a product of the shift from "theatrical" public events dependent on the mutual presence of performer and audience to mass-mediated events that compensate for the audience's distance by using attributes of narrative spectacle associated with the Hollywood cinema to frame the event. This definition of the media event provides a useful framework for thinking about the inspiration behind *Light's Diamond Jubilee*. The celebration's organizers wanted to create a television program that would demonstrate the "wonder" of electronic technology, a program that would disrupt the flow of normal television, a program that would transform the many segments of the TV audience into a single, national audience. In other words, the electric industry wanted to create its own media event—a single television program that would dominate the entire medium for an evening, placing the electric industry at the symbolic center of American life.

The electric industry discovered an opportunity to monopolize the airwaves as a result of the TV networks' experimentation with blockbuster programming in the mid-1950s. During 1953 and 1954, NBC and CBS began to test a programming format that NBC programming chief Sylvester "Pat" Weaver referred to as "spectaculars." These were prestigious, live programs either modeled after or directly adapted from Broadway dramas, musicals, and variety revues. With running times of at least ninety minutes and budgets from $200,000 to $500,000, these were the lengthiest and most expensive entertainment programs ever broadcast. By scheduling them occasionally— usually once or twice per month—the networks gambled on capturing a massive audience share with programming designed to interrupt the prime-time schedule and, in Weaver's words, "challenge the robotry of habit viewing." In its sales pitch to potential sponsors, NBC suggested that this costly programming strategy could revolutionize the network's efforts to deliver viewers to advertisers. Unlike existing programming strategies, which targeted portions of the viewing audience, the spectacular was conceived "with the idea of reaching the *total* TV audience—not just a segment of it."[33] But the spectacular wasn't just an attempt to maximize the viewing audience; it also represented a potential strategy in the networks' early efforts to constitute the experience of television viewing, in this case as an extraordinary national event delivered to the American home. As a programming strategy, spectaculars were the networks' attempt to create media events.

Although network radio schedules had sometimes included special events, the radio model of programming adopted by the television networks relied on familiar, regularly scheduled programs with standardized formats.[34] Network schedules organized these programs to fit and, in a very real sense, structure the family's household routine, its daily and weekly alternation of labor and leisure.[35] Television originally had possessed a certain novelty appeal, but by 1953 the medium as it was typically experienced had become merely another element in the ordinary domestic life of the family. The dominant programming strategy made it possible for the networks to guarantee predictable audience ratings to advertisers by encouraging viewer loyalty to familiar daily or weekly programs. But while this strategy for minimizing risk made sense from an economic standpoint, Weaver felt that it was slowly degrading the *meaning* of television, defining the experience as something so banal that it was in danger of being ignored. "I could see that the whole programming service was running downhill, with sponsors and agencies seeking the cheap way of getting their messages across—quiz programs, audience participation and mystery shows, and low-cost talent shows that, in the long run, would be bound to reduce the importance of the network service generally in the lives of the people."[36]

By occasionally disrupting the familiar schedule with expensive programs of more than an hour's length, Weaver broke with the radio model of programming that dominated early TV and with the definition of the viewing experience implicit in that model. This effort to restore the novelty of television was particularly valuable as NBC introduced color television in January 1954 and hoped to spur color-TV sales. NBC subsequently achieved its greatest success and set a single-network ratings record when 65 million viewers tuned in to watch its color adaptation of *Peter Pan,* starring Mary Martin.[37]

Weaver had conceived of spectaculars as a way not only to escape radio's pattern of habitual programming but also to end the radio model of sponsorship. Since sponsors placed programs in the network schedule in a time slot that the sponsor essentially controlled as a franchise, they held inordinate power in shaping network schedules as well as in the production of programs. Under the radio model, Weaver argued, "Programs landed next to each other by mere chance with each agency building its own show in a way that was aimed at nothing more than keeping its client happy. There was no planned relationship of one program and another or to the competition, and no particular attempt to create a lasting pattern for people at home."[38]

As big-budget spectaculars raised the cost of production beyond the reach of most individual companies, Weaver hoped to limit the role of sponsors in general, to champion participating sponsorship as the dominant model for television in order to shift the balance of power to the networks. "In what Weaver dubbed the 'magazine concept,'" historian Vance Kepley writes, "multiple advertisers were urged to buy segments of time on programs so that no one advertiser would exercise undue leverage. Just as magazine advertisers had no editorial authority over the articles, so NBC would offer a schedule of shows to advertisers as vehicles for the commercials while retaining the ultimate control of that schedule."[39]

The networks gradually gained control from sponsors and began to conceive of the broadcast schedule as a coherent, integrated text in which each component was designed to hold a viewer's attention, while it also constructed a public identity for the network. In this early stage of the spectacular, however, well-capitalized sponsors still were able to purchase broadcast time from the networks and, in certain instances, to dictate the placement of their programs in the network schedule. That sole sponsorship of these expensive programs was limited to only the largest companies imbued the programs with a meaning that exceeded their particular content: Spectaculars became monuments to corporate stature. By their very scarcity, single-sponsor spectaculars signified economic and social power, and the effect was only magnified when the program appeared on more than one network.

At the time that the electric industry planned *Light's Diamond Jubilee*, Ford Motor Company and General Foods had produced the only other multi-network spectaculars. Orchestrated by theatrical producer Leland Hayward, the Ford Fiftieth Anniversary show aired on all four networks in June 1953, establishing the sole precedent for *Light's Diamond Jubilee*'s domination of the airwaves. The General Foods show was broadcast in March 1954 on CBS and NBC and featured a star-filled homage to Rodgers and Hammerstein. These spectaculars aired on multiple networks simultaneously because the networks had not yet escaped the radio pattern of sponsorship. The networks were willing to sell broadcast time to big-ticket sponsors without worrying about disrupting their regular schedules or effacing network identity by offering the same programming as their competitors.

The value of this programming strategy was debated in the advertising and TV industries. By appearing on multiple networks, each of these programs reached over 75 percent of the nation's TV households and more than 70 million viewers, easily providing the sponsors with their largest audiences ever. But budgets of nearly $1 million for production and broadcast time meant that these programs were viable advertising options for only the wealthiest companies. For those who could afford the expense, however, the enormous audience exposure actually made the programs an economical method for reaching consumers, with a lower cost-per-thousand-viewers than the average prime-time series had.[40]

The advertising industry speculated that the significance of these spectaculars exceeded the goal of addressing consumers with specific advertising messages. As corporate public relations efforts, their influence was more diffuse and yet more lasting. They created an identifiable corporate image for the sponsor, influencing not only consumers but also retailers who marketed the products at the local level. As NBC argued in its sales pitch to sponsors, while most television programming was unremarkable, these spectaculars promised "to return to television the excitement and thrills which are inherent in it . . . to become a national conversation piece . . . [to express] a 'quality' feeling, a luster to the show that rubs off on the product."[41]

As the Edison Electric Institute and the Ayer agency planned the Diamond Jubilee, they took advantage of these conditions in the television industry in order to place *Light's Diamond Jubilee* simultaneously on virtually every television station in the country. Although General Electric and Westinghouse, the Diamond Jubilee's primary sponsors, advertised on a number of regular prime-time series, neither company purchased advertising time on any of the other spectaculars during the 1954–1955 TV season.[42] Their financial resources were concentrated on this single program because it promised to pay huge dividends by reaching everyone in the United States who owned a TV set.

At the same time that Diamond Jubilee organizers planned the most expansive television broadcast in history, however, they also worried about the effectiveness of simply imposing the Edison celebration on the public via the mass media. Concerned that neither a massive, televised pageant nor a multitude of disconnected local events would achieve the goal of shaping national policy, they decided that the Edison celebration should be carried out on two fronts. First would come public events staged in local communities by utility companies, with the goal of weaving the Diamond Jubilee's themes into traditional community ceremonies and festivals—the parades, fairs, and other civic activities through which a community achieves a sense of collective identity. National media coverage would form the campaign's second front, with advertisements, publicity, and sponsored television programs providing a broader context for local events. The Edison Electric Institute helped to coordinate the nationwide activities on both fronts by mailing thousands of copies of a *Jubilee Plan Book* and a *Jubilee Fact Book* to local utilities, manufacturers, retail stores, chambers of commerce, schools, and any other interested organization or community group.[43]

In spite of the Diamond Jubilee's reliance on the mass media, small-scale community activities were seen as the campaign's "backbone." Community activities, the plan book stated, "can present the story of electrical progress in terms of the community, in a manner that is familiar and real to everyone who lives in it. They can give to electrical progress a very local and personal meaning. The closer this story can be brought to [community members], the more effective it will be." According to the plan book, the celebration of Edison would give local utilities an excuse to organize self-promoting civic lighting projects. Some of these projects, such as campaigns to improve street lighting, might have practical value; others would use electric lighting solely to stage striking visual displays—bathing monuments, scenic sights, and major buildings in brilliant floodlights or emblazoning the night sky with high-powered beacons. General Electric actually produced ceremonial 75,000-watt Diamond Jubilee light bulbs, which the organizers made available to cities that wanted to create spectacular visual effects. The organizers also recommended that utilities organize a variety of instructional projects that would stress the Diamond Jubilee's educational value. These included window displays in community businesses, presentations for schools and civic groups, plant tours, and coordinating "electrical safety" weeks in the community.

If local activities were to succeed in engaging citizens in the cause of the electric industry, however, not all activities could be perceived as originating from the vested interests of local utilities and retailers. Some activities had to appear to emerge from within the community as spontaneous expressions of civic or national pride. Therefore, the plan book also contained strategies for stimulating community participation and tactics for insinuating Diamond Jubilee themes into traditional local events. The campaign's success depended on the ability to entice community members into becoming performers in the Diamond Jubilee, into seeing themselves as actors in a local celebration rather than as mere observers of a distant national event. These activities, the handbook stated, "require participation on the part of the audience. Thus, these acts will have an additional effect through the very participation."

The most important opportunity for eliciting community participation involved traditional civic events, such as parades and pageants, which the Diamond Jubilee committee conceived as ideal vehicles for expressing the celebration's themes. The plan book described sample pageants and parades in considerable detail in order to provide models for community festivities. Most of the suggestions set forth strategies for representing a causal link between images of technological and social progress, using dramatic vignettes, such as moments from Edison's life, or episodes dramatizing events in the story of "electrical progress." For comic effect, it recommended, each vignette should contain one character who is "agin" all forms of change—"thus providing a positive statement of the benefits of electricity, then knocking down these consistently old-fashioned ideas." Parades could adopt similar strategies, employing floats featuring a "Then and Now" motif in which, for instance, one woman might slave over a washtub while her counterpart reads a book and does laundry in a modern washing machine. The contrast between past and present, built on good-natured ridicule of previous times and previous products, was meant to represent the inevitability of progress and to emphasize electricity's transformative effect on local communities. D. C. Luce, one of the celebration's primary architects at the Edison Electric Institute, advised local utilities that the Diamond Jubilee's most important goal was to remind the public that "electricity has reached into local communities throughout our land and transformed them in seemingly miraculous ways."[44]

It is not clear how many communities actually incorporated these suggestions into their celebrations, or how many even participated formally in the Diamond Jubilee. The *Edison Electric Institute Bulletin* reported activities across the country, and by its count, 1,200 communities celebrated the Diamond Jubilee in some manner. It appears that most commercial utility companies commemorated the event at least by organizing small-scale activities—lunches, banquets, speeches, school presentations, and demonstrations of electrical lighting and appliances. But very few events seem to have been devoted solely to the celebration. Instead, the Diamond Jubilee was incorporated into existing civic events, as the national organizers suggested.

For instance, Miami's Orange Bowl Parade on New Year's Eve inaugurated 1954 as the year of the Diamond Jubilee. During the Orange Bowl festivities, two barges floated side by side in Biscayne Bay, illuminated against the night sky. One barge held an enormous figure of King Orange, the other had a huge birthday cake with seventy-five candles. Lights strung between the barges spelled out "Light's Diamond Jubilee." Other cities integrated the Diamond Jubilee into civic celebrations. Atlantic City unveiled civic lighting projects, such as "the world's most modern boulevard lighting." The centennial parade in Sioux City, Iowa, featured a Diamond Jubilee motif, including a float on which a man dressed as Edison stood surrounded by modern electrical appliances. General Electric's ceremonial 75,000-watt Diamond Jubilee lamp served as the centerpiece of many civic lighting displays and spectacles at fairs. When Denver switched on its huge lamp atop its tallest downtown building, the light from it reportedly surpassed even the streetlights below. Each city visited by the Ice Capades, the touring theatrical ice-skating troupe, witnessed a tribute to the Diamond Jubilee during the show's opening number, since the year's tour was sponsored in part by the electric industry. Diamond Jubilee themes and motifs worked their way into many other local activities, including museum exhibits, displays at state and county fairs, holiday parades, and halftime shows at college football games. Light's Diamond Jubilee queens were crowned in a number of cities and at county and state fairs, including the New York State Fair. San Diego paid homage to its "Queen of Light" by bestowing upon her a bouquet of light bulbs.[45]

These local Diamond Jubilee activities served mainly to legitimize the celebration of Edison by defining it as an event that merited civic remembrance. Some events represented the historical origins of the electric industry and the rise of electrical goods; others displayed technological innovation as a dramatic spectacle. In spite of its reverence for Edison, however, the Diamond Jubilee was designed primarily to shape the present and the future. History was of consequence only to the extent that it legitimized the industry's vision of progress. "The solid accomplishments of the past seventy-five years," the plan book stated, "will be presented not as nostalgic monuments but as springboards to the future." While the organizers expected that local events would be most effective at implicating individual citizens in the Diamond Jubilee, their greatest concern was that these events might be too disparate, fragmented, or unfocused to leave participants with any meaning other than a vague sense of nostalgia. Consequently, national media coverage and sponsored television programs served an essential role in their plans, "providing a background against which community Jubilee activities will have added meaning."

The national campaign began with the Diamond Jubilee slogan, "Light for Freedom, Power for Progress." This slogan—in which "freedom" ultimately meant freedom from government intervention and "progress" depended on the continued growth of the electric industry—appeared on all publicity and on a variety of items that the Diamond Jubilee committee provided for local organizers, including stationery, window stickers, displays, and medallions. The medallion expressed the celebration's themes in a highly concentrated form. On one side, an open hand holds Edison's first light bulb. Encircling the hand is an iconic representation of an electron's flight. On the opposite side, the Diamond Jubilee's slogan rests above an olive branch. In this image, Edison's familiar invention, which had come to be identified as the electric industry's foundation, provides the core around which orbits the peaceful atom. The image proclaims an ahistorical, mythic association, an assertion that the future of atomic energy was inherent in Edison's primitive electronic experiments.

Through the national media, the organizers planned to achieve three goals: to provide the celebration's historical context, to integrate local events into the greater celebration, and to create a vision of the future that demonstrated the imminent value of atomic energy. First, organizers wanted to provide enough information about Edison, the development of the electric industry, and the social changes made possible by electrical service to create a meaningful context for the celebration's historical spectacles. Press releases and staged publicity events spread information through the print media, radio, and television. Articles and advertisements stressed the growth of the consumer market for electrical appliances. Sponsored programs recounted the myth of Edison. During the week before the broadcast of *Light's Diamond Jubilee*, for instance, the industry sponsored three other network programs devoted to the inventor: an episode of the historical drama series *You Are There* titled "Edison's Miracle of Light," an episode of *General Electric Theater* (1953–1962) starring Burgess Meredith as "Edison the Man," and an episode of the Westinghouse-sponsored *Studio One* (1948–1958) titled "The Boy Who Changed the World." At least ten other national network radio and TV programs during October gave substantial treatment to the Diamond Jubilee.[46]

Since local celebrations were separated from one another by time and distance, national media coverage next provided local communities with a sense that they were participating in a national event. This type of coverage is an example of television's tendency, as described by Dayan and Katz, to represent national events through the image of an epidemic, a cultural contagion in which isolated celebrations merge into each other as their participants perceive that they are all engaged in a vast celebration.[47] In order to unite community and local celebrations, the plan book even suggested organizing local projects related to the *Light's Diamond Jubilee* TV program—including store displays devoted to the program, speeches about the program made to local organizations, school projects, contests ("prizes might be given for the best letters on what the Jubilee television show meant to the writer"), and collective viewing of the broadcast by members of local civic or school groups. The goal of these activities was to ensure that the TV program was experienced as an integral component of local celebrations, not as a distant product of the mass media.

Finally, the organizers imagined that national television coverage would be responsible for directing the attention of local participants toward the utopian future promised by atomic energy. "Television itself is the acme of electrical progress in the field of communication," the plan book stated. "A dynamic presence, the television show will point the way from the dreams of today to the realities of tomorrow." Since both television and atomic energy could be perceived as the epitome of "electrical progress," the campaign for the peaceful atom invoked an identification that already existed in the culture of the era, a figurative link between television and atomic energy—the two most prominent technological innovations to emerge since World War II.

By the mid-1950s, however, the identification of television and atomic energy seldom heralded a utopian destiny. Many who attempted to make sense of television's social impact following World War II were drawn to metaphors associated with the dark legacy of atomic warfare rather than with the brilliant future of atomic energy. NBC vice president John F. Royal expressed this metaphor most succinctly when shortly after the war he declared, "Television is the atomic bomb of culture." An agent for the William Morris talent agency later demonstrated the cultural confusion surrounding the metaphor when he claimed, "Television has the impact of an atomic bomb. It is increasing the people's intellect in proportion to a bomb's destructive power for blowing them to pieces."[48]

Just as postwar responses to atomic energy were contradictory, mingling expressions of terror and hope, responses to television were a tangle of utopian assurances and dystopian fears. Consequently, as historian Lynn Spigel has noted, the destructive powers of atomic warfare provided a metaphor for expressing anxieties about television's potentially harmful social impact.[49] The associative link between television and the atomic bomb was enacted more directly when television became the preferred medium for representing the spectacle of atomic blasts once nuclear weapons testing began within the borders of the United States in 1951.

The first bomb test to be broadcast on television took place in April 1952, when the AEC staged a public detonation designed to prove its complete confidence in handling the bomb. More than 35 million Americans watched the event live—and the audience might have been larger had the AEC been able to schedule the blast for prime time. This first televised bomb blast was constructed as a media event, simultaneous evidence that television and the atomic bomb were the most wondrous technologies of the postwar era. *Life* magazine's story about the test focused on its coverage by broadcasters, emphasizing television's unprecedented ability to provide live, democratic, and safe access to the spectacle of the atomic blast. Under the headline "Everyone Gets a Look," the magazine contrasted photos of two groups of viewers. In one, Senators Margaret Chase Smith, Leverett Saltonstall, and Lyndon Johnson gaze intently at a television set in the Senate building, while in the other, customers at Chicago's Merchandise Mart watch the televised explosion through a display window. With their depiction of viewers pausing in the flow of their lives to gather in public settings and gaze fixedly at the TV screen, these photos contrast the experience of viewing a media event with that of viewing normal TV shows. In addition, these juxtaposed images construct a particular social meaning of television, defining it as a medium uniquely capable of representing the bomb's sublime force and of sharing that experience immediately with viewers from any social class and any region of the country.[50]

By the mid-1950s, the television industry had learned both to depict the weapons tests as media events and, when necessary, to integrate them into the routine flow of TV programming. For one televised test in 1955, CBS and NBC joined forces for an unprecedented broadcast, sharing responsibility for the $200,000 production cost, a crew of eighty, and $500,000 worth of equipment. News personalities Dave Garroway, John Cameron Swayze, Charles Collingwood, and Walter Cronkite were on the scene as witnesses for their respective networks. Known as an occasional companion to chimpanzee J. Fred Muggs on NBC's *Today* show, Garroway was selected by lottery to be the only reporter on the front lines. His subdued response contrasted with his normally jovial persona. "I ain't gonna tell no jokes," he said. "I'm going to personalize the bomb."[51] In fact, this desire to "personalize" the bomb gave the event a grisly undertone. The networks seemed to feel that there was something lurid or irresponsible about merely displaying the sheer spectacle of destructive force. Therefore, they chose to frame the test as an object lesson by using it to imagine the repercussions of a nuclear strike on the United States.

In order to simulate the bomb's effect on a typical American city, the networks visited "Survival City," a cluster of typically furnished 1950s American homes constructed for the broadcast just a short distance down "Doomsday Drive" from Ground Zero. During the days leading up to the blast, the networks featured a number of news reports from the fateful city. TV reporters introduced viewers to the Darling family, a suburban middle-class family like many others depicted on television, except that this was a family of fashion-store mannequins. Kit Finne, food editor of *Home*, NBC's midday information program directed mainly at housewives, took viewers on a tour of the Darlings' ranch-style house. She conducted mock interviews with the mute family, looked into their kitchen cupboards, and specu-

Life magazine documented viewers' reactions to the first televised atomic weapons test in 1952. In the top photo, Margaret Chase Smith, Leverett Saltonstall, and Lyndon Johnson observe from the U.S. Senate.
(Mark Kaufmann, *Life* Magazine © Time Warner)
In the bottom photo, a crowd gathers around a TV set displayed in a window at Chicago's Merchandise Mart.
(Ralph Crane, *Life* Magazine © Time Warner)

lated on the blast's probable effects on household items like baby food, dishwashers, and children's clothing. In the days leading up to the blast, television domesticated the event through its coverage but didn't try to tame the bomb. Instead, television created a typical middle-class family in a typical American town, like those from any of its domestic situation comedies, in order to see the family obliterated.

This nightmarish vision seems to have sprung from the same cultural impulse that critic Susan Sontag has described as "the imagination of disaster." Through the spectacle of post-Hiroshima science-fiction films, Sontag argues, one could "participate in the fantasy of living through one's own death and more, the death of cities, the destruction of humanity itself. . . . Thus, the science-fiction film . . . is concerned with the aesthetics of destruction, with the peculiar beauties to be found in wreaking havoc, making a mess." Similarly, historian Paul Boyer has claimed that the nuclear devastation in Hiroshima at the end of the war left Americans feeling "naked and vulnerable" in victory. "Sole possessors and users of a devastating new instrument of mass destruction, Americans envisioned themselves not as potential threats to other peoples, but as potential victims," he states.[52] Although the networks framed their coverage as having instructional value, their efforts to "personalize" the bomb's impact seemed designed to appeal to the culture's fascination with visualizing its own destruction. In the fantasy scenario constructed by the network news coverage, the link between television and the bomb created a particularly morbid media event—the technology of mass communication uniting viewers across the nation to imagine humanity's annihilation by the technology of mass destruction.

Ultimately, however, the network media event fizzled. Inclement weather caused so many postponements that the eminent TV journalists had all gone home and most of the expensive equipment had been packed away when the blast finally occurred. *Newsweek*'s report captured the gruesome irony of the coverage as it finally appeared: "*Home* gave a filmed version of the explosion a brief five-minutes between a lesson in meringue whipping and a plug for Mother's Day; the next day, second-string network men explored the ruins of Survival City."[53] In many ways, this outcome is even more disturbing than the nihilistic fantasy that the networks originally had concocted. Instead of a spectacular media event, television ultimately transformed the explosion and the incinerated Darling family into an indistinct element in the banal flow of daytime TV.

If Light's Diamond Jubilee and Atoms for Peace were going to direct national attention from the destructive capacity of nuclear energy to its productive potential, the campaign for the peaceful atom also needed to reorient TV coverage from its fascination with the spectacle of nuclear holocaust. In late August 1954, Congress passed the Atomic Energy Act of 1954, opening the door for the commercial production of atomic energy. To mark the occasion, public relations experts in the Eisenhower administration devised a media event that would demonstrate atomic energy's constructive character by capitalizing on television's uncanny ability to bridge enormous distances.

On Labor Day 1954, one week after signing the legislation, President Eisenhower appeared in a Denver television station to break ground on the first commercial nuclear power plant—which was located 1,300 miles away in Shippingport, Pennsylvania. The simultaneous display of distant locales was a common visual device of early television, having been used most memorably in the 1951 premiere broadcast of Edward R. Murrow's news series, *See It Now*, which demonstrated the wonder of television using a live, split-screen shot of the Golden Gate Bridge and the Brooklyn Bridge. Still, Eisenhower's ground-breaking ceremony was unique because it was an explicitly political event, an example of politics conducted as show business. While millions of Americans watched the multiple-network broadcast, Eisenhower juggled events occurring in two separate locations united only by television, displaying the agility of a television emcee.

With the inauguration of Eisenhower, the electric industry had discovered not only a great supporter who was prepared to roll back New Deal–era legislation that restricted its participation in the field of atomic energy but also a political figure who appreciated the value of public relations in the age of television. Although reportedly skeptical of television in the early days of his presidential campaign, Eisenhower was associated with the medium's transformation of national politics, becoming the first candidate to announce his candidacy on live TV, the first to use TV commercials, and the first to hold televised press conferences.[54]

The popular press depicted Eisenhower as a man struggling mightily to adapt to the television era. "On television sets in millions of American homes," *TV Guide* reported, "there appears a relaxed Dwight Eisenhower. . . . It seems so simple and informal. Yet back of it are days of planning, arranging, and rehearsing." In fact, at the beginning of 1954 the White House invited actor and TV producer Robert Montgomery to coach the president on his TV performances, to share advice about how to behave naturally in front of early TV's intrusive cameras and blinding lights.[55] Since Eisenhower claimed to have distrusted television as a tool of demagogues, he wasn't depicted as a natural TV performer, even though he was closely identified with the medium.

Consequently, Eisenhower was an ideal master of ceremonies for the first nuclear power plant ground-breaking ceremony, a broadcast designed to demonstrate the most advanced capabilities of science and technology. An avuncular figure, he seemed to derive his mastery of the medium not from some preternatural bond with the technology but rather from an old soldier's dogged determination to keep pace with progress. After a brief speech in which he proclaimed confidence that "the atom will not be devoted exclusively to the destruction of man, but will be his mighty and tireless benefactor," Eisenhower waved a zirconium-handled wand over a cabinet which newspaper accounts described as "about the size of a television console." The tip of the wand contained radioactive minerals that triggered a "neutron counter" in the cabinet, tripping a relay that sent a signal through telephone wires to start an automated bulldozer at the construction site. The bulldozer scooped up three tons of earth, rumbled forward, and dumped its load on the ground, while AEC chairman Lewis L. Strauss and Representative W. Sterling Cole, chairman of the Joint Congressional Committee on Atomic Energy, looked on.[56]

Eisenhower's magic wand conjured up images of wizardry, and atomic energy had been depicted as a magical power, a genie released from its bottle (as in the Disney short film *Our Friend the Atom* [1957]). But Eisenhower's magic wand also framed the event as a dramatic spectacle instead of a scientific demonstration. The technical capability that made it possible for Eisenhower to control events at the construction site were obscured behind a display of television's ability to link acts separated by a great distance. Eisenhower waved the wand over a device that resembled a television console, and if his performance was meant to invoke a magical transformation, television was the object transformed.

Once Eisenhower triggered the switch in Denver, he settled back into an upholstered chair to watch the bulldozer on a television set situated alongside the triggering device. In this telling moment Eisenhower shifted from controlling the event to being merely another viewer, a transition which acknowledged that the television viewer had the best vantage from which to observe an event staged solely for the benefit of TV cameras. Unlike the nuclear weapons tests that preceded it, there was no original event that existed autonomously from television's coverage. There was nothing to be gained, and much to be lost, from being present at either site. With little to see in the Denver TV studio and scarcely more than an unmanned tractor in Pennsylvania, the only way to comprehend the entire ground-breaking ceremony was by watching television. Not only did the viewers have

In September 1954, President Eisenhower participated in the televised ground-breaking ceremony for the country's first commercial atomic energy plant. From a TV studio in Denver he started an unmanned bulldozer on a Pennsylvania construction site by waving a wand over a triggering device described in the press as resembling a television console.
(Source Unknown/Courtesy of Dwight D. Eisenhower Library
National Park Service Collection)

privileged access to the event but the event existed *solely* for television, a product of electronic reproduction. By creating a performance that was wholly accessible only through television, this media event designated television as the only medium fully capable of expressing the peaceful atom's potentially revolutionary benefits for American society. In other words, the campaign for the peaceful atom used television to pacify atomic energy.

The campaign for the peaceful atom circulated throughout the mass media, but focused most intensively on television. It might have been possible for the electric industry to achieve its promotional goals by sponsoring normal TV programs, but television represented more than a means for diffusing advertising messages. Its rapid and seemingly democratic expansion into American homes gave television the potential to embody the figurative bond between technological and social progress that was central to the Diamond Jubilee's strategies for winning approval of a revised atomic energy policy. In order to entwine television and atomic energy together within the electric industry's narrative of progress, the organizers of both Light's Diamond Jubilee and Atoms for Peace chose to stage media events that would revive the sense of television as a modern miracle and that would distract the networks from their morbid fascination with nuclear destruction. By deciding that the Diamond Jubilee should climax with a broadcast that filled virtually every TV screen in the nation, the electric industry guaranteed that its program would be an unprecedented media event.

Still, the broadcast time was an empty vessel; the sponsors needed to complete it with a program suited to their imperial programming gesture. Since previous spectaculars had used Broadway talent, the Diamond Jubilee's organizers decided on a different direction, looking instead to Hollywood and David Selznick, a producer whose acclaimed movies epitomized the motion picture industry at its most extravagant. Indeed, as historian Ronald Haver has suggested, Selznick's *Gone with the Wind* was probably the greatest event in Hollywood's history. "It is impossible at this remove to reconstruct the impact of *Gone with the Wind*, the phenomenon that it represented to the industry and to the public," Haver says. "It was the first true 'event' movie of the sound era, and its production and marketing set the pattern for all subsequent large-scale efforts in the picture business; the *Gone with the Wind* syndrome would dominate the industry's thinking and goals for the next thirty-five years as everybody tried to duplicate its success."[57]

The electric industry turned to Selznick because they envisioned *Light's Diamond Jubilee* as a similar sort of event, one that would dwarf anything ever seen on television. Selznick's production of *Light's Diamond Jubilee* is an intriguing artifact from Hollywood's early engagement with television, therefore, because it represents an attempt to create a single television program with the cultural impact of Hollywood's most celebrated movie. Whether Selznick liked it or not, his premiere television program was rooted deeply in the campaign for the peaceful atom, a campaign orchestrated by the most powerful political and economic forces in America during the 1950s.

·V·
David O. Selznick
and the Making of
Light's Diamond Jubilee

"The terrible thing about television," David O. Selznick confessed in the *New York Times* of 24 October 1954, "is that you have no idea—everything becomes such a nightmare in the hour before broadcast—whether you have a hit or a flop until the show is on, and then it is too late to do anything about it."[1] Anticipating the most grueling opening night of his career, Selznick could barely hide his apprehension. Later that evening his first television production, *Light's Diamond Jubilee*, would be broadcast to more than 70 million viewers over all four TV networks. Live television's merciless deadline dangled like a sword over his head, and his ambition to create the most distinguished program ever seen on TV only sharpened the blade. The national press had reported widely on the production, wondering whether the producer of *Gone with the Wind* still had the touch that once had made him Hollywood's master showman and questioning whether it would be deft enough for this more intimate medium. Selznick himself intended *Light's Diamond Jubilee* to announce his ambitions in television, heralding his name as "the first television trademark."[2] Considering the weight of expectations and responsibilities, it's no wonder that Selznick described television production in terms that expressed his fear of losing control: the "nightmare" of live production, the inscrutable TV audience, the experience of bearing helpless witness to the verdict of 70 million viewers.

Movies always had promised Selznick the potential for mastery, an opportunity to command every stage of the creative process. Elaborate market research, test screenings, and endless tinkering through editing and reshooting had tempted him with dreams of crafting the perfect motion picture, one completely responsive to the desires of its audience. Movies had seldom rewarded this fantasy of control, but at least they held out the promise. For Selznick, the terrible thing

David O. Selznick on the set of *Light's Diamond Jubilee*
with actress Judith Anderson.
(Courtesy of Film Collection, Harry Ransom Humanities Research Center,
University of Texas at Austin © David O. Selznick Productions)

about television on the eve of *Light's Diamond Jubilee* was that it had come to signify abandonment, a reluctant submission to forces beyond his control. In part these concerns reflected his diminished capacity to orchestrate a major production, but they also expressed the frustrations of a movie producer struggling to define the role of a producer in a medium dominated by broadcast networks, commercial sponsors, and advertising agencies.

Although he was only fifty-two years old at the time of *Light's Diamond Jubilee*, David Selznick hadn't made a feature film in Hollywood for nearly six years. During the studio era, independent production—with its huge risks and rewards—had given him unprecedented control over his movies. He embraced independence because it meant freedom from the routine movies, bureaucratic management, and assembly-line production procedures enforced by the studio system. No New York office ordered him to make a designated series of pictures; no studio supervisor enforced production schedules or budget limits. Liberated from the studios, Selznick joined Samuel Goldwyn as the only independent producers able to pursue an ideal of prestige filmmaking that rivaled anything imagined at MGM or Paramount.

Sacrificing the studio system's efficiency in order to concentrate on individual, big-budget projects, Selznick cultivated a chaotic mode of production that flouted the studios' "rules," enabling him to oversee virtually every element of the filmmaking process. He pursued this strategy first because it suited his sensibility and his conception of the producer's artistic control. "In the making of good pictures," Selznick once explained, it is "so essential for a producer to collaborate on every inch of the script, to be available for every conference, and to go over all details of production that it is physically impossible for him to give his best efforts to more than a limited number of pictures."[3] Selznick also believed that concentrating on a few lavish productions represented the most lucrative financial strategy—a belief vindicated by the success of *Gone with the Wind* and *Rebecca*.

At the same time, however, Selznick also discovered the dangers of this relatively artisanal approach to film production. "In terms of efficiency and productivity," historian Thomas Schatz has argued, "Selznick clearly was lost without the discipline of a full-blown factory grinding away or a New York office controlling finances and demanding a steady output."[4] Selznick's freedom from a studio's constraints encouraged the obsessive behavior that was at least partially responsible for his decline as a filmmaker during the late 1940s. "In usurping more and more control over the entire production process," Schatz has claimed, "Selznick upset the delicate balance of power and division of labor that was so essential to effective filmmaking, particularly in the heady realm of prestige production where Hollywood's top artists were involved." Selznick's constant interference in the production process—his incessant rewriting and reshooting—drove up the cost of production and ultimately led to the box office catastrophes of

The Paradine Case in 1947 and *Portrait of Jennie* in 1948. Burdened there-
after by huge debts that made it practically impossible to continue
producing feature films in Hollywood, Selznick found himself during
the late 1940s and early 1950s in a "downward spiral, working in self-
indulgent isolation."[5]

During the fallow years of the early 1950s, Selznick re-released his
earlier pictures, produced a few films in Europe, and investigated his
prospects for returning to production in the United States. When he
decided in late 1953 that he and his organization had recovered sufficiently to resume production in Hollywood, he returned to a film industry that during the preceding five years had undergone its most
radical changes since the introduction of sound. One result of these
changes was the rapid growth of independent production. Capital
gains tax incentives had encouraged actors, directors, writers, and
producers to establish their own production companies. The major
studios supported this trend in order to reduce fixed costs and financial risk in the face of shrinking profits. Consequently, the percentage
of independent productions among feature films increased steadily
during the early 1950s, from 25 percent in 1950 to 53 percent in 1956.[6]

An environment conducive to the independent producer seemed
to offer fertile ground for Selznick's reemergence in the film industry.
But Selznick's prospects upon returning to Hollywood weren't promising. A still-sizable debt and a reputation for profligacy made it difficult for him to secure financial backing. The movie industry was
adapting to independent production, yet Hollywood's most famous
independent producer was locked out.

Selznick turned to television partially in response to bad fortunes
in the movie business, but it was a transition that he had anticipated
for nearly two decades. He had tried unsuccessfully since the 1930s
to move into broadcasting, but he had grown accustomed to a degree
of autonomy seldom awarded to television producers by sponsors or
networks. With its minimal budgets, weekly production schedules,
and meddlesome sponsors, network television offered little promise
of accommodating the idiosyncrasies that Selznick had acquired during years as an unfettered monarch of the movie industry—especially
his stubborn refusal to compromise his authority as a producer.

Selznick remained stalled at this impasse until February 1954, when
Charles Miller, an agent with Hollywood's most powerful talent
agency, MCA, presented an offer from the N. W. Ayer and Son advertising agency to produce the electric industry's *Light's Diamond
Jubilee*. Among Hollywood's independent *movie* producers, Selznick
now stood somewhere in the middle of a growing pack, but his repu-

tation clearly overshadowed any of Hollywood's reigning *television* producers. With TV sets in more than half the country's homes and *Light's Diamond Jubilee* on nearly every set, the program promised national exposure, a chance for Selznick to restore his reputation and demonstrate to the entertainment industry that he could operate within television's budgetary constraints and unyielding production schedules. Television represented uncharted territory in which Selznick could display his skills as a producer without having to battle the major studios, whose executives he scornfully described as "incurably reactionary former and frustrated monopolists."[7]

But there were reasons for Selznick to be cautious about the electric industry's offer, even though the sponsors were willing to finance the most expensive program in TV history. The scheduled October broadcast date was only eight months away—not much time to prepare a two-hour production. The live broadcast's irrevocable deadline was an unfamiliar constraint, differing markedly from a feature film's flexible release date. Because of his impetuous filmmaking style, Selznick often postponed his productions' scheduled premieres, but the broadcast deadline would permit no such luxury. Selznick also recognized that his company was ill-prepared to enter television on any terms, much less under a strict deadline. Late-1940s budget cutbacks left Selznick Productions with only a skeletal staff in the New York distribution office and no production staff or contract actors in Hollywood. Neither Selznick nor any of his employees were familiar with the economics of the television industry or with the medium's programming formats.

Such conditions may have warranted caution, but Selznick negotiated with the Diamond Jubilee sponsors because he couldn't resist the chance to restore his reputation while staking out a position in the new medium. Selznick assumed that two decades in the movie business had given him the experience to become one of television's major producers. The making of *Light's Diamond Jubilee*, however, proved to be a costly lesson in the hazards facing the independent movie producer in television. Precisely because of his experience in the studio era, Selznick anticipated neither the challenge of forming a new TV production company nor the annoyance of battling the corporate sponsors upon whose patronage he would depend.

With *Light's Diamond Jubilee*, David Selznick discovered television sponsors who were willing at least to entertain his notions of creative autonomy and costly prestige production. Selznick—as he had during all previous negotiations with broadcasters—presented the Ayer advertising agency with a list of demands that would allow him to enter television on his own terms. He requested a nonexclusive contract to produce *Light's Diamond Jubilee,* for which the sponsors would pay $375,000 a huge sum by television standards, but a fraction of the $4 million budget on *Portrait of Jennie,* his last Hollywood feature. Selznick Productions would bear all production costs, while the sponsors would purchase broadcast time and rent network facilities. In exchange for assuming the risk of production, Selznick would retain all subsequent rights to the program after the single network broadcast. The program would blend filmed and live segments, but an effort would be made to film as much as possible in order to take advantage of Selznick's expertise as a movie producer.[8]

Selznick's desire for autonomy was signified by his efforts to shape the program according to his agenda, and not that of the sponsors. In effect, he attempted to efface any marks of a sponsor's presence. Although the Diamond Jubilee was planned as a celebration of Edison, Selznick was a reluctant biographer, refusing to be restricted by the industry's hagiography. He expected complete freedom in determining the program's content and demanded that there be no commercial interruptions; the program should use only two commercials, placed as bookends at the broadcast's beginning and end. Selznick was so determined to produce an absolutely unique television program that he promised to employ only performers who hadn't yet appeared in the medium. Finally, he asked that the program bear the trademark of Selznick Productions rather than that of a sponsor. "I have long been eager to establish the first television trademark," he explained, "and it will be a lot easier to establish it on this show than it will be on a future continuing show or series."[9] Resisting the sponsor's direct input during the production process, eliminating marks of sponsorship within the program, and rejecting the conventions of TV entertainment, Selznick in these negotiations envisioned television production as an extension of his established filmmaking procedures. If the electric industry wanted to import Hollywood spectacle into television, it would have to accept Selznick's conception of TV production.

During these initial negotiations, Selznick offered no compromises. Surprisingly, the Ayer agency and the sponsors agreed to nearly all of his terms, including his demand for a commercial-free broadcast. The sponsors guaranteed that Selznick would be given a free hand in all matters relating to "showmanship, casting, and production" but insisted that he agree to consult with the advertising agency "about reaching the objective" of the greater Diamond Jubilee celebration. Selznick balked at this condition, perceiving its division of labor as a sign of the sponsor's reservations in ceding authority to him. "This is obviously fraught with all kinds of dangers," he explained to his agent, "because the moment I have Ayer as an executive producer, I am doomed in my thinking and in my operations; I am operating entirely differently than in the past twenty-five years."[10]

In spite of his apprehensions about the potential conflicts between his sense of "showmanship" and the sponsor's promotional objectives, Selznick signed the production agreement during March 1954, and both parties pledged that "good faith" would guide their relations during the eight months until the broadcast. In fact, from the outset their alliance was driven more by mutual suspicion than by a spirit of cooperation. Because Selznick and the advertising agency hadn't drawn the lines of power in the production agreement, they spent weeks afterward in protracted negotiations, each championing a different conception of the program.

The Ayer agency wanted Selznick's guarantee that his goal of creative autonomy wouldn't compromise the sponsors' promotional ambitions. From their perspective, this program climaxed a public relations campaign that was too expensive and too important to be diverted by the impulse of a single individual—even by the program's producer. The production agreement had specified that the program's purpose was "to demonstrate and emphasize the contributions electricity is making to modern living." James Hanna, Ayer's executive in charge of the Diamond Jubilee account, reinforced this purpose in a letter to Selznick following the signing. According to Hanna, the program should promote better lighting, the great need for electrical wiring of homes, the future use of electricity on farms, new electric home heating appliances, and, most important, the future of atomic energy for the development of electric power. "I doubt if you want the specifics on these points at this time," he concluded, "but I thought it might be helpful for you to know the general area of promotional thinking which the industry expects will receive recognition in our show."[11] Hanna's communication expressed the sponsors' utilitarian view of the program, their expectation that it deliver specific messages about consumer goods no matter what its final form.

Selznick was stunned by this instrumental conception of sponsored entertainment. Although he had no clear vision of the program to offer in contrast, he perceived *Light's Diamond Jubilee* as a national pageant, an opportunity to sell not just consumer goods but "the American Spirit and what America stands for, and the progress America has made and the spirit of the American future." Although Selznick's conception of the program suited the electric industry's broader

While performing in *Light's Diamond Jubilee,* Kim Novak paused in this
publicity still to celebrate Edison's invention.
(Courtesy of Film Collection, Harry Ransom Humanities Research Center,
University of Texas at Austin © David O. Selznick Productions)

ideological goals, he and the advertising agency disagreed about
strategies for achieving these goals. Throughout the negotiations the
advertising agency took the role of strident propagandist, while Selznick championed persuasive techniques that seem more characteristic of contemporary advertising. The agency wanted to inculcate the

public with explicit messages about the electric industry's goods and services; Selznick countered by suggesting that the program bathe the electric industry in the ambience of civic virtue and national pride. By weaving electrical motifs subtly through the mise-en-scène and by celebrating a general vision of progress that identified national interests with technological development, Selznick hoped to demonstrate subtly "the change in the American home and the progress of American living as a result of the wires coming into the home that started with Edison's invention of the electric light." [12] The negotiation process, the antagonistic dialogue with the agency, actually helped Selznick to articulate his conception of the program. The more the agency argued for an explicit discourse about products, the more Selznick responded with increasingly ethereal ideas about social progress and national identity.

During these ongoing negotiations, Selznick gradually began to recognize his folly at having leapt into television production before considering the implications of his decision. He had gloated momentarily at the $375,000 that Selznick Productions would receive for the project, since it was a huge sum by television standards. But it also represented the first time in decades that Selznick would have to work within a fixed, minimal budget. In the movie industry, the promise of windfall profits at the box office had encouraged his freewheeling spending. Now Selznick feared that the entire budget for *Light's Diamond Jubilee* would barely cover his company's typical operating expenses during the months of production. "I am enormously worried that if we are not careful we are not only going to go over budget, but are going to exaggerate, rather than reduce, our reputation for not caring what we pay for anything," he complained. [13] Selznick had been motivated to produce *Light's Diamond Jubilee* by a desire to restore his reputation as a producer; instead, his hasty decision threatened to reinforce his undisciplined image.

Selznick despaired over his entrapment in the production agreement until he received a telephone call from Charles Glett, once the manager of Selznick's studio and now an employee at CBS. Glett offered Selznick a new outlook on the program by introducing him to the standard telefilm practice of deficit financing and the profit potential of ancillary markets, including syndication and foreign theatrical release. A spectacular production that stood on its own merits, independent of the Diamond Jubilee celebration, might deliver profits for years to come. "I want to think about the show in terms of use not just for this one broadcast," Selznick now realized, "but also for possible theatrical release abroad, and very importantly, for subsequent TV use here—possibly even theatrical use here, for I feel the day is not far off when important TV shows will be used not only subsequently on TV but even in theaters."[14]

In developing a strategy for potentially limitless profits through subsequent distribution, Selznick eliminated what in his mind was one of television's most pressing constraints. The ambition to create a lasting product distinguished Selznick's production from previous live TV shows, which disappeared into the ether during the initial broadcast. This concept of the program as a permanent artifact required the company to work quickly in order to shoot the entire production on film. It also demanded that Selznick Productions control all subsequent rights to every aspect of the program—including copyright clearances and residual agreements for cast and crew. Finally, Selznick's new vision of residual profits ensured a continuing antagonistic relationship between the producer and his sponsors. Selznick believed more strongly than ever that *Light's Diamond Jubilee* shouldn't merely promote electricity; its long-term value depended on its being a truly unique television program.

This new ambition to create a production with value beyond the context of the Edison celebration demanded that Selznick free himself from the creative constraints imposed by the sponsors. But by the end of March the Ayer agency had raised its demands, requesting a single commercial placed midway through the program. During the following week, Ayer questioned Selznick about the possibility of more commercials, mailing him a letter of agreement supplementary to the contract. Selznick responded angrily to the sponsor's seemingly inevitable encroachment into the program. "Even though it is now already apparent to me that I probably made a very serious mistake in agreeing to do this show," he told his agent, "I see no reason why we should not insist upon [the advertising agency's] fulfilling their end of the bargain."[15]

Selznick instructed his agent to free him from the agreement at any cost. In just a few short weeks, he already had grown weary of the advertising agency's interference in the project, trying "to prove its producing abilities." Selznick worried that if he allowed its representatives to continue interfering, "they could completely undo anything I attempted by deciding at the last minute to insert something at the beginning or middle or end which would completely undermine everything that I have struggled to achieve." As a last-minute compromise, Selznick's agent negotiated a new deal in which Ayer would finance the writing of an initial script during the next month. At the end of that period, either Ayer or Selznick could abandon the project if either was dissatisfied. In addition, Selznick would retain the rights to any scripts or treatments generated during this process, an important provision in the event that Selznick and prospective writers developed an idea that could be used for future projects. Although Selznick agreed to the terms of the new deal, he was far from enthusiastic about the prospects for *Light's Diamond Jubilee*. Peering into his future, he offered a keen assessment of the impending production process. "I am undertaking a backbreaking six-month job," he said, "that is actually far more difficult than making a ten- or twenty-million dollar grossing film, that at best is difficult and profitless, and that at worst can be disastrous."[16]

After only two months of dealing with corporate patrons, Selznick had lost sight of the potential benefits of producing *Light's Diamond Jubilee*. The best contract in the history of Hollywood TV production now seemed a burden. Selznick understood that he had accepted the project recklessly and had gotten himself into an untenable situation, yet bailing out would further damage his reputation. The broadcast date was just six months away, and still he hadn't developed any specific ideas for a script, nor had he hired a production staff. Selznick experienced the decline of his company since the 1940s most profoundly at this point. "What I really need," he admitted, "is some fine creative mind . . . someone who is very widely and deeply read, someone of intelligence and taste . . . to kick this thing around with. . . . I find myself terribly handicapped by having not one single person in our employ in either the editorial or creative fields with whom I can even discuss such problems." He instructed employees in his New York distribution office to stroll through bookstores looking for any book that might spark his imagination or might suggest a collaborator.[17]

In mid-May, Selznick turned to his longtime collaborator, screenwriter Ben Hecht. One of the finest and most prolific writers of the studio era, Hecht (often without credit) had worked on almost every Selznick production since the 1930s, including *Gone with the Wind* and *Notorious* (1946).[18] Hecht and Selznick immediately brainstormed through a number of concepts for the script. They considered giving the program a unified narrative structure, the saga of a single American family during the years of electricity's development. Although this idea appealed to Selznick and Hecht because of its resemblance to feature-film narrative, they decided that it would be impossible to guide a respectable two-hour filmed narrative from the script stage to broadcast in just six months. For practical reasons, they began to develop an alternative structure, conceiving of the program as a "mosaic" or "tapestry" that could include a number of discrete narrative and performance segments that would be less challenging to produce.[19] This type of program—modeled after the revue format already made popular on TV by comedy-variety performers like Milton Berle—would be less costly and would provide greater flexibility during the production process, since individual segments could be altered or replaced without disrupting the entire production.

Selznick also argued that the eclectic structure would enable him to represent what he perceived as the diversity of the American experience and the accomplishments of American culture. In essence, Selznick imagined the program's textual heterogeneity as reflecting the nation's diversity. "Believe it or not," he told the press, "we had a chart drawn up, with people divided by geographical areas, by income, by education, and so on, so that some portion of the program would interest everybody." Selznick imagined the audience as a collection of social groups, rather than as an undifferentiated mass—though his conception of social difference was narrowed to include only variations in age. His chart, he explained, focused primarily on "elements that would appeal to babies, adolescents, young married people, the middle-aged, and the old folks."[20]

Selznick's image of the audience suppressed ethnic, racial, or class differences in favor of an idealized image of the extended family. In fact, Selznick became so nervous about the propriety of even considering a story with black characters that he wrote directly to Diamond Jubilee chairman Charles Wilson, requesting his advice. Given his antagonism toward the sponsors, Selznick was surprisingly deferential on this issue. "There are presumably millions of potential buyers among colored people who are just as interested in electrical equipment as their lighter-skinned brethren," he wrote, but "if you must turn thumbs down on this story . . . it will be for good and sufficient reasons that I shall not further challenge, I assure you."[21] In moments like this, it became evident that Selznick's opposition to the sponsors was based less on principled differences than on his reluctance to compromise his autonomy as a producer. During the writing process, Selznick articulated an ideological agenda that was virtually indistinguishable from that of his sponsors.

Selznick came to see the national broadcast as an extraordinary forum that placed upon him a responsibility to deliver an uplifting message to a nation which he perceived as torn by a dilemma—simultaneously enchanted by the promise of atomic energy and anguished by the terror of nuclear weapons. He viewed the program not merely as a symbolic reflection of the nation but also as an active "contribution to the American way of life, on which depends not only the future well-being of all American citizens of every class and creed, but also . . . the future of private enterprise and the progress and health of American corporations." His goal was to portray the benevolent face of nuclear research, "to give the people of the country a better feeling about the future, during these times when everyone is so depressed, consciously or subconsciously, by the fear that we are on the edge of disaster and annihilation."[22]

The desire to reassure Americans about a future that protected private enterprise and the progress of corporate America was an ambition perfectly suited to the electric industry's agenda, which stated that the program's accent should be "more upon the electrical future than upon achievements of the past," especially considering that the past achievements of nuclear technology had been only destructive. Selznick's conception of the program, however, made nuclear annihilation the inescapable undercurrent of a promising nuclear future. Indeed, this tendency ran throughout postwar American culture. As historian Paul Boyer has observed, "Along with the shock waves of fear, one also finds exalted prophecies of the bright promise of atomic energy. The more euphoric of these predictions soon faded, but the upbeat theme proved remarkably tenacious. These two responses that seem so contradictory—the terror of atomic war and vision of an atomic Utopia—were in fact complexly interwoven."[23]

Hecht helped Selznick to narrow the program's focus by deciding to adapt a few short stories whose variety would represent both the breadth of the American experience and the unifying value of American individualism. Hecht, familiar with writing to suit a client after years in the studio system, came up with a structure that satisfied both Selznick and the sponsors—the notion of using light as a structural metaphor throughout the show, to associate the electric industry's most apparent product with the notion of enlightenment.[24] Although Selznick wouldn't deny the nuclear threat, his determined optimism began to structure the program and influence the type of stories selected—stories that, in his words, could be "twisted" to reflect "either the development of electricity or of American individualism."[25] Selznick purchased broadcast rights to seven short stories: Irwin Shaw's "Girls in Summer Dresses," Arthur Gordon's "A Kiss for the Lieutenant," Ray Bradbury's "Powerhouse," E. C. Keifer's "Men Are Maddening," Max Shulman's "A Chance for Adventure," Dorothy Parker's "Here We Are," and John Steinbeck's "Leader of the People."

The program's utopian vision influenced the selection and shaped the adaptation of these stories, most obviously in the transformation of Steinbeck's "Leader of the People," a melancholy meditation on the closing of the American frontier. Selznick decided to change the story's bittersweet climax because he thought it unsuited to the program's general tone. As a member of Selznick's staff told Steinbeck's agent at the time of the purchase, "Since [Selznick's] plan is to use this story to lead into an optimistic portrayal of the future, he would like Mr. Steinbeck to know at the outset that he plans to end the story on an optimistic, rather than the present contrary note, and he would like the concluding speech to be from the boy refusing to accept grandfather's declaration that frontiers are closed." [26] Ultimately, Selznick intended to conclude the program with "an optimistic portent of the future," a rapturous climax in which the various strains of the program would culminate at the pinnacle of church and state: "three distinguished ministers of the three great American faiths"—Protestant, Catholic, and Jewish—would remind viewers that eternal truths endure, and then President Eisenhower would implore viewers to have faith in the future of American ingenuity and enterprise. Selznick toyed with the idea of changing the program's title to "The American Dream." [27]

Selznick and Hecht completed a first draft of the script by the beginning of July, and Selznick finally began to organize the myriad details that go into a production. With only three months until the broadcast, the script was still rough, the key production positions were vacant, and casting hadn't even begun. In late July Selznick hired a production supervisor, William Phillipson, who had been general manager of West Coast operations for ABC. Phillipson took charge immediately, hiring researchers and the first members of a production staff. [28] Selznick still worried that the production couldn't be organized in time to shoot the various segments on film. His original plans called for filming as much of the program as the budget would allow—to ensure better-quality prints for subsequent distribution—but it now became apparent that there wouldn't be enough time for production and post-production if the entire program was filmed. He feared that the program might have to be broadcast live, which would substantially reduce its resale value since a kinescope copy would be less satisfactory for distribution than original film footage. Production delays intensified the pressure, because they undermined the program's only chance to earn a profit.

Selznick felt the constant strain of being an independent movie producer in an unfamiliar medium. He had wanted to retain the option of using both film and live sequences in the program, and of using personnel from both the movie and the TV industries, but he hadn't appreciated the jurisdictional conflicts that might arise. He hadn't considered how difficult it would be to control residual rights, or even to determine pay scale, when dealing with performers and technicians from television, stage, and film, all of whom were covered by different union agreements which contained separate provisions for live and filmed production. After lawyers examined Ben Hecht's contract, for instance, Selznick learned that the production company still hadn't secured future rights to Hecht's script. With the company's profit margin dependent on the potential residual value of the program, this sort of contractual loophole could be devastating. In a panic at the end of July, Selznick ordered his distribution chief, Frank Davis, to leave his duties in New York and assist in contract negotiations, because the production company was getting itself into "a terrible snarl as a result of awful conflicts on union and guild contracts." "I simply cannot any longer be negotiator, lawyer, and businessman on this show and be its creator," Selznick complained. "I will fail miserably if I have to go through this even a little while longer."[29]

Forced to press his distribution chief into service with the live broadcast looming ever closer, Selznick faced the difficulty of attempting to meet television's rigorous production schedule without a standing production company or the active support of an advertising agency or TV network. When he signed the production agreement, he had known that his existing organization couldn't produce the program alone. He was counting on support from the Ayer agency, his agent at MCA, and the networks, since the agencies and the networks generally worked together to produce and broadcast spectaculars. By the end of July, however, Selznick saw that aid from these organizations wasn't about to materialize.

Since *Light's Diamond Jubilee* was to be broadcast on all four networks, no single network would be identified with the program; therefore, no network offered assistance. Worse, the agencies had failed to deliver promised talent. The Ayer agency had assured Selznick that it could provide Bing Crosby, since the performer was closely associated with General Electric, one of the Diamond Jubilee's primary sponsors. But no amount of effort, including Selznick himself directly imploring Crosby, could convince the singer to appear. Selznick had similar problems with the producers of the Westinghouse-sponsored TV series, *Studio One*, who refused to share broadcast rights to stories that they controlled.[30] Despite repeated assurances that they would, Selznick's representatives at MCA couldn't provide even an experienced TV director. "If this were film or we were set up for a consistent TV operation," Selznick informed his agent, "we would have an organization; but in accepting this show, I recognized that we did not have the staff for TV, that we could not afford to assemble one, and took at face value the statements of both MCA and Ayer that I could count upon them for help."[31]

The advertising agency came to represent the worst of the institutional forces that impeded Selznick's ability to produce the program. Nowhere were these forces more evident to Selznick than during casting and the hiring of production personnel, when Selznick ran up against the blacklisting practices that had developed in the broadcasting industries because of pressure from anti-communist groups during the 1950s. Although political blacklisting in the entertainment industry was never explicitly acknowledged, its effects were felt forcefully in television because of the networks' susceptibility to pressure from advertisers. The practices of blacklisting, including checking the "clearance" of individuals with liberal political affiliations, were institutionalized by advertising agencies and networks as a component in the production process.

Selznick initially had expressed concern that Ayer's contractual prohibition against using personnel connected with "subversive" movements was an expression of "hysteria," and not a concern for "equity and justice." Nevertheless, he submitted to the clearance process, although he found its actual procedures to be obscure. During pre-production, writer Lillian Hellman and director Lewis Milestone were rejected by the advertising agency after lengthy, ambiguous negotiations. Selznick complained bitterly about the delays caused by the clearance process. "I wish you would get to the bottom of just who it is we should check with on these and related matters," he told Frank Davis. "Isn't there someone at the FBI that we are permitted to check with directly?"[32] As this statement indicates, the blacklist was less a political issue for Selznick than just another of the TV industry's inconveniences; the political implications of blacklisting wouldn't temper his celebration of "the American dream."

Selznick's company finally adapted to blacklisting by establishing a procedure whereby Frank Davis would contact CBS's Daniel O'Shea with requests for clearance. O'Shea had been Selznick's own administrative right-hand man until their falling-out in 1950. Since leaving Selznick, O'Shea had become the individual primarily responsible for the clearance process at CBS, the network whose reputation for zealotry in institutionalized blacklisting led historian Erik Barnouw to name it "purge headquarters."[33] Selznick paid little heed to O'Shea's recommendations concerning writers whose stories were being adapted, but he required that all actors considered for the program be cleared before contract negotiations. Writers John Steinbeck, Irwin Shaw, and Dorothy Parker were rejected by O'Shea, but their association with the program would be minimal, especially as Selznick and Hecht adapted their stories to suit the program's celebratory spirit. Actors, in contrast, were more visible and, therefore, more likely to provoke sponsor concern or public censure. Actresses Lena Horne, Uta Hagen, and actor Jose Ferrer were deemed unsuitable for television, Ferrer merely because the blacklisting organizations found his attempt to clear himself before the House Un-American Activities Committee "unimpressive." Other prospective performers, such as Edward G. Robinson, Kirk Douglas, Joseph Cotten, Lauren Bacall, Orson Welles, and Frederic March were cleared—though reluctantly, because of their involvement with a variety of liberal political causes.[34]

Casting and other hiring began in earnest during August. Most of the participants from the movie industry agreed to work for minimal fees as a favor to Selznick. Longtime Selznick actor Joseph Cotten agreed to serve as on-screen narrator, while established screen and stage actors such as Lauren Bacall, David Niven, Thomas Mitchell, Helen Hayes, and Judith Anderson agreed to perform in the narrative sketches. The company also hired a number of the movie industry's most notable production personnel. Victor Young, who recently had scored such movies as *The Greatest Show on Earth* (1952) and *Shane* (1953), was hired to compose the score. Furth Ullman, the production designer for such Broadway productions as *South Pacific* and *The King and I*, was brought in to design both the filmed and the live segments. MGM cameraman Ray June was signed as director of photography for the filmed segments. Carey Wilson, who for years produced MGM's Andy Hardy and Dr. Kildare series, signed on to produce the nonfiction segments of the program, which would demonstrate the scientific achievements of the electric industry. Famed cinematographer James Wong Howe agreed to shoot these segments. Finally, King Vidor was brought aboard to direct the filmed short-story adaptations.

By early September, with only six weeks until the broadcast, crucial aspects of the production were still unresolved. Selznick, who wasn't yet satisfied with the script, instructed his staff to comb bookstores for love scenes from great novels or dramatic scenes involving electricity. Although King Vidor had agreed to direct the film segments, he so far had not contacted Selznick about his assignment. Furth Ullman had yet to begin designing the production. Many smaller casting decisions remained. The production also needed at least two more directors, one who could direct the filmed bridging sequences featuring narrator Joseph Cotten and another who could direct the segments of the broadcast that would have to be produced live. And finally, Selznick still hadn't hired anyone to be responsible for calculating a production budget. As difficult as it is to believe, the company had begun signing contracts before even determining a detailed budget.[35] Selznick Productions was living up to its reputation for economic waste and inefficiency.

However disorganized, the company had to go into production by mid-September for there to be any hope of producing filmed sequences for the broadcast. During the first week of September, William Phillipson hired Riley Jackson as production manager and budget coordinator. He then rented soundstage space at RKO's Pathe Studios for $500 a day beginning 20 September. After one day of rehearsal, King Vidor directed Steinbeck's "Leader of the People," starring Walter Brennan and Brandon De Wilde, on 21 and 22 September. Then, after one more day of rehearsal, Vidor directed Arthur Gordon's "A Kiss for the Lieutenant," starring Guy Madison and Kim Novak, on 24 and 25 September. In the meantime, Christian Nyby, a former editor who had gone on to direct low-budget films like *The Thing* (1951) and had begun to establish a reputation as a TV director at Hal Roach's studio, directed narrator Joseph Cotten in the filmed scenes that would bridge the various segments.[36]

Because of the hectic pace, Selznick couldn't oversee the production process with his customary diligence. Furth Ullman, for instance, had designed sets for the filmed sequences but hadn't had time to produce continuity sketches that would guide the director and crew in lighting sets, blocking action, and framing compositions. Faced with little preparation time, Vidor shot sequences off the cuff. "Some of my disappointments in the show to date," Selznick responded after viewing the rushes, "have been due to our having to shoot without these sketches, and my having insufficient time to substitute my own personal supervision of these camera angles."[37]

Once the editing began, Selznick came up against the faults of the frenzied production schedule. Whereas in movies he had the freedom to improvise on the set, secure in the knowledge that he could reshoot problem footage, the budget and time constraints of television made it essential to work from a precise shooting plan, recorded with continuity sketches. Without the sketches, Vidor and company made many mistakes, including using extreme long shots that wouldn't register on the small TV screen, filming shots that wouldn't cut together well, and failing to provide the proper shots for editing the scenes effectively. "We are in bad, bad trouble on the end of 'Leader of the People,'" Selznick warned, "because we don't have the angles we need to salvage pieces of what otherwise is a performance that would satisfy [Walter] Brennan no more than it satisfies us." As the date of the live broadcast approached, Selznick implored the production staff to work overtime to provide the continuity sketches that would be necessary for keeping the live segments within budget and on schedule. "Now we are in the live show, and I cannot have any surprises as to the camera treatment of it," he warned Ullman.[38]

David O. Selznick, President Eisenhower, and director William Wellman on the
Denver set where the president filmed his closing statement.
(Source Unknown/Courtesy of Dwight D. Eisenhower Library
National Park Service Collection)

In early October Selznick received his first precise cost estimate and
learned that he was about to lose thousands of dollars in the process
of glorifying the electric industry. Tensions between Selznick and the
Ayer agency were running high as the producer and another of his
longtime associates, director William Wellman, flew to Denver to film
the show's denouement, an inspirational speech by President Eisenhower. Selznick wrote a brief speech in which Eisenhower would deliver an uplifting message about national pride without actually tout-
ing the electric industry. The Ayer agency wanted the president to
recognize the Diamond Jubilee during his speech, but Selznick refused. Though Selznick prevailed in this confrontation, his relations
with the advertising agency had reached their worst stage yet.[39]

After returning from Denver during the first week of October, Selznick hired two television directors for the live broadcast—Bud Yorkin
to rehearse and direct the onstage performers and Alan Handley to

call the shots from the control booth.[40] As the program neared its broadcast date, crew members worked eighteen-hour days to complete the editing of the film sequences, to construct sets for the live sequences, and to rehearse the live performances. Selznick privately feared that the production wouldn't live up to expectations for his television debut. In his search for reasonably priced talent, he hadn't been able to avoid performers familiar to TV audiences. In fact, some of the performers, like comedian George Gobel and singer Eddie Fisher, had achieved fame mainly as a result of their exposure on TV. In the final tally, Selznick found time to film only two of the adapted short stories. For safety's sake, he had incorporated two other filmed segments, a clip from his 1938 feature *The Adventures of Tom Sawyer* and an MGM-produced Robert Benchley film short from the 1940s, neither of which represented the novelty he originally had intended for the program. While the filmed segments would fill much of the program's first hour, its second hour would consist primarily of musical numbers and dramatic adaptations to be performed live. Even if his company could carry off the live sequences, the program's residual value had been compromised by the poor planning which had made it impossible to film much of the script.

The structure of *Light's Diamond Jubilee*, which Selznick described as "a tapestry of entertainment woven around the theme of light," provides a context for combining discrete sketches and musical performances with sequences that promote consumer use of electricity. No single mode of address dominates the program; instead, the program shifts between expository and dramatic sequences, pausing occasionally for live performances. Since there are no commercials, the sponsors' presence is signified explicitly only during the program's introduction. Against the image of a magnificent sunrise an announcer welcomes the viewer: "Your hosts for the next two hours are the millions of Americans who own our electrical industries through investment, by their own free will, of their personal savings. These join with the many thousands of men and women who supply electricity and who design and produce electrical equipment for America's mills and factories, and farms and homes, and the defense forces, in hoping that you will find something entertaining and informative in this program." This populist greeting represents one of the Diamond Jubilee's central strategies—its efforts to mask the campaign's actual corporate patrons and their proprietary interests behind the more benign image of a spontaneous, popular celebration orchestrated by hardworking Americans. Following this introduction, the sponsors' presence disperses into the text, never emerging explicitly through commercial interruptions but returning implicitly during expository passages about the future of electrical research, technology, and consumer goods.

Joseph Cotten acts as on-screen narrator, weaving the "tapestry" from the various sequences of narrative and performance: the whitewashing scene from Selznick's 1938 production of *The Adventures of*

Light's Diamond Jubilee host Joseph Cotten.
(Courtesy of Film Collection, Harry Ransom Humanities Research Center,
University of Texas at Austin © David O. Selznick Productions)

Tom Sawyer; "A Kiss for the Lieutenant," a filmed sketch starring Kim Novak and Guy Madison as a young Air Force widow and a pilot who share a brief emotional encounter as he is about to leave for active duty; the Robert Benchley comic film about raising children; Eddie Fisher at a college dance singing a live version of "Sweetheart of the Sigma Chi" (with an uncredited cameo appearance by his wife, Debbie Reynolds); Lauren Bacall and David Niven starring as a married couple who momentarily question the husband's restlessness in a live adaptation of "The Girls in Their Summer Dresses"; comedian George Gobel performing a monologue about "electronic brains"; Helen Hayes and Thomas Mitchell starring as an elderly small-town couple who find they've inherited money from a lost uncle in a live performance of "A Chance for Adventure"; singer Dorothy Dandridge performing a pair of Gershwin tunes; and, finally, Walter Brennan and Brandon De Wilde starring as a former wagon train leader and his young grandson in a filmed adaptation of Steinbeck's "Leader of the People." Interwoven with these sequences are expository scenes depicting a comic history of electrical appliances, a preview of "tomorrow's gadgets," references to the threat posed by nuclear weapons, and the efforts of scientists to tame the atom and create the nuclear-powered world of the future.

In attempting to redeem the atom, *Light's Diamond Jubilee* oscillates between two poles identified by Susan Sontag in her description of American life after Hiroshima. "Ours is indeed an age of extremity," she writes. "For we live under the threat of two equally fearful, but seemingly opposed, destinies: unremitting banality and inconceivable terror."[41] Sontag's stark opposition describes *Light's Diamond Jubilee*. For ninety minutes the program meanders through sentimental drama, homespun comedy, and romantic ballads with no apparent narrative direction or rhetorical goal. After the unremitting banality of these early sequences, however, the program arrives at the adaptation of "Leader of the People" and finally confronts the inconceivable terror hidden within the campaign for the peaceful atom.

In Steinbeck's original story, an aging pioneer of the American West visits his grandson in California. The old man once led wagon trains to the coast, but now he admits sadly that the frontier is closed and the pioneer spirit that drove the restless movement westward is dead. "When we saw the mountains at last, we cried," he tells his grandson. "But it wasn't getting here that mattered, it was movement and westering. . . . The westering was as big as God, and the slow steps that made the movement piled up and piled up until the continent was crossed." Now that civilization has pushed to the bluffs overlooking the Pacific Ocean, there is nothing left to discover. "But that's not

Brandon De Wilde and Walter Brennan in the adaptation of John Steinbeck's
"Leader of the People."
(Courtesy of Film Collection, Harry Ransom Humanities Research Center,
University of Texas at Austin © David O. Selznick Productions)

the worst," he explains. "Westering isn't a hunger anymore. It's all
done."[42] The old man's disappointment is purposely ambiguous. To
the grandfather, the nation's western migration represented the spirit
of progress, but it isn't clear whether, in observing the closing of the
frontier, he laments the end of progress or regrets its meager rewards.

The story's appeal to Selznick is evident. The grandfather's weary judgment echoes Selznick's sentiments about Hollywood's decline during the 1950s—particularly his belief that the pioneer spirit had been extinguished in the movie industry. But his adaptation of "Leader of the People" does not conclude with this passage; instead, it transcends Steinbeck's despair by having the boy refuse to accept his grandfather's resignation. "Grandpa, no!" the grandson cries. "There must be other kinds of westering—in balloons maybe, to the moon and the stars!" Cheered by his grandson's faith, the old man suddenly rises, exclaiming, "Now that's the kind of spirit I haven't seen since we cleared the Donner Pass!" As the boy points to the ocean, he shouts, "Just wait till you hear the story of my westering!" Smiling and gazing seaward, the grandfather sighs, "I'll be glad to listen." The old man's sudden reversal occurs without warning or narrative motivation. In an instant, he rejects nostalgia and recognizes progress as inexorable, inextinguishable. Even when humanity seems to have driven itself to the very limits of its ambition for mastering the world, he recognizes, there are new frontiers to discover.

Having revised Steinbeck by opening his closed frontier, the scene dissolves to a series of images representing productive factories and research laboratories—the products of an unquenchable pioneer spirit that continues to inspire Americans. In voice-over, Joseph Cotten explains, "And that boy found his frontier more stupendous than any known to man . . . and then . . ." Cotten's voice trails off, the screen goes black, and suddenly an atomic bomb detonates. An ominous drumbeat sounds a funeral dirge as the bomb explodes into a mushroom cloud, soon replaced by images of other nuclear blasts that dissolve one into another. The words "radioactive," "uranium," "fusion," "fission," and "H-bomb" appear on the screen, superimposed on the bomb footage. "These are the words that bring to mind not science, but the Four Horsemen of the Apocalypse," Cotten intones. "And the gossip is that laboratories are busily at work on a missile no bigger than a bean bag that will blow the world to smithereens. Atomic power is destructive, but so is a pencil—which can write a poem, but can also write a death warrant. It would have been foolish to worry about the invention of the pencil because it could be used to write wrong things. It would be just as foolish to look with dread on the new power that has come into the world. It will not destroy the world!" The sudden reversal at the conclusion of "Leader of the People"—the grandfather's unexpected shift from pessimism to optimism—echoes through the subsequent sequences: in the move from narrative to exposition, from the recognition of nuclear terror to its immediate disavowal. These abrupt, unmotivated transitions signal the figurative return of the sponsors, submerged since the opening credits. Any pretense of entertainment fades away; the remainder of the program is dominated by expository sequences representing the electric industry's utopian vision of the future.

As the screen fills with images of research laboratories, models of future cities powered by atomic energy, and images of futuristic medical devices, Cotten explains, "In the research laboratories of our electric industry, thousands of research scientists and chemists are coaxing the atom's magic powers into new uses and devices to ease the strains of living, to increase the sources of diversion, and to reduce the hazards of disease. . . . Through the black fist of the atomic bomb, these are the bright visions we can see of tomorrow—and in their coming lies a deeper promise: man working for the salvation of man means the growth of human goodness, the deepening of human faith and the growing love of God. This is an American light that has never failed—the light of faith."

The futurist social fantasy expressed in the final half-hour of *Light's Diamond Jubilee* depicts atomic energy's effects in utopian terms characteristic of a discourse that critics James Carey and John J. Quirk have termed the "electrical sublime." The futurist discourse characteristic of the electrical sublime "identifies electricity and electrical power, electronics and cybernetics, computers and information with a new birth of community, decentralization, ecological balance, and social harmony." The various versions of this discourse "convey an impression that electrical technology is the great benefactor of mankind. Simultaneously, they hail electrical techniques as the motive force of desired social change, the key to the re-creation of a humane community, the means for returning to a cherished naturalistic bliss."[43]

Rather than express tendencies inherent in electricity or electrical power, the electrical sublime displaces a utopian desire for social transformation onto electrical research and technology, conflating notions of technological and social progress. As Carolyn Marvin has noted, however, "In its most tangible aspect, electricity came to existing groups less as a transformative agent . . . than as a set of concrete opportunities or threats to be weighed and figured into the pursuit of ongoing social objectives."[44] In this sense, utopian discourses about electricity's future benefits may have been the language used to express a genuine desire among the disenfranchised for social reform, but too often, as Carey and Quirk recognize, "the real beneficiaries of the rhetoric of the electrical sublime were the electrical light and power companies that presided over the new technologies."[45]

Both the government's Atoms for Peace campaign and the electric industry's Diamond Jubilee employed the rhetoric of the electrical sublime to legitimize the commercial production of atomic energy by implicating it in the promise of social reform. The Atoms for Peace campaign was focused mainly on the utopian promise of atomic energy, suggesting a futurist narrative that returned insistently to the figure of Eisenhower, the visionary leader of the atom's peaceful era. The Diamond Jubilee linked Eisenhower's atomic future with electricity's origins, embodied by Thomas Edison, the industry's spiritual father. The link between Edison and Eisenhower as the figures at the center of these campaigns recurs at the conclusion of *Light's Diamond Jubilee*, when the program that began as a celebration of Edison concludes with an appearance by Eisenhower.

An image of Washington crossing the Delaware appears on-screen, then dissolves into a scene of Lincoln in his chamber, anguished by the decision to engage the South in war. This image dissolves into a shot of the Lincoln Memorial. As the camera tracks backward from the memorial, however, it reveals that this Lincoln Memorial is actually an image on the screen of a television set. Pulling back farther, the camera reveals that the TV set belongs to President Eisenhower, who is experiencing the immediacy of live television by watching *Light's Diamond Jubilee* along with every TV viewer in America; indeed, the president's attention to the program signifies its importance as a national event.

Sensing the presence of the TV camera, Eisenhower turns from the TV set to speak directly to the audience, the action emphasizing his peculiar relationship to the new medium, through which he was simultaneously a typical television viewer and one of the medium's masters. This self-reflexive moment represents Selznick's one attempt to imagine television as a unique communications medium, with qualities distinguishable from the cinema. As Eisenhower discards his role as anonymous observer in order to take command of the broadcast, *Light's Diamond Jubilee* celebrates the wonder of television technology—the immediacy of live broadcast, the ability to collapse time and space, the power to address an entire nation at once. But unlike Eisenhower's televised ground-breaking ceremony for the first nuclear power plant, the Diamond Jubilee performance is a sham. Instead of staging a live event, Selznick simulated television's immediacy by filming Eisenhower's appearance three weeks earlier in a Denver TV studio. Because he never conceived of live broadcast as anything but a nuisance, Selznick was content to fabricate an image of television's immediacy.

Feigning spontaneity, Eisenhower concludes a brief speech about Edison by reminding television viewers of the importance of family and the value of sharing family experiences. But while television viewing was generally depicted as a primary family experience during this era, Eisenhower's family is curiously absent from this scene of domestic life in the White House. In order to foster communal participation in the celebration, the Diamond Jubilee's organizers had recommended forming groups to view the program, but Eisenhower is alone watching *Light's Diamond Jubilee.* As the camera tracks away from the president after his speech, he sits in a sanctuary constructed on a soundstage in Denver, a cavernous study containing only a fireplace, the television set, and an upholstered chair—an austere vision of domestic life in the White House.

The broadcast completed, Eisenhower's blank television screen now stares impassively. Alone with the TV set, absolutely disconnected from his family or the nation of TV viewers that he has just addressed, the president turns awkwardly and gazes at the fire burning in the fireplace. Television was supposed to have united the nation in a celebration of Edison, but instead it has created this unsettling image of isolation—an emptiness at the symbolic center of American life. This image, of the president alone with a blank TV set, is what lingers at the conclusion of *Light's Diamond Jubilee.*

As an unprecedented Hollywood TV production, *Light's Diamond Jubilee* represented one potential strategy for the corporate sponsorship of Hollywood programming and one model by which independent movie producers could enter television production. Ultimately, the program appeared on nearly every existing TV station in the country—broadcast live or using same-day kinescopes over 329 stations and given delayed broadcast on 26 others. Thanks to this programming strategy and the promotional campaign that accompanied it, the program's audience exceeded 70 million viewers, a result that gratified the electric industry. One industry report noted happily that "the industry was able to entertain some 70 million people for two hours at an individual cost less than that of a post card." The industry also reported that the majority of the fan mail and reviews were extremely positive, although reviews in major publications were mixed.[46]

Depictions of Edison in the media were so seemingly ubiquitous during the days leading up to the broadcast that *New York Herald Tribune* critic John Crosby commended *Light's Diamond Jubilee* because "the one thing the show did not have, thank heaven, was a dramatization of Thomas Edison's discovery of the electric light." On the other hand, he was thankful that the program concluded "in the nick of time, before [its] sentimentality got completely out of hand." Writing in *Variety,* industry reporter George Rosen was even more critical: "Not in a month of spectaculars will you come across the kind of marquee values as were superimposed over the $1,000,000 (and plus) *Light's Diamond Jubilee* attraction. More's the pity, then, that it had to wind up largely as a glorified paean of faith in the American individual more suggestive of 'Voice of America' programming. And it seemed to go on interminably." Striking a more enthusiastic note, *New York Times* critic Jack Gould said, "Except for the overly solemn note sounded in the last twenty minutes or so, it was a remarkable achievement. . . . All in all, Mr. Selznick made a most impressive debut in the TV medium." *Time* offered the most encouraging assessment when its critic claimed that *Light's Diamond Jubilee* "was easily the best single TV program" of the year. But *Time* also recognized that the program was an anomaly and not likely to be embraced as standard practice in the industry. "Shows of this excellence require staggering amounts of money and exhaustive preparation," the review noted. "Ordinary TV is not geared to operate on this kind of [production] schedule, nor can ordinary sponsors regularly pay this sort of money."[47]

As the climactic event in the Diamond Jubilee celebration, the TV broadcast was embedded in the elaborate array of texts and public performances that unfolded during the months leading up to the broadcast. Intended as the culmination of the yearlong publicity campaign, the TV program was expected to reconstitute the myriad elements of the Diamond Jubilee in a single text, to provide the moment when an individual's unfocused and distracted experience of the celebration on a community level would crystallize into a greater understanding.

The campaign for atomic energy had told the industry's story of "electrical progress" but never in a single text. Consequently, the industry intended to conclude its campaign by representing the story of electricity with the production values and narrative strategies of a Hollywood spectacular. But since television's images and sound were still impoverished in comparison with those of the cinema, the television broadcast created an alternative sense of spectacle by broadcasting the program simultaneously on all of the nation's TV stations.

It might seem excessive, even irrational, for a single sponsor to broadcast the same program on every existing channel, but the meaning of *Light's Diamond Jubilee* was expressed most clearly by its very ubiquity, by its ability to place television in the service of the electric industry. For one evening, watching television meant watching *Light's Diamond Jubilee*. The difference between the general experience of watching TV and the specific experience of watching a particular program was erased; television became *Light's Diamond Jubilee*. The industry displayed its social and economic power through its ability to unify the heterogeneity of TV's typical programming flow, and this symbolic expression of power was in many ways more important than the content of the program.

The sponsors provided Selznick with the opportunity to create a national pageant, a monument to one of the most powerful industries in the world, but Selznick had neither the means nor the imagination to match their ambitions. In spite of his reputation as a master of Hollywood spectacle, Selznick valued sentiment more than power. He mounted huge productions not to stage historical epics in the style of De Mille but to provide the most lavish setting for the emotional conflicts of melodrama. Inspired by a melodramatic sensibility, Selznick was more sensitive to the pastoral values lost with the origins of modernity than enthusiastic about the technocratic future envisioned by the electric industry. But, the organizers of the Diamond Jubilee, sold on Selznick's ability to orchestrate elaborate productions, failed to notice the potential conflicts posed by the sentimentality of his movies. A devout believer in the decline and fall of Hollywood, skeptical of modernity's influence on traditional values, Selznick ultimately did not share his sponsors' rapturous belief in progress. Still, his sensibility never threatened to undermine the program or subvert the industry's goals. In fact, although Selznick and the sponsors argued over the producer's authority, the program actually articulated many of the themes circulating throughout the Diamond Jubilee, including the utopian promise of atomic energy.

Yet it was precisely Selznick's nostalgia that made it impossible for him to envision a program that embodied the industry's definition of progress with anything approaching the inspiration of the sponsor's decision to take over the airwaves. Selznick might have used television technology to identify the medium itself with the guarantee of progress—as the Eisenhower administration had with the televised ground-breaking ceremony for the first nuclear power plant. Instead, Selznick saw live broadcasting as a hindrance. Because of the logistical demands of live production and the limited financial value of a production captured only on kinescope prints, Selznick was disappointed that he hadn't been able to film the entire program.

Since the production agreement for *Light's Diamond Jubilee* stated that Selznick Productions would bear all production costs, the burden of the program's expense fell more heavily on Selznick than on his sponsors. With a final production cost of $424,000, Selznick Productions lost $87,000 on the program.[48] Selznick was shocked to learn that costs had jumped more than $80,000 in the final two weeks of production. When he demanded that his staff account for the discrepancy, it became clear that the principal cause of nearly every excessive cost was the inflexibility of scheduling caused by the live broadcast. Delays in defining the show's content, last-minute changes, expansion of the cast, and the demand for technical perfection could be tolerated by Selznick's typical film schedule but not by a television schedule, and overtime labor charges in constructing sets and post-production inflated the budget during the final days.[49]

After studying the report, Selznick recognized that the problem centered on the inefficiency of his company, which had not been prepared to engage in television production. Selznick offered his own rambling, but accurate, critique of the situation. "We had been out of production for a long time," he noted. "We were short-handed from an executive standpoint, and I suppose we can find excuses for ourselves in these factors, and in the further fact that we found to our horror having signed for this show on all networks, that we could not rely upon one of them instead of all of them, and that we had to build an organization from scratch. When we go back into production, we are going to need more expert controls over physical production and cost factors through the services of a first-rate production manager."[50] In suffering the losses, Selznick learned the absolute necessity of having an efficient, organized production company in order to deal with television's rigid broadcast schedules.

Since Selznick had undertaken the production of *Light's Diamond Jubilee* to prove his ability to handle a strict budget, he warned his colleagues about the danger of announcing their financial loss. "I think we must be careful not to spread information or even gossip about the overage, lest it be damaging to us," he reminded his staff. Selznick pleaded with the Ayer agency and MCA to rescue him from his financial setback, but both agencies declined. In a memo, Selznick expressed his anger over the way that the advertising agency had abandoned him during production and had failed to deliver on its promises of production support. "If I am forced to take a financial beating in consequence of what I should regard as unethical and unfair and incredibly ungrateful attitude on the parts of your agency and of your sponsors," he wrote, "I shall simply charge it up to experience, remember it thoroughly, and be guided in the future accordingly."[51]

When the electric industry's Diamond Jubilee committee met to conclude business at the end of December 1954, its members listened to reports of Selznick's financial woes and sent only regrets. N. W. Ayer vice president Jim Hanna reported to Selznick's MCA agent, Charles Miller: "The committee is very sorry to hear [about Selznick's troubles], but unfortunately there is no action the committee can possibly take. . . . This is a business letter giving the business facts. But I do not want to conclude it without expressing again our great appreciation for the tremendous and unquestionably successful job done by Mr. Selznick, and our regrets that he was unable to make something for himself out of the project." By personally lobbying members of the committee, many of whom were acquaintances, Selznick later persuaded the Diamond Jubilee planning committee to pay an additional $20,000. But the stigma of the experience, including the indifference of the advertising and talent agencies, left him feeling bitter and abandoned. He was determined that during any future interaction with the television industry, he would negotiate directly with networks and avoid dealing with advertising agencies.[52] He vowed never again to be subservient to commercial sponsors.

During January 1955, after reflecting on the *Light's Diamond Jubilee* experience, Selznick wrote a long letter to NBC executive Emanuel Sacks outlining his future TV production plans and his perspective on the emerging field of telefilm production.[53] Selznick offered an astute assessment of the differences between his brand of independent production and the series television production that already dominated the telefilm industry, comparing series production to his early experience at MGM and RKO. "Whereas I am known primarily as the maker of a relatively small number of films," he explained, "my experience has also encompassed the management of very large enterprises, dealing in quantity output. It was not by either necessity or limitation of knowledge or experience that I became the producer of a small number of films, but by choice, because of my recognition that in the motion picture field a very small number of top motion pictures was preferable to quantity output from every standpoint, including the financing. By contrast, I recognize that the reverse is true in television."

Based on his experience with *Light's Diamond Jubilee,* Selznick believed that expensive TV spectaculars weren't economically feasible for Hollywood producers; until advertisers could afford larger budgets, the trend in television programming leaned toward the mass production of telefilm series. Nevertheless, he hoped to position his company as television's first prestige production firm. "As I visualize this enterprise," said Selznick of his TV production plans, "it would be the first major film producing unit devoted exclusively to quality productions in television. The Selznick name should, for purposes of television, become associated with 'quality' in the same manner as it has for so many years in motion pictures." In spite of his bitter lesson, Selznick still tended toward extravagance. Because he wanted to limit the financial resources tied up in television by his company, he promised to produce "only" five or six series during the upcoming 1955–1956 TV season, with three or four more premiering during fall 1956.[54]

While Selznick was producing *Light's Diamond Jubilee*, the ABC-TV network began to court rival Hollywood producers like Walt Disney. As Selznick licked his wounds in the days immediately following *Light's Diamond Jubilee*, he witnessed the premiere of *Disneyland*, which, in contrast with Selznick's production, introduced Disney as the producer of a low-budget TV series. Later Selznick observed that a number of Hollywood's major studios seemed likely to follow Disney into the production of television series. Ever disdainful of mass production in Hollywood, Selznick warned ABC president Leonard Goldenson that the network would regret its alliance with the studios. "Good films for television, like good films for theaters," Selznick wrote, "will come from individual producers of talent and showmanship, not from assembly-line machines, as will be learned very rapidly by all the networks."[55] In fact, Selznick's predictions couldn't have been more mistaken. As *Light's Diamond Jubilee*—and the TV spectacular—faded into memory, the TV networks turned increasingly to Hollywood studios like Disney, which were capable of meeting the demands of series production. "Assembly-line" series came to dominate television in the years following *Light's Diamond Jubilee*, but David Selznick never produced another television program.

·VI·
Disneyland

The broadcast of *Light's Diamond Jubilee* helped to make October 1954 a watershed for television production in Hollywood. Alongside those marginal movie industry figures who had labored to wring profits from telefilm production during the late 1940s and early 1950s, there appeared a new breed of producer attracted by television's explosive growth following the end of the FCC's station application freeze in 1952.[1] Columbia set the stage in early October when its TV subsidiary, Screen Gems, debuted *Father Knows Best* on CBS and *The Adventures of Rin Tin Tin* on ABC. Selznick followed with his prime-time spectacular during the final week of October, and three days later he was joined by fellow independent producer Walt Disney, whose premiere television series, *Disneyland*, entered ABC's regular Wednesday night schedule on 27 October. Like Selznick, the television producers who emerged in Hollywood during 1954 were established members of the movie industry who diversified into TV production without leaving movies behind. The first to link production for the two media, these producers sparked the full-scale integration of movie and TV production in Hollywood.

As the recipient of nearly two dozen Academy Awards for his studio's cartoon animation, Walt Disney rivaled David Selznick as one of the studio era's most acclaimed independent producers and shared his status as the most celebrated Hollywood producer to enter television by 1954. Disney possessed the independent producer's belief in television as an alternative to the restrictive studio system, but his conception of television's role in a new Hollywood was more sweeping than that of his predecessors, who saw the electronic medium as little more than a new market for traditional film production. Unlike almost every other telefilm producer in Hollywood, however, Disney harbored no illusions about dominating TV production; his modest production plans initially involved only the *Disneyland* series. Still, Disney was the first Hollywood executive during the 1950s to envision a future built on television's technical achievements—the scope of its signal, the access it provided to the American home. For Disney, network television arrived as an invitation to reinvent the movie business, to explore horizons beyond the realm of filmmaking.

Disney later admitted that he was "never much interested" in radio, but television, with its ability to display the visual appeal of Disney products, was another matter entirely. The studio aired its first television program on NBC during December 1950. Sponsored by Coca-Cola, "One Hour in Wonderland" was set at a Disney Christmas party and featured excerpts promoting the studio's upcoming theatrical release, *Alice in Wonderland* (1951). In 1951 Disney produced its second hour-long program for NBC, a special sponsored by Johnson and Johnson. Disney's subsequent plans for a television series started with a demand as outlandish as anything ever dreamed by Selznick: To obtain the first Disney TV series, a network would have to purchase the series and agree to invest at least $500,000 for a one-third share in the studio's most ambitious project, the Disneyland amusement park planned for construction in suburban Los Angeles. NBC and CBS balked at these terms, but ABC, mired in third place, decided to accept.[2]

In uniting the TV program and the amusement park under a single name, Disney made one of the most influential commercial decisions in postwar American culture. Expanding upon the lucrative character merchandising market that the studio had joined in the early 1930s, Disney now planned to create an all-encompassing consumer environment that he described as "total merchandising." Products aimed at baby boom families and stamped with the Disney imprint—movies, amusement park rides, books, comic books, clothing, toys, TV programs, and more—would weave a vast commercial web, a tangle of advertising and entertainment in which each Disney product, from the movie *Snow White & the Seven Dwarfs* (1937) to a ride on Disneyland's Matterhorn, promoted all Disney products. And television was the beacon that would draw the American public to the domain of Disney. "We wanted to start off running," Walt later recalled. "The investment was going to be too big to wait for a slow buildup. We needed terrific initial impact, and television seemed the answer."[3]

Television served a crucial role in Disney's plans to create an economic and cultural phenomenon that would exceed the boundaries of any single communications medium. By raising capital through the ABC investment and raising consciousness through its depiction of the park's construction, television's figurative representation of Disneyland actually called the amusement park into existence, making it possible for the first time to unite the disparate realms of the Disney empire. With the home as its primary exhibition site, television gave Disney unparalleled access to a family audience that he had already cultivated more effectively than any Hollywood producer in the studio era. As a result of the postwar baby boom, Disney's target audience of children between the ages of five and fourteen grew from 22 million in 1940 to 35 million in 1960.[4] Television provided the surest route to this lucrative market.

As a text, the *Disneyland* television program also marked a rite of passage for the Disney studio. Its broadcast signaled the studio's transition from the prewar culture of motion pictures to a postwar culture in which Disney's movies were subsumed into an increasingly integrated leisure market that also included television, recorded music, theme parks, tourism, and consumer merchandise. By depicting the new amusement park as another of Walt's fantasies brought to life by the skilled craftsmen at the Disney studio, the *Disneyland* TV program gave a recognizable symbolic form to Disney's elaborate economic transformation. It is only a slight exaggeration, therefore, to claim that Disney mounted an entertainment empire on the cornerstone of this first television series.

In the six years between the *Paramount* decision and the premiere of *Disneyland,* the Disney studio and ABC-TV experienced a series of dramatic changes that set the stage for Disney's appearance on network TV. Both the Disney studio's plans for expansion and ABC's goal of recruiting Hollywood producers for its network schedule represented responses to a new media environment created by the disintegration of the studio system, the growth of independent production in the movie industry, the national expansion of network television, and the continued dominance of two networks, CBS and NBC. The union forged by ABC and Disney was a critical stage in the revival of both companies and in the integration of the movie and television industries.

Unlike many who groped for a response to the changes that swept the movie industry following World War II, Walt Disney and his brother, Roy, answered uncertainty with a calculated plan for diversification. Biographer Richard Schickel has suggested that the Disneys addressed the unstable postwar conditions more aggressively than other Hollywood leaders did because their company had suffered misfortunes during the early 1940s, when virtually everyone else in Hollywood had prospered. In this regard, the contrast between Disney and fellow independent producer David Selznick is striking. During the late 1930s, Disney and Selznick stood together for a moment at the pinnacle of the movie industry. Although they were independent producers who worked outside the security of the major studios, Disney and Selznick took extraordinary financial risks that ultimately paid off in the two most profitable Hollywood movies of the 1930s: Disney's *Snow White* and Selznick's *Gone with the Wind*.[5]

But Disney and Selznick shared good fortune only briefly. Following *Snow White*, Disney nearly buried his studio beneath ambitious plans for expansion. With box office disappointments like the costly animated feature *Fantasia* (1940), the closing of foreign markets because of the war, and overinvestment in new studio facilities, Disney faced burdensome corporate debts that weighed even more heavily once the banks shut off credit to the studio in 1940. Disney raised funds reluctantly by offering stock to the public, but only government contracts to produce educational cartoons kept the studio active during the war. "The only good thing about the situation," according to Schickel, "was that the problems that were later to plague the rest of the industry had been met by Disney at a time when the government could help out and when the general buoyancy of the industry could at least keep him afloat. The result, of course, was a head start in gathering know-how to meet the crisis that was coming—a head start in planning for diversification first of the company's motion picture products, then of its overall activities."[6]

In contrast with Disney, Selznick rode the crest of the movie industry's most prosperous decade, with each risky project repaid by profits that masked the wastefulness and inefficiency in the Selznick organization. Selznick diversified by forming a distribution division and by attempting to break into television, but he continued to produce the type of expensive, prestige productions that had become his trademark. As industrywide profits dwindled during the late 1940s, this costly strategy made Selznick's company vulnerable in a capricious movie marketplace and led to its sudden collapse following the failures of *The Paradine Case* and *Portrait of Jennie*. The conditions that subsequently encouraged the growth of independent production during the 1950s might have rejuvenated a longtime independent like Selznick, but he floundered in the new environment, encumbered by huge debts and an inflexible conception of his role as producer. As an ironic result of Selznick's triumphs during much of the 1940s, therefore, he was less adept than Disney at navigating through a new Hollywood. His decision to produce *Light's Diamond Jubilee* was a typically ill-conceived reaction to changes in the movie industry, more an attempt to revive a stalled movie career than a real strategy to diversify into television.

Plagued by adversity during the 1940s, Walt and Roy Disney entered the new decade with a plan to transform the Disney studio from an independent producer of feature films and cartoon short subjects into a diversified leisure and entertainment corporation. Instead of retrenching, as others had, the Disneys fortified their company through a careful process of diversification. Beginning in 1953, the company implemented a series of changes designed to redefine its role in Hollywood. Disney established its own theatrical distribution subsidiary, Buena Vista, in order to end its reliance on distribution through the major studios. The studio also ceased production on its by-then-unprofitable cartoon short subjects, cut back on expensive animated features, and began to concentrate on nature documentaries and live-action movies following the success of *Treasure Island* (1950) and *Robin Hood* (1952).[7] Blueprints for Disneyland and ideas about television production took shape during this period of corporate transition.

As Disney's schemes for expansion pointed toward television, the reorganization of ABC-TV during the early 1950s spun the network in the direction of Hollywood. Like the reorganized Disney company, ABC-TV was a product of the Justice Department consent decree that followed the *Paramount* decision in 1948. The consent decree had required Paramount Pictures to divest its theater chain and to reduce the chain from 1,400 to 650 theaters within five years. Once the separation took effect, in January 1950, the newly independent theater company, United Paramount Theaters (UPT), led by chairman Leonard Goldenson, looked to television as a potential site for reinvesting profits from the sale of its theaters. Paramount Pictures had spearheaded the movie industry's efforts to integrate broadcasting into the studio system—from its merger with CBS radio in the late 1920s to its investment in theater TV and the DuMont Television Network in the 1940s and 1950s. Influenced by this tradition and anticipating television's imminent growth, UPT decided to diversify by purchasing television stations. The theater company already owned a single station, Chicago's WBKB, which earned its first profit in 1950. When the FCC's freeze on station applications dragged on into the early 1950s, however, UPT became impatient and chose instead to purchase the ABC-TV network in 1951.[8]

At this time, ABC and DuMont were the weakest television networks, lagging far behind NBC and CBS in affiliates and earnings.

ABC owned and operated stations in five of the six largest television markets, but the network had only fourteen primary affiliates in the rest of country, while NBC had sixty-three and CBS had thirty. ABC trailed the two major networks in audience size, advertising revenues, and live clearance rates (the proportion of affiliates broadcasting the network signal live).[9] Unable to match the financial resources of the dominant networks, ABC couldn't compete effectively in program acquisition. Therefore, when the FCC finally approved the UPT-ABC merger in 1953, UPT's first priority was to inject $30 million into the network, initiating a five-year plan to boost ABC into full competition. While $7.5 million was used for improvements in network facilities, $22.5 million went directly to purchase programming.[10] Able at last to pay competitive prices, ABC made an unprecedented commitment to acquire filmed programming produced in Hollywood—a decision influenced by the network's low live clearance rates, its search for a programming source other than the advertising agencies, its need to distinguish itself from the other networks, and its hope of attracting new sponsors to television.

At the time of the merger with UPT, ABC had a live clearance rate of only 34 percent. This low figure was a result of FCC policy decisions during the early years of commercial network television. The FCC's allotment of only two VHF channels in the vast majority of markets created what William Boddy describes as an "artificial scarcity" that gave a competitive advantage in the new medium to the two dominant radio networks, NBC and CBS. The licensing freeze of 1948–1952 increased this advantage by enabling NBC and CBS to solidify their positions in local markets during a period of limited competition. As a result, ABC had fewer affiliates and a lower live clearance rate than both of the other networks throughout the 1950s.[11] Because ABC depended inordinately on delayed broadcasts by its affiliates, the network had to use either kinescopes of live broadcasts or programs shot directly on film. Filmed programs offered a superior image quality and retained greater potential residual value in syndication and international distribution. Consequently, ABC became the first network to stock the majority of its prime-time schedule with filmed programs.[12]

ABC also chose filmed programming in order to cultivate ties with the motion picture industry, a neglected source of program production. By establishing a relationship with Hollywood studios, ABC could avoid both direct competition with the major networks and dependence on programs produced by advertising agencies. NBC and CBS had a firm lock on traditional broadcasting performers like Bob Hope and Jack Benny, and ABC was reluctant to engage in bidding wars. At the same time, the network hoped to avoid the traditional radio model of production, in which advertising agencies supplied programming for the networks. Not only were major sponsors reluctant to bring their programs to ABC, since its audience was relatively small, but once an agency-produced program proved successful on ABC, sponsors had the freedom to shift the program to NBC or CBS in search of a larger audience.[13] This happened with a number of series, perhaps most prominently with the Danny Thomas sitcom *Make Room for Daddy* (1953–1964), which departed for CBS after its third season. Consequently, ABC was faced with the problem of improving its programming without relying on two of the broadcasting industry's most common strategies for filling prime-time schedules: using established star performers and acquiring programs supplied by sponsors.

One alternative would have been for ABC to produce its own programs independently of sponsors, an approach that NBC and CBS had begun to use. Yet ABC did not have the financial leverage or security to undertake such a venture. By necessity, if not by design, ABC relied on outside producers to fill its broadcast schedule.[14] Although ABC did not entirely purge its schedule of sponsor-produced programming during the 1950s, the network increasingly looked to Hollywood, since established movie studios were among the few potential TV producers who could afford to generate programming without financial or technical support from advertisers. In addition, ABC could sign these companies to exclusive contracts, ensuring that its programs would not be uprooted and sold to another network after being developed on ABC. The network's 1953 production agreement with Hal Roach, Jr., which resulted in such series as *The Stu Erwin Show*, was its first with an established—though admittedly a minor—Hollywood producer.[15]

Hollywood-produced television series also suited ABC's plans for differentiating the network from NBC and CBS. As the third-place network, ABC chose to build its audience in direct opposition to those of the established networks. During a period in which the other networks were experimenting with spectaculars and the possibility of attracting viewers with unique video events, ABC remained committed to the traditional strategy of programming familiar weekly series that defined television viewing as a consistent feature in the family's domestic routine. Robert Weitman, the network's vice president in charge of programming, emphasized the importance of habitual viewing in ABC's programming strategies. "The answer seems to be in established patterns of viewing," he explained. "People are annoyed when their favorite show is pre-empted, even for a super-special spectacular." Leonard Goldenson, who had spent decades in the business of movie distribution and exhibition, recognized the similarities between television viewing and the experience of movie-going during the studio era. "The real strength and vitality of television," he claimed, "is in your regular week-in and week-out programs. The strength of motion pictures was always the habit of going to motion pictures on a regular basis, and that habit was, in part, taken away from motion pictures by television."[16] ABC's programming strategy was built on the belief that television's fundamental appeal was less its ability to deliver exotic events than its promise of a familiar cultural experience.

As a result, ABC's regularly scheduled series would serve as the basis for network counterprogramming, the principal tactic in the assault on CBS and NBC. Rather than compete with an established series or live event by scheduling a program of similar appeal, ABC hoped to offer alternative programming in order to attract segments of the audience not being served by the other networks. The network would construct and project a specific identity by treating its schedule as the expression of a unique relationship to the broadcast audience. "Whatever the audience is not watching at any given time makes for new possibilities," Goldenson noted. "We are not trying to take away audiences from CBS and NBC. . . . We are trying to carve our own network character, to create new audiences."[17]

This tactic was based on a related aspect of ABC's programming philosophy—its attention to audience demographics. Governed by the belief that "a network can't be all things to all people," ABC chose to target "the youthful families" with children, a section of the audience whose numbers had increased rapidly since World War II. "We're after a specific audience," stated Goldenson, "the young housewife—one cut above the teenager—with two to four kids, who has to buy the clothing, the food, the soaps, the home remedies." As this statement implies, ABC chose to align itself with small-ticket advertisers, those selling the types of products that young families might be more likely to need and afford. Goldenson justified ABC's entire programming strategy when he remarked, "We're in the Woolworth's business, not in Tiffany's. Last year Tiffany made only $30,000."[18]

While economic considerations may have influenced ABC's shift to filmed television programming, the network's commitment to a specific concept of product differentiation also influenced its interaction with Hollywood producers. ABC's related strategies of counterprogramming, demographic targeting, and reliance on small-ticket sponsors made it imperative that the Hollywood producers with whom ABC collaborated deliver a particular type of product—a weekly series of films that would display movie industry production values while invoking traditional Hollywood genres and story-telling skills. Ideally, Hollywood production values would differentiate the series from live television, while Hollywood genres might appeal to an audience dissatisfied with the radio-style fare of variety shows, situation comedies, and anthology dramas. Finally, the network also hoped that the reputations of individual Hollywood producers might attract sponsors that had not previously advertised on ABC, or on television in general.

Eager to acquire more-prestigious programming, the third-place network gambled on Disney by committing $2 million for a fifty-two-week series (with a seven-year renewal option) and by purchasing a 35 percent share in the park for $500,000. Without even a prospective format to present to advertisers, ABC invoked the Disney reputation alone to sell the program under a joint-sponsorship package to American Motors, the American Dairy Association, and Derby Food. Sponsorship of the season's twenty original episodes was sold at $65,000 per episode, and the network time was billed to advertisers at $70,000 per hour. During the late 1950s, when ABC's ratings and advertising revenue finally approached the levels of NBC and CBS, Leonard Goldenson consistently referred to the Disney deal as the network's "turning point." Indeed, *Disneyland* attracted nearly half of ABC's advertising billings during 1954, the final year during which the network operated at a loss.[19]

Although Walt Disney repeatedly assured the press that the *Disneyland* TV series would stand on its own terms as entertainment, the program served mainly to publicize Disney products. *Disneyland*'s identification of the amusement park and the TV series was confirmed during the first episode when Walt informed viewers that "Disneyland the place and *Disneyland* the show are all the same." Both the series and the park were divided into four familiar movie industry genres: Fantasyland (animated cartoons), Adventureland (exotic action-adventure), Frontierland (Westerns), and Tomorrowland (science fiction). Introduced by Walt himself, each week's episode represented one of the park's imaginary lands through a compilation of sequences drawn from the studio's cartoon short subjects, nature documentaries, animated and live-action features, or short films produced as outright promotions for Disney movies about to enter theatrical release. According to William Boddy, as a television series *Disneyland* "was unprecedented in both the number of reruns per season, the number of commercial breaks per hour, and the amount of each program devoted to direct promotion of Disney's feature films, comic books, trademark merchandise, and the new amusement park."[20]

Disneyland's format and pervasive self-promotion were new to television, but these strategies had roots in the popular radio programs broadcast from Hollywood during the 1930s and 1940s. Hosted by actors, directors, or celebrity journalists, programs like *Hollywood Hotel* and *Lux Radio Theatre* offered musical performances or dramatizations of studio feature films, but their strongest lure was the glimpse they provided into the culture of Hollywood. Through informal chats with performers and other members of the industry, these radio programs perpetuated an image of Hollywood glamour while promoting recent studio releases.[21] Disney simply adapted this format for television. As the master of ceremonies, he turned himself into a media celebrity, much as director Cecil B. De Mille earlier had ridden *Lux Radio Theatre* to national fame.[22]

The actual production of *Disneyland* required a minimal financial investment by the Disney studio. At a time when the typical network series featured thirty-nine new episodes each season, Disney's contract with ABC called for only twenty original episodes, with each one repeated once, and twelve broadcast a third time during the summer. Instead of viewing the deal as an obligation to produce twenty episodes of new television programming each season, Disney saw it as an opportunity to capitalize on the studio's library of films dating back to the debut of Mickey Mouse in the late 1920s. The wisdom of this format, as Richard Schickel has noted, "was that it allowed the studio to participate in TV without surrendering control of its precious film library."[23] Long after many of the major studios had sold the TV rights to their films, the Disneys boasted that they still owned every film they ever made. Although it is not generally remembered, during the first three years of *Disneyland*, the studio produced only one narrative film made expressly for the series—the three-part "Davy Crockett" serial that took the nation by storm during that first season.[24] More typically, the *Disneyland* TV series introduced a new generation of children to the studio's storehouse of cartoons.

Even with a program that consisted largely of recycled material, the studio admitted that it would not turn a profit from its first year in television. There were production costs in preparing the theatrical product for broadcast (editing compilation episodes or filming Walt's introductory appearances) and in producing its limited amount of original programming. But these costs generally were defrayed throughout the studio's various operations. The three hour-long episodes of the "Davy Crockett" series, for instance, cost $600,000—more than three times the industry standard for telefilm production—and yet,

The subject of a three-episode serial during the first season of *Disneyland*, Davy Crockett became a national phenomenon. In this publicity still, actor Fess Parker is joined on the set by Walt Disney and director Norman Foster.
(Courtesy of Wisconsin Center for Film and Theater Research
© Walt Disney Productions)

during that year alone, the cost was spread over two separate network broadcasts and a theatrical release. By employing up to 80 percent of the studio's production staff, the television operation also enabled the Disney studio to meet the expense of remaining at full productivity. In addition, all costs not covered by the network's payments were charged to the studio's promotion budget—another indication of the program's primary purpose.[25]

Nearly one-third of each *Disneyland* episode was devoted directly to studio promotion, but the entire series blurred any distinction between publicity and entertainment. Indeed, *Disneyland* capitalized on the unspoken recognition that commercial broadcasting had made it almost impossible to distinguish between entertainment and advertising. One episode, "Operation Underseas," provided a behind-the-scenes glimpse at the making of *20,000 Leagues under the Sea* (1954) just one week before Disney released the film to theaters.[26] This episode was later followed by "Monsters of the Deep," a nature documentary that provided another opportunity to plug the studio's most recent theatrical release. An episode titled "A Story of Dogs" preceded the release of *Lady and the Tramp* (1955), Disney's second major feature distributed to theaters during the initial TV season.

Viewers didn't mind that *Disneyland* was simply a new form of Hollywood ballyhoo, because Disney framed the program within an educational discourse, reassuring viewers that they inhabited a position of privileged knowledge that was available only through television. Amid paternalistic fears over the pernicious influence of television, comic books, and other forms of mass culture, Disney's middlebrow didacticism was disarming. In each episode, *Disneyland* rewarded its viewers with an encyclopedic array of general information borrowed loosely from the fields of history, science, and anthropology, while also sharing more-specialized knowledge about the history of the Disney studio and its filmmaking procedures. Through this specialized knowledge about the Disney studio, the *Disneyland* TV series defined a particular relationship between television and movies, one in which television served an inchoate critical function by providing commentary on Disney movies. Though produced by the studio itself, *Disneyland* nevertheless contained elements of a critical discourse on the cinema. It educated viewers to perceive continuities among Disney films, to analyze certain aspects of the production process, and to recognize the studio's body of work as a unified product of Walt's authorial vision.

Disneyland's most obvious strategy for educating viewers was its use of behind-the-scenes footage from the Disney studio. The first episode introduced the Disney studio through images of Kirk Douglas playing with his sons on the studio lot, James Mason fighting a man-made hurricane on the stage of *20,000 Leagues under the Sea*, animators sketching models, and musicians recording the score for a cartoon. By representing the studio as an active, self-contained creative community bustling with activity, these scenes evoke impressions of studio-era Hollywood while masking the fact that historical conditions had rendered those very images obsolete.

Disney also used behind-the-scenes footage to demonstrate the elaborate process of filmmaking, particularly the intricacies of animation. Although one might think that a filmmaker like Disney would be afraid of ruining the mystery of animation by revealing how its effects are achieved, Richard Schickel has observed that "Disney always enjoyed showing people around his studio and explaining to them exactly how the exotic process of creating an animated film proceeded." In fact, Disney originally planned for the amusement park to be located at the studio, with demonstrations of the filmmaking process as one of its major attractions.[27] In one feature film, *The Reluctant Dragon* (1941), Disney displayed the animation process by allowing Robert Benchley to lead moviegoers on a tour of the Disney studio. But this was a one-shot experiment that couldn't be repeated in other movies without becoming a distracting gimmick. Following in the tradition of the earlier Hollywood radio shows, therefore, Disney defined television as a companion medium to the cinema, an informational medium that could be used to reveal the process of filmmaking—since that impulse could not be indulged in the movies themselves. While Disney movies were presented as seamless narratives, television gave Disney the license to expose their seams.

Disney's willingness to display the process of filmmaking suggests that reflexivity in itself is not a radical impulse. More a disciple of Barnum than Brecht, Disney had no intention of distancing his audience from the illusion in his movies. Instead, he appealed to the audience's fascination with cinematic trickery. Disney exhibited what historian Neil Harris describes as an "American vernacular tradition" perhaps best exemplified by P. T. Barnum. Barnum's showmanship depended on his recognition that the public delights both in being fooled by a hoax and in discovering the mechanisms that make the hoax successful. Through his fanciful exhibitions, Barnum encouraged "an aesthetic of the operational, a delight in observing process and examining for literal truth."[28] Far from being hoodwinked by Barnum's artifice, the audiences that witnessed his exhibitions took pleasure in uncovering the process by which these hoaxes were perpetrated.

Inheriting Barnum's sense of showmanship, Disney developed his own "operational aesthetic" through television, enhancing his audience's pleasure—and anticipation—by offering precious glimpses of the filmmaking process. Of course, Disney's depiction of the production process was selective; it ignored the economics of filmmaking in favor of focusing on the studio's technical accomplishments. *Disneyland* never explored such issues as labor relations at the Disney studio or the economics of merchandising that sent the largest share of profits into Walt's pockets. Instead, in what has become a cliché of "behind-the-scenes" reporting on filmmaking, *Disneyland* treated each movie as a problem to be solved by the ingenuity of Disney craftsmen. This approach created a secondary narrative that accompanied the movie into theaters, a story of craftsmen overcoming obstacles to produce a masterful illusion. With this strategy, viewers were given an incentive to see the completed movie, because the movie itself provided the resolution to the story of the filmmaking process as depicted on *Disneyland*.

The program also educated viewers through its attention to Disney studio history. The determination to recycle the Disney library shaped the series during its early seasons, making *Disneyland* an electronic museum devoted to the studio's artistic achievements. Before the arrival of television, Hollywood's history was virtually inaccessible to the general public, available only sporadically through the unpredictable re-release of studio features and short subjects. Movies themselves may have been preserved in studio vaults, but for moviegoers accustomed to an ever-changing program at local theaters, the Hollywood cinema during the studio era was much like live television—an ephemeral cultural experience in which each text inevitably dissolved into memory, swept away in the endless flow of serial production. Although much of television in the mid-1950s traded on the immediacy of live broadcast, the sale of motion pictures to broadcasters meant that television also became the unofficial archive of the American cinema, in which Hollywood's past surfaced in bits and pieces, like fragments of a dream. One of the pleasures of *Disneyland* was the chance it offered to halt the flow of mass culture by remembering relics from the Disney vaults.

Although *Disneyland* may have struck a nostalgic chord for older viewers, the program's presentation of studio history was less sentimental than reverential. Cartoons nearly forgotten were resurrected with a solemnity normally reserved for the most venerable works of art. This attitude is apparent from the first episode, when Walt announces that the end of each episode will be reserved for Mickey Mouse. After leading the viewer through an elaborate description of the proposed amusement park and other studio activities, Disney stands behind a lectern and turns the pages of a massive bound volume, an illustrated chronicle of Mickey's adventures. In spite of the flurry of changes at the studio, he explains, one should not lose sight of an eternal truth: "It all started with Mickey . . . The story of Mickey is the story of Disneyland." As he continues, the scene segues into Mickey's first appearance, in the cartoon "Plane Crazy," and then dissolves to one of his most famous appearances, as the Sorcerer's Apprentice in *Fantasia*.

The tone of the scene—Disney's scholarly disposition, the sight of Mickey's history contained in a stately book—implies that the Disney studio's products are not the disposable commodities of pop culture but artifacts worthy of remembrance. Walt's role as narrator is to recall forgotten cartoons in the public's cultural memory by demonstrating their canonical status within the artistic history of the Disney studio. As an electronic museum, *Disneyland* invoked the cultural memory of its audience mainly to publicize new Disney products. In spite of its commercial motives, however, the series also made it possible to conceive of Hollywood as having a history worthy of consideration.

"Monsters of the Deep," a typical episode from the first season of *Disneyland*, demonstrates the strategies for situating new Disney movies in the context of the studio's history and production practices. The episode introduces Walt in his studio's research department. Surrounded by books and charts, he appears professorial. Inspired by knowledge, yet free from scholastic pretension, he is television's image of an intellectual, kindly and inviting. Speaking directly to the camera, he leads the viewer through a discussion of dinosaurs, using illustrations from enormous books to punctuate his presentation.

This lecture seems motivated only by Disney's inquisitive character until the Disney sales pitch gradually seeps in. "We told the story of dinosaurs large and small in *Fantasia*," Disney reminds viewers, as the screen dissolves to images from the animated feature. As Disney explains the habitat, feeding patterns, and behavior of dinosaurs, the

As host of *Disneyland*, Walt Disney adopted a scholarly demeanor.
(Courtesy of Photofest © Walt Disney Productions)

footage from *Fantasia* becomes recontextualized, as though it were a segment from a nature documentary, a reminder that even Disney's most fantastic films have educational value. Disney segues into a report on sea monsters, asking whether giant squids have existed among the mysteries of the ocean, tracing the enigma through debates over the veracity of historical accounts. This query provides a transition to a discussion of the problems involved in creating a plausible giant squid for the Disney feature *20,000 Leagues under the Sea*. From the research department, the scene dissolves to a studio soundstage where star Kirk Douglas performs a song from the movie and then guides the television viewer through a behind-the-scenes glimpse of the special effects used to stage the movie's spectacular battle sequence featuring the giant squid.

Afterward, Disney draws a line of continuity through the studio's present and past accomplishments by introducing viewers to an extended sequence from the studio's most famous scene of undersea adventure, Pinocchio's escape from the whale, Monstro, in the 1940 feature *Pinocchio*. Even the last two sequences, so clearly intended to advertise Disney products, carry the promise of edification as they define a limited and specialized knowledge—the Disney canon, the production of Disney movies—that is directed toward enhancing the experience of *20,000 Leagues under the Sea*.

Because the *Disneyland* TV series delivered viewers like no program in ABC history had, even the program's advertisers didn't mind subsidizing Disney's opportunity for self-promotion. *Disneyland* concluded the season as the first ABC program ever to appear among the year's ten highest-rated series. It was viewed weekly in nearly 40 percent of the nation's 26 million TV households.[29] The trade magazine *Sponsor* applauded Disney's skill at blending entertainment and salesmanship, quoting an unnamed ABC executive who quipped, "Never before have so many people made so little objection to so much selling."[30] Through its Emmy Awards, the television industry affirmed its approval of Disney's venture, nominating Walt as TV's "Most Outstanding New Personality" and honoring "Operation Underseas"—an episode about the making of *20,000 Leagues under the Sea*—as TV's Best Documentary.[31]

For the movie industry, the most telling detail in the entire Disney phenomenon was the surprising performance of the studio's feature films. By releasing its features through its own distribution company, Buena Vista, and by timing the release dates to coincide with simultaneous promotion on the television program, Disney emerged as the top-grossing independent production company of 1955. Undoubtedly aided by its exposure on the TV series, *20,000 Leagues under the Sea* grossed $8 million when it finally played in movie theaters—the largest sum ever reached by a Disney movie on its initial release. It finished the year as Hollywood's fourth-highest-grossing movie and became the first Disney movie ever to crack the list of twenty all-time top-grossing films. In addition, Disney's new animated feature, *Lady and the Tramp,* pulled in $6.5 million—the highest figure for any of Disney's animated films since *Snow White.* Even the first feature-length True-Life Adventure, *The Vanishing Prairie* (1955), grossed a respectable $1.8 million.[32]

The most startling evidence of TV's marketing potential came from the studio's experience with Davy Crockett. Disney edited together the "Davy Crockett" episodes that already had aired twice on TV and released them as a feature film during the summer of 1955. *Davy Crockett: King of the Wild Frontier* may have been a typical "program oater," as *Variety* claimed, but it earned another $2 million at the box office because it had been transformed by television into a national phenomenon.[33] The accompanying Crockett merchandising craze gathered steam throughout the year, ultimately surpassing the Hopalong Cassidy boom of the early 1950s. By mid-1955, as "The Ballad of Davy Crockett" climbed the pop music charts, Crockett products—including jeans, pistols, powder horns, lunch boxes, the ubiquitous coonskin caps, and much more—accounted for nearly 10 percent of all consumer purchases for children, with sales figures for Crockett merchandise projected to exceed $100 million by the end of the year.[34] Disney's apparent golden touch during 1954 and 1955 demonstrated to Hollywood that the studio had tapped into a rich promotional vein by integrating its various activities around television and the family audience.

The *Disneyland* TV program's most significant accomplishment, however, was the fanatical interest it generated in the Disneyland amusement park. Without the growth of national network television and the access it provided to the American family, Disney would not have gambled on the park. "I saw that if I was ever going to have my park," he explained, "here, at last, was a way to tell millions of people about it—with TV."[35] Disney needed television not simply to publicize the park but to position it properly as a new type of suburban amusement, a bourgeois park designed to provide edifying adventures for baby-boom families instead of cheap thrills for the urban masses.

To distinguish his park from such decaying relics as Luna Park at Coney Island, Disney assured the public that any amusement experienced in his park would be tempered by middle-class educational values. Disneyland wouldn't be another park trading in the temporal gratifications of the flesh; instead, it would be a popular monument to human knowledge, a "permanent world's fair" built around familiar Disney characters and a number of unifying social goals, including educating the public about history and science.[36] The park was inextricably linked to television, because TV enabled Disney to redefine the traditional amusement park as a "theme park." With the assistance of the *Disneyland* TV series, Disney brought discipline to the unruly pleasures of the amusement park, organizing them around the unifying theme of Disney's authorial vision. By invoking cultural memories of Disney films, the TV series encouraged an impulse to re-experience texts that became one of the theme park's central attractions.

Just as it hooked American television viewers with the serialized story of Davy Crockett, the *Disneyland* TV series also bound up its audience in the ongoing story of what came to be mythologized as "Walt's dream." The seriality of *Disneyland*—and its direct relationship to the creation and continued development of the park—were crucial to the program's success. Before Disney, prime-time series were episodic; narrative conflicts were introduced and resolved in the course of a single episode. Open-ended serials were confined to daytime's soap opera genre. Disney certainly wasn't concerned about issues of TV narrative, but the *Disneyland* series demonstrated an incipient understanding of the appeal of serial narrative for network television. The success of the three-part "Davy Crockett" serial was attributable at least in part to its ability to engage viewers in an ongoing narrative. Similarly, with Walt as on-screen narrator, the *Disneyland* series, in effect, narrated the construction of Disney's amusement park, making the project a matter of continued concern for the show's viewers by creating a story out of the construction process and certifying it as the crowning achievement of an American entrepreneurial genius in the same league as Thomas Edison and Henry Ford.

No less than three entire episodes, and portions of others, were devoted to the process of conceiving, building, and inaugurating the park. At the climax of the construction process, viewers witnessed the park's opening ceremonies on 17 July 1955, in a live, two-hour broadcast hosted by Art Linkletter, Robert Cummings, and Ronald Reagan. It was only appropriate that the first amusement park created by television should be introduced in a ceremony designed explicitly for television as a media event.[37] The first season of *Disneyland* was a unique type of television text, an open-ended series in which the episodes built toward a final resolution, staged as a television spectacular not unlike *Light's Diamond Jubilee*. Just as the electric industry spent the year before its broadcast stirring up interest in the celebration of Edison, Disney orchestrated a yearlong narrative that concluded with the opening ceremony of Disneyland the park.

By constructing a story around the events of the park's development, and by creating an analogy between the TV program and the park, the Disney organization provided a narrative framework for the experience of Disneyland. The series represented the transition from movie studio to theme park by treating the park as the studio's most ambitious production. In the first episode, "The Disneyland Story," Walt introduces viewers to the park as an idea, shifting constantly between a huge map of the park, a scale-model replica, and stock footage that invokes each of the park's imaginary lands. The first season of *Disneyland*, he explains, will enable viewers "to see and share with us the experience of building this dream into a reality."

The second construction episode, "A Progress Report," initiates the journey from the studio to the park as Walt takes a helicopter

Walt Disney captured the TV audience with the ongoing story of his efforts to realize his "dream," the Disneyland amusement park.
(Courtesy of Photofest © Walt Disney Productions)

flight from his office to the new location. This episode also begins the process of identifying Disneyland with the culture of the automobile and the superhighway. Although the transition to the construction site could have been managed by a straight cut or a dissolve, the helicopter flight instead laboriously tracks the highway that a typical traveler would follow to reach the park. With Walt providing commentary, the flight depicts both a literal and a figurative passage from Hollywood to Disneyland, tracing a path from the Disney studio in Burbank, over the heart of Hollywood, down the Hollywood Freeway, connecting to the Santa Ana Freeway, and finally reaching the Disneyland exit in Anaheim—"a spot chosen by traffic experts as the most accessible spot in Southern California." Once at the construction site, the labor of construction is depicted through fast-motion photography. Accompanied by ragtime music, the scurrying workers driving bulldozers, digging ditches, and planting trees seem like animated figures; their labor takes on a cartoonish quality. In keeping with the tradition of the program's behind-the-scenes footage, Walt pauses to demonstrate how the technical feat of time-lapse photography works, but he never addresses the actual labor of the workers whose activities are represented.

The third episode picks up the construction after the park's major structures have been built, as the various rides and special effects are being installed. Again, the series demonstrates how these devices, such as authentic-looking mechanical crocodiles, were designed and created at the Disney studio. This episode establishes continuity between motion picture production and the creation of the park, demonstrating studio activities that have been reoriented to service the park. The underwater monorail employed to move the submarine in *20,000 Leagues under the Sea* has become the basis for the Disneyland monorail train; the stage where Davy Crockett recently fought the Battle of the Alamo is now the site of construction for the park's authentic Mississippi River steamboat; the sculptors and technicians who created the squid in *20,000 Leagues under the Sea* are now making a mechanical zoo for the park. Once these devices are loaded onto trucks, they are transported to the park. As voice-over commentary reviews the route, viewers again follow the highway from the studio to the park, making the journey at ground level this time.

Television made the entire Disney operation more enticing by fashioning it as a narrative experience which the family TV audience could enhance—and actually perform—by visiting the park. Here again Disney shrewdly perceived television's ability to link diverse cultural practices that intersected in the domestic sphere of the home. In effect, Walt identified the program with the park in order to create an inhabitable text, one that would never be complete for a television-viewing family until they had taken full advantage of the postwar boom in automobile travel and tourism and made a pilgrimage to the park itself. A trip to Disneyland—using the conceptual map provided by the program—offered the family viewer a chance to perform in the Disneyland narrative, to provide unity and closure through personal experience, to witness the "aura" to which television's reproductive apparatus could only allude.

In a sense, Disney succeeded by exploiting the quest for authentic experience that has become central to the culture of modernity. In fact, tourism, as Dean MacCannell suggests, is based on the modern quest for authenticity, the belief that authentic experience exists somewhere outside the realm of daily experience in industrial society.[38] While Walter Benjamin predicted that mass reproduction would diminish the aura surrounding works of art, Disney seems to have recognized that the mass media instead only intensify the desire for authenticity by invoking a sublime, unmediated experience that is forever absent, just beyond the grasp of a hand reaching for the television dial.

As a tourist attraction, Disneyland became the destination of a secular pilgrimage anchored firmly by the family home, which served not only as the origin and the terminus of the journey but also as the site of the television set that would confirm the social meaning of the vacation experience. A father visiting the park expressed something of this sentiment. "Disneyland may be just another damned amusement park," he explained, "but to my kids its the Taj Mahal, Niagara Falls, Sherwood Forest, and Davy Crockett all rolled into one. After years of sitting in front of the television set, the youngsters are sure it's a fairyland before they ever get there."[39] Television defined Disneyland as a national amusement park, not a park of local or regional interest like previous amusement parks but a destination for a nation of television viewers. In the first six months alone, one million paying customers passed through the gates at Disneyland, 43 percent of them from out of state. After the first full year of operation the park had grossed $10 million, one-third of the company's revenue for the year and more than any Disney feature had ever grossed during its initial release.[40]

Disney's integration of television into movie industry marketing schemes identified television as a worthy investment for Hollywood's major studios. Events leading up to Disney's debut may have suggested to executives of the major studios that they reconsider television production, but only Columbia, through its Screen Gems subsidiary, had acted decisively before Disney's triumph during the 1954–1955 TV season. Disney's immediate success convinced the major studios that production for the new medium at last held some value. "I'm not sure just where the initiative started," Warner Bros. executive Benjamin Kalmenson later explained when recounting the origins of television production at Warner Bros., "but as a result of the success Mr. Disney was having with a feature motion picture called *20,000 Leagues under the Sea*, I personally felt that his ability to exploit his pictures on television was of great value, and began to wonder why we couldn't do likewise." [41] As Kalmenson's comment implies, it was not the *Disneyland* TV series itself that fascinated the Hollywood studios. The revenue generated by network license fees was relatively insignificant; the episodes were mainly an outlet for cartoons, short subjects, travelogues, and other ephemera that the studios had purged from their production schedules. What impressed the major studios was the program's ability to ignite enthusiasm for Disney features, especially among families with young children.

While the major studios had been able to rationalize the production of motion pictures during the studio era, they never brought the same sort of predictability to the marketing of their pictures. They never succeeded at developing advertising or publicity strategies which guaranteed that the variety of promotions used to publicize a film—whether transmitted by the media or staged by local exhibitors—actually reached a film's potential audience. This marketing problem was compounded by the industry's reorganization following the *Paramount* decision. Forced to distribute each film separately to independent theater chains, the studios now also had to market each picture individually.

The emergence of national network radio, with a signal that crossed both socioeconomic and geographic boundaries, had provided the most efficient national medium for film promotion. Disney's video success made it apparent that television had become the dominant national advertising medium by the mid-1950s. Providing a channel to a rapidly growing audience, television could become the most effective marketing tool ever imagined by the movie industry. By following Disney's example and forming alliances with television networks, rather than with advertisers, the studios could ensure their access to the medium without surrendering autonomy to television's traditionally powerful sponsors.

Disney expanded his role in television during the fall of 1955 with the premiere of *The Mickey Mouse Club* in ABC's weekday afternoon schedule. With this new program and the ongoing *Disneyland* series, Disney continued to use television mainly as an opportunity for studio publicity. Besides producing a sequel to "Davy Crockett," for instance, Disney created no original programming for *Disneyland* until the 1957–1958 season. Disney's concept of "total merchandising" continued to shape the type of text that his company produced for television. Whereas traditional notions of textuality assume that a text is singular, unified, and autonomous, with a structure that draws the viewer inward, Disney's television texts were, from the outset, fragmented, propelled by a centrifugal force that guided the viewer away from the immediate textual experience toward a more pervasive sense of textuality, one that encouraged the consumption of further Disney texts, further Disney products, further Disney experiences. *Disneyland* drew the attention of viewers to the TV text only to disperse it outward, toward Disney products.[42]

Television made possible Disney's vision of "total merchandising" because it gave him the ability to integrate apparently isolated segments of the national commercial culture that developed after the war. In this sense, the entire Disneyland phenomenon may have been the first harbinger of Max Horkheimer and Theodor Adorno's prediction for the apotheosis of the television age, the moment when "the thinly veiled identity of all industrial culture products can come triumphantly out into the open, derisively fulfilling the Wagnerian dream of the *Gesamtkunstwerk*—the fusion of all the arts in one work."[43] By offering the first glimpse of a new Hollywood—in which television profitably obscured conventional distinctions among the media—Disney provided the impulse for the major studios to enter television and a blueprint for the future development of the media industries.

·VII·
Origins of
Warner Bros. Television

Disneyland provided the incentive for Hollywood's major studios to reconsider television production because it proved that a movie studio could profit from simply supplying programs to the networks. Although the major studios once had hoped to control their own TV stations and networks, Disneyland showed that television production alone could benefit a studio. First, network television offered a market for the type of low-budget productions that allowed a studio to make full use of its equipment and facilities. During the 1950s, as the studios shifted into financing and distributing independently produced feature films—with many of these films shot on location—on-site activity at the studios diminished. Although the studios had planned to cut fixed costs, without some modest production activity they now faced the prospect of abandoned backlots, silent soundstages, and warehouses filled with dusty equipment. Second, thanks to the ever-expanding broadcast signal, network television revealed an uncanny aptitude for publicity. In fact, once the studios learned to exploit commercial television's blend of entertainment and advertising, Disneyland was only the most obvious example of the cross-promotion taking place between the media during the early 1950s. While promoting feature films on TV, the major studios also began to sign contracts with TV stars and to adapt TV series into feature films.

After witnessing Disney's success, Warner Bros., Twentieth Century–Fox, and MGM decided to diversify into TV production during 1955. Warner Bros. and MGM signed initial contracts with ABC, while Twentieth Century–Fox committed to CBS. Like Disney, each studio entered television with a flagship series that carried its name: Warner Bros. Presents, MGM Parade, and The Twentieth Century–Fox Hour (though Fox also agreed to produce a series based on its 1943 movie My Friend Flicka). Each of the studios expected to restore activity on its lot and hoped at least to break even on the expense of production, but—as the titles suggest—their overriding motive was to publicize themselves and their new theatrical releases before a nationwide audience. In fact, Jack Warner openly admitted that Warner Bros. was producing a TV series "only to secure advertisements through television."[1]

In order to gain access to a national audience, however, Warner Bros. had to win the approval of its network gatekeeper, ABC, and it had to create a program that would appeal to television audiences. Because the network held the keys to the airwaves, Warner Bros. was forced to compromise when it discovered that its commercial motives—and its narrow conception of television programming—often didn't coincide with those of a TV network. Warner Bros. wanted a forum for studio advertising, but in order to carve out a distinct identity in the competition among networks, ABC needed a program with the qualities of a major studio production. The subsequent negotiations between Warner Bros. and ABC—echoed certainly in discussions at MGM and Twentieth Century–Fox—revolved around several questions: What form should a major studio-produced television program take? What role should the network and advertisers play in the production process? Could a major studio organize the production process efficiently enough to meet network broadcast schedules and TV budgets? How could the program be designed to serve both the studio's self-promotional goals and the network's need to attract a competitive audience share? Would advertisers sponsor a program devoted primarily to publicizing other products, specifically a studio's feature films?

Warner Bros. decided in 1955 that the time was right to enter television, not only because Disney had made the transition successfully but also because the studio had found its footing in the movie industry. Contrary to the assumption that the movie studios finally turned to television in a state of panic, Warner Bros. actually began television production only after recovering from the financial instability of the late 1940s and early 1950s. Following a period of retrenchment in which Warner Bros. cut fixed costs and began to finance independent production, the studio rebounded, along with the entire movie industry starting in late 1953. Spurred by the success of CinemaScope features, the growth of independent production, and changing patterns of theatrical exhibition, the movie industry experienced a startling resurgence. Until 1953, only about one hundred movies in the history of Hollywood had ever earned more than $5 million. In the year and a half following the September 1953 release of *The Robe,* Twentieth Century–Fox's first CinemaScope feature, thirty pictures cracked the $5 million barrier.[2]

This boom reinforced changes that had begun to take place in the movie industry after the *Paramount* decision. As expensive independent films replaced the routine studio productions formerly handled by contract employees, movies were coming to be conceived as individual projects that could be marketed as events. Since most theaters were no longer affiliated with the major studios, competitive bidding among independent theater chains drove up the price on the most distinctive and eagerly anticipated movies. At the same time, theaters earned back this investment by keeping successful movies on their screens for longer periods of time. Consequently, the major studios faced a situation in which a single hit movie could account for most of a studio's annual earnings—a marked change from the studio era, when earnings were distributed fairly evenly among numerous releases.

In 1948, for instance, Paramount's *The Road to Rio* was the industry's biggest hit with gross revenues of only $4.5 million. By 1952, the two biggest films, Paramount's *The Greatest Show on Earth* and MGM's *Quo Vadis*, grossed $12 million and $10.5 million, respectively. Three major hits during 1954 sent Columbia's gross revenue from $60 million to $80 million in a single year.[3] In other words, by 1954 industrywide profits equaled those of the immediate postwar era, but these profits were earned by fewer and fewer movies. Since the most successful movies often had the largest budgets and the most celebrated stars, the studios were encouraged to raise budgets and gamble on hitting the jackpot. As each studio began the elusive quest for the single hit that could mean the difference between profit and loss, the first stirring of the blockbuster syndrome swept through the industry.

Warner Bros. certainly encouraged the growth of blockbusters. In January 1954, Jack Warner announced that the studio's next sixteen features would cost as much as its previous forty-two. The studio's three-year-old policy of discontinuing long-term contracts and throwing open the doors to independent producers had begun to pay off. Only two producers, Henry Blanke and David Weisbart, remained under contract. The majority of production deals now were signed with independent producer-directors, such as Mervyn LeRoy, John Ford, Alfred Hitchcock, Howard Hawks, Raoul Walsh, William Wellman, John Huston, Elia Kazan, and Billy Wilder, or with stars, such as Burt Lancaster, Doris Day, and the studio's most successful independent producer, John Wayne. Warner Bros. financed an industry-record twenty-one independent features during 1954, a year in which the studio was responsible for a number of the industry's biggest hits—*Dial M for Murder, Dragnet, A Star Is Born, Hondo,* and *The High and the Mighty.* Profits for the year rose to nearly $4 million, far below the studio's 1946 high-water mark but a significant turnaround nonetheless.[4]

Jack Warner entered 1955 by declaring his devotion to the "new realities" of Hollywood. After the uncertainty of the previous years, he welcomed the ballooning budgets and cascading box office receipts that fueled the blockbuster syndrome. "This is film's Cadillac Age," he told the press. "Nothing is exorbitant if it's the right thing." During the same interview in which Warner swore allegiance to Hollywood's first manifestation of the blockbuster syndrome, however, he also admitted that the time had come to begin producing for television. With a disdain for the broadcast medium cultivated over the last four years, Warner announced the studio's intentions by acknowledging simply, "We can't assume that television is going to blow over."[5] It was no coincidence that Warner Bros. executives turned their attention back to television production at the same time that they embraced the movie industry's "Cadillac Age." The studio's commitment to the blockbuster syndrome and its decision to engage in television production were intertwined elements of a new corporate strategy, one designed to take advantage of the changing conditions in Hollywood.

Expensive independent productions had the potential for huge payoffs, but they also carried a major liability. Funded by advance loans from Warner Bros., these productions tied up studio finances for increasingly extended lengths of time. It frequently took six or eight months to complete just the principal photography for such extravagant productions. By the time pre- and post-production were considered, the studio often didn't see a return on its investment for up to two years. In 1954 the studio advanced $18.5 million to independent companies, with another $20 million scheduled for 1955. Three films alone—*Moby Dick, Giant,* and *The Spirit of St. Louis*—accounted for $16 million of the studio's production budget. More and more frequently, advances to independent producers left Warner Bros. with as much as $45 million tied up in unfinished or unreleased projects. Because these films were released individually to exhibitors who were no longer bound to the studio through an integrated system, the studio could not count on a steady cash flow—even as its features became more costly. To stabilize the uncertain fortunes of the blockbuster syndrome, Warner Bros. had to find a way of meeting the expense of studio overhead and also a means of improving its cash flow.[6]

In January 1955, while still affirming its commitment to high-cost, independent production, Warner Bros. also decided to resuscitate the low end of its production schedule. The studio reintroduced a series of modestly budgeted studio-produced features and doubled its number of contract producers by signing William Goldbeck and Frank Rosenberg to oversee them.[7] At the same time, the studio decided to negotiate a production agreement with a television network. Television production became a viable option for Warner Bros. and the other major studios when they began to seek both a counterbalance to the skyrocketing costs and unpredictable profits of blockbuster production and an effective means for promoting these new movie events.

Although Disney's resurgence made television impossible to ignore, the idea of using television to promote feature films didn't start with Disney. Beginning in 1951, television variety show host Ed Sullivan crafted a shrewd arrangement with the movie industry by regularly converting his series, *Toast of the Town,* into an hour-long advertisement for Hollywood. Sullivan frequently distinguished his program from other TV variety shows by paying homage to individual movies, to famous Hollywood figures, such as Samuel Goldwyn and David Selznick, or to particular studios, like MGM. To the major studios he offered free publicity in exchange for the prestige and popular appeal that Hollywood could bring to his program. With studios clamoring for airtime, Sullivan's policy became firmly entrenched by 1954; during that year *Toast of the Town* leapt into the five top-rated network programs, remaining there for the next three seasons.[8] Other variety shows, such as the *Colgate Comedy Hour,* soon began courting Hollywood studios.

When Sullivan initially decided to celebrate the movie industry in 1951, Warner Bros.—still hostile toward television—refused to participate, even when Sullivan offered to devote an entire program to the studio's release of *A Streetcar Named Desire* (1951). By 1954, however, network exposure had become crucial to the studios' promotional campaigns, and an appearance on the Sullivan show was actively pursued and jealously guarded. Therefore, Warner Bros. scored a major coup in March 1955, when Sullivan devoted an entire episode to "The Warner Story." The event was so important that Jack Warner flew from Los Angeles to appear on the program.

Later in the summer, Warner Bros. used television to launch two of its releases, *Mr. Roberts* and *Pete Kelly's Blues.* In June, Sullivan devoted an entire program to *Mr. Roberts,* featuring live interviews with stars James Cagney, Henry Fonda, and Jack Lemmon, scenes enacted onstage by the stars, clips from the film itself, and interviews with the producer, Leland Hayward, the director, Mervyn LeRoy, and members of the original Broadway cast. A few weeks later, the *Colgate Comedy Hour* saluted *Pete Kelly's Blues* with a documentary tracing the creation of the film, from scriptwriting through the laboratory work on the finished print. Television publicity launched both films on successful theatrical runs. Although Warner Bros. did not measure the effect of television promotions, the box office success of *Mr. Roberts* and *Pete Kelly's Blues*—the second and fourteenth top-grossing films of 1955, respectively—provided sufficient evidence of television's value.[9]

Since *Mr. Roberts* and *Pete Kelly's Blues* represented the extremes of movie production at Warner Bros. by the mid-1950s, the performance of *Mr. Roberts* at the box office was gratifying, but the success of *Pete Kelly's Blues* was astonishing. Adapted from a famous Broadway play and produced by stage producer Leland Hayward, *Mr. Roberts* was a prestige production, filmed on location, and loaded with stars—the epitome of the blockbuster movie. *Pete Kelly's Blues*, on the other hand, was a modest production, shot entirely at the Warner Bros. studio and featuring no movie stars. Although in many ways unremarkable, *Pete Kelly's Blues* was distinguished by its identification with network television, through the presence of Jack Webb, who produced, directed, and starred in the movie. Webb first came to Warner Bros. to produce a 1954 feature film version of his hit TV series *Dragnet*, and his emergence as a leading star and independent producer for Warner Bros. signaled the rise of cross-promotion between the media.

In response to the unpredictability of theater attendance during the 1950s, the movie industry increasingly sought projects with proven appeal, using "pre-sold" story properties already familiar from other media. Although the industry had always produced adaptations of novels, plays, and radio programs, the 1950s saw a dramatic increase in the number of adaptations. Fierce bidding wars surrounded most new Broadway shows, driving the price for motion picture rights as high as $1 million by mid-decade.[10] While Warner Bros. entered the battle for Broadway plays like *Mr. Roberts,* it also began looking for television properties that might attract an audience at a lower cost. The studio had pursued this idea once before, in 1949 when it attempted to capitalize on the first wave of excitement surrounding network television by producing *Always Leave Them Laughing*, a movie that starred television's first comedy sensation, Milton Berle. Although Berle was a genuine television star, he was not necessarily a pre-sold commodity; after all, broadcast television reached only 2 percent of the nation in 1949. With such a small built-in audience, the production failed at the box office.

Jack Webb and Ben Alexander in the 1950s version of the TV series *Dragnet*. The feature-film adaptation of *Dragnet* became the second-highest-grossing movie for Warner Bros. in 1954.
(Courtesy of Wisconsin Center for Film and Theater Research
© Mark VII Productions)

By 1954, however, the television audience had grown to include 56 percent of the national population. Since *Dragnet* was seen regularly by more than half of these TV households, Warner Bros. financed an adaptation of the TV series to be produced independently by Jack Webb's company, Mark VII Productions. The gamble paid off handsomely for Warner Bros., with the movie version of *Dragnet* grossing $4.3 million—more than any 1954 Warner Bros. release except John Wayne's *The High and the Mighty*.[11] Since MGM also had great success in 1954 with *The Long, Long Trailer*, a film starring the red-hot television duo of Lucille Ball and Desi Arnaz, Warner Bros. stepped up its plans for television adaptations. Jack Warner's staff drew up a list of thirty TV series that would be likely candidates, and the studio conducted negotiations with TV personalities like Ball and Arnaz, Jackie Gleason, and Sid Caesar. Warner Bros. considered producing movies based on programs like *Wild Bill Hickok, Medic,* and even *Toast of the Town*—assigning contract writer Irving Wallace to write a script for a movie version of the Sullivan show. After much consideration, the studio financed two more television adaptations, *The Lone Ranger* (1956) and *Our Miss Brooks* (1956). Using the same stars and production teams from the TV versions, both films were produced on budgets larger than the TV standard, but much smaller than a typical feature-film budget.[12]

By 1955 Warner Bros. certainly recognized the value of cross-promotion with television. The broadcast medium served the studio both by providing the opportunity to publicize recent studio releases and by developing popular TV programs that could be adapted for theatrical distribution. *Disneyland* crystallized thinking about television because it demonstrated that both functions could be consolidated more efficiently in a program that Warner Bros. actually produced and controlled. Instead of waiting for *Toast of the Town* or the *Colgate Comedy Hour* to offer an invitation, Warner Bros. could produce a program of its own that would make it possible for the studio to orchestrate its own publicity by coordinating television exposure with a movie's larger marketing campaign. In addition, a Warner Bros. series might be useful for developing popular programs or stars which could be spun off into motion pictures—just as Disney had adapted *Davy Crockett* for theatrical release. By creating its own TV properties, the studio would avoid the need to negotiate for series created by outside producers.[13]

As president of Warner Bros. Distribution in New York, Benjamin Kalmenson was assigned to negotiate a production agreement with one of the television networks. During the early 1950s, Harry Warner had gradually withdrawn from the day-to-day management of Warner Bros., leaving room for Kalmenson to become the most influential policymaker in the New York office. Kalmenson began his career in film distribution with the Pittsburgh branch of First National Pictures in 1927 and reached the position of vice president and sales manager for all of Warner Bros. Distribution in 1941.

Like many of those involved with motion picture distribution and exhibition, Kalmenson had devoted his life to the proposition that theatrical exhibition, in which the public purchased the right to view each individual movie, was the only way to run the entertainment business. Never mind that broadcast television was an equally commercial proposition. "I am against the entire principle of entertainment for nothing," he said when asked about television. But since Kalmenson had to secure markets for Warner Bros. products under the new conditions of Hollywood, he laid aside his personal convictions in pursuit of a TV contract. During his years in distribution, Kalmenson had developed close contacts with Leonard Goldenson and his staff at United Paramount Theaters. When UPT merged with ABC in 1953, Kalmenson found himself with excellent connections to the broadcasting industry. As he recalled, "We had quite a number of discussions with ABC because the boys at ABC are friends of mine; some of them came from United Paramount Theaters, so we had been accustomed to dealing with them in the past."[14]

Given the studio's primary interest in publicity, Kalmenson entered negotiations with ABC during the winter of 1954–1955 hoping to strike a deal in which Warner Bros. would commit as few of its resources as possible to the project while still being able "to reach the vast television audience." He hoped to sell the network a series of hour-long episodes, with each episode consisting of an extended trailer for a current studio release and a re-edited version of a studio feature from the 1930s. This first round of negotiations faltered when ABC offered to pay no more for a Warner Bros. series than the $2 million it had paid Disney. Buoyed by the success of *Disneyland*, ABC was in a stronger bargaining position than ever before and was unwilling to accept a deal solely on the studio's terms. In order to make the series palatable to advertisers, ABC also wanted something more attractive than films that had been buried in the Warner Bros. vaults for twenty years. According to Kalmenson, the network wanted to draw "the cream of our entire product," including recent hits and classic films like *Casablanca* (1942). "The whole idea collapsed," he recalled, "when I was convinced they weren't satisfied with my selection of films." Jack Warner ordered his staff to abandon the negotiations, later explaining, "The money was so small an amount, so insignificant in comparison with the money we deal with in our practice in general, that we decided not to sell the pictures."[15]

Although these preliminary negotiations failed, they opened the door for continuing conversations with ABC and fueled what Kalmenson described as the studio's search "to find some way of using television to exploit our new product." In January 1955 ABC's Leonard Goldenson made a diplomatic journey to the major studios in Los Angeles. Over the course of this visit, ABC and Warner Bros. came to an informal agreement about the conditions under which the studio would sign its first TV contract.[16] Despite his continued apprehension about television production, Jack Warner conferred with Goldenson again during March 1955, while Warner was in New York to appear on *Toast of the Town*. Afterward, representatives from Warner Bros. and ABC signed a preliminary agreement that called for the studio to supply one television series—*Warner Bros. Presents*—for network broadcast beginning in September 1955.

A press release issued jointly by Warner Bros. and ABC—while filtered through the hyperbole of public relations—provided an early indication of the conflicts inherent in their relationship. Eager to convince Hollywood observers that the Warner Bros.–ABC agreement would benefit the entire movie industry, Jack Warner invoked the mythic image of the Warner brothers as movie industry pioneers. "My brothers and I approach this new relationship between motion pictures and television with the same zeal and enthusiasm as we had when we first presented commercially successful talking pictures," he proclaimed. Warner left little doubt, however, that feature films overshadowed television production in the studio's concerns. "We believe that *Warner Bros. Presents* will prove a major factor in developing new entertainment talent for motion pictures," he said, "and in telling the important story of the motion pictures to the public. . . . The new Warner Bros. television show will exploit to the fullest extent the value of the television medium in the marketing of the motion picture."[17]

In amplifying Warner's remarks, Benjamin Kalmenson directed his comments primarily at motion picture exhibitors. Anticipating criticism from theater owners, Kalmenson appeared eager to forestall their rancor; he spoke only of the benefits that exhibitors would derive from *Warner Bros. Presents*. Asserting that the television program would provide "a tremendous lift to our methods of marketing new pictures," Kalmenson assured theater owners that the TV program would not steal away the movie audience but would instead attract new segments of the public to movie theaters. "This forward-looking step on the part of the Warner brothers," he explained, "will contribute greatly toward the continuing development of new audiences for the motion picture theater. *Warner Bros. Presents* makes available to the motion picture theater the benefits of the greatest advance merchandising program ever conceived by the industry."[18]

While the studio executives directed their remarks to the movie industry, ABC president Robert Kintner tried to convince TV advertisers that a Warner Bros. series would draw viewers to the network. He informed potential sponsors that *Warner Bros. Presents* would differ from previous telefilm series because it would be the first series produced by a major motion picture studio. Displaying production values "unmatched and unmatchable in all television," *Warner Bros. Presents* would be the evidence of ABC's newfound commitment to "quality" programming.[19]

The conflicting interests expressed by Kintner and the studio executives suggest that *Warner Bros. Presents* was riddled by contradictions from the moment that the companies agreed to the production deal. Warner Bros. hoped to produce the least challenging program possible, conceiving of it mainly as an opportunity for studio publicity. ABC was willing to grant the studio its promotional ambitions, but also expected the first filmed television series to have production values that evoked the Hollywood cinema's commitment to spectacle. These tensions would strain the working relationship between Warner Bros. and ABC throughout the production of *Warner Bros. Presents*.

Even before the ABC–Warner Bros. agreement was officially announced, NBC dispatched its own representatives to the studio to propose a counteroffer. The details of these negotiations suggest just how differently Warner Bros. might have engaged in television production had it signed with another network. Fred Wile and Tom Sarnoff from NBC's West Coast television division arranged a meeting with Steve Trilling, Jack Warner's executive assistant, and with Jack Warner, Jr., son of the studio production chief. During the course of his presentation, Wile professed NBC's eagerness to invite the participation of Hollywood's major studios "in either TV production or promotion or both." Wile informed Trilling and Warner that the studio's participation could take any of a variety of forms: a series of half-hour or hour episodes, live or filmed programs, weekly or monthly scheduling, even occasional shows, such as a yearly series of three or four spectaculars. Wile also attempted to raise the stakes by making a proposition that the financially insecure ABC couldn't match: To ease the studio's shift to television production, NBC would make available the network's best producers, facilities, equipment, and technical personnel. Wile reinforced the distinction between the two networks by reminding Trilling and Warner that only NBC had the means to sell the Warner Bros. product to advertisers and to promote it in a manner appropriate to the studio's stature in the entertainment industry. "Please," he concluded, "don't close [a deal] with anybody without first talking to us."[20]

Wile and Sarnoff had approached Trilling in Hollywood because they assumed that the studio's TV production business would be handled on the West Coast. Trilling informed them that they were mistaken; the entire television matter was being handled by Kalmenson in New York—a confusion that revealed that Warner Bros. and NBC had never developed strong ties. Wile flew east to discuss the subject with Kalmenson, but nothing emerged from the conversations. Warner Bros. apparently thought that its promotional goals would best be achieved through the single program that it had agreed to produce for ABC. Because the studio had no further plans for establishing itself in television, one series was sufficient; there really was no need to negotiate other deals, to risk more studio capital, or to burden the studio's production operations with more than one series. Considering NBC's offer, it is still possible to imagine an entirely different Warner Bros. program that might have developed—perhaps three or four Warner Bros. spectaculars a year, produced by renowned TV producers like Fred Coe—if the studio had negotiated seriously with NBC before entering its agreement with ABC.

Warner Bros. and ABC initially forged their relationship while negotiating the studio's production agreement. The contract passed through two stages—a preliminary agreement dated 8 March 1955 and a final contract that wasn't signed until 22 September 1955, more than a week after the series premiered.[21] By providing a glimpse into the process of negotiation that shaped *Warner Bros. Presents*, these documents reveal two companies laboring to define the relationship between a broadcast network and a major Hollywood studio.

The deal called for Warner Bros. to produce thirty-nine new episodes per year, with ABC repeating thirteen during the summer. In contrast with ABC's Disney contract, which allowed Disney to supply the network with a mélange of programming extracted from the company's vaults, the contract with Warner Bros. protected ABC from becoming a dumping ground for films that no longer had value in theatrical re-release. The contract explicitly required the studio to provide "newly filmed programs . . . produced under the general supervision of Mr. Jack L. Warner." Like *Disneyland*, the Warner Bros. program would have a general title identifying it with the production company, but the program would consist of alternating dramatic series adapted from successful Warner Bros. movies—initially four series consisting of ten episodes each, later reduced to three series of thirteen episodes.[22]

From hundreds of movies in the Warner Bros. library, the studio and ABC finally agreed on a few that represented some of Hollywood's most easily identifiable and, therefore, marketable genres. *Warner Bros. Presents* was to be divided into four general categories: "romantic-intrigue," "mystery," an "adventure type of adult Western," and a "teenage comedy." *Casablanca* (1942) and *The Maltese Falcon* (1941) would serve as the models for the romantic-intrigue and mystery categories, respectively. The source films for the other two categories had not been firmly established, but the Western prototypes were considered to be *Hondo* (1953) and *The Treasure of the Sierra Madre* (1948), while the teenage comedy was to resemble *Janie* (1944) or *Brother Rat* (1938). By the time the final contract was signed, the two companies had reduced the number of series to three and had settled on the specific movies to be adapted for the series: *Casablanca*, *Cheyenne* (1947), and *King's Row* (1942). While the reasons for omitting the mystery and comedy genres weren't specified, *King's Row* was added so the series would include at least one genre—the family melodrama—designed to appeal primarily to women.

The alternating format of *Warner Bros. Presents* offered both the studio and the network a chance to test the prime-time waters. In fact, the production agreement assumed that not all three series would find an audience; in case any of the series failed in the ratings, the contract specified that ABC and Warner Bros. would substitute one from an entirely different genre. As far as both companies were concerned, *Warner Bros. Presents* was something like a fishing expedition in which alternating series, identified with specific genres, would be used to attract certain elements of the TV audience. The alternating format represented an unsystematic effort to acquire greater knowledge about television viewers through a process of trial and error. *Variety*'s review of the series speculated that *Cheyenne* was designed for children, *Casablanca* for teenagers, and *King's Row* for adults.[23]

ABC evidently hoped to acquire the prestige associated with specific Warner Bros. features as a substitute for acquiring the features themselves. Therefore, it was agreed that each series not only would use the title of the chosen Warner Bros. film but also would use the narrative structure of the film prototype as its model; each series would be "similar in format and plot to the motion picture of the same title." ABC and Warner Bros. chose these titles for their "marquee value," to capitalize on what the network described as the "familiarity factor." But they were chosen also because they possessed specific characteristics that made them valuable as "models" in their respective genres. Each movie provided "the best story line, the best setting, and the most flexible formats for a continuing series."[24]

Once the studio began the work of transforming the feature film's single narrative into the infinitely repeatable structure of an episodic series, however, it became apparent that fidelity to the source film would prove to be a severe constraint. The final contract, therefore, relieved some of the studio's creative restrictions by amending this requirement to state that each series could be based not only on the feature film and its screenplay but also on "the characters, plot, title, dialogue, scenes, incidents, background, setting, locales, situations, action, language, themes, or general nature" of the entire feature or any part of it. In other words, as the final contract states explicitly,

Warner Bros. was free to add new elements or to alter the series according to its "uncontrolled discretion."

Indeed, the final contract was a testament to the clout of a major studio, because it gave Warner Bros. complete creative control over the series but for just two restrictions. First, the episodes had to meet National Association of Broadcasters standards, television's guidelines for propriety similar to those in the movie industry's Production Code. Second, although Warner Bros. was allowed to extend a series plot across two episodes, the series could not adopt a serial structure. Because open-ended narratives were still the province of daytime soap operas, ABC wanted to associate prime time with the closed narrative of the episodic series. The network seemed to believe that audiences could be engaged by the daily episodes of a daytime serial, but that too much time passed between the weekly episodes of a prime-time series for audiences to remain engaged by stories left perpetually unresolved. ABC took great pains to assure potential sponsors that individual episodes would consist of "complete, self-contained stories."

Each episode would contain a narrator's introduction featuring host Gig Young, followed by the forty-five-minute "entertainment portion of the program," a three-minute trailer for the next week's program, and a six- to eight-minute segment of "general publicity and promotional material" devoted to recent Warner Bros. releases. This final segment, titled "Behind the Cameras at Warner Bros.," would consist of an excerpt from a current release and appearances by movie stars in exclusive behind-the-scenes production footage. It was the presumed appeal of movie stars that encouraged ABC to accept the studio's promotional segment as part of the program. ABC assumed that a Hollywood studio's most important contribution to broadcast TV would be the value of established motion picture stars—even if those stars were tacked on to the program in publicity features.

For the thirty-nine original episodes of *Warner Bros. Presents*, Warner Bros. would receive a minimum guarantee of $2.25 million—$50,000 per episode for the first broadcast, $25,000 each for twelve repeats. ABC would seek a higher price from sponsors—$65,000 per original, $39,000 per repeat, for a total of $3 million. Warner Bros. and ABC also agreed that the network license fee would not constitute the studio's full compensation for the program; the telecast of the "Behind the Cameras" segment each week would serve as partial compensation for the studio's expense. In effect, ABC traded broadcast time with the publicity-hungry studio in exchange for a lower license fee than a studio otherwise might have demanded. Neither company publicly acknowledged this aspect of the deal, probably because ABC feared alienating potential sponsors by admitting that Warner Bros. planned to use the series for self-promotion.

In exchange for the license fee, ABC had the right for one year to televise the series at the day and hour of its choosing. It could broadcast the program on a sustaining or commercial basis and could arrange for any type of sponsorship—single, multiple, or participating. Significantly, at this stage of the relationship, all residual and licensing rights remained exclusively with Warner Bros. ABC did not yet have the power to demand a share in these ancillary markets.

Once the initial agreement had been reached, ABC faced the task of selling *Warner Bros. Presents* to advertisers. With the confidence required in a sales pitch, ABC billed *Warner Bros. Presents* as "the greatest new programming concept yet to come to the television screen" and "a milestone in the progress of mass entertainment." Because there was no evidence to substantiate these claims—no cast lists, completed scripts, prospective budgets, or pilot episode—ABC traded entirely on the Warner Bros. name. For the purpose of attracting advertisers, the real value of the Warner Bros. deal was the studio's prestige and reputation, not the material asset of an actual series. "In coming to the home screen for the first time," the network promised, "Warner Bros. will throw all its resources behind *Warner Bros. Presents* to give the TV production all the craftsmanship and quality that has been the hallmark of Warner Bros. motion pictures."

By invoking the quality of Warner Bros. movies and the values associated with Hollywood studios, ABC used sleight of hand to distract advertisers from the fact that major motion picture stars and Hollywood production values could not be delivered on the budget for *Warner Bros. Presents*. The $3 million that Warner Bros. received from ABC might have financed two or three of the studio's moderately priced feature films, but a season of *Warner Bros. Presents* would require the studio to produce the equivalent of *twenty* feature films. Once the $3 million network license fee was allocated to thirty-nine hour-long episodes, the studio would have to produce the series on a budget equivalent to a feature-film budget of $150,000.

In 1955, even the most disreputable Poverty Row potboilers cost more than Warner Bros. could spend on an episode of *Warner Bros. Presents*. ABC implied, however, that *Warner Bros. Presents* would not reflect its paltry budget; instead it would somehow transcend the economic constraints with a touch of Hollywood magic. "The production values Warner Bros. will put into each of these new 'pictures-for-television' will exceed many times their selling price," the sales brochure promised. The sales presentation bathed the entire series in the aura of the Warner Bros. tradition and the image of Hollywood. Invoking the titles of thirty-five famous Warner Bros. movies and promising that the series would be supervised personally by Jack L. Warner, the network further identified *Warner Bros. Presents* as a product of the movie industry by claiming that its hour-long episode length—at a time when all other telefilm series ran only a half-hour—would make the program a "blockbuster" television series.

While the movie industry had developed a number of marketing strategies to differentiate its theatrical features from standard television series (including such technological innovations as wide screen, 3-D, and stereophonic sound), ABC was just as actively attempting to associate its programming with the movie industry. The network tried to appropriate the cultural values associated with the motion picture industry—such as the term "blockbuster"—and to rearticulate these values for television. For this reason, the brochure repeatedly stressed the "Hollywood" qualities that Warner Bros. would bring to television for the first time—"glamorous settings," "compelling stories," "memorable characters."

An idealized image of Hollywood served as the imagined referent for *Warner Bros. Presents*. ABC assured potential sponsors that "the high point of each week's program" would be the "Behind the Cameras" segment, "the most glamorous and looked-forward-to feature of the program." Offering a glimpse of Hollywood sets and interviews with major movie stars, such as John Wayne, Alan Ladd, Gary Cooper, and James Stewart, "Behind the Cameras" would give *Warner Bros. Presents* the "glamour" and "star value" promised to advertisers. Grafted onto each week's narrative episode, "Behind the Cameras" would provide the Hollywood flavor needed to distinguish *Warner Bros. Presents* from other telefilm series.

ABC's terms for the program's sale reflected the industrywide movement away from sponsor control of programming. The network planned to line up two to four alternating sponsors, which would be allowed to advertise one or two of their products but would not be permitted to promote the company in general or to plug an entire array of products. The sponsor's costs would total $133,917 per week—$68,822 for the program and $65,095 for an hour of network time. ABC made it clear that Warner Bros. had complete creative control over the series, with the studio and the network free even to change the program's format if they found it necessary. Despite the studio's lack of television experience, the contract required a firm fifty-two-week commitment. In essence, the TV sponsors, like exhibitors during the studio era, were forced by ABC to purchase an entire block of Warner Bros. product without being able to inspect a single episode beforehand. Such contractual provisions resembled the practices of blind-bidding and block-booking that had characterized distribution at the height of the studio era. For Warner Bros., this provision seemed to provide a buffer between the studio and demanding sponsors, guaranteeing a degree of autonomy that most television producers did not share—and that a major motion picture studio feared to lose.

Without even a pilot episode, Robert Kintner and his sales staff at ABC signed a full slate of sponsors within a month. The cigarette company Liggett and Myers purchased a half-hour each week for $3.3 million. General Electric and Monsanto shared the other half-hour on alternate weeks, each paying $1.7 million. Neither Liggett and Myers nor General Electric, two of the television industry's largest advertising clients, had ever before purchased time on ABC; Monsanto had never advertised on television at all. The sale clearly demonstrated the importance of Warner Bros. to the network's plans for expansion.[25]

Kintner immediately wired the news to Jack Warner, and in the telegram he accurately attributed the sales to the studio's value as a cultural commodity. "Congratulations on the sale ABC made to Liggett & Myers for cigarettes and to GE for radios, TVs, and small appliances," said Kintner. "I say congratulations because I was able to sell these accounts only because of your past reputation and the reputation of your studio, and because of the confidence of these clients and advertising agencies in your ability to produce the top television program. Basically our representation in making this sale was that the people were buying the ability of Warner Bros. and you particularly."[26] Now that the series had been successfully marketed, and the contractual relations between Warner Bros., ABC, and the sponsors had been established, Kintner appeared confident that *Warner Bros. Presents* would be "of a technical and creative quality equal to anything on television."

Even though *Warner Bros. Presents* had been sold to advertisers, Warner Bros. still had not faced the most pressing question of all: Since the studio had shifted primarily into financing and distributing independent films, how would it meet the challenge of producing low-budget, episodic TV series? The studio's reputation and previous experience alone could not guarantee a smooth transition. The formation of a television production division at Warner Bros. required the studio to resurrect its dormant tradition of B-movie production and retool to operate on budgets barely adequate even on Poverty Row.

Television production would share two important features with B-feature production: limited budgets and tight production schedules.

In the studio system, B features were produced on a fixed budget because their rental income was highly predictable; B-feature rentals were charged at a flat rate, while A features received a percentage of the box office gross. Television production at Warner Bros. would face the same restrictions as B-film production, since the network's weekly broadcast schedule would necessitate rigidly enforced production timetables and the studio's contract fixed the income for *Warner Bros. Presents* at $3 million. Looking back in 1960, William T. Orr, the head of Warner Bros. TV, claimed that these factors were what most distinguished the production of television films and feature films. In motion pictures, he claimed, Warner Bros. prepared a flexible budget and production schedule based on the picture's projected performance at the box office; in television, however, programs were produced within a proscribed budget and an unyielding production schedule because their income was predetermined. "And as a matter of good business practice," he added, "you can go over budget, but then it is your decision to spend money you are not receiving for the show."[27]

Network television programs did not have to be produced on a fixed budget if the production company was willing to gamble on future revenue from syndication and merchandising. Deficit financing of this sort had become standard practice for telefilm producers as early as 1951, and Columbia's Screen Gems subsidiary had established the viability of the practice for Hollywood studios. Yet, as Orr's statement indicates, even five years after Warner Bros. had begun TV production, the studio paid little attention to deferred revenue possibilities when estimating the budgets for its television series. During the studio's initial stage of TV production this attitude can be explained by the company's single-minded concern with exploiting television to its short-term promotional advantage. Although other telefilm producers had already begun to earn profits through syndicated reruns, Warner Bros. initially failed to anticipate the long-term value of its TV productions.

The studio's reliance solely on network license fees and its failure to consider deficit financing meant that it could produce *Warner Bros. Presents* only by resuming the highly rationalized mode of production employed for B movies. Following the successful transition to independent production, studio executives were ambivalent about returning to a system of inexpensive mass production.[28] Warner Bros. had begun to thrive again during the movie industry's Cadillac Age, in which the profits from a single prestigious blockbuster could dwarf those generated by an entire season of B features. But once the decision was made, the company could draw on a tradition of low-budget production in planning the new division. Over the decades Warner Bros. had developed a reputation for being one of the industry's most fiscally conservative studios, one that produced films inexpensively and efficiently, seldom purposely gambling on the sort of prestige pictures that characterized a studio like MGM. Instead, Warner Bros. relied on strict budget controls and the steady rewards of a relatively narrow profit margin, producing features on the smallest budgets of any of the five largest studios.[29]

Hollywood's major studios began systematically producing B movies during the Depression, when exhibitors started programming double features in order to boost attendance. Needing low-cost features to fill out the second half of these bills, major studios like Warner Bros. formed B-movie units that soon stabilized the studio's revenue base by turning out a series of relatively undifferentiated features that accounted for as much as half of the studio's annual output. B movies at Warner Bros. not only provided a consistent source of income but also supported studio expenses, since Warner Bros. added overhead charges of 30 to 40 percent to the budget of each B movie. B-movie production also offered a low-stakes training ground for actors, writers, directors, and producers. Indeed, Harry Warner claimed in 1937, "You can run a movie business without any A's sooner than you can run it without any B's." Under the supervision of Bryan Foy, the B-movie unit at Warner Bros. produced roughly twenty-five movies a year during the late 1930s, on a total annual budget of only $5 million. Individual production budgets were held below $150,000, and shooting schedules ran anywhere from fourteen to twenty-eight days.[30] Obviously, B-movie narrative strategies and production values were shaped by this strict economy.

During the early 1940s, Warner Bros. and the other major studios phased out the systematic production of B movies, primarily because of a 1940 Justice Department consent decree that altered the major studios' practice of blind-bidding and block-booking by reducing the groups in which features could be sold to theaters from thirty movies or more in each block to a maximum of five. Like the other major studios, Warner Bros. had to upgrade the narrative and production values of each movie in these smaller blocks in order to differentiate them in a more competitive market. Most of the major studios expunged the label "B movies" from their vocabularies because the negative connotation associated with the term made it difficult to sell such movies in these smaller blocks. The increased emphasis on A movies was reinforced by the box office boom of the war years, in which top-grossing movies commanded longer runs. It soon became apparent that a small number of A movies could earn greater profits than a combined program of A's and B's. From the mid-1940s until 1948, therefore, Warner Bros. eliminated almost all feature film production below the level of $500,000 and shifted to a full program of productions with established stars.[31]

In January 1948, however, the studio quietly reintroduced B-movie production as one of its strategies to combat inflated production costs and declining theater attendance. Saul Elkins was assigned to supervise production on a series of genre features—mainly crime stories and Westerns—with budgets under $300,000.[32] During the next three and a half years, Elkins produced fourteen features using a consistent set of writers, directors, actors, and technicians. The primary difference between these B features and the earlier ones produced during the 1930s, however, was that these weren't scheduled as fodder for the lower end of double bills. Instead, following the success of two low-budget features, Twentieth Century–Fox's *Boomerang* (1947) and RKO's *Crossfire* (1947), Warner Bros. joined the rest of the industry in gambling on B-budgeted movies that would be treated in distribution like A features.[33] This trend continued at Warner Bros. until the studio shifted to financing and distributing big-budget independent features in 1951.

In order to revive full-scale B-level production for its TV series in 1955, Warner Bros. followed the precedent Columbia had established with Screen Gems and initially formed a television production company from Sunset Productions, a wholly owned subsidiary that produced the studio's short subjects, travelogues, documentaries, and, occasionally during the 1950s, low-budget "featurettes" of forty to fifty minutes in length. Since its early production of Vitaphone musical shorts in the late 1920s, Warner Bros. had been one of the most active studios in the field of short subjects, producing not only the typical series of westerns and comedies, but even Academy Award–winning miniature dramas that used some of the studio's most important directors, writers, and stars. With historical documentaries, CinemaScope travelogues, and the "Joe McDoakes" comedy series in production at Sunset, Warner Bros. remained dominant in the admittedly shrinking field of short subjects through the mid-1950s.[34] In spite of its relative success, however, Sunset Productions was unquestionably a ghetto housing the curiosities produced by a studio whose primary activity, like that of the other major studios, was the production of high-cost, feature-length films. In early 1955, the studio administration decided that TV production would be at home in the milieu of Sunset. Jack Warner's son, Jack Junior, was named vice president in charge of television production at the company, while Norman Moray, the subsidiary's New York–based head of distribution, managed the entire operation.[35]

For a short time it looked as though all Warner Bros. TV activity would be channeled through this subsidiary, just as Columbia had directed its TV business to Screen Gems. Industry rumors speculated that Warner Bros., like Columbia and Universal before it, had established Sunset as a separate entity in order to avoid antagonizing exhibitors. The trade press assumed that the subsidiary would produce all telefilm programming and, perhaps, serve as the distributor of the studio's film library to TV. Indeed, the studio's March 1955 preliminary agreement to produce a TV series for ABC, though negotiated by Benjamin Kalmenson in New York, was signed not with Warner Bros. Pictures but with Sunset Productions.[36]

By April, however, Warner Bros. realized that Sunset could not move quickly enough to have a program on the air by early September. The small-scale subsidiary simply couldn't marshal the resources necessary for such an ambitious project. Only the studio's feature-film division could mobilize the facilities and personnel that would be needed to produce a TV series in that brief time span. In addition, studio executives recognized that if the series was to serve its promotional purpose, it needed to advertise the Warner Bros. trademark, not to obscure the studio's role behind the name of a subsidiary. In early April, therefore, the studio decided to organize two separate TV operations. Warner Bros. Pictures would produce TV series wholly owned by the studio, while Sunset Productions would finance and produce series developed by independent producers. Sunset would own these series, but the producers would receive a percentage of the profits. Warner Bros. also charged Sunset with the responsibility for developing new programs.[37] Throughout much of its first two years in television production, Warner Bros. had no intention of expanding or developing new series; instead, the company focused entirely on sustaining week-to-week production demands.

While Sunset took responsibility for program development, the feature-film division accepted the task of constructing a TV production unit. Studio executives believed that network television—with its demand for increased productivity and its promise of guaranteed revenue—offered an ideal opportunity to reassert aspects of the studio system at Warner Bros. After beginning to encourage independent production in the late 1940s, Warner Bros. had shifted toward what Janet Staiger has termed the "'package-unit' system of production." Staiger describes this mode of production: "Rather than an individual company containing the source of the labor and materials, the entire industry became the pool for these. A producer organized a film project: he or she secured financing and combined the necessary laborers . . . and the means of production." [38] Although Warner Bros. had supported the "package-unit" system as a means for reducing costs and attracting independent producers, television production offered the studio a chance to revive its various departments and the "producer-unit" system of management which it had used throughout much of the studio era. In this model, individual producers working under the general supervision of Jack Warner had supervised six to eight individual films per year, with each producer usually specializing in a particular type of film. [39] This is precisely the model of hierarchical management that Warner Bros. used to organize TV production.

Although Warner Bros. executives felt capable of reviving mass production at the studio, they nevertheless perceived television production to be different from the company's previous activities. Because of the peculiar demands of television production—namely, the requirements of dealing with networks, sponsors, and advertising agencies for the first time—studio executives believed that no one within the organization possessed sufficient experience in broadcasting or adequate contacts within the broadcasting industry to lead Warner Bros. into the TV business. In early April, therefore, Warner Bros. hired Gary Stevens to supervise the TV operations. Brother of 1950s TV star and producer Mark Stevens (*Big Town* [1950–1956]), Gary Stevens had gained most of his television experience at small advertising agencies and by working as a press agent; he had never managed a studio. [40]

As a studio neophyte, Stevens was not intended to have the same control over TV production that Jack Warner wielded over theatrical feature production. General strategic decisions regarding television were the responsibility of Warner and his executive assistants, Steve Trilling and William Orr. Stevens's job was to oversee the day-to-day operations, to carry out decisions passed down by the studio bosses. When the TV operation officially began functioning on 14 April 1955, Warner immediately informed Stevens that the TV supervisor would have to seek authorization at the executive level for the hiring of any above-the-line talent—writers, directors, producers, and actors. Stevens could hire on his own authority only below-the-line personnel—directors of photography, camera operators, editors, and so forth—who would be placed under general contract with the TV division and would work on all of the series. On one occasion in July, Stevens inadvertently tested Warner's directive by hiring a supporting actor without first seeking the proper authorization. Warner's response was swift and stern. "Do not do this again under any consideration," he warned.[41]

The studio created two supervisory positions under Stevens to oversee the story and production departments for the entire TV division. It was decided that TV production would operate most efficiently by having these departments supervise all television activity, rather than establishing separate story and production departments for each series. Oren Haglund was given the job of TV production manager. His task was to coordinate the physical activities of all TV production—lining up crews, supervising set construction, and so forth. Shortly after Stevens was hired, the studio brought in Richard Diggs to head the TV story department. The studio considered a number of movie industry story editors for the job but chose Diggs because he was the only one who also had radio and TV experience, having served time on Don Ameche's radio series, on Louella Parson's TV program, and in the production departments at two advertising agencies.[42]

The position of story editor already had become one of the most crucial in television production because the story editor was responsible for monitoring the series narrative over the course of a season. At the most general level, Diggs's task was to acquire story properties that seemed appropriate for the series and to coordinate the hiring of writers—the function of any movie studio's story department. More important, however, it was his responsibility also to ensure that the many different writers who worked on a series understood the narrative formula, with its recurring characters, situations, and conflicts. When these writers submitted scripts that inevitably brought unique inflections to the formula, the story editor had to make the individual scripts conform to the logic of the entire series, ensuring the stability of the overall series narrative by maintaining the consistency of characters, situations, and structure or, if the series was meant to change, by overseeing adjustments.

Warner Bros. realized that the most active television production companies, such as Ziv, Screen Gems, Revue, and Four Star, hired a writer to devise a pilot script and then allowed that writer to supervise the work of other writers on subsequent episodes.[43] At these studios, a single story editor (or sometimes a two-person team) was responsible for maintaining the series' formula, and each series was supervised individually. But the Warner Bros. conception of television production was more factorylike, emphasizing efficient management-level control. Since general studio output took precedence over the autonomy of creative personnel or the production of individual series, no single person was responsible for creating a series formula; the scripts for all three series were channeled through Diggs, a studio-level story editor who was not associated with any single series.

In order to attract talent from the movie or radio industries, other large television production companies like Screen Gems and Revue offered profit-participation deals with actors and producers, such as the deal signed in 1955 by Alfred Hitchcock to produce and host *Alfred Hitchcock Presents* for Revue. These deals gave individual producers or stars a degree of autonomy in developing series and allowed them to share the rewards of syndication. Warner Bros., of course, negotiated similar deals for feature films. But in television, Warner Bros. chose to reassert elements of the studio system by enforcing a rigorously controlled production process and creating a number of policies that limited the autonomy of its above-the-line personnel. Each of these policies differed from those already established at many of the independent TV companies. First, the studio decided not to sign profit-participation deals in TV; instead, Warner Bros. signed producers, directors, and actors who appeared in recurring roles to exclusive contracts much like those of the studio era. Second, Warner Bros. would not allow producers to create series; instead, the studio assigned producers and directors to existing series for which the studio owned all rights. Third, Warner Bros. elected not to sign term contracts with writers, choosing instead to hire all writers on a free-lance basis.

Each of the three individual series within *Warner Bros. Presents* was supervised by a team consisting of a producer and a director, who were placed under short-term contract to the studio. The initial producer-director teams were

	King's Row	Cheyenne	Casablanca
PRODUCER:	Roy Huggins	Harve Foster	Jerry Robinson
DIRECTOR:	Paul Stewart	Richard Bare	John Peyser

Following the practice of the studio era, Warner Bros. initially paid the directors higher salaries ($650 per week) than it paid the supervising producers ($500 per week). In fact, *Cheyenne* director Richard Bare, who previously had directed a number of low-budget features at Warner Bros., was offered the chance to produce *Cheyenne,* but he turned it down when he learned that directors would be paid better.

Although it is generally acknowledged that the producer holds the most influential creative role in TV series production, it is interesting to note that this hierarchy was not immediately established or universally accepted during the early days of television production at

Warner Bros.[44] Warner Bros. producers initially were not given the autonomy enjoyed by producers working at Screen Gems and Four Star,
but once production at the studio got under way, it became apparent
that the producer's supervisory position provided the most effective
vantage point from which to orchestrate the various personnel involved in production and maintain the continuity of the series narrative across an entire season. Since the director was immersed in the
physical production of each episode, he did not have the same opportunity. Through experience, Warner Bros. gradually decided that
producers should have more authority than directors in the hierarchy
of television production, a decision that became evident over the next
two years when the studio hired directors solely on a free-lance basis,
while giving producers term contracts and larger salaries.

The actors who played the recurring characters in the series were
signed to term contracts with guarantees of thirteen or twenty-six
weeks. Their salaries ranged between $300 and $750 per week. Since
the TV series were considered to be training ground for new talent,
Warner Bros. was careful to ensure that its contracts allowed the
studio to assign these actors to other series or to theatrical features.
Writers, on the other hand, were hired solely on a free-lance basis.
Whereas a number of TV companies hired a staff of writers for their
series, Warner Bros. made nonexclusive, flat-rate deals with writers
in order to avoid the cost of daily rates or long-term commitments. As
a result, no single writer could gain leverage in contract negotiations
by becoming indispensable to a particular series. At the outset, the
terms for these deals were relatively meager: $500 for an original
story, $810 for a first draft, $690 for a final draft—a total of $2,000 for
an original script. Understandably, the $2,000 limit placed severe con-
straints on the caliber of writers who would work for Warner Bros.
on the TV series.[45]

The creation of television series at Warner Bros. conformed closely to
the studio's earlier B-movie operations. Every Hollywood studio during the studio era had to balance efforts to control costs by organizing
a regulated and efficient production process with the need to create
movies that were sufficiently distinctive to appeal to audiences. Consequently, the production process at the major studios involved a tension between the impulses of standardization and differentiation.[46]
Because of its low budgets, Warner Bros. tilted the balance toward
standardization whenever possible, demonstrating a willingness to
sacrifice originality for economy. During the studio era, Warner Bros.
developed an extremely materialistic conception of Hollywood narrative, one in which each studio movie was seen less as a coherent

whole than as a collection of parts that could be disassembled, maintained in a storehouse of studio tradition, and then selected and reassembled according to need. This process of recycling occurred throughout the studio system, most literally when studios used the same costumes, props, and scenery in movie after movie; it also occurred in less tangible forms, such as the repetition inherent in star performances and genre films or the creation of remakes and sequels. Warner Bros. took this approach to the extreme, recycling screenplays—and even footage—with abandon.

From all appearances, producers at Warner Bros. seldom suffered anxiety over the source of their creative inspiration. Jack Warner once proudly shared with *Fortune* magazine his advice for writers who suffered creative blocks: Just look back in the studio's story files for ideas. "That's how we do it," Warner explained. "Whenever I go by the projection room and hear them running off *Moby Dick* I know the boys are working on *Captain Blood*." [47] Remakes were a common practice at Warner Bros., especially in the B unit, where story costs were held to a minimum. Production chief Bryan Foy claimed that he chose new projects from a pile of scripts on his desk; after one was filmed it went to the bottom of the pile and then worked its way back to the top. Often a film would be remade three or four times by transposing its narrative into other genres or by increasing or decreasing its production values and the relative status of its stars. Thus the gangster film *High Sierra* (1941) was made into the Western *Colorado Territory* (1949); the seagoing A feature *Tiger Shark* (1932) was given a circus setting in the B film *Bengal Tiger* (1936).

This process of incorporation reached more-literal levels in the production of a number of studio remakes. On remakes of *20,000 Years in Sing Sing* (1933), *The Dawn Patrol* (1932), and *The Crowd Roars* (1932), for instance, the creative process began with the producer, editor, and art director printing all the footage from the original film in which the main actors were not obviously recognizable (generally medium and long shots). The remainder of the remake was then planned so that shots could be inserted into the existing footage, with the original film serving as a blueprint. During principal photography, a Movieola was kept on the set in order to match past and present shot composition, set design, and even the relative size of the actors who would correspond to the actors in the original films. Frequently footage was transferred from film to film within a particular genre, for instance when original footage from *The Divine Lady* (1929) was used in *Captain Blood* (1935) and, later, in *The Sea Hawk* (1940). [48]

Many of these practices were transferred directly to television production. Writer David Harmon, who had been hired to write the first episode of *Casablanca* but who had no experience working for Warner Bros., lobbied for a research junket to the Moroccan city. Since the studio had decided to place the series in the present, instead of in the World War II setting of the original film, Harmon wanted to see how the city had changed since the war. "I would be able to see the truth and use it as fiction," he explained to Gary Stevens. Harmon's plan was probably greeted with amusement and, as one might imagine, it was quickly rejected. Considering budget restrictions, verisimilitude was a less highly esteemed narrative value than pastiche, the inventive recombination of components from previous texts. When it came time for writers and producers to begin script preparations on the three series of *Warner Bros. Presents,* therefore, Jack Warner suggested a research junket more in line with typical procedures at the studio: He arranged a screening of the three prototype films.[49]

During pre-production, the writers and producers saw no problems in generating episodic stories based on *King's Row* and *Casablanca,* but they began to see problems with *Cheyenne.* The movie version of *King's Row,* starring Robert Cummings and Ronald Reagan, was a small-town melodrama centering on the return of a prodigal-son psychiatrist following medical school; his reappearance triggers a series of intertwined conflicts that have bubbled for years beneath the town's placid surface. *Casablanca,* starring Humphrey Bogart and Ingrid Bergman, was a wartime adventure about the romantic wanderers, political refugees, and social outcasts who, on their passage through the North African city during World War II, gravitate to Rick's Cafe, a casino owned by an American expatriate. With an ensemble of characters and a central setting, both of these movies presented the writers with opportunities for spinning out stories based on the prototype. *Cheyenne* posed difficulties, however, because its structure left the writers uncertain as to how it might provide a model for generating new episodes. Although the movie version was set in Cheyenne, Wyoming, the location was not terribly important to the fairly conventional Western about a reformed gambler (Dennis Morgan) who agrees to help Wells Fargo capture a troublesome bandit known as the Poet. The writers questioned whether the series should be centered on the city of Cheyenne—as *King's Row* and *Casablanca* were structured around a location and a stable set of characters—or whether "Cheyenne" should be the name of a central character who would serve as the narrative focus of the series.

A certain vagueness had surrounded the Western segment of *Warner Bros. Presents* from the time of the agreement between the studio and the network. While the "romance" and "adventure" formats were tied to the specific titles of *King's Row* and *Casablanca,* the Western wasn't immediately identified with a single title. Although ABC wanted to exploit the familiarity of *King's Row* and *Casablanca*, it was not so much interested in a specific Western film as in the Western as a genre. Indeed, there was nothing about the feature film *Cheyenne* that distinguished it from any number of other studio Westerns. In effect, Warner Bros. borrowed the title *Cheyenne* and then created a new and entirely unrelated TV Western using combined fragments from the studio's library of Westerns. The writers chosen for the first episodes screened a number of studio Westerns and read scripts and stories from the files. The decision was made to organize the series around a central character loosely modeled after the Errol Flynn character in the Warner Bros. Western *Rocky Mountain* (1950). Maurice Geraghty based his script for the first episode, "Julesburg," on portions of three separate features—*Dodge City* (1939), *Colt .45* (1950), and *Dallas* (1950). The finished episode contained footage from these films and from the feature version of *Cheyenne*. Don Martin, the writer for the second episode, "Mountain Fortress," modeled his effort on the feature *Rocky Mountain*.[50]

This peculiar creative process, with its emphasis on the reassembly of components from movies already produced within the studio system, became the preferred model for textual production at Warner Bros. TV. It was not only economical, but it played havoc with conventional notions of authorship, because no single writer could claim to be the creator of a Warner Bros. TV series. For legal purposes, all Warner Bros. TV series were based on previous studio productions, even if they bore a relationship in name only. This method of storytelling favored the studio's proprietary claims to authorship on each series, even if the process of assembling fragments from studio films ultimately created a new series that resembled no particular film. Writers received residual payments for individual episodes, but no writer could claim the rights to an entire series because no writer was ever listed as the creator of a Warner Bros. series.

The studio's institutionalized recombination led to a number of fascinating legal disputes as the labor guilds attempted to define the concept of authorship in terms more favorable to its members. The Screen Directors Guild, for instance, considered requesting residual payments for director Gordon Douglas because so much footage from his film *The Charge at Feather River* (1953) was used in a first-season *Cheyenne* episode adapted from the feature. In the early 1960s, the Writers Guild of America filed for arbitration against Warner Bros. on behalf of Maurice Geraghty, claiming that Geraghty deserved residual payments for having created *Cheyenne*. Geraghty reasoned that since no pilot script existed before his script for the first episode and since the series obviously was not based on the Warner Bros. feature version of *Cheyenne*, he deserved full rights for having created the series. Warner Bros. countered with the claim that Geraghty's episode had been based not on a single Warner Bros. film but on four different films. It also claimed that Geraghty had not completely defined the Cheyenne character's traits during this initial episode, nor had he established the structure of the series. His script had not formed a prototype, the studio claimed, because the defining features of the series had developed over a number of episodes.

Faced with this rebuttal, the Writers Guild expanded its case to claim that all of the writers who worked on *Cheyenne* during the first season actually authored the series and therefore deserved residual payments as creators.[51] Ultimately, the guild's arbitration panel ruled that neither Geraghty nor any of the other first-season writers could claim to have originated *Cheyenne*. The panel upheld the studio's rights to *Cheyenne* because the series was based on studio-owned properties. Since no individual in Warner Bros. management could actually claim to have created the series, and the series was not based on the movie *Cheyenne*, the television series essentially was defined as an "authorless" text—one without a creator or a moment of creation. Because of management ingenuity in protecting residual rights to the series, *Cheyenne* was defined by Warner Bros. and the Writers Guild as a series without a prototype, each episode a variation of a model that didn't actually exist. This became the standard form of authorship at Warner Bros.

Once the studio's TV operation had been established and the three series had been defined, Warner Bros. still faced a number of problems in running the organization smoothly and efficiently. Principal photography on *Cheyenne*, the first series to go into production, was pushed back from the first week of June to the second in order to complete the transformation of inexperienced actor Norman Walker into TV star Clint Walker. Along with rechristening Walker, the studio put him through an intensive weeklong course that consisted of lessons in horsemanship, gunslinging, and dancing—to help him develop the grace and poise needed to play a legendary hero. Although the "Behind the Cameras" segment would have seemed to be the least difficult aspect of the entire series to produce, the segment immediately ran into trouble when Warner Bros. feature stars—Alan Ladd and Gary Cooper, for example—refused to cooperate in the production of this promotional feature. In spite of Jack Warner's orders that everyone on the lot cooperate with the studio's promotional

With intensive lessons in horsemanship and gunslinging, Warner Bros.
transformed inexperienced actor Norman Walker into Clint Walker,
the star of *Cheyenne*.
(Courtesy of Wisconsin Center for Film and Theater Research
© Warner Bros.)

crew, these stars didn't feel obliged under their independent con-tracts to participate in the studio's new public relations endeavor. Only Warner's personal intervention convinced Ladd and Cooper that they should spare the time to film sequences for the "Behind the Cameras" crew.[52]

As production began on the individual episodes, the entire televi-sion division ran consistently overschedule and overbudget. No epi-sode of *Cheyenne* finished on schedule until production of the tenth episode, and *Casablanca* met its schedule only once in its first nine episodes. Studio personnel soon began to realize that Warner Bros. had underestimated the budgets for television production. While each *Cheyenne* episode was budgeted at approximately $50,000, the actual cost of the individual episodes ranged from $63,000 to $76,000. The figures for *Casablanca* and *King's Row* were comparable.[53] To make matters worse, the Screen Actors Guild went on strike during Au-gust, halting production on the series for nearly the entire month.

When Jack Warner departed in the midst of this confusion for his summer vacation in the south of France, he left orders with his lieu-tenants, Steve Trilling and William Orr, to keep a close watch on Gary Stevens and the TV operation. While Warner was overseas, Stevens began to assert himself, giving self-aggrandizing interviews to the Los Angeles newspapers. Stevens told reporters that he was attempting to deal with the fact that *Warner Bros. Presents* was strictly a low-rent operation, a characterization that Warner Bros. and ABC had denied. With reckless flippancy, he also joked that, nevertheless, Warner Bros. should be able to produce the best show on television, or the studio should be turned into a parking lot, with its executives as at-tendants. Monitoring the L.A. newspapers from his French villa, Jack Warner failed to see the humor. He sent a wire to Trilling demanding that Stevens be fired and immediately locked out of the studio. Ste-vens begged for a chance to speak with Warner, but the studio chief was in no mood to negotiate. He had already been dissatisfied with the production delays and cost overruns, and this transgression gave him the reason he needed to fire Stevens.[54]

Since William Orr had monitored the TV operation from his posi-tion as head of talent at the studio, Warner ordered him to take over the TV production and get it under control. In spite of Warner's desire to score valuable publicity on network TV, he couldn't afford to fail in front of a national audience or to lose money on a project whose sole purpose was to generate publicity. Orr moved into an office in the TV building on 20 August 1955, armed with Jack Warner's direct order to reduce the cost of each episode to less than $49,000.

Orr's first telegram to Warner demonstrated just how little he or anyone else at the studio understood television production at the time. In the wire, Orr explained the company's excessive costs by describing the unforeseen intricacy of assembling a television program:

> The many different component parts of this hour show—the opening, closing, intermediate cuts where Gig Young comes back for a few seconds at a time to make lead-ins and lead-outs, the commercials, the drama itself, the "Behind The Cameras," and, last but not least, the trailers for the following week's show—take a great deal of coordinating as everything has to be split-second timing so that the show will come out in exactly the right number of feet. It makes it doubly difficult to cut a picture. Just when you think you have it right dramatically, you find out you are over footage and have to start re-viewing it for places to make added cuts. Naturally, there has been much confusion until all departments—lab, duping, music, cutting, etc.—get into the routine necessary to turn these things out once a week.[55]

Because of the complications involved in assembling the program, it appeared virtually impossible to produce *Casablanca* at under $50,000 per episode, *Cheyenne* below $52,000, or *King's Row* for less than $43,000. After including the cost of "Behind the Cameras" and studio overhead charges, Orr reported, "the kind of show we have undertaken . . . will not be produced for $65,000." Given that Orr did not express these concerns until August—two months after TV production had begun at the studio—his report gives a sense of the uncertainty that surrounded the studio's inauguration of television production. Upon reflection, Orr reminded Warner that the program's financial losses could be justified if the desired goal of promoting Warner Bros. features was thus served. "Even though the entire series, including [summer] reruns, might net us no profit," he reminded Warner, "I believe the overall result for Warner Bros. will be well worth the expenditure."[56]

Warner Bros. was not the only major studio experiencing turbulence during the transition to television production in late August 1955. Twentieth Century–Fox and MGM also had announced plans to unveil prime-time television series in September. The major studios had come under attack almost since the moment they signed network deals, and many people in the media industries predicted that the studios would fail in this new venture. Advertising agencies, sponsors, the industry press, and even some individuals at the networks resented the majors' colonizing television with programs whose primary function was to promote theatrical features. Independent telefilm producers fired their own criticisms at the majors because they feared being completely squeezed out of the network and syndication markets.[57] Articles in the trade papers during the late summer further stirred up sentiment against the majors by revealing that television operations were not running smoothly at any of the studios. Along with the management shakeup at Warner Bros., both Twentieth Century–Fox and MGM came under critical scrutiny.

Twentieth Century–Fox had agreed to produce two initial series for CBS. The first, *Twentieth Century–Fox Theater,* was sponsored entirely by General Electric and was designed as an hour-long anthology series featuring weekly adaptations of movies from the studio's past. Like the Warner Bros. program, this series also would feature promotional segments, including tours of the studio lot and excerpts from recent theatrical releases. The second series, a half-hour Western based on the feature film *My Friend Flicka,* was commissioned by CBS, which planned to schedule the series after locating a sponsor.

Turmoil on the Twentieth Century–Fox lot came to public attention as early as July, when it was reported that the first half-hour episode of *My Friend Flicka* had cost $44,000—$6,500 more than CBS had agreed to pay. With future episodes expected to cost at least $40,000, Fox was on the verge of losing nearly $100,000 over the course of a thirty-nine-episode season. Similarly, the twenty episodes of *Twentieth Century–Fox Theater* that General Electric had purchased for $100,000 each were now running at $150,000, saddling the studio with a projected loss of another $1 million. Like Warner Bros., Fox had not yet considered the strategy of recovering such losses through subsequent distribution in the syndication market.

In late August, General Electric and CBS requested that Fox studio chief Darryl F. Zanuck personally intervene to reorganize the studio's TV operations. The first hour-long episode of *Twentieth Century–Fox Theater,* an adaptation of *The Ox-Bow Incident* (1943), had been shot, but—in spite of its inflated cost—it was deemed unacceptable by the sponsor, the network, and Zanuck. The studio boss immediately brought in Otto Lang to act as executive producer for the TV division, replacing Sid Rogell, who returned to his former duties as Fox's studio production manager, while remaining in charge of the TV division's business affairs. Zanuck recruited David Brown and Julian Johnson from the studio's story department to provide editorial guidance for a new set of TV writers that included Alistair Cooke, Mel Dinnelli, and Carroll Carroll. The premiere of *The Twentieth Century–Fox Hour* was postponed for two weeks, and an adaptation of Noel Coward's *Cavalcade* (1953) was moved into the premiere slot while Zanuck supervised extensive reshooting for *The Ox-Bow Incident. My*

Friend Flicka was in a similarly desperate situation. CBS had purchased the series for its fall schedule, and five episodes had been completed, but these episodes were so poor that the network couldn't sell them to a single sponsor. While CBS postponed the series indefinitely, Zanuck junked all existing episodes and started from scratch.[58]

MGM was much more ambivalent about television than either Warner Bros. or Twentieth Century–Fox. By waiting until mid-July to sign a contract for its first TV series, MGM wound up with precious little time to prepare for the fall 1955 season. ABC offered a one-hour time slot, but MGM chose the half-hour format because the studio didn't want to commit to full-scale TV production. MGM soon announced that its series, *MGM Parade*, would consist entirely of clips from old and new MGM movies, leading a *Variety* reporter to speculate that this halfhearted attempt at TV production, nothing more than the studio plugging its own products, would prove to be "the sorest spot of all in network-studio relations." MGM's ambivalent efforts at television production seemed to be the least-adulterated example of an attitude shared by all the major studios: Television was an electronic medicine show that deserved to be used only for hawking the studio's wares.

MGM underscored this belief when it chose for its inaugural TV broadcast to promote its recent release of the Stanley Donen–Gene Kelly musical *It's Always Fair Weather* (1955).[59] A wicked satire of the television and advertising industries, *It's Always Fair Weather* depicts both television personalities and advertising executives as shallow-minded boobs enslaved by the mania of the electronic marketplace. Throughout the film, commercial television is generally identified with the deterioration of the musical's traditional values, its utopian vision of community, family, and romantic love. The irony, of course, is that MGM, along with the other major studios, exploited the commercial impulse that underlies all network programming—precisely the quality that the studio's movie ridiculed.

Despite Warner Bros.'s more active involvement in television production, the attitude toward television at that studio was equally conflicted. Benjamin Kalmenson, head of the studio's New York offices, still had reservations about producing a network series, even if the studio's theatrical releases benefited from the exposure. "As a matter of fact," he remarked in the fall of 1955, "*Warner Bros. Presents* is in the nature of an experiment, and I'm not too sure that the whole idea is going to be worthwhile. The whole industry is in such a state of transition that nobody can be too sure of anything. . . . And if you have the responsibility that we have—with some negatives costing us

$5 million or more—you would be awfully careful about picking up the few nickels that television has to offer, when you are positive it will have a destructive effect by keeping more people in the home."[60]

Kalmenson's ambivalence about television, expressed even as Warner Bros. crossed the threshold into television production, suggests just how conservative a major studio could be. In spite of the conditions that had shaken the movie industry since World War II, Kalmenson was still reluctant to tamper with a familiar system in which the studio received most of its income from the distribution of feature-length motion pictures to movie theaters. As studio executives prepared for the premiere of the first Warner Bros. television series, they approached television apprehensively, neglecting its potential as a source of income and gambling solely on its ability to promote feature films. As Kalmenson admitted, the decision to produce *Warner Bros. Presents* represented not the studio's total commitment to television but only a tentative experiment conducted over the nation's airwaves. The major studios' common belief that they were producing extended advertisements set the stage for conflict among the studios, the networks, and the advertisers, who, after all, had to foot the bill for the studios' unprecedented promotional opportunity.

·VIII·
Negotiating
the Television Text:
Warner Bros. Presents

On the day before the network premiere of *Warner Bros. Presents,* ABC president Robert Kintner wired a telegram to his new business associate, Warner Bros. president Jack Warner. Kintner was writing before the studio's prime-time debut, he explained, simply to express his gratitude and confidence. Whether the program was judged a success or a failure, ABC valued its new relationship with Warner Bros. and planned to order a second series for the next season. Warner responded by thanking Kintner and assuring him that his studio was prepared to supply the network with more programming.[1] In this tranquil moment before the broadcast, both executives shared a small luxury: They appeared to be satisfied with their partnership. For the moment, ABC could imagine that it had purchased another *Disneyland,* another Hollywood series that would strike a chord with television viewers. At the same time, Warner Bros. could believe that it had finally navigated the rocky passage into television after a decade of unrealized ambitions. Kintner and Warner indulged themselves because they would soon face the judgment of television viewers, critics, and their peers in the motion picture, broadcasting, and advertising industries. After years of experience, both men knew that soon they would not have the luxury of wishful thinking.

At 7:30 P.M. on Tuesday, 13 September 1955, an image of the Warner Bros. studio, an aerial view displaying twenty soundstages and a sprawling backlot, heralded the premiere of *Warner Bros. Presents* on ABC-TV. As horns sounded a fanfare, the famous Warner Bros. logo grew from a pinpoint to fill the screen, and an announcer spoke: "From the entertainment capital of the world comes *Warner Bros. Presents*—the hour that presents Hollywood to you—made for television by one of the great motion picture studios." The screen dissolved to images of activity at the studio—cameras circling on cranes, carpenters carrying scenic flats, actors bustling around soundstages—as the announcer continued: "Each week Warner Bros. takes you behind the cameras to see how motion pictures are made. And each week you'll see a different story based on one of these famous Warner Bros. productions: *Casablanca, King's Row,* and *Cheyenne.*" With images meant to evoke a working movie factory and narration that promised first and foremost to reveal the process of Hollywood filmmaking, the title sequence introduced *Warner Bros. Presents* as a program about the Warner Bros. studio. In this sequence, which would be repeated at the beginning of each episode, the three continuing series appear to be almost an afterthought, memento mori recalling movies from the studio's past.

Introduced by host Gig Young, each individual installment of *Warner Bros. Presents* offered a complete episode from one of these series but gave top billing to the eight-minute feature that concluded the program—"Behind the Cameras at Warner Bros.," a segment offering backstage glimpses of stars like John Wayne, Gary Cooper, and Elizabeth Taylor, or an insider's view of studio productions like *The Searchers* (1956) and *The Spirit of St. Louis* (1957). Inspired by Disney's success on television, Warner Bros. continued to mimic Disney by using television to create a marketable identity for the Warner Bros. studio. Warner Bros. no longer functioned the way it had during the studio era—as a movie factory thriving with legions of contract employees—because of conditions epitomized by the rise of television. But like Disney, Warner Bros. planned to use television to revive its *image* as a traditional Hollywood studio, an identity far more marketable than its new identity as a distributor of independently produced movies.

Warner Bros. Presents debuted with an episode of *King's Row* in which the protagonist, a young small-town psychiatrist played by Jack Kelly, dispels the townspeople's suspicion of psychotherapy by curing a woman whose paralysis is the symptom of a childhood trauma. The "Behind the Cameras" segment featured *The McConnell Story,* a 1955 film directed by Gordon Douglas and starring Alan Ladd. The episode captured a respectable 34 percent of the viewing audience, but it triggered an immediate critical barrage from the press, which felt that it failed to demonstrate the production values and story-telling skills associated with a major motion picture studio.[2] When the first installments of *Cheyenne* and *Casablanca* sank below 15 in the ratings, the sponsors—General Electric, Monsanto, and Liggett and Myers Tobacco Company—joined the press in attacking the stu-

Warner Bros. Presents debuted with an episode of *King's Row,*
starring Nan Leslie and Jack Kelly.
(Courtesy of Photofest © Warner Bros.)

dio. "Their criticisms are so persistent and so severe," Kintner informed Warner, "as to raise the most serious problems for both Warner Bros. and ABC. *King's Row* and *Cheyenne* are far below the quality
of most TV. The series represents a below-standard operation that can
only detrimentally affect the advertisers, ABC, and Warner Bros. The
series has gotten off to such a bad start that it will take emergency
measures to make it a success."[3]

Instead of marking a smooth passage into television, the premiere
and subsequent early episodes of *Warner Bros. Presents* sparked a new
and often acrimonious round of negotiations among Warner Bros.,
ABC, and the program's sponsors. Informing Jack Warner that the
sponsors had demanded immediate conferences to discuss the fate
of *Warner Bros. Presents*, Kintner joked with the studio chief, "This
is worse than the picture business, isn't it?"[4] Warner undoubtedly
agreed. Since the studio's production agreement with ABC expressly

prohibited any sort of interference from the network or the sponsors, Warner was not prepared for the possibility that commercial television might force him to compromise his studio's customary autonomy in the conception and execution of its products. Warner Bros. had accepted the contract based on ABC's assurance that—contrary to industry standards—sponsors would not be allowed to meddle with studio productions.[5] Only after the program premiered, however, did Warner Bros. executives realize just how substantially the studio's traditional production practices would be altered by the intricate set of relationships which bound together the studio, the network, and the sponsors.

Although the sponsors were contractually forbidden from interfering in the production of *Warner Bros. Presents*, their financial leverage as the source of network income made it impossible for ABC to ignore their complaints. In commercial television, even a major Hollywood studio wielded far less power than did the networks and advertisers. Consequently, Warner Bros. would not be the sole author of *Warner Bros. Presents*; instead, the studio's first TV series would be the product of this new economic affiliation, shaped by expectations that each participant brought to the relationship. As the studio, the network, and the sponsors struggled to define *Warner Bros. Presents* in accordance with their own economic goals and differing conceptions of television entertainment, the ongoing negotiations forced the series into a state of perpetual contestation and transformation. How should a TV series produced by a major Hollywood studio serve the commercial goals of network television? *Warner Bros. Presents*, which Warner Bros. executives described as an "experiment," served as a laboratory for testing possible answers.[6]

Because of its lack of experience in television, Warner Bros. initially gave little thought to the ways in which the conditions of commercial television might influence its creation of a television program. Warner Bros. had two primary goals in producing the series: to diversify its production operations and to publicize studio features. Given the financial restrictions imposed by the network license fee, the studio conceived of the continuing series as undistinguished B-grade productions and didn't worry about differentiating its dramatic series from others on TV. Warner Bros. hoped to produce the least-expensive program possible, conceiving it solely as a framework from which to suspend studio publicity. The studio's economic interests and its previous experience in producing feature films led it to overlook the context into which *Warner Bros. Presents* would be inserted—its relationship to other programs in the network schedule, to the sponsors' commercials, or to the conditions of home viewing. The studio was concerned only with questions relevant to the task of organizing an efficient and economical production process. Within the financial and temporal constraints of network television, how could a major studio produce thirty-nine hours of programming?

ABC and the sponsors demonstrated a more complicated conception of the television text because of their familiarity with the conventions of the broadcast industry. ABC's approach to the TV text was more audience-oriented, defining the text in relation to the network's conception of TV audiences and their activities as viewers. How should the TV text's mode of address take into account its mode of reception—the domestic conditions of television viewing? The network felt both that the family gathered around the living room TV set was the subject of address for the TV broadcast and that the home viewer was an inherently distracted viewer whose attention had to be actively focused on the TV screen.[7] While ABC clearly granted the studio its promotional ambitions in order to acquire the allure of Hollywood stars, the third-place network intended to appeal to home viewers also by broadcasting the first filmed television series with production values and narrative strategies matching those of major studio feature films. At a time when all filmed TV series were produced on a shoestring budget, ABC hoped that Warner Bros. would distinguish itself by displaying the Hollywood cinema's sense of spectacle. ABC also assumed that the studio's skill in producing such Hollywood genres as the melodrama (*King's Row*), the romantic adventure (*Casablanca*), and the Western (*Cheyenne*) would give the network an edge in counterprogramming by providing an alternative to the other networks' dominance in such traditional broadcast genres as situation comedy, variety shows, and live drama.

While the studio conceived of *Warner Bros. Presents* as an autonomous text, the network and the sponsors recognized that the series should also be conceptualized in relation to network television's other texts—commercials and other programs in the network schedule. Concerned about the fragmentation of *Warner Bros. Presents*, they asked how the program could hold a viewer's attention during the many abrupt shifts from the episodic narrative to commercials to studio self-promotion. Similarly, ABC was concerned with the program's position as an element in the larger organization of network schedules. How would the series fit in with other programs on ABC's schedule and in contrast to competing programs on other networks? These concerns demonstrate ABC's interest in promoting two of commercial television's most significant textual characteristics: segmentation and flow. Critic Raymond Williams was the first to suggest that, in spite of the fact that TV listings set programs out as separate from one another, the television experience actually is not one of single, discrete programs interrupted by commercials and other intrusions. Rather, commercial television consists of a planned, continuous sequence of often unrelated images and sounds which Williams refers to as "flow."[8] From the network's perspective, flow developed as a programming strategy designed to hold the attention of distracted viewers by minimizing the sense of discontinuity during abrupt shifts from one of these arbitrarily connected segments to another.

The Warner Bros. program played a prominent role in ABC's strategy for managing the flow of its prime-time schedule. The network intended to counterprogram against the other networks by scheduling a unique hour-long show—a "keystone" program—in the 7:30 P.M. time slot each evening and then to build the evening's schedule on that foundation.[9] NBC and CBS were relatively uncompetitive before 8:00 P.M. NBC, for instance, split the 7:30–8:00 time slot with a fifteen-minute newscast and the Dinah Shore variety show, while CBS aired a game show, *Name That Tune*. ABC hoped to capitalize on the minimal competition during the time slot in order to capture viewers early and hold them throughout the evening. The same strategy had given ABC its first hit with *Disneyland* on Wednesday nights in 1954, and now the network aimed to repeat its success with *Warner Bros. Presents* on Tuesday. Because of the large percentage of children viewing television at 7:30, however, Warner Bros. also would have to repeat Disney's success with the younger age groups in order to garner competitive ratings and to set the stage for the remainder of ABC's Tuesday night schedule.[10]

Although the sponsors were only slightly concerned with the scheduling of *Warner Bros. Presents*, they wanted the Warner Bros. series to provide a suitable "environment" for their advertisements. That their sponsorship provided Warner Bros. with a forum for free publicity rankled, but they had agreed to the deal once ABC had satisfied their doubts by promising a miracle in which Warner Bros. would use its movie industry expertise to produce a program that transcended the constraints posed by telefilm budgets.[11] Expecting the same stars and production values as those found in the studio's theatrical features, the sponsors agreed to tolerate the self-promotion as long as the program delivered the highest possible ratings—at least equal to *Disneyland*'s 39 rating during the previous season.

After meetings with the sponsors during the program's first weeks, ABC's programming chief Robert Kintner sent a pessimistic telegram to Warner that turned up the heat in the laboratory of *Warner Bros.*

Presents. The episodes came under attack for their impoverished sets and generic costumes, their amateurish acting and clichéd writing, their bland visual style and confused editing. The sponsors complained most vociferously about the "overcommercialization" of the program, represented primarily by host Gig Young's incessant plugs for the studio. In his role as host, Young introduced the episodes, bridged the transitions between the program and commercials, and conducted the backstage tours. The sponsors felt that Young, like Walt Disney in his series, should manage the textual flow more gracefully, weaving the diverse discourses of narrative, commercials, and studio promotion into a seamless whole. Instead, Young's brusque narration contained constant references to the "Behind the Cameras" segment that concluded the program. Because the studio lacked an understanding of flow, the program's segmentation seemed too obvious, its organization too arbitrary. The sponsors' solution to this "overcommercialization" was to decrease the emphasis on "Behind the Cameras," a reaction they justified by citing the decline in ratings that occurred during the last quarter of the program.[12]

The critics and sponsors weren't alone in grumbling about *Warner Bros. Presents.* Even studio personnel recognized that it was less distinguished than other filmed TV series. Hectic production schedules caused by an August Screen Actors Guild strike, the demands of television's weekly broadcast schedule, and the difficulty of organizing the new television production unit left little time for perfection, and sometimes even for simple craftsmanship. *Cheyenne* made an inauspicious debut when writer Maurice Geraghty asked to have his name removed from the premiere script, which he felt had been ruined during the episode's production and post-production.[13]

The pace at Warner Bros. was so frantic that *Casablanca* director John Peyser didn't view the final cut of his episodes until they aired on his home television set. Like the sponsors, Peyser complained that Gig Young's insistent studio promotion created the impression that "Behind the Cameras" was the real subject of each episode and that *Casablanca*'s narrative was little more than an unfortunate intrusion. He was even more startled to witness the results of the obviously rushed and haphazard process of post-production. Glaring errors, the product of carelessness, appeared frequently. Black film leader used during editing was left in the final cut; as a result, the image intermittently disappeared, replaced by a black screen. In other instances, dialogue and action begun in one shot were repeated in the succeeding shot as the editor cut to a reverse angle yet picked up the character's movement or speech at a point before the moment when the cut occurred.[14] Since professional editors working for a major studio

generally wouldn't make such obvious mistakes, these problems indicated the studio's initial difficulty in adapting to the pace of TV
production.

Throughout the opening weeks of the TV season, ABC and the
sponsors applied relentless pressure to Warner Bros., reminding the
studio that less expensive new series, like *Gunsmoke* (1955–1975),
were drawing much higher ratings. Monsanto's advertising agency
mailed an article from the trade magazine *Advertising Age* to executives at Warner Bros. and ABC. Chronicling the shortcomings of the
new studio-produced series, the article warned advertisers that "buying a show from a big movie studio is no guarantee of quality entertainment." In addition, the article argued against "overcommercialization," stating that "a film company should not be allowed to compete
with the advertiser for commercials on a TV show the advertiser is
paying for."[15]

Representatives of Monsanto actually flew to Los Angeles for a
three-hour meeting with Jack Warner and the studio's television supervisor, William Orr. Since Monsanto had never before advertised
on television and had been drawn to this sponsorship deal by the
tradition of motion picture production associated with Warner Bros.,
it turned out to be the most demanding sponsor, expecting the studio
to make good on all of ABC's vague marketing promises. Surprised
that Warner Bros. had not delivered the anticipated production values or stars, Monsanto requested that the studio give the show a
"shot in the arm" by adding major stars on a one-shot or recurring
basis, thereby enabling the network to publicize the series more
heavily. "In my opinion," Warner told Kintner, "[the sponsors] expect too much. They left me feeling that they would be pleased only
if we could get John Wayne to play the part of 'Cheyenne' and com-
parable stars for *Casablanca* and *King's Row*." Warner countered ABC's
exaggerated assurances by explaining to Monsanto's representatives
the economic realities of the entertainment business. "I told them that
if we could secure the Wayne type of star we would be happy to," he
said, "but for the money they are paying us it would be just impossible. . . . These people are getting a good bargain for the $65,000 they
are paying us."[16]

As early as mid-October, distress signals echoed through the soundstages of Warner Bros. and in the hallways at ABC. "We are in a most
serious crisis," Kintner told Warner, "and by 'we' I mean both ABC and
Warner Bros., because neither of us can afford to fail in TV."[17] On the
West Coast, Jack Warner, William Orr, and the four *Warner Bros. Presents* producers huddled with ABC's vice president in charge of West
Coast programming, Robert Lewine, and with the network's Warner

Bros. liaison, J. English Smith, to concoct a plan for salvaging the program. The participants reached two conclusions. First, Warner Bros. had to make a greater effort to unify the four different elements contained within the program's general structure. The host's direct-address segments, the episodic narrative, the commercials, and the studio promotions should be restructured so that transitions from one to the other seemed less arbitrary. If the differences among these elements were less apparent, *Warner Bros. Presents* would have a better chance of holding viewer attention throughout the hour. Second, the studio had to clarify the narrative strategies of each individual series, both to generate more-compelling stories from the series formula and to hold the attention of the audience by increasing their investment in the episodic narrative.[18]

At this point, Warner Bros. adopted a number of textual strategies that had been established in broadcast radio. The studio began by introducing a dramatic "vignette" to lead off the program, a "teaser" that offered an enigmatic trace of the impending narrative to provoke the viewer's desire to experience the entire program. Orr described the structure and function of the vignette to his producers: "This is to be a visual device narrated by Gig Young consisting of exciting film, perhaps one or two shots, placing a slab of drama before the audience to tell them what our show is about. It should be brief, exciting, and dramatic." The vignette should not be merely an excerpt from the episode, he argued, but should be conceived at the time of scripting as a structured prologue to the narrative's first act. "The action in the vignette," he added, "can take place some time prior to the story's actual opening, from seconds to hours, days, or months, as long as it predicts the story to be told in the main drama and is itself dramatic action."[19]

A typical vignette introduces a *Casablanca* episode titled "The Return." Following the title sequence, the scene fades up on a low-angle, stylized shot of an unknown man in silhouette passing through large iron gates. As the man strides slowly toward the camera in a single take, Gig Young speaks in voice-over: "A prison camp behind the Iron Curtain. This man has been dead for four years. Now he lives again in *Casablanca*." The scene dissolves to a shot of Young standing in a book-lined study. "Good evening," he says, addressing the camera. "My name is Gig Young and it is my great pleasure to be with you again. In this hour, you and I are going to find out exactly who that man was and why he was released." The structure of this sequence suggests that the narrative vignette was adopted to solicit the attention of distracted television viewers and to focus it on a compelling narrative enigma. As a narrative device, the vignette may have been awkwardly executed by appealing so explicitly to the viewer, but it represented the studio's first concerted effort to devise a mode of address that responded to the conditions of television viewing rather than to those of the cinema.

Though forced upon the studio by the sponsors and the network, the initiation of the vignette marked an important moment in the development of series television at Warner Bros. For the first time, the program's primary emphasis shifted, however slightly, from studio promotion to the narrative episode that filled the bulk of the broadcast. Whereas the viewer initially had been faced with a seemingly arbitrary spectacle of narrative and advertising, this structural feature was meant to direct the viewer's attention to the primacy of the narrative. By planting this enigmatic sequence at the beginning of the program and by giving it authority through the host's narration, the studio hoped that the narrative would become the program's organizing frame, that the text's flow would be orchestrated by the narrative, and that desire for narrative closure would hold the viewer's attention for the length of the program, regardless of transitions among the program's many other elements.[20] By subtly shifting the emphasis away from self-promotion, therefore, Warner Bros. hoped not only to appease the sponsors but also to serve its promotional goals more effectively by ensuring that viewers would still be watching when "Behind the Cameras" aired.

Along with the effort to integrate the program's various elements by encouraging investment in the narrative, the studio made other significant changes. Most of them were borrowed from radio and were designed to support the text's flow by providing less-abrupt transitions between the narrative and the commercials. It was agreed that Gig Young would appear more frequently and would begin "to project more warmth and sincerity" in his role as a bridge between narrative and advertising. His introductory comments would be directed more toward the narrative episode and his segues returning from commercials would be used to reiterate the plot—another change designed to organize the program's structure for the distracted television viewer. The studio and the network agreed also on a standard format for transitions into commercials and back to the narrative. The musical score would punctuate the scene, bringing it to a definite conclusion, before a "gentle" fade to black and a fade-up would lead into the commercial—thereby providing a "graceful and unhurried presentation" to showcase the commercial.

ABC also negotiated another change designed to encourage viewer interest throughout the hour: Instead of being divided into three segments, the narrative would now consist of four segments. With this alteration the network could schedule three commercial breaks during the program's first half-hour, when competition on the other networks wasn't as strong and more viewers tended to be watching. This structural change also ensured that the third segment would not end until at least thirty-nine minutes into the program—well beyond the 8:00 P.M. starting time of the other networks' more competitive programs. In other words, the network hoped that the narrative's second-act complications would be compelling enough to carry viewers beyond the point at which they might switch to the other networks. J. English Smith, ABC's studio liaison, hoped that these changes, taken as a whole, would "provide a more smoothly integrated presentation which will result in a better pace, greater sustained viewer interest, and a reduced possibility of tuneout during the last fifteen minutes of the program." [21]

While ABC and Warner Bros. restructured the program's format, they also examined each of the individual series, since all three had come under attack. *Casablanca,* which starred Charles McGraw in the role made famous by Humphrey Bogart, was criticized for its routine plots, its superficial, undifferentiated characters, and its slow pace. As a partial remedy, Warner Bros. picked up the pace by chopping over three minutes off the second episode. Of course, this last-minute editing further offended the sponsors because the lost time had to be recovered by padding "Behind the Cameras." [22] The network thought that *King's Row* should branch out from the central psychiatrist character and generate future narratives by focusing also on other characters in the community. "I suggest this possibility," Kintner remarked, "because there has been so much question about whether the stories directly tied to the young psychiatrist can have an interest for the entire family, including children." Jack Warner responded, "We do not and never did intend to make *King's Row* a series on psychiatry. It is and will be more of an anthology . . . with stories of different residents of the city." [23]

The negotiations over *King's Row* explicitly introduced the question of the intended audience for *Warner Bros. Presents* and suggested to studio executives that ABC had conflicting ideas about how to use the studio most effectively. ABC had signed the production agreement with Warner Bros. in part because of the studio's reputation for sophisticated genre films. The network had selected *Casablanca* and *King's Row,* a romance and a melodrama, because of their appeal to a mature audience. Later, the network had marketed the program to sponsors by emphasizing that the studio's legacy of high-quality production would provide a sophisticated environment for their advertisements. At the same time, however, ABC primarily wanted to build a unified schedule that would attract steady, routinized viewership. Instead of developing a few random hits scattered throughout the schedule, the network intended to structure its schedule around nightly blocks of programming anchored by the leadoff "keystone" programs. Through contacts at the Young and Rubicam advertising agency, however, story editor Richard Diggs had learned that the TV industry considered the 7:30 P.M. viewing audience to be immutably top-heavy with children; television industry wisdom held that no program could achieve impressive ratings during this period without appealing primarily to the younger audience.[24]

Studio personnel argued that the network had unfairly exploited Warner Bros. in order to achieve conflicting goals. On the one hand, ABC wanted to market a "mature" program in order to entice new advertisers to television; on the other hand, the network wanted to serve its general programming strategies and was less concerned with whether the time slot suited the series. Warner Bros. attributed the program's low ratings not to its questionable quality but to what the studio perceived as ABC's misguided scheduling practices. From the studio's perspective, the audience for *Warner Bros. Presents* existed, but not in the time slot that ABC had forced upon it. This argument began to arise after a late-September article in *Variety* asserted that the program had faced a difficult challenge from the outset because dramatic programs had never been successful before 9:00 P.M. Richard Diggs began a running debate with ABC's Robert Lewine about whether *Warner Bros. Presents* would find an audience in the early time slot. "I feel that in our time slot we are in very much the same position the Theater Guild would be in if Barnum and Bailey asked it to play *Death of a Salesman* in the center ring of the circus," he complained. "I question if the finest script in the world would have much of a reception in this situation."[25] As Warner Bros. personnel saw it, ABC gambled in the face of clear precedent by forcing *Warner Bros. Presents* into the 7:30 time slot when a later slot "would have almost automatically guaranteed a higher rating."[26]

After listening to his advisers, Jack Warner confronted Robert Kintner with the studio's criticisms of network programming policy and chastised ABC for its contradictory attitude toward *Warner Bros. Presents*. Warner asked Kintner to explain why the network expected narratives that attracted mature viewers, while broadcasting the program at a time when high ratings were possible only by appealing to children. In his response, Kintner never mentioned the general network strategy that justified scheduling *Warner Bros. Presents* at 7:30 P.M., but he advised Warner that the time slot from 7:30 to 8:00 P.M. represented the greatest potential in television because it had not yet been dominated by the other networks. "Actually, 7:30–8:00 P.M. has the minimum competition that you can find in television, with only *Name That Tune,* Dinah Shore and John Cameron Swayze against you, and this is the real reason we have done as well as we have," he said. "If you moved to the 8:00–9:00 P.M. spot, you would be on against Milton Berle, Martha Raye, and Bob Hope, and, I must be candid, but I believe that would really knock your rating down." Because the network simply wouldn't move the program from this time slot, the problem of targeting an audience remained—and Kintner merely rearticulated the contradiction. "I agree with you that there is confusion concerning an 'adult' show vs. a 'children's' show," he admitted. "I think that what we were groping for was an adult show that would hold the attention of children who were older than nine or ten years of age."[27]

Cheyenne, in particular, suffered from the tension of trying to create a series that would appeal to both children and adults. When the market for television programming opened in the late 1940s, the producers of B Westerns were among the first to fill the new programming needs. By the mid-1950s, low-budget cowboy stars like William "Hopalong Cassidy" Boyd, Roy Rogers, and Gene Autry had resurrected themselves as TV stars. In short measure, new TV Western series, such as *The Lone Ranger* (1949–1957), *The Cisco Kid, Wild Bill Hickok,* and *The Adventures of Rin Tin Tin,* filled the airwaves. As more independent telefilm producers turned to the Western genre because of its adaptability to low-budget production, the B Western's backlot landscapes, shrieking Indian raids, and stolid lawmen epitomized the worst of television programming to those who disparaged the new medium.[28]

At the same time, however, the motion picture industry was developing a contrasting variation of the Western genre, a type that came to be known as the "adult" Western. As postwar conditions in the film industry encouraged increased differentiation within the movie industry's traditional genres, Westerns began to employ narrative strategies more commonly associated with modernist fiction or with the contemporary American theater of Arthur Miller and Tennessee Williams—strategies such as formal self-consciousness, a revisionist attitude toward generic conventions, ambiguous or troubled characters, psychological conflicts, and ambitious social and political allegory.[29] The industry began to distinguish Westerns such as *The*

Gunfighter (1950), *High Noon* (1952), and *Shane* (1953) from traditional Westerns by referring to them as "adult" Westerns. While it is not clear how the term "adult" Western originated, the industry quickly cultivated it as a marketing device, and the popular press regularly discussed the features of this type of Western.[30] Managed to a certain degree by studio publicity, the discourse about adult Westerns constructed a subgenre with appeal to moviegoers who had grown tired of the traditional Western's most common conventions, especially as they were displayed daily on television.

Although the point is not to define the adult Western, nor to contrast it with other types of Westerns, one might roughly describe the early TV Westerns as emphasizing the same qualities that had always characterized B Westerns. Action and plot take precedence over dialogue and characterization. Characters are identified by a simple collection of stereotyped traits; they seldom display long-term goals or recall a past that impinges upon present events. Instead, B-Western characters exist primarily as plot functions; their narrative agency provides the most expedient support for the narrative's efforts to create and resolve conflicts. For this reason, narrative conflicts are generally unambiguous, enacted by clearly distinguishable antagonists— hero versus villain, cowboys versus Indians.

These intrinsic characteristics, however, do not really mark the differences between traditional and adult Westerns. In fact, the adult Western was defined almost exclusively by the discourse of the industry and its critics. It is important to recognize this because critics often have discussed the adult Western as though it emerged full-blown through a process of generic evolution. Historian J. Fred MacDonald exemplifies this approach when he discusses the rise of adult Westerns on TV by remarking that "adult Westerns were recognizable immediately by their [TV] sponsors."[31] The point is not that the adult Western was an ideal type that sponsors were able to recognize, but that the entertainment industry actively constructed the category of adult Westerns as a marketing category, to distinguish one type of product—expensive, feature-length Westerns—from the low-budget, formulaic movies and TV series which it resembled. For instance, during the 1950s Warner Bros. produced three different types of Westerns for three different exhibition settings. The studio financed independently produced prestige Westerns like *The Searchers* (1956), *Giant* (1956), and *Rio Bravo* (1958) for exhibition in first-run theaters, while producing its own low-budget Westerns like *Fort Dobbs* (1958) and *Westbound* (1959) for the second-run theater and drive-in-movie market. Finally, the studio produced its Western television series for

TV broadcast. Discussions of the adult Western genre in the popular press helped to construct a different value for each set of films.

The adult Western reached television during September 1955 when three series—*Cheyenne* and *The Life and Legend of Wyatt Earp* (1955–1961) on ABC and *Gunsmoke* on CBS—claimed the label for the first time. Along with the acquisition of new studio-produced series, the introduction of adult Westerns represented another of the networks' strategies for associating themselves with Hollywood's more prestigious products. The premiere episode of *Gunsmoke* demonstrated just how self-consciously the movie and TV industries worked to define the adult Western by calling attention to the expectations that a viewer should bring to the genre. In a sequence that appeared before *Gunsmoke*'s opening credits, John Wayne welcomed viewers to the new series. Standing behind a hitching post and speaking directly to the camera, Wayne informed viewers that this was the first TV Western in which he would have liked to appear. "I think it's the best thing of its kind that's come along," he said. "It's honest; it's adult; it's realistic." As the star of Hollywood's most celebrated Westerns for more than a decade, Wayne legitimized *Gunsmoke* by giving his endorsement and by explicitly labeling the supposed differences between the new, adult Westerns and typical TV fare.[32]

The ongoing negotiation of the adult Western produced many conflicts around the Warner Bros. series *Cheyenne,* which ABC's sales presentation had described as an "adult Western—featuring a mature story." The network invoked these terms to identify the series with a type of Hollywood movie that had been created in the first place to differentiate feature-film Westerns from their TV counterparts. By distinguishing its new Western from the low-budget telefilm Westerns that had been marketed primarily to appeal to children, ABC hoped to use the promise of a more desirable audience of consumers to attract prestigious sponsors. The contradiction for *Cheyenne* was obvious: The series was sold on its promised appeal to an adult market, and yet it was designed according to network specifications to draw an audience of children, an audience that would inflate the program's ratings even if it didn't supply the type of viewer most desirable to the sponsors.

For Warner Bros., the 7:30 P.M. time slot initially meant that *Cheyenne* should follow the narrative model provided by existing television Westerns. When the first episode featured various conventions of the B Western—infallible hero Cheyenne Bodie (Clint Walker), a comic sidekick (L. Q. Jones), an extended Indian attack, and a conflict based on action rather than character psychology the sponsors were not pleased. According to Kintner, the sponsors repudiated the series because it didn't provide the proper setting for the products advertised in their commercials. Liggett and Myers, which also sponsored *Gunsmoke*, cried that they had purchased an adult Western "along the lines of *Hondo* or *Gunsmoke*" but had received instead a mere "Cowboys and Indians story." Kintner immediately asked the studio to reformulate the series. Warner Bros. agreed without hesitation. "Some Indians may pop up now and then," Jack Warner assured Kintner, "but we are switching to adult Westerns." Kintner returned to the sponsors with news of the change and explained how the mistake had occurred. "While *Cheyenne* was attempting to attract an 'all-family audience,'" he said, "it will turn to an 'adult Western' conception rather than a program that is mostly designed to hold younger people. Perhaps the first *Cheyenne* was an error, but it was a legitimate error whose purpose was to try to hold as many sets at 7:30 as possible."[33]

For Warner Bros., the first adjustment in salvaging *Cheyenne* was to replace producer Harve Foster with *King's Row* producer Roy Huggins. At the same time, Warner authorized larger salaries for writers on all three series, and although script payments were still only $2,500 to $2,900 per episode, the increase enabled the producers to recruit more experienced writers who previously had been too expensive. After Huggins became producer, an effort was made to rid *Cheyenne* of its B-movie conventions and to emphasize elements of the adult Western. Cheyenne's humorous sidekick was unceremoniously dropped. Since the revisionist adult Westerns had attempted to remove the Western from an unspecific, mythic West and place it in a landscape invested with historical authority, Huggins tried to bring a sense of verisimilitude to the series, going so far as to order a dozen historical reference books, a "minimum reference investment" for the series.[34] He also commissioned scripts with plots motivated by character psychology, rather than simply by conventional action. The most successful of these was an adaptation of the studio's 1948 movie *Treasure of the Sierra Madre*. Once these changes had been made, Warner Bros. tipped off the industry press that *Cheyenne* had been transformed into an adult Western, hoping that publicity would help to resituate the series in the public eye. *Variety* reviewed the new *Cheyenne* in November, just one month after it had called the series "strictly kiddo fare." While the reviewer admitted that the episode "resembled a watered-down *Treasure of the Sierra Madre*," he also applauded the "astonishing" change in the series, calling the episode "the most adult of the 'adult Westerns' seen this season on TV."[35] By mid-November the effort expended to acquire the "adult" label appeared to have been justified. Although still action-oriented, the more reflective *Cheyenne* episodes began to pull higher ratings than competing NBC and CBS programs over the course of the entire hour.[36]

In spite of the improvements in *Cheyenne*, however, ABC and the sponsors continued to apply pressure to Warner Bros. because the overall rating for *Warner Bros. Presents* remained between 15 and 20. Kintner promised that the sponsors would stop complaining when the series regularly reached a rating between 25 and 30.[37] While ratings for *Cheyenne* easily hit the mark, those for *King's Row* and *Casablanca* were seldom much more than half that figure. In order for the entire program to achieve ratings that would satisfy the sponsors, both Kintner and Warner agreed that the weaker series—both of which had been designed to appeal to women—would have to undergo further alterations.

After meeting with sponsors, Kintner complained to William Orr that *King's Row* had become too nostalgic and sweet-tempered, that the series was not "sufficiently lusty to be true to the era or to be attractive to the viewer." Later, he warned that the series "may lack appeal for the male element unless the stories are very lusty and combative." Following the network's suggestions, Warner Bros. commissioned scripts that introduced violent conflict and threats of danger into the pastoral melodrama of *King's Row*. Its soothing tales of moral welfare became "lusty and combative" as both studio and network sought "to minimize the serenity and gentleness inherent in the series." In one typical script written under this new policy, an escaped criminal seizes control of the local elementary school and holds the teacher and students captive during a lengthy confrontation with the police. Soon Warner Bros. adopted a new policy in acquiring stories for each series. In the words of *King's Row* producer Ellis St. John, the episodes for all three series now had to be "action stories that also appeal to adults."[38] This approach involved a startling departure from the original conception of *King's Row* and *Casablanca*. Although neither Warner Bros. nor the network ever explicitly articulated the new policy, its unspoken goal was to make *King's Row* and *Casablanca* more "masculine," more like *Cheyenne*, by adding action and the element of jeopardy to both series. ABC used the comparative failure of *King's Row* and *Casablanca* as a rationale for ending its efforts to appeal to women viewers.

While some of the changes in these series involved mere shifts in tone, the most interesting changes required major transformations in the narrative structure of *King's Row* and *Casablanca* and compelled the network and studio to question the development of narrative strategies for TV series. In general, the structure of *Cheyenne*, on the one hand, and of *King's Row* and *Casablanca*, on the other, represented two alternative forms of the episodic series narrative. *Cheyenne*, with its redeemer figure wandering from community to community through the old West, proved to have an ideal structure for generating series narratives and for appealing to viewers. In essence, this type of structure gave the series many similarities to the anthology format, in which a series consists of diverse, unrelated narrative episodes. In the case of *Cheyenne*, each episode contained conflicts involving new characters, and the episodes were unified only by the recurring character of the protagonist, who functioned as the force of moral order able to resolve any narrative conflict. Each time Cheyenne entered a new community, he either witnessed or provoked a new story in which he would participate to varying degrees. Like many of the telefilm genre series developed at this time, including most Westerns and crime series, *Cheyenne* could be described as a disguised anthology series.

King's Row and *Casablanca*, on the other hand, took place in the very sort of community through which Cheyenne merely wandered. Centered around a single location, a community with a fixed population, these series generated stories through the ongoing interaction of an established ensemble of characters. Although other characters occasionally entered the community from outside, these external figures were always peripheral to the episodic narrative. Like the conflicts in TV's situation comedy, therefore, those in the prime-time melodramas *King's Row* and *Casablanca* generally involved the potential disintegration and ultimate reintegration of the community structure. Warner Bros. and ABC began to feel that this community imposed too many restrictions on the series. Because of its episodic structure—a single locale, a limited set of characters, and the need to impose closure at the end of each episode—the series didn't offer the potential for a wide variety of stories. In addition, because conflicts were restricted to a small cast of recurring characters, the series presented few possibilities for violent conflicts or jeopardy.

King's Row director Paul Stewart had warned the studio about these narrative constraints before the series even went into production. Stewart worried that the studio's contractual commitment to five actors in recurring roles might restrict the narrative possibilities for the series, especially if Warner Bros. demanded that all of the actors be used in order to get the most value from them. "I cannot be too emphatic about this," he explained, "since I feel that as we progress with the writers, and we place upon them this restriction of having to create stories only about these individuals, we will have an ingrown quality in our shows."[39] The network and studio might have solved this dilemma if they had been willing to sacrifice episodic closure and transform these melodramas into the serial format of the daytime soap opera. At the time, however, soap operas were a somewhat disreputable form of programming locked in the women's ghetto of daytime TV. In spite of ABC's concern with demographics, the network seemed convinced that the appeal of soap operas was too limited for prime time and expressly prohibited Warner Bros. from producing open-ended serials for *Warner Bros. Presents*.[40]

Eager to escape the limitations of the episodic format, ABC repeatedly requested the studio to move beyond the cafe setting of *Casablanca* and the town of *King's Row* in order to stir up more diverse, action-filled stories. *Casablanca* episodes began to change in ways similar to the siege episode of *King's Row*. Narratives were structured around murder mysteries and characters in peril; deadlines were added to provide a thrust to the narrative. In an episode titled "Killer at Large," for instance, an assassin stalks a diplomatic conference taking place in the city, and the protagonists discover that the villain has planted a bomb scheduled to detonate at precisely 11:00 P.M.

Kintner offered the most fascinating strategy for diversifying the episodic narratives when he suggested adapting the screenplays of old Warner Bros. features to fit the series. *Cheyenne* had successfully adapted not only *The Treasure of the Sierra Madre* but also *Rocky Mountain* (1950), *Along the Great Divide* (1951), *The Charge at Feather River* (1953), *Bordertown* (1935), and *To Have and Have Not* (1944). *Cheyenne's* structure, however, made this sort of adaptation easy, since the lone protagonist either could be inserted into these narratives as an active participant or could be added as an observer. But the structure of *King's Row* and *Casablanca* did not allow such facile narrative transposition. Eager to guide these series in the direction of *Cheyenne's* disguised anthology structure, Kintner offered an ingenious solution. "Story lines from previously made Warner Bros. pictures might be adapted," he said, "even if a technique like flashbacks were used to get away from the set characters and into a different story setting."[41] Kintner's suggested use of flashbacks to diverge almost entirely from the established characters might have transformed *King's Row* and *Casablanca* into anthology series in everything but name.

By early December, ABC and Warner Bros. considered *King's Row* moribund. To salvage the series and add variety to its episodes, Warner Bros. weighed the possibility of shifting *King's Row* away from its established characters and making it a full-fledged anthology of stories situated in and around the town, featuring new characters and unrelated stories each week. From the studio's standpoint this seemed like a shrewd maneuver. According to the industry's agreement with the Writers Guild, Warner Bros. retained all subsequent rights to scripts written for an established episodic series, including serialization, sequel, and merchandising rights, but the studio held only TV film rights to an anthology script. In addition, minimum payments and residuals for an anthology script were $200 to $300 higher than those for an episodic series script.

Warner Bros. thought that it might retain all rights to future scripts and circumvent the extra payments by making *King's Row* an anthology series without officially declaring the change in format. The studio quickly realized, however, that such a strategy would not be accepted by the Writers Guild, because the union agreement clearly defined an episodic series, and a setting alone could not serve as the basis for such a series. According to the agreement, "'Episodic series' means a series of films each of which contains a separate complete story with a character or characters common to each of the films." Since episodic series were contractually defined as being organized solely around recurring characters, Warner Bros. feared that if the series changed in midstream from an episodic to an anthology format the Writers Guild might claim payments for future episodes as anthology scripts, and also might demand retroactive payment for completed episodes, claiming that the series had always been an anthology.[42]

Thwarted in the attempt to transform *King's Row* into an anthology series, ABC, Warner Bros., and the sponsors agreed in mid-December to drop *King's Row* from *Warner Bros. Presents* and to gradually phase out *Casablanca*. *King's Row* was replaced in the rotation by a full-fledged anthology series whose blunt title, *Conflict*, promised to deliver exactly what ABC thought *King's Row* had lacked. *Conflict* premiered with an episode based upon the school-siege script written but never produced for *King's Row*.[43]

Even though *Cheyenne* was broadcast only every third week and each of its episodes was buried within studio self-promotion, the Western series grew to be one of the year's most popular new programs, averaging a 33 rating by midseason. If its individual ratings had been calculated separately from those of the other series in *Warner Bros. Presents*, *Cheyenne* would have finished the season among the twenty top-rated programs. The popularity of *Cheyenne*, a solid hit in a year that saw the emergence of other hit Westerns like *Gunsmoke* and *The Life and Legend of Wyatt Earp*, demonstrated that the negotiations between Warner Bros., ABC, and the sponsors had at least generated a tentative strategy for producing popular series television. Still, War-

Cheyenne emerged from *Warner Bros. Presents* as the studio's first television hit. (Courtesy of Wisconsin Center for Film and Theater Research © Warner Bros.)

ner Bros. was never satisfied with its unwanted collaborators. Once it became apparent that the studio would suffer financial losses, Jack Warner lost patience with the network and the sponsors. He complained to Robert Kintner that Warner Bros. had not received adequate financial compensation for its program and that the series was still handicapped by its time slot. He also requested that ABC simply dismiss the disgruntled sponsors from their contracts and replace them with more congenial companies.[44]

The sponsors, ABC, and Warner Bros. never agreed about "Behind the Cameras," but other elements of the negotiations provoked Warner Bros. to consider the TV text as something different from the cinematic text. Prompted by its partners, the movie studio began to consider such issues as television's modes of reception, the TV text's flow, and the implications of series narrative. ABC and the sponsors convinced Warner Bros. to emphasize its episodic narratives in order to unify the program's unrelated elements and to sustain the home viewer's experience of flow. After gradually rejecting the ensemble series, *Casablanca* and *King's Row*, Warner Bros. and ABC found that

Cheyenne's disguised anthology structure proved to be the most effective conjunction of economic and textual practices.

Organizing stories around the wandering redeemer figure enabled Warner Bros. to create a disguised anthology series that provided the distinctiveness of anthology episodes and the standardization of an established character and a narrative formula. Because the series relied on only a single recurring character who moved freely through a backlot Western landscape, episodic narratives could be generated easily and produced at a relatively low cost. At the same time, the moral certainty associated with this redeemer hero proved appealing to the television audience at a time when Westerns were becoming the dominant prime-time television genre.

Whatever the moral certainty of its TV hero, however, the first year of television production at Warner Bros. was one of confusion and uncertainty, a protracted period of unsystematic trial and error in which the studio lost nearly $500,000 because of its inability to work within a budget established by the fixed network license fee. This was true not only for Warner Bros. but also for MGM and Twentieth Century–Fox, the other major studios that entered television in 1955.

Throughout the season, MGM and ABC tinkered with *MGM Parade,* attempting to transform the program into something more than a weekly advertisement for new MGM releases. As with the Warner Bros. program, *MGM Parade* began to emphasize individual narratives while devoting less time to studio promotion. MGM, however, did not produce original episodes for television; instead, it broadcast two of its feature films—*Captains Courageous* (1937) and *Gaslight* (1944)—presenting them in severely edited versions that ran over two half-hour episodes. ABC canceled the program at the end of the season and didn't bother to order another.

Twentieth Century–Fox experienced similar turmoil during a debut season that saw studio management twice replace the executive in charge of the TV division. After many production delays and considerable time spent reshooting early episodes, *My Friend Flicka* sat on the shelf until February 1956. In addition, the studio lost nearly $2 million on its flagship program, *The Twentieth Century–Fox Hour.* Although CBS renewed the series for a second season, a disappointed General Electric chose not to return for another year as sponsor.[45]

Together the three major studios lost almost $3 million during their first season of television production. This financial setback was compounded by the fact that each of the studios ignored the established telefilm industry practice of recovering short-term losses through subsequent sales of reruns in syndication. The time allotted to publicity in *Warner Bros. Presents* and *The Twentieth Century–Fox Hour* left the episodic narratives contained in both series with running times of approximately forty minutes. Since this length couldn't fill standard one-hour or half-hour time slots on local stations, both series were unmarketable in syndication. And *MGM Parade,* consisting solely of studio promotions, had even less value beyond its initial run. Blinded by their short-term plans for publicizing feature films, Warner Bros., Twentieth Century–Fox, and MGM produced something rare in the telefilm industry—programs that *Variety* aptly described as "properties with little or no residual value."[46] As the trade papers noted, it was already clear that programs could not return their investment during the first run; profits were made in reruns. The failure of the major studios to create a product with long-term value was an astounding blunder. More than anything else during the first season, it demonstrated how haphazardly Hollywood's major powers had entered the field of television production.

The popularity of *Cheyenne* was the sole factor that led to the renewal of *Warner Bros. Presents* for a second season. Yet neither ABC nor Warner Bros. suggested scheduling the Western series in its own time slot. Instead, it was agreed that the format for *Warner Bros. Presents* would alternate *Cheyenne* and the anthology series *Conflict.* The decision to juxtapose *Cheyenne,* an emerging hit, with the anthology format's unproven potpourri of stories provides the most revealing evidence of the ambivalent relations between Warner Bros. and ABC at the end of the first season. Kintner's rationale for the switch to an anthology format suggests that *Warner Bros. Presents* was still something of a laboratory for both ABC and Warner Bros. "Making these anthology episodes will not only bolster up the series," he explained while canceling *King's Row* and *Casablanca,* "but will give us a chance to study a different format for possible use in the 1956–1957 season."[47]

The decision to retain the alternating format showed that both companies were stalled in a holding pattern at the end of the first season. ABC couldn't decide what type of programming it wanted from the studio. Should the network continue to market the Warner Bros. name and reputation in the *Warner Bros. Presents* format, or should it solicit individual series like *Cheyenne,* whose episodic narratives would stand alone, unencumbered by the studio's hard sell? For its part, Warner Bros. was still uncertain of its intentions toward television. Was the money in prime time sufficient to justify a complete commitment to series production? Or should the studio continue to hedge its bets by producing a program that contained both narrative episodes and studio promotion?

When it came time to renegotiate the studio's contract, neither Warner Bros. nor ABC expressed long-term goals. Although Kintner and Warner had agreed before the season to increase the studio's presence in ABC's prime time schedule, no one suggested expansion plans during this round of negotiations. Instead of capitalizing on the success of *Cheyenne,* or laying the groundwork for other Warner Bros. series, contract talks for the second season determined only that *Warner Bros. Presents* would be renewed in the alternating-series format. The debut season may have enabled Warner Bros. to cross the threshold into the television industry, but it signaled neither a firm decision about the value of television production at the studio nor certainty about the type of television text that the studio would produce. With the studio's annual earnings holding steady at $4 million, it wasn't even clear that the network publicity had been effective.[48]

Only one year earlier, Disney had made the transition to television look remarkably easy—so easy, in fact, that *Disneyland* seemed to provide clear evidence of the social power wielded by media industries in the age of television. In Disney's hands, television appeared to be a spellbinding instrument of social persuasion. As Disney's sophisticated publicity campaigns reverberated through the electronic medium, the Disney phenomenon seemed less the product of industrial design than a popular mandate, the answer to a voice that bubbled forth from the American public and begged for Disney's indulgence. When Warner Bros. decided to follow Disney's path into television during 1955, studio executives were inspired by this fantasy of social power, driven by television's potential for channeling unpredictable, and increasingly unmanageable, popular tastes into a disciplined market for Hollywood movies.

But cultural events like *Disneyland* occur rarely. Although there is a tendency to describe the culture industries as economic and ideological juggernauts that roll across the landscape of modern culture, carrying out elaborate schemes to expand and consolidate their power, the truth is that media companies do not often achieve the calculated success witnessed in Disney's transition to television. Seldom has any media company matched Disney's skill in developing strategic goals, marshaling financial resources and technical expertise, and enlisting other media companies in the creation of a cultural product able to strike such a resonant chord with a wide range of audiences. The performance of media companies just as frequently resembles that of Warner Bros. during its first year of television production. Limited conceptually by assumptions and predispositions formed during the studio era, Warner Bros. executives responded to immediate conditions instead of developing coherent, long-range plans;

they struggled through conflicts with their new partners, groped to unlock the enigma of popular taste, and generally failed to achieve their single-minded goal because they tried merely to mimic Disney's success instead of making an effort to understand how and why it had occurred.

·IX·
Reviving the Studio System at Warner Bros. Television

The short-sightedness that Warner Bros. exhibited during its first year of television production did not improve when the studio agreed to a second year in 1956, nor even as the studio came to supply one-third of ABC's prime-time schedule by 1960. Despite a commitment to broadcasting that dated back to the silent era, Warner Bros. television policy during the 1950s blended a profound ambivalence for television with a nostalgia for the economic stability of the studio system. In contrast to Disney, therefore, Warner Bros. never fully calculated television's future influence in Hollywood. Reluctant to tamper with the movie industry status quo, Warner Bros. focused on short-term goals, gauging television as a source of immediate income and as an excuse to revive elements of the studio system lost in the transition to independent production. Otherwise, studio executives typically improvised television policy only when external events provoked a response.

Because Warner Bros. failed to formulate long-range plans for television, ABC actually set the studio's agenda, bringing Warner Bros. into prime time and prompting its expansion with orders for new series. As Warner Bros. developed an exclusive alliance with ABC, the intertwined fates of the two companies epitomized the movement by all three networks to forge ties with large Hollywood studios. By tapping Hollywood as a source of filmed, hour-long programs that were too expensive for single sponsors to afford, the networks imposed a new pattern of participating sponsorship, virtually barring sponsors and advertising agencies from the realm of program production and scheduling.

Thanks to the networks' increased reliance on filmed programs, the industry prospered, but power in the industry became increasingly concentrated in the few diversified studios capable of supplying the networks with a variety of series at once. The ascendance of major movie studios and a select group of independent producers—Desilu, Revue, and Four Star—signaled the third stage in the development of the telefilm industry, the period of economic concentration in which massive production factories replaced the small, specialized producers who had defined the industry during its earlier stages. In the tightened market that resulted from the networks' alliance with Hollywood studios, the networks began to consolidate power over advertisers, affiliates, and producers alike.

Warner Bros. welcomed ABC's patronage because network contracts made it possible to resume a full production schedule at the studio. Though a strong proponent of independent production in the movie industry, Warner Bros. used television to reestablish the mode of production that had characterized the studio era—signing exclusive contracts with actors and producers, rebuilding production departments and an administrative staff, reviving activity on the studio lot. This restoration project, however, took place within the context of broadcasting's rigid deadlines and tight budgets, constraints that turned the entire enterprise into a supercharged version of B-movie production. At the height of its productivity during the studio era, Warner Bros. Pictures seldom produced more than one feature film per week. By the late 1950s, Warner Bros. Television churned out the equivalent of a feature film *each day*.

Television's frantic pace demanded a regimented production process, and Warner Bros. rose in the telefilm industry through its sheer productive capacity, its ability to organize the most economical and efficient telefilm enterprise in Hollywood. The pace and scale of production placed enormous stress on the studio, taxing both the facilities and the personnel; these industrial pressures justified strict administrative control over every phase of the production process. Therefore, while other telefilm studios experimented with a variety of alternatives for organizing production, creating new programs, and rewarding personnel, Warner Bros. stood alone in its commitment to a studio-era management style. As studio executives attempted to revive, and then sustain, a mode of production from the studio era, Warner Bros. Television represented the last gasp of the Hollywood studio system.

Preparing for a second year in television during the summer of 1956, Warner Bros. lacked a coherent direction. Responsibility for TV production was divided between Sunset Productions, the official TV subsidiary, and the still-untitled division of Warner Bros. Pictures that had produced the first season of *Warner Bros. Presents*. Under the leadership of Jack Warner, Jr., Sunset Productions held a mandate to create and produce the studio's new series, but after a year of activity Sunset still hadn't sold a single program. In the meantime, William Orr's production unit geared up to produce another season of *Warner Bros. Presents*. Although the series had failed in the eyes of ABC and its advertisers, Warner Bros. didn't anticipate changing the format in the second season; once again, each episode would conclude with the promotional segment "Behind the Cameras at Warner Bros."

Network executives Robert Kintner and Robert Lewine spent weeks persuading the studio to change the title and to eliminate the "Behind the Cameras" segment. Faced with sponsors reluctant to enlist for another round of *Warner Bros. Presents*, ABC reported that the studio's reputation no longer reassured wary TV advertisers. "Our research department affirms that ratings will be better by titling *Cheyenne* and *Conflict* separately, rather than as *Warner Bros. Presents*," Kintner explained. "General Electric has wanted this for some time, because titles associated with film production companies have not guaranteed success. Since *Cheyenne* dominated the ratings for *Warner Bros. Presents*, a change in title would only help to identify the property and its entertainment value."[1] Warner Bros. agreed, but reluctantly; to discontinue the *Warner Bros. Presents* format meant losing the opportunity for publicity that had been the main reason to produce a TV series in the first place. In essence, by accepting ABC's proposal to let *Cheyenne* and *Conflict* stand alone, Warner Bros. redefined its role in television, becoming a movie studio that produced TV programming instead of one that exploited television to publicize feature films. This crucial transition—so important to the development of TV production at the studio—resulted not from a conscious policy decision but from an obligation to respond to the network.

If there is an explanation for this myopic view of television at Warner Bros., it might be traced to the conservative economic policies of the studio era. Historian Richard Maltby has argued that the studio system encouraged fiscal conservatism because the economic stability of the studios rested on a precarious foundation of costly, short-term investment in production followed by a rapid payoff at the box office. This financial strategy "led inevitably to short-term accounting procedures, by which studios wrote films off their books after at most two years, regarding any further earnings as windfall profits." Along with emphasizing short-term profits, these economic practices encouraged an allegiance to the industry status quo because the studio system provided the most obvious answer to Hollywood's "need for long-term economic stability to provide a secure base for short-term financial adventurism."[2] Twenty-five years of experience in the studio system had conditioned Warner Bros. management to accept the status quo while concentrating on short-term rewards. From the security of the studio system, Warner Bros. had been willing to imagine investing in television, but the uncertainty of the movie business following the *Paramount* decision discouraged even modest speculation.

The disintegration of the studio system, along with the accompanying rise of the blockbuster syndrome, had magnified the financial risk in moviemaking, while stripping away the economic stability maintained through vertical integration. The risk inherent in the industry's new hit-driven, "boom-or-bust" philosophy was exemplified by Warner Bros.'s 1956 movie *Giant*. During the previous two years, the studio had advanced more than $38 million to independent producers. By financing the production of expensive independent features like *Giant, Moby Dick,* and *Spirit of St. Louis* during 1955 and 1956, Warner Bros. suffered excruciating cash-flow problems, with more than $45 million locked up in unreleased features by March 1956. Those financial woes were forgotten temporarily when *Giant* became a huge hit, but even *Giant*'s success reinforced the studio's vulnerability in the new era, since that movie alone accounted for almost 90 percent of the studio's $3.4 million annual profits.[3] In blockbuster-era Hollywood a single movie quite literally could mean the difference between success and failure for an entire studio. Dependent on costly investment in production without guaranteed box office returns, the movie industry became increasingly volatile, and in this environment Warner Bros. executives may not have been capable of creating a visionary master plan for television.

Based on studio-era economics, then, Warner Bros. was accustomed to realizing quick profits from a movie's initial release. But by 1956 television networks, sponsors, and producers already had established a very different economic pattern in TV production. In television, the license fees paid by networks and sponsors for a program's initial broadcast seldom matched production costs. Instead, television had become a futures market in which producers and distributors gambled that profits lay in reruns, which promised untold rewards for patient and well-financed companies able to sustain a lengthy financial commitment. Independent telefilm producers like Desilu had produced their series on film in order to have a permanent product that could be distributed to local stations after an initial network broadcast; the wisdom of this decision became apparent as television's demand for programming fueled the market for reruns. In the mid-1950s Desi Arnaz and Lucille Ball became the first telefilm producers to earn $1 million solely from television when they expanded to produce series like *Our Miss Brooks* (1952–1956) and *December Bride* (1954–1959), while licensing episodes of *I Love Lucy* to CBS for repeat broadcasts on the network's morning schedule.[4]

Although there were no guarantees that a series would even survive its initial network run, those series that sold as reruns often repaid their investment many times over. Independent producer Jack Chertok, for instance, premiered *Private Secretary* (1953–1957), starring Ann Sothern, in 1953. Sponsored by American Tobacco and broadcast on CBS, the series earned a modest profit of $104,000 on the first 104 episodes aired in prime time. In 1955, with new episodes still in prime time, Chertok sold the previously televised episodes to Television Programs of America (TPA), a distributor of syndicated programs, for $1 million and a percentage of future sales. TPA subsequently licensed these episodes to CBS for summer repeats and marketed them to local stations that televised them in "strips" of five weekly episodes. In the first year of syndication alone, TPA grossed $3 million.[5]

Television syndication deals of this sort turned Hollywood topsyturvy. Because of profits from reruns, telefilm series with three-day shooting schedules and budgets of only $30,000 to $40,000 per halfhour episode could be as profitable as all but the most lucrative feature films. With fading Hollywood stars forming their own production companies or signing profit-participation deals to appear in TV series, many of the major studios' former contract players—cut loose from the studio system after the war—found themselves inhabiting the realm of the nouveau riche. Desi Arnaz and Lucille Ball, once contract performers at RKO, were the first to earn a fortune in television, but a number of former Warner Bros. actors also became millionaires in the mid-1950s. Ann Sothern signed a profit-participation deal to star in *Private Secretary* and received more than $1 million from her 25 percent interest in the series. As the president of Four Star Productions, Dick Powell became a millionaire when early episodes of *Four Star Playhouse* were sold to a distribution company in 1956. Even Ronald Reagan, whose career had stumbled badly since his days at Warner Bros., joined the ranks of TV's new millionaires when his agent, MCA, rewarded him in 1959 with a part-ownership in *General Electric Theater*, the Reagan-hosted anthology series produced through the agency's TV subsidiary, Revue Productions.[6]

If executives at Warner Bros. paid attention to the fortunes of their former contract performers or other independent producers, it wasn't evident in their plans for television. Warner Bros. was ambivalent about television because studio executives observed the paltry sums earned in the first-run TV market and seemed to ignore reruns as a rationale for long-term investment. The studio's failure to anticipate the value of reruns in the case of *Warner Bros. Presents* showed the residue of conservative fiscal policies from the studio era. This initially conservative approach to television production, then, set the pattern for many subsequent decisions about television. Warner Bros. consistently sought the most immediate benefits from broadcasting, only to lose out on the greater rewards that might have accompanied patience and a more careful plan for integrating television into the studio's future. Nowhere was this more evident than in the studio's decision to sell its feature-film library to television.

By January 1956, Warner Bros. executives believed that the time had come to negotiate a deal for the broadcast rights to the studio's library of feature films. RKO had opened the market for the major studios in July 1955, when Howard Hughes sold the studio's pre-1948 features to General Teleradio, the broadcasting subsidiary of General Tire and Rubber Company. In January 1956, Columbia began releasing features to television through its own subsidiary, Screen Gems. With mounting production debts, Warner Bros. management needed a quick infusion of cash and assumed that they should act quickly to sell the studio's library before a TV market flooded with features drove down the value. The studio first negotiated with ABC, but the two companies failed to come to terms. Instead, during late February, Warner Bros. reached an agreement with P.R.M., a metal-processing company with plans to diversify into media ownership through its subsidiary, Associated Artists Productions (AAP). In March 1956, Warner Bros. sold all rights to its library of 750 features, 100 silent films, and 1,500 short subjects, which included the studio's famed cartoon series. Warner Bros. received $21 million; taxed as capital gains, this windfall provided the studio with $15 million in after-tax profits.[7]

The Hollywood studios released their feature films to television using one of three methods: selling all television rights to the studio library as a package, retaining the rights and licensing them to a TV distributor for only a limited period of time, or setting up their own TV distribution division in order to retain all rights and to control syndication.[8] The most conservative approach was to sell the library outright, since this strategy traded potential long-term rewards for a quick payoff. Only Warner Bros., RKO, and Paramount took this route, and in each case distributors subsequently earned enormous profits by peddling the studios' legacy to local TV stations. Since the Warner Bros. library no longer held much value in theatrical markets, the television sale may have seemed like a handsome profit, but once again it demonstrated the studio's failure to imagine the future of tele-

vision in Hollywood. Within two years, AAP had collected $30 mil-
lion in rentals from the Warner Bros. library; it then sold the property
to United Artists for $35 million.[9]

The ambivalence that both shaped television policy at Warner Bros.
and strained the studio's relations with ABC might have continued
indefinitely had both companies not been shaken by management
changes in 1956. By early 1956 the Warner brothers—Jack, Harry, and
Abe—were uncertain not only about the future of television but also
about the movie business in general. Indeed, the brothers may have
ignored the long-term value of their feature-film library simply because they were seeking a liquidation sale instead of an investment.
Even as the Warner brothers negotiated to sell the studio's library,
they also decided to offer the studio itself for sale.

   During February 1956 the brothers arranged to sell their interest in
the company to a syndicate of investment bankers and brokerage
firms led by Boston banker Serge Semenenko, whose First National
Bank of Boston had become a major source of film industry financing.
The deal took months to unfold as both parties maneuvered for advantage. Initially, brothers Abe (who played almost no role at the studio) and Jack supported the sale, while oldest brother Harry opposed
it. Harry relented in May, however, and the Warner family agreed to
sell 800,000 shares of Warner Bros. Pictures for $22 million. The syn-
dicate would gain controlling interest in Warner Bros., with 28 percent of the stock, while the brothers would retain 10 percent and continue serving on the board of directors. Reports indicated that Harry
and Jack Warner would vacate their offices and that former Warner
Bros. producers Jerry Wald and Hal Wallis, along with independent
producer David Selznick, headed the list of likely candidates to replace Jack as head of production.[10]

   The agreement began to unravel, however, when the Justice Department discovered that one of the purchasing syndicate's central
figures was Si Fabian, owner of Stanley Warner Company, the firm
that had purchased the Warner Bros. theater chain. After the Justice
Department announced that it would block any arrangement that
involved the theater company's return to production, Semenenko
scrambled to locate a replacement investor. He discovered a candidate
at the helm of Warner Bros. studio in Hollywood. Although Jack Warner initially had been the one to inspire the decision to sell the studio,
he seized the opportunity to join the purchasing syndicate and to
remain in the movie business. Harry, who had been convinced by
Jack to sell his stock and step down as president, felt betrayed by his
brother's reversal, but Jack nevertheless joined the purchasing syndi-

cate. Since Jack retained his stock, the purchase price was reduced to $17 million for 200,000 shares. When the dust settled, Jack emerged not only as the company's single largest shareholder, with 10 percent of the stock, but also as the new president of a reorganized Warner Bros. Pictures.[11]

Following United Artists, Universal, and RKO, Warner Bros. was the fourth major studio to undergo a change of management during the tumultuous 1950s. Like those studios, Warner Bros. immediately felt the impact of new management. Shortly after the Semenenko purchase, the new board of directors authorized Jack Warner to begin an expansion program designed to take advantage of the new conditions in Hollywood. Warner announced that during the second half of 1956 the studio would concentrate on resuming a full production schedule by strengthening its commitment to the production of independent features and television series.[12] This announcement provided the first indication that Warner Bros. would consider expanding its television operations beyond the level required to produce a single network series.

During the reorganization at Warner Bros., ABC was experiencing unrest within its own management. As president of the parent company, American Broadcasting–Paramount Theaters, Leonard Goldenson had never been satisfied with Robert Kintner's leadership of the network. Kintner had been ABC's president before the merger, and network chairman Edward Noble had insisted that he remain in office afterward. From the outset, Goldenson and his colleagues at United Paramount Theaters had disapproved of Kintner's management style, questioning both his tight grip on the reins of power and his caution in building the network. Kintner's success was undeniable; ABC had earned an annual profit for the first time in 1955, helping to push the parent company's earnings to $8.2 million, a 74 percent increase over the previous year. Still, Goldenson complained that the network had begun to stagnate under Kintner's guidance because he was slow to capitalize on the early successes.

Goldenson gradually acquired more influence with the board of directors, and, in the process, he began to orchestrate a campaign aimed at removing Kintner from office. Following a spirited battle that lasted through much of 1956, Goldenson convinced the board to fire Kintner in October. Immediately afterward, Goldenson moved from his office at United Paramount into one at ABC and began to oversee the network's day-to-day operations, inserting Oliver Treyz as vice president in charge of the network and James Aubrey as vice president in charge of programming.[13]

The change of management did not alter ABC's programming strategies, but it accelerated the pace of its assault on NBC and CBS. Since Goldenson had been dissatisfied with Kintner's reluctance to take risks in acquiring new programming, he urged Treyz and Aubrey to be more aggressive. Within weeks of deposing Kintner, Goldenson secured $60 million in loans to support a bid for more-competitive programming. To signal the network's new ambition, ABC immediately signed Frank Sinatra to a $3 million contract for a live variety series. Teen idol Pat Boone was lined up for a similar program aimed at a younger audience.[14] Goldenson also vowed to strengthen his network's bonds with the Hollywood studios. Since the excitement of the ABC deals with Disney, MGM, and Warner Bros. in 1954 and 1955, the network hadn't shown much enthusiasm for cultivating its relationship with the Hollywood studios. In particular, Goldenson had questioned Kintner's failure to build stronger ties with Warner Bros. following the studio's premiere season. To demonstrate the network's newly assertive posture, Goldenson believed that it was essential to persuade Warner Bros. to assume a greater role in television.

Shortly after Goldenson moved into the network office, therefore, he dispatched Robert Lewine to Warner Bros. with instructions to purchase new series for ABC's 1957–1958 season. By coincidence, the management changes at Warner Bros. had prompted a new attitude about television, a willingness to accept television production as an integral part of the activities of a Hollywood studio. Lewine arrived at Warner Bros. in late October 1956 for a meeting attended by Warner Bros. TV production supervisor William Orr, *Conflict* producer Roy Huggins, *Cheyenne* producer Art Silver, story editor Jack Emanuel, and Sunset Productions chief Jack Warner, Jr. During the course of the meeting, the Warner Bros. representatives pitched a number of ideas for new series, including two proposed by Jack Warner, Jr., as projects in development at Sunset.

Producer Roy Huggins made the strongest impression, describing two series that captured Lewine's attention. Huggins first proposed a Western series with an iconoclastic lead character, an irrepressible gambler who resembled traditional Western heroes, except that he had "more than a little larceny in his soul." Like Cheyenne Bodie, the studio's first Western hero, this character would be a drifter whose occupation varied with his opportunities, but unlike Cheyenne, this protagonist would skirt the edges of the law, with the series being careful "to see that he cheats only cheaters and steals only from thieves." In his second proposal, Huggins described a private-detective series based on a novel that he had written before joining Warner Bros. The series would be distinguished by a new type of private eye—a young, urbane, intellectual living the good life in sunny Southern California. Lewine received both proposals enthusiastically and agreed that ABC would finance production of pilots that could be aired as episodes of the anthology series *Conflict*. In retrospect, this was a turning point in the Warner Bros.–ABC partnership. By approving Huggins's proposals, Lewine set in motion a series of events that ultimately produced two of the studio's most popular and influential TV series— *Maverick* and *77 Sunset Strip*.[15]

The October 1956 meeting represented a crucial moment in the institutionalization of television production at Warner Bros., the process by which television production changed from a speculative publicity gambit to an integral component in the studio's activities. In its efforts to divine the secret of Disney's promotional magic, Warner Bros. had up to now organized TV production on an ad hoc basis, with responsibility for television divided between William Orr's production unit at Warner Bros. Pictures and Jack Warner, Jr.'s Sunset Productions. By agreeing to create a number of new TV series for ABC's 1957–1958 season, however, the studio for the first time accepted television production as a viable source of income and a logical element in a major studio's production schedule. The decision to expand in television, however, was soon followed by the recognition that television production had to be organized more systematically in order to be profitable. The time had come to clarify the relationship between Orr's unit and Sunset Productions.

Under the guidance of Jack Warner, Jr., Sunset Productions had shown considerable initial promise. Along with producer Cedric Francis, Jack Junior had developed at least twenty prospective series by 1956. Sunset had commissioned scripts for pilot episodes of such series as *High Venture*, an Air Force action series; *96 Williams Street*, a crime series about an insurance investigator; and *Joe McDoakes*, a situation comedy based on the Warner Bros. short subjects created by studio director Richard Bare. By this time, Sunset also had produced a fifteen-minute presentation for another series, *Port of Call*, which featured veteran actor John Ireland and studio contract actor Dennis Hopper in a story about adventures aboard a cargo ship.[16]

Both Jack Junior and Cedric Francis envisioned Sunset as a stripped-down alternative to the parent studio. For example, Francis proposed revising the studio's traditional filmmaking process by learning from the methods of TV production. "I want to adopt a flexible, mobile type of shooting, somewhat similar to that used in live TV," he claimed, "even though there will be great resistance in the old dinosaur-like production departments at Warners." Jack Junior also proposed that Sunset, in contrast with the parent studio, form co-production partnerships with independent TV producers. "One thing we must determine," he told Orr, "is basic policy on participation series. Very often in the past we have lost excellent series ideas because we have not been willing to consider such deals."[17] Warner and Francis were never able to see their ideas put into practice, however, because Sunset produced nothing but a flurry of activity and a mounting sense of failure—an alarming contrast to the explosive rise of its most obvious predecessor, Columbia's Screen Gems subsidiary. Sunset had hired the William Morris agency to market the studio's prospective series, and Jack Warner, Jr., had traveled to New York to meet personally with advertising agencies, but none of the proposed series attracted a buyer.[18]

Sunset was able to convince ABC to finance the production of a pilot for the steamy jungle adventure, *Amazon Trader*, but even this modest accomplishment ultimately backfired. Hoping to save money and to gain authenticity, Sunset dispatched independent producer Thomas MacGowan to shoot the pilot in the mountains of Peru, transporting only a small cast and crew. The production turned out to be a nightmare. The wardrobe was lost in transit, the star came down with typhoid, and Peru's rainy season settled in just as shooting began. After finishing over schedule and over budget, the pilot was deemed so unsatisfactory by ABC's Robert Lewine that veteran studio director Gordon Douglas ultimately had to reshoot the entire project on a studio soundstage. When ABC also rejected the new version, the network and the studio shared the loss of nearly $80,000 for the half-hour pilot.[19]

Observing this debacle as it unfolded, Jack Warner decided to pull the plug on Sunset Productions, worried that its failures might reflect badly on the entire studio. By fall 1956 it had become evident that television production at Warner Bros. would function more efficiently if coordinated under one command. The *Amazon Trader* incident simply provided the final incentive to consolidate power in the hands of William Orr. "I definitely want our TV division to be under your supervision," Jack Warner informed Orr. "The making of pictures and the okaying of scripts is to be entirely in your hands. . . . I cannot make it any plainer than this, Bill. If you are going to sit idly by and have . . . others do things without your knowledge, we will have turmoil in our TV department. You are the executive in charge, as the trade papers say, and I want you to be in charge of everything that happens."[20]

The many failures of Sunset Productions forced Warner Bros. to reorganize television production at the studio. Following the *Amazon Trader* failure, Orr's TV unit, which was officially christened Warner

Bros. Television, assumed responsibility for developing and producing television series. Sunset Productions shifted away from series television and toward TV commercials. According to Jack Warner, Jr., the Sunset staff began to explore the possibility of producing TV commercials during the summer of 1956. Sunset entered the field "with a good bit of trepidation," but by November 1956 it had produced its first commercial, an assignment for Eastman Kodak arranged by the J. Walter Thompson advertising agency. Three months later, Warner Bros. fully committed itself to commercials by opening sales offices in New York and Chicago, announcing at the same time that it would produce both TV commercials and industrial films. In April 1957, the transformation became official when Sunset Productions was dissolved and reestablished as Warner Bros. TV Commercial and Industrial Films. Norman Moray, former distribution chief of Sunset, was installed as president, with Jack Warner, Jr., in charge of commercials. Within the first year of operation, the company hoped to produce more than $1 million worth of TV commercials.[21]

The decision to create new series for ABC had signaled a nascent acceptance of television at Warner Bros., but television production became a fully functioning component of the studio only after the demise of Sunset Productions and the consolidation of Warner Bros. Television under the sole guidance of William Orr. Facing a heightened demand for TV production during 1957, Warner Bros. demonstrated its new commitment to television by constructing on the studio grounds a $1 million complex devoted entirely to Warner Bros. Television. Opened during the summer of 1957, the new building housed executive offices, a story department, and editing facilities—with space enough to handle the production of ten to fifteen different series.[22] By creating a permanent structure to house the TV division, Warner Bros. sent a signal that the studio's ad hoc approach to television had ended. Preparing for a third season in television production, Warner Bros. was fully committed to television for the first time.

ABC ordered three new Western series from Warner Bros. for the 1957–1958 season, fueling the rise of the TV Western in 1957, a year in which fifteen Westerns appeared in prime time. Although ABC hoped ultimately to control all of the programs in its prime-time schedule, in this transitional season the schedule was a mixture of programs sponsored by a single advertiser and those for which the network simply sold commercial time. While one Warner Bros. series, *Sugarfoot* (1957–1961), was commissioned by the network in order to sell individual commercials, the other series, *Colt .45* and *Maverick*, were created expressly for sponsors.

Because of *Cheyenne*'s success, three new Western series entered production
at Warner Bros. during the 1957–1958 TV season. Pictured (*left to right*)
are Will Hutchins (*Sugarfoot*), James Garner (*Maverick*), Wayde Preston
(*Colt .45*), and Clint Walker (*Cheyenne*).
(Courtesy of Wisconsin Center for Film and Theater Research
© Warner Bros.)

Following the 1956–1957 season, ABC chose not to renew *Conflict*, the Warner Bros. series that had alternated biweekly in the time slot shared with *Cheyenne*. At the time, ABC offered to purchase a full season of thirty-nine *Cheyenne* episodes for the 1957–1958 season, but Warner Bros. declined. Since each hour-long episode took six working days for principal photography alone, it was impossible for the studio to supply a new episode of the hour-long series each week. Because Clint Walker appeared in virtually every scene, it also was impossible to shoot more than one episode at a time. Consequently, Warner Bros. developed *Sugarfoot* to alternate with *Cheyenne*. By introducing a new lead character and a second production unit, the studio could film multiple episodes simultaneously. In a gesture that would come to characterize the tendency to avoid risk at Warner Bros. Television, the studio designed *Sugarfoot* and the other new series, *Colt .45* and *Maverick,* as slight variations on the narrative model established by *Cheyenne*. In *Sugarfoot*, Will Hutchins played Tom Brewster, a goodhearted young drifter who traveled the West while studying to become a lawyer. Toting a stack of books and an aversion to violence, he shared Cheyenne Bodie's penchant for meddling in the affairs of others. But whereas Cheyenne usually dispatched conflicts with firepower, Tom Brewster attempted to replace gunplay with a gift for rhetoric—though he knew how to handle a weapon when persuasion failed.

ABC ordered the second Warner Bros. series, *Colt .45*, for Campbell's Soup, which asked to sponsor a half-hour Western. Wayde Preston played Christopher Colt, a handgun salesman whose travels through the West inevitably land him in the middle of local conflicts. Chris Colt differed from Cheyenne Bodie only in the premise for his travels. Otherwise, given the constraints of the half-hour format, *Colt .45* was a condensed version of the *Cheyenne* model, its half-hour episodes providing even less screen time to develop characters that were anything more than generic conventions. Because *Colt .45* had the smallest budget of any Warner Bros. series, Orr considered it to be the studio's "tryout show," the production used to judge new writers and directors.[23]

Maverick, the third new Warner Bros. series of 1957–1958, held a unique status as the only Warner Bros. series created in direct partnership with a sponsor. At ABC's instigation, Warner Bros. developed *Maverick* in order to convince industrialist Henry Kaiser to advertise on the network. Kaiser was a metals manufacturer who had prospered as a defense contractor during World War II; now he planned to become more competitive in consumer goods, such as aluminum foil. With little experience in television, Kaiser hired former

NBC president Pat Weaver in 1957 to coordinate and direct his company's TV advertising. Kaiser originally wanted to sponsor "prestige" programming, such as a series of feature films newly released to television. Together, ABC and Warner Bros. persuaded the industrialist to sponsor *Maverick* instead.

The three companies formed a partnership in which each company owned one-third of the series—sharing the rights to residual profits and merchandising. To purchase its share of the series and the network broadcast time, Kaiser Aluminum paid a combined cost of $7 million during the first season. Although Kaiser joined a partnership with one of Hollywood's most famous studios, the sponsor demonstrated little faith in Warner Bros., requesting a contract that freed the sponsor from further financial obligation should *Maverick* fail to achieve respectable ratings by January 1958. Not only did ABC receive its largest advertising billing in years from the sale, but it also got a viable new series that could be scheduled in the 7:30 P.M. Sunday time slot against the other networks' seemingly indomitable competition, NBC's *The Steve Allen Show* (1956–1961) and CBS's *The Ed Sullivan Show* (1948–1971).[24]

Maverick was a refreshing variation on the *Cheyenne* archetype because producer Roy Huggins created *Maverick* in reaction against Cheyenne Bodie, a character with whom he had become all too familiar during his stint as *Cheyenne*'s first-season producer. For Huggins, Cheyenne exhibited the worst traits of the stereotypical Western heroes who had come to populate prime time. Assuming that he was not alone in having tired of unambiguously virtuous heroes, Huggins decided to introduce a more complicated character, one capable of deflating the clichéd moral lessons that concluded most episodic Westerns. In a memo outlining the creation of *Maverick,* Huggins recalled that he invented the character of Bret Maverick because he wanted to "do a Western series with a hero who was exactly the opposite of 'Cheyenne Bodie.' A hero with humor, who gambled for a living, who was not concerned with the troubles of others, and who was, in fact, a kind of 'gentle grafter.' "[25]

Like other Warner Bros. Westerns, *Maverick* was not an absolute departure from *Cheyenne* but a subtle variation on its narrative formula. Like *Cheyenne* and the other new Westerns, *Maverick* chronicled the adventures of a charismatic drifter who was compelled—by the conventions of the genre more than his own moral code—to solve the problems of others. As a prime-time hero in the 1950s, Bret Maverick had to be essentially virtuous, but at least he displayed few traces of what Huggins described as Cheyenne Bodie's "irritating perfection." The wanderer Cheyenne Bodie sometimes ran afoul of local lawmen, political bosses, or self-appointed civic guardians, but he possessed the moral certainty of the Western hero and ultimately triumphed through the strength of his unswerving principles. In contrast, Maverick embodied another archetypal Western character—the gambler, the con artist whose only allegiance is profit, the trickster whose moral code is molded by expediency and self-preservation.

In nearly every episode, Maverick is an unwelcome outsider whose motives are suspect. Ultimately, Maverick's decency emerges, but he is neither infallible nor a self-appointed moral guardian. Drawn into conflict reluctantly, Maverick is a flawed redeemer who succeeds as a satirist, resolving conflict by revealing hypocrisy and stripping away the masks that hide corruption. Huggins claimed that *Maverick* was simply *Cheyenne* "turned inside-out," a satirical commentary on Cheyenne Bodie's "rugged individualism, lofty moral principles, lack of humor, fanatical courage, mechanical marksmanship, physical perfection, unflinching honesty, and commendable generosity." [26]

Though Roy Huggins was given considerable freedom to develop the series, he was never given credit for its creation, because Warner Bros. intended to control all residual rights to its TV series. Huggins had devised the concept for the series, but when authorized to write a pilot script, he was informed that he could not use his original pilot idea. In order to control sequelization rights to any subsequent episodes based on a pilot episode, Warner Bros. demanded that *Maverick*'s pilot script be based on a story property owned by the studio. Studio attorney Bryan Moore explained the rationale to William Orr: "Our plan for developing new TV series underscores the importance of developing projects . . . to avoid sequelization payment obligation. The only sure way is, when assigning writers to new series, to furnish them with nothing less than a complete story owned by us. It is not sufficient to give the writer a format, characters, locale, background, scenes, and other elements which are short of a story." Later, he elaborated: "Our initial or pilot teleplay should be based upon a story (nothing less will do) and the teleplay writer should not be permitted to create or develop a new and different central character. We must start with a complete story and completely delineated characters all of whom are wholly owned by us without restriction." [27] In other words, by leaving any room for the creative intervention of the writer, Warner Bros. risked opening the door for a writer to claim authorship—and ultimately to demand residual payments for the full series.

The entire process of series "creation" was really an elaborate fiction to which Huggins and other writers submitted by contract. The studio's goal was not to find a studio-owned story that actually would serve as the source for a series, but to locate a story that could be identified plausibly as the source, should series ownership be challenged. After searching through the files of studio-owned story properties, Huggins selected "War of the Copper Kings," by C. B. Glasscock, as the source for the first episode, and hence for the entire series. Using only Glasscock's premise, Huggins and writer James O'Hanlon created a new story by inserting the Bret Maverick character as an outsider who aids a community in standing up to an exploitative mine owner. Still, by declaring the Glasscock story as the source of *Maverick*, Warner Bros.—and not Roy Huggins—retained all rights to the series. Huggins subsequently shifted his original pilot story, "Point Blank," to the second episode.[28]

Along with developing new story properties, Warner Bros. had decided to expand into TV production in order to reestablish its pool of contract talent, signing young performers for television with the goal of developing new stars who could be used in feature films. *Maverick* star James Garner was the embodiment of the studio's strategy. After signing his first contract with Warner Bros. in 1955, Garner was shuttled through supporting roles in several low-budget studio features and in episodes of *Cheyenne* and *Conflict*. In early 1957, Garner was cast as Bret Maverick, but before shooting the pilot he was selected by director Joshua Logan to play Marlon Brando's sidekick in the studio's big-budget feature, *Sayonara* (1957). Although this casting decision sparked tensions between the TV and feature divisions by delaying production of the *Maverick* pilot, it also meant that Garner was on the verge of breaking out of supporting roles even before *Maverick* premiered.[29] In fact, when Garner returned from Japan, Warner Bros. quickly rushed him through the shooting for the pilot of *Maverick* and then placed him in a starring role in another feature, *Darby's Rangers* (1958). Between January and July 1957, when the studio began filming episodes of *Maverick*, Garner performed in two feature films and the series pilot. In a period when the rising salaries of established actors were driving up the cost of independent productions, Warner Bros. capitalized as fully as possible on Garner's studio contract—which paid him only $250 per week in 1957.[30]

Both ABC and Kaiser hoped to take advantage of Garner's rising fame by having him star in all forty of the season's *Maverick* episodes. From the beginning, however, Warner Bros. had informed its partners that it would be necessary to cast more than one leading man in any hour-long Warner Bros. series, because each episode required a shooting schedule of six working days. To accomplish the feat of delivering an episode per week, the studio would need two units in production simultaneously, and this would require more than one lead actor.[31] Warner Bros. agreed to produce as many episodes as possible starring Garner—and ABC promoted the series as though it starred Garner alone—but William Orr repeatedly warned both the network and the sponsor that the studio could not sustain production with a single star.

Warner Bros. tested actors for the second role throughout the summer of 1957, but ABC and Kaiser dragged their feet on approving the casting. In a late September meeting with representatives of ABC and Kaiser, Orr reported that the studio had reached a crisis. *Maverick* had debuted two weeks earlier, and already it was on the verge of falling dangerously behind schedule. With their backs against the wall, ABC and Kaiser approved actor Jack Kelly, who had starred in the studio's short-lived *King's Row* series, to play Bart Maverick, Bret's gambler brother. To assure audiences that Kelly wasn't being "sloughed off as a Garner substitute," Warner Bros. agreed that Bret Maverick would appear in the early episodes featuring brother Bart. As insurance, the studio also prepared a form letter for the press and angry fans, explaining that Bart had always been intended as a central character.[32]

In these early episodes, as Huggins later admitted, *Maverick* was still a fairly conventional Western. "It would have been too risky," he once claimed, "to break the rules right away." Budd Boetticher, director of a number of critically acclaimed Randolph Scott Westerns during the 1950s, directed the first two episodes of *Maverick*. The series may have appeared to be a conventional drama at this point, but Boetticher's vision of Western heroism still didn't correspond with Huggins's ironic conception of the character. "Boetticher changed the character completely in the early days of *Maverick*, and I never used him again," Huggins later recalled. "He was a director who took the cowardly lines away from Maverick and gave them to another guy on the grounds that heroes didn't talk like that."[33]

Gradually, Huggins gathered a number of collaborators who shared his conception of *Maverick*. Together, this group—which included writer Marion Hargrove, writer-director Douglas Heyes, writer-director Montgomery Pittman, and director Les Martinson—accounted for a majority of the episodes during the first two seasons. As Garner and Kelly proved adept at balancing a subtle blend of comedy and adventure, Huggins and his team gently prodded *Maverick* in the direction of comedy. In a well-publicized set of guidelines drafted for *Maverick* writers, Huggins described his hero as "a happy existentialist." "His motives," Huggins explained, "always derive from himself, never from others, or from the 'community.'" Huggins provided writers with instructions for breaking nearly every Western convention. "In the traditional Western," he wrote, "the situation is always serious, but never hopeless. In a *Maverick* story, the situation

The Maverick brothers: James Garner as Bret (*above*)
and Jack Kelly as Bart (*right*).
(Both photos courtesy of Wisconsin Center for Film and Theater Research
© Warner Bros.)

is always hopeless, but never serious. . . . The whole spirit of *Maverick* is out of Ben Johnson. Johnson got fun out of larcenous people and treated them warmly and humorously." [34] Both of the Maverick brothers were to evade honest labor, to flee danger rather than protect a woman, and to resolve narrative conflicts through subterfuge or dumb luck—while avoiding bravery whenever possible.

Huggins and his writers considered it their duty to puncture the Western genre, including both the unquestioned heroism of the traditional Western and the strained sophistication of "adult" Westerns. Writer Marion Hargrove explained, "If the average Western is a reaction against the realities of modern life, *Maverick* is a reaction against the unrealities of the average Western." Each episode of *Maverick* parodied the Western genre in general, but some episodes provided more explicit parodies of other TV Westerns, particularly such respected Westerns as *Gunsmoke* and *Bonanza*. *Bonanza* was parodied in "Three Queens Full," an episode in which Bart is hired to guard three women who are about to become the brides of rancher Joe Weelwright's strange sons, Moose, Henry, and Small Paul.

Gunsmoke, which Hargrove described as "the solid, solemn daddy" of all TV Westerns, came under attack in an episode titled "Gun Shy." In this episode, Marshall Mort Dooley and his rustic sidekick, Deputy Clyde Diefendorfer, attempt to evict the gambler Bret Maverick from their town, though Maverick has done nothing to warrant their animosity. As a suspicious outsider with a disreputable occupation, Maverick simply resembled the type of character who was often the antagonist in *Gunsmoke*. The episode begins with voice-over narration by Marshall Dooley, mimicking the narrative structure of *Gunsmoke*, but Maverick gradually steals the narration and the episode shifts to his perspective—from which Marshall Dooley's apparently sensitive demeanor begins to look like camouflage for a man who is really dimwitted, trigger-happy, and power-mad. By rewriting *Gunsmoke* from the outsider's perspective, *Maverick* gently ridiculed *Gunsmoke*'s "serious" tone, exposing the violent, formulaic Western hidden behind its grave facade. As Hargrove gleefully admitted, *Maverick* was engaged in satirical guerrilla raids on "straight" Westerns, though its targets couldn't fight back. "*Maverick* is perhaps the only Western that could do such a thing," he laughed. "*Gunsmoke* can do nothing in retaliation. It cannot parody *Maverick* without endangering its own impressive dignity, and *Maverick* has no dignity to attack." [35]

Aside from the initial casting decisions, Kaiser actually didn't interfere in the production, even though it owned one-third of the series. Kaiser and ABC gave Warner Bros. free rein with *Maverick,* and the studio passed that freedom along to Huggins, because the program was an immediate hit. *Maverick*'s second episode passed Steve Allen in the ratings, and by November the series also led Ed Sullivan in major markets. As with previous ABC series, *Maverick* would have been one of the season's biggest hits if only ABC had enough affiliates to compete with NBC and CBS in all of the country's markets. Nevertheless, Kaiser was clearly satisfied. After its first season of sponsoring *Maverick,* the company reported an 11 percent increase in its total aluminum foil sales and a 22 percent increase in its market share.[36]

For Warner Bros., *Maverick* demonstrated television's ability to transform an unknown, $250-per-week contract player into both a TV and a movie star. Watching *Maverick* pass its competitors in the ratings, Warner Bros. released *Sayonara* in December 1957 and *Darby's Rangers* in January 1958. In the course of a single year, James Garner had become a national sensation. To capitalize on Garner's growing fame, Warner Bros. immediately rushed him into another feature, *Up Periscope* (1959), which was filmed during the summer hiatus that followed the first season of *Maverick*.

The only cloud on the horizon at the end of the first season appeared when Roy Huggins began to question his status at Warner Bros. In order to maintain the quality of *Maverick*, Huggins personally rewrote almost every episode and contributed more than half of the original stories—without receiving credit or royalty payments. In addition, Huggins wrote the pilot scripts for *Maverick*, *Colt .45*, and the private detective series *77 Sunset Strip*, which was in development at the studio. Considering that he also had guided *Cheyenne* through its first-season transformation into a hit, Huggins came to the not-unreasonable conclusion that Warner Bros. hadn't adequately compensated him for extraordinary service. According to his lawyer, Huggins wanted to be recognized as "the man who conceived *Maverick*, produced the pilot, and gave it the style that has set it apart from the other Westerns on the air."

In February 1958, with negotiations deadlocked, Huggins asked to be released from his contract. If Warner Bros. wouldn't release him, he warned, he would refuse to write another *Maverick* script; following the letter of his contract, he would only supervise production. Reluctantly, Orr renegotiated Huggins's contract in March 1958, nearly doubling his salary, to $1,100 per week.[37] This particular crisis was averted, but it set the stage for more problems to come as Warner Bros. attempted to sustain the studio system's use of long-term exclusive contracts at a time when its producers and actors couldn't fail to notice the rewards reaped by others in the television industry.

The second major crisis at Warner Bros. Television followed close on the heels of the dispute with Roy Huggins. In May 1958 Clint Walker, the star of *Cheyenne*, demanded to renegotiate his contract before he would return for another season. Walker had signed his first contract with Warner Bros. in 1955 as a virtual unknown and had received an initial salary of $175 per week, which rose to $500 per

week the following year.[38] After the second season of *Cheyenne,* Warner Bros. decided to capitalize on Walker's rising popularity by casting him in a feature film, *Fort Dobbs* (1958), which was shot on location during his summer hiatus from the series. By the time Walker
ended his third season of *Cheyenne,* he had begun to chafe under the
conditions of the studio's seven-year contracts. Walker timed his
ultimatum carefully, assuming that he had acquired leverage power
with the studio once *Cheyenne* finished the 1957–1958 season among
the twenty top-rated series and as ABC's second-highest-rated series
after *The Life and Legend of Wyatt Earp.*

Warner Bros. had entered television production determined to develop inexpensive contract performers and not to use established
stars. Consequently, William Orr, who had been the studio's talent
director before taking over the television division, believed that the
division's primary duty was to build stars, while enforcing term contracts in order to suppress the inflationary contract demands that inevitably accompanied stardom. Orr described the studio's strategy in
an article titled "The TV Stairway to Stardom," published in the *Hollywood Reporter*: "Under a policy set by Jack L. Warner, the studio
combines motion pictures and television in the development of new
talent and new stars. . . . Since the entrance of the major motion
picture companies into television, it has become possible to develop
more stars in a shorter period of time than ever before in the history
of the entertainment business."[39] Under the terms of the studio's
contracts, actors were required to work forty weeks per year in any
vehicle selected for them by the studio—whether it be television or
feature films. The first significant integration of movie and TV production at Warner Bros., therefore, centered on the use of contract
performers.

Some agents countered the studio's policy by attempting to negotiate separate movie and TV contracts that would pay their clients a
larger salary for feature-film work, but Warner Bros. refused to make
such deals. "Whatever the salary is," Orr stated, "it encompasses all
phases of film production. I have fought very hard with agents to sign
people to all-encompassing contracts . . . our stand being that TV is
not a sideline with Warner Bros. but an important adjunct to the
building of solid careers."[40] For their services in television, the studio's new contract actors received only a salary and the Screen Actors
Guild minimum residual payment per episode. The studio had no
intention of sharing profits with actors.

When not engaged in production, Warner Bros. TV stars still
earned money for the studio. When they made personal appearances,
the studio received half of their earnings. In this way, the studio ac-

tually forced the actors to pay a percentage of their own salaries, since the money earned by the studio through an actor's personal appearances could be channeled back into paying the actor's salary. As one studio executive explained it, "If we clear $10,000 from appearances by actors when we pay $50,000 per year, the actor really only costs us $40,000." [41] The studio also earned money from its performers by licensing their likenesses for use on trademark merchandise such as comic books, games, and toys—for which the performer received nothing more than the SAG minimum royalty. In addition, the TV stars were encouraged to exploit their popularity by launching recording careers, but they were obliged to record for Warner Bros. Records—which, again, channeled the largest portion of their earnings back to the studio. Warner Bros. justified these restrictive contractual conditions by arguing that the studio was almost completely responsible for the market value of its actors; its guidance and marketing skills had delivered them from anonymity to stardom.

Clint Walker became the first Warner Bros. performer to revolt against this new manifestation of the star system, simply because he was the first star to emerge at Warner Bros. Television. Walker decided to hold out for an entirely different kind of contract, with provisions that gave him a larger percentage of residuals and merchandising profits, more time off between productions, the right to make public appearances without returning half the earnings to the studio, and the freedom to sign a separate recording contract. Walker's salary had reached $1,250 per week, but his residual payments remained at the SAG minimum. Walker noted that equally popular Western stars, like James Arness from *Gunsmoke* and Hugh O'Brian from *The Life and Legend of Wyatt Earp*, collected a percentage of the profits from their programs and retained all of their earnings from personal appearances. "Television is a vicious, tiring business," Walker lamented, "and all I'm asking is a fair share." Announcing that he was prepared, if necessary, to return to his previous occupation as a carpenter until his contract expired in 1962, Walker refused to work for the entire 1958–1959 season. [42]

From the perspective of Warner Bros. management, there was only one possible response to Walker's demands. If Walker succeeded in "blackmailing" the studio, as management perceived his holdout, the entire television division would collapse as each rising Warner Bros. star in succession demanded a larger piece of the studio's TV profits. After meeting with representatives of ABC and its advertisers, Orr acted swiftly, replacing Walker in *Cheyenne*. Though the series was still titled *Cheyenne* through the entire season, Cheyenne Bodie disappeared without a trace. In his place, Warner Bros. simply substituted a new heroic loner, Bronco Layne, played by energetic new-comer Ty Hardin, while offering virtually no narrative justification for the change. Warner Bros. received some puzzled fan mail questioning Cheyenne's absence from a series that still carried his name, but the studio sustained an entire season without Walker—and finished among the top twenty programs—by interspersing episodes featuring Bronco Layne with reruns of *Cheyenne* from previous seasons.

Warner Bros. was so successful in calling Walker's bluff that it repeated the tactic later in the season when Wayde Preston walked off the set of *Colt .45*, complaining about mediocre scripts and lousy pay. Though Preston had already filmed eight of the season's episodes, Orr simply replaced him in the series with Donald May, another contract actor. Preston never returned to the lot. Television viewers received no explanation within the series narrative when Christopher Colt ceased being the protagonist of *Colt .45*, and the series began to chronicle the exploits of his previously unmentioned cousin, Sam Colt, Jr.[43]

By the time ABC and Warner Bros. entered into negotiations about the 1958–1959 season, the studio's fourth year in television, the network and the studio had formed an exclusive relationship that proved to be mutually advantageous. So closely had Warner Bros. and ABC begun to collaborate that they never signed a production agreement after the second season. Even the contract for *Maverick*, which included Kaiser as a partner, was drafted but never officially approved. Subsequently, ABC and Warner Bros. shared a handshake agreement that gave ABC the right of first refusal on all Warner Bros. series. As their relationship grew more informal, the two companies became increasingly intertwined. Warner Bros. agreed to share merchandising and syndication rights with ABC in exchange for network financing on pilots. Beginning with *Colt .45* and *Maverick*, therefore, ABC participated in the subsidiary rights to every subsequent Warner Bros. series.[44]

Executives at Warner Bros. felt responsible for much of the network's success and hoped that the network would demonstrate its appreciation when it came time to bargain over license fees. In a lengthy memo outlining the studio's position in negotiations, William Orr reminded his staff, "Up to this point, Warner Bros. has not failed to deliver anything but top-grade merchandise to ABC." Even on *Warner Bros. Presents*, its least successful effort, the studio had provided "complete cooperation in changing, shifting, complying, conceiving, and spending in order to constantly improve the show." Pointing out that *Cheyenne* was network television's top-rated series in markets with affiliates for all three networks, Orr argued that Warner Bros. series would be among the highest-rated in prime time if only ABC had more affiliates. Orr also noted that many of ABC's more expensive gambles had failed, while the Warner Bros. series succeeded. "We have had no failures [this season]," he said, "whereas a show such as *Frank Sinatra,* for which fantastic sums of money were paid, has constantly been three or four ratings points lower than *Colt .45* [the lowest-rated Warner Bros. series]."[45]

For the 1958–1959 season ABC renewed all of the Warner Bros. series from the previous season: *Cheyenne* (without Clint Walker) and *Sugarfoot* (which would continue to alternate with *Cheyenne*), *Maverick*, and *Colt .45*. In addition, the network ordered two new series: *Lawman* and *77 Sunset Strip*. A half-hour series, *Lawman* contributed to the glut of Westerns that flooded TV during 1958, when twenty-four different Western series appeared in prime time. Starring John Russell as Marshal Dan Troop and Peter Brown as young Deputy Johnny McKay, *Lawman* was set in Laramie, Wyoming, and was the first Warner Bros. Western to depart from the *Cheyenne* archetype. Instead, *Lawman* bore a striking resemblance to *Gunsmoke*, the other archetype for TV Westerns. A towering, solemn figure, armed with a piercing stare and an unwavering sense of dignity, Russell played Dan Troop as a frontier patriarch, maintaining law and order in a town routinely beset by the sort of drifters who starred in the other Warner Bros. series.

With *77 Sunset Strip* Warner Bros. escaped the Western genre for the first time since *Cheyenne* had emerged as the breakout hit in *Warner Bros. Presents*. Created by Roy Huggins, who once again received no official credit, *77 Sunset Strip* shared the same self-deprecating humor that distinguished *Maverick* from other TV Westerns. Although never as sharply satirical as *Maverick*, *77 Sunset Strip* revived the crime genre on television simply by injecting humor into a genre trapped under the influence of *Dragnet's* grim rites of law and order. Before *77 Sunset Strip* appeared, even new crime series like *Naked City* seemed duty-bound to maintain a tone of humorless determination. Along with *Richard Diamond, Private Detective* and *Peter Gunn,* which were both produced by Blake Edwards and which also premiered at almost the same time, *77 Sunset Strip* transformed the TV crime genre by substituting an updated version of the hard-boiled private detective for the stolid cops who governed most crime series. The blend of action and humor introduced by these new private eyes soon spread throughout prime time—and is still the predominant characteristic of TV's private-detective genre.

77 Sunset Strip evolved through many stages on its way to becoming a TV series. Before arriving at Warner Bros., Roy Huggins had written crime fiction, published in popular magazines and novels. Stuart Bailey, the protagonist of *77 Sunset Strip*, first appeared in Huggins's 1952 *Esquire* story "Death and the Skylark." When ABC offered to finance the development of a detective series in October 1956, Huggins adapted this story as an episode of *Conflict* titled "Anything for Money," which starred Efrem Zimbalist, Jr., as Stuart Bailey. In this version, Bailey was not officially a private detective but more a thrill-seeker who falls into a crime investigation; he also wasn't yet located at the Hollywood address made famous by the series.[46] ABC chose not to add the series to its fall 1957 schedule, but Warner Bros. liked the premise enough to produce another pilot episode at its own expense.

In spring 1958, William Orr authorized Huggins to produce a new ninety-minute pilot film starring Zimbalist. Huggins borrowed Marion Hargrove from *Maverick* to adapt one of his unpublished stories, "Girl on the Run." The pilot was shot in eleven days during early 1958 on a budget of only $130,000. In this version, Stuart Bailey works alone to protect a young woman who has witnessed a mob-related murder. He has no partner, and his office is fairly seedy. Although different in many ways from the series that followed, the episode does establish that Bailey holds a Ph.D. in Indo-European Languages, and that he would have been the youngest Ph.D. in the history of Columbia University had World War II not intervened. After serving in the OSS during the war, he tried to take a position in the hallowed halls of an Ivy League school but realized that he couldn't be happy in such "cloistered surroundings." Thus he became a private detective. Although he is not surrounded by the attributes of wealth, Bailey is a seasoned traveler, a gourmet chef, a man of considerable worldliness.

In July 1958, ABC finally decided to pick up the series for an October premiere. In the limited amount of time before the broadcast, Warner Bros. made a number of changes to supplement the cast and strengthen the series' Hollywood location. First, Orr suggested adding a second detective to the agency in order to speed the pace of production—just as the studio had added Jack Kelly to *Maverick*—and also to ensure against a replay of Clint Walker's holdout. By this time, Orr wanted to guarantee that no single actor could throw a wrench into the machinery of production at the studio. As in *Maverick*, the two characters occasionally would appear in a single episode, but generally they alternated each week. Once again, Huggins found his single protagonist replicated for institutional—not narrative—reasons. Until August, this second detective was known as Ben Royce, but he ultimately came to be known as Jeff Spenser. As played by

Roger Smith, Spenser was as young, attractive, and contemporary as Stuart Bailey, if slightly less urbane. Like his partner, Jeff Spenser was educated, having worked his way through school to receive a law degree and, ultimately, to work for the FBI.

The studio also added another supporting character, who initially was going to be called Rickey, but finally became Kookie. The Kookie character was written for Edd Byrnes, who appeared in the "Girl on the Run" pilot episode as a callow, hipster assassin. During a February 1958 preview in a local theater, Byrnes tested so well among women and younger audience members that the studio decided to

Efrem Zimbalist, Jr., Roger Smith, and Edd Byrnes of
77 Sunset Strip, the studio's first and most popular
private-detective series.
(Courtesy of Bison Archives © Warner Bros.)

inject his teen appeal into the series by changing him into a likable character, a parking attendant at the restaurant next door to the agency. The series description registered with the Writers Guild gives some idea of the studio's shrewd demographic justification for adding Kookie: "He's a 'real cool cat.' He's hep but likable, and, despite his 'beat generation' dialogue, he's *not* a juvenile delinquent. Rickey [Kookie] is ambitious and sharp; he'd rather be a private-eye than anything else in the world. His role in the series should have definite appeal to teenagers." Two other recurring characters were added to the agency after the pilot: Suzanne Fabry (Jacqueline Beer), an attractive French secretary, and Roscoe (Louis Quine), a streetwise older man who aided the detectives by supplying information. Along with adding these characters, Orr also suggested sharpening the sense of location by substituting a real Sunset Strip restaurant for the fictional restaurant located next door to the agency. Orr persuaded Dean Martin to allow the series to use the name of his restaurant, Dino's.[47] Although the series was never shot anywhere but the studio after the pilot episode, the inclusion of a real Hollywood landmark helped to place *77 Sunset Strip* at the epicenter of TV hipness in the late 1950s.

In creating the series, Huggins was not interested in playing out traditional mystery stories, which, in the hands of *Dragnet* and other series, left little time for anything other than resolving an obvious narrative enigma. The series description warned prospective writers, "Our protagonists will not wander about, asking interminable questions, and being slugged from behind. Their adventures will be basically suspense-melodrama, with a leavening of humor." As he prepared the series for production, Huggins complained to studio story editor Jack Emanuel that the story department had delivered too many prospective stories that were "similar in several dreary ways which make them unsuitable for '77.'" Huggins argued that the stories submitted to him were typical of other crime series, but not what he had in mind for this new series. He claimed that a private detective story should be different from a police procedural, that the private eye shouldn't simply be a de facto cop. He also complained that the submitted stories "emphasize the mysteries to such an extent that . . . the protagonist merely runs about asking questions or being hit on the head." Consequently, the stories "end up with a twenty-page explanation of what's been going on." Huggins concluded, "If we are looking for a series that will be unusual, our only hope is to get as far away from the cliched private-eye story as we possibly can." He advised searching for "suspense novels rather than mysteries—the chief difference being that in the suspense novel the emphasis is on the predicament of the hero, with the mystery secondary or entirely dispensed with."[48]

Huggins selected one of his own published stories, "Lovely Lady, Pity Me," for the first regular episode and borrowed another *Maverick* colleague, Douglas Heyes, to write the screenplay. Heyes worked day and night, finishing the script just hours before shooting began on September 12—for an episode scheduled to air on October 17. The brief turnaround time for this first episode meant that the series' production schedule had a very slim margin for error from the beginning, leaving the studio no more than three episodes ahead of the broadcast date throughout the season. Although Huggins had a distinct vision of the series, he never actually produced a single episode. He returned to *Maverick* as soon as *77 Sunset Strip* entered production, leaving Howie Horwitz to assume the role of producer on the detective series.[49] Burdened by a frantic production schedule, and lacking Huggins's guidance, *77 Sunset Strip* was never as consistently distinctive as Huggins had intended; too often, the episodes relied on the sort of predictable, by-the-numbers mystery plots that Huggins abhorred.

Nevertheless, *77 Sunset Strip*'s blend of humor and action succeeded beyond any expectation, enabling the series to win its Friday time slot consistently. With two handsome young detectives, the hippest milieu on TV, and teen sensation Edd Byrnes, *77 Sunset Strip* established itself as one of the most attractive series for advertisers seeking young viewers. Pepsi-Cola, for instance, used the series to launch a challenge to Coca-Cola's long-standing dominance in the cola market, introducing a slogan exclaiming, "Now it's Pepsi for those who think young." Over images of fun-loving teenagers and young adults, the voice-over narration reminded viewers: "Reach for a Pepsi and you make the modern move. Think young and say Pepsi." For ABC chairman Leonard Goldenson and network vice president Oliver Treyz, *77 Sunset Strip* was practically the ideal embodiment of the network's programming strategy, which targeted "the post-war families, the big consumers of TV and of the products advertised on it." By pointing out the youth of such Warner Bros. performers as Garner, Zimbalist, and Smith, Goldenson explicitly contrasted his network with the more powerful networks, which had cornered the market on established stars. "These are our marquee [names]," he said. "When you compare them with the Jack Bennys and the Groucho Marxes, you have a difference in age that literally represents a gap between generations." Although ABC still trailed the other networks in sheer number of affiliates and, consequently,

earned barely half of the gross revenues that the others did, its advertising billings were rising at a dizzying pace, climbing 24 percent in
1958 alone. In fact, in the four years since the debut of *Disneyland*,
ABC's gross billings had tripled, rising from $34.7 million in 1954 to
$103 million in 1958.[50]

Warner Bros. received much of the credit for ABC's vast improve-
ment, since its series helped ABC to capture ratings victories on four
nights each week in the top twenty-four markets. By the end of 1958,
Warner Bros. had become the most heralded success story in Hollywood since the end of World War II. According to the trade journals,
Wall Street investors now perceived Warner Bros. as the model for
the movie studio of the future. Warner Bros. announced that it now
planned to produce only twelve to fourteen movies per year. But with
an average budget of $2.5 million, these would be marketed as A pic-
tures, giving them the potential for lucrative returns at the box office.
Since such a small number of movies couldn't be expected to pay for
studio overhead, Warner Bros. relied on television to support studio
expenses by adding nearly 40 percent in overhead charges to the
average TV budget. In addition to paying overhead, television production continued to serve as a valuable training ground for inexperienced writers, directors, producers, and actors. With this new production strategy, of course, Warner Bros. now experienced periods in
which feature production was absent from the studio. "The Warners
lot would resemble a ghost town," *Variety*'s George Rosen reported
in 1959, "if it weren't for the two *Mavericks* shooting simultaneously,
the *Cheyennes*, *Sugarfoots*, *77 Sunset Strips*, and the *Lawmans*." During
the 1958–1959 season, Warner Bros. grossed $12.6 million from net-
work license fees on its six prime-time series. With a boost from television revenues, the studio's annual profits rebounded to $15.8 mil-
lion during the fiscal year ending in July 1959. Jack Warner called it
the studio's best year since 1953, the year when the sale of the theater
chain ended the studio's vertical integration.[51]

After the success of the 1958–1959 season, ABC eagerly returned to
Warner Bros. and ordered seven and a half hours of programming for
the 1959–1960 season. Warner Bros. now had sole responsibility for
30 percent of the network's prime-time schedule. ABC renewed all of
the series from the previous season except *Colt .45*. Clint Walker returned to the studio after his yearlong holdout. Though Walker negotiated a new contract that reduced his workload to only thirteen
new episodes per season, ABC renewed *Cheyenne*, scheduling it in its
own time slot for the first time. The network also renewed *Lawman*,
Maverick, *Sugarfoot*, and *Bronco*, with the last two alternating each

week. ABC ordered one new Western as well, an example of the exotic variations being tested during a TV season in which twenty-eight Western series monopolized more than one-quarter of prime time.[52] To exploit topical interest in Alaska's bid for statehood, this new series, *The Alaskans*, starred Roger Moore, Jeff York, and Dorothy Provine as fortune-seekers during the late-nineteenth-century gold rush. Once again, Warner Bros. created a new series simply by transposing the elements of its successful series. *The Alaskans* resembled *Maverick* in many ways, not least of which was the main characters' collective obsession with getting rich as quickly as possible while assiduously avoiding hard work.

ABC was eager to renew *77 Sunset Strip* but was faced with a new and pleasant dilemma: an overabundance of advertisers lined up requesting advertising time on the detective series. The Ted Bates advertising agency informed ABC that it could guarantee advertisers for another Warner Bros. private-eye series, particularly if the studio would agree to cross-promote the series by occasionally sending Efrem Zimbalist, Jr., and Roger Smith to the other series. In an event that epitomized the informality of the relationship between Warner Bros. and ABC, William Orr and Oliver Treyz agreed on a pair of new detective series while standing on the steps of the Warner Bros. commissary after lunch. In order to duplicate the ratings of *77 Sunset Strip*, the solution for both the studio and the network seemed to be to duplicate the series itself as closely as possible. Warner Bros. considered a number of suitably sunny locales for its new detective franchises, including the Caribbean and Florida, but settled on Hawaii and New Orleans. Thus *77 Sunset Strip* became *Hawaiian Eye* and *Bourbon Street Beat* (1959–1960).[53] These new series were veritable carbon copies of the original, with interchangeable characters and virtually identical narrative strategies. Both series featured two attractive detectives—one well-bred and highly educated, the other a little rough around the edges—who were accompanied by a young sidekick, a faithful female companion, and a crusty, streetwise older man. The Warner Bros. backlots and soundstages served as the exotic milieu within which one of these detectives solved a new case each week.

With the order from ABC for eight prime-time series, including three new series sold without a pilot, Warner Bros. suddenly became the largest telefilm producer in Hollywood. In 1958–1959, the studio produced 127 hours of television; with ABC's order for the 1959–1960 season, Warner Bros. would produce 260 hours—the equivalent of 170 feature-length films. By 1959, twenty-three soundstages were devoted solely to TV production; the television division employed three hundred permanent personnel, including ten producers, twenty-seven contract actors, and more than sixty free-lance writers at any given time. The editing department grew from a staff of thirty-three in 1957 to ninety in 1959.[54] To manufacture 260 hours of TV drama within a year required an amazing degree of organization and discipline. The goal of simply meeting production deadlines assumed the highest priority in this context. In order to make the deadlines, Warner Bros. had to function with the efficiency of a factory.

As in the first years of Warner Bros. Television, production was organized according to the unit-producer system adopted from the studio era. Studio production chief William Orr, along with his assistant Hugh Benson, supervised all activity at the studio and served as the liaison with both the studio administration and the TV industry. Under Orr in the management hierarchy, individual producers supervised each series, taking responsibility for the scripts and for assigning writers, directors, and actors (both those under contract and those hired on an individual free-lance basis). When the volume of production became too great for Orr to oversee all of the series, he added another layer of management by appointing supervising producers who were responsible for overseeing the work of individual producers on two or three series.[55]

Centralized studio departments provided services to each series. Because these departments were independent of any specific series, Orr instructed his producers that each was responsible for the work of the individual departments on his series. "You must be aware," Orr warned, "that in addition to good stories, production values and the mechanics of segments must be constantly supervised. EVERY DETAIL MUST BE SUPERVISED TO THE NTH DEGREE. I realize we're involved in volume production, but this cannot under any circumstances be used to justify sloppiness in performance, direction, makeup, hairdressing, wardrobe, or any other facet of production."[56] The story department supplied a steady stream of story ideas for the entire television division, monitoring hundreds of books, magazines, and script submissions each week, as well as negotiating with writers, agents, and the network's department of standards and practices, which checked studio scripts for "inappropriate" content.[57] The studio casting department coordinated the use of studio contract performers and free-lance actors. Production manager Oren Haglund held responsibility for assigning crews, and the crews passed from series to series, depending on production schedules. Finally, the editing department took care of post-production for all of the series on the lot, and when even a couple of episodes were delayed in production, this department became a bottleneck that stalled activity throughout the studio. In 1958, because ABC had been slow to sign *77 Sunset*

Strip, Warner Bros. completed many episodes only a few weeks ahead of the scheduled network broadcast date. Production throughout the studio frequently stalled while *77 Sunset Strip* episodes were being edited, and Warner Bros. was penalized more than $100,000 in overtime charges at the labs.[58]

By the late 1950s, Warner Bros. Television was an intricately organized, high-volume factory system with little margin for error. By falling behind schedule at any stage of the production process, the studio not only risked additional expenses, which would cut into the small profit margin, but also faced the danger of failing to meet network broadcast deadlines. The responsibility for maintaining shooting schedules and holding down costs belonged to the producer, who was to be certain that shooting scripts were completed on time and that they provided an adequate blueprint for a narrative that could be shot in six days, within the allotted budget, with a running time that fit the network time slot without elaborate tinkering in the editing room.[59]

The writing process was streamlined by having all of the Warner Bros. series share the same narrative formula. Although the series that followed *Cheyenne* adopted multiple protagonists, each of the studio's series produced before 1960 (except *Lawman*) employed the disguised anthology format established with *Cheyenne*. Each of the episodes in the subsequent series focused on one of the male protagonists, inserting that character into a self-contained crisis that the protagonist resolved. Whether a Western or a crime series, the plot always involved giving aid to some beleaguered victim and usually depended on solving a crime. Afterward, the protagonist simply moved on to another situation. The multiple protagonists in each series seldom collaborated in individual episodes; instead, they alternated as episodic protagonists.

Since the heroes of the various Warner Bros. series served practically the same narrative function, and the episodes seldom moved beyond the barest elements of the plot, there was little to distinguish one character from another. This made the writing process easier to manage, because a script written for *Maverick* or *77 Sunset Strip* could be exchanged between either of the lead characters with only minimal alterations. As scripted, Bret and Bart Maverick were almost identical; the same was true for Stuart Bailey and Jeff Spenser. In fact, the Warner Bros. protagonists varied so little that scripts could be passed from series to series, or even from the detective to the Western genre—as when "Lovely Lady, Pity Me," the first regular episode of *77 Sunset Strip,* was remade on *Maverick* as "The Lass with the Poisonous Air."

To distinguish its relatively undifferentiated characters, Warner Bros. defined a minimal backstory for each character, which was invoked occasionally, but the producers concentrated primarily on identifying one or two character traits that could be repeated in episode after episode, to condense the character into a single, unmistakable trait which was referred to as the character's "shtick." The *Maverick* brothers had their shtick—moments when they invoked their pappy's wisdom. On *Bourbon Street Beat,* the detectives were distinguished by the fact that one loved to cook and the other was untidy. The most famous shtick involved Kookie's incessant hair-combing on *77 Sunset Strip,* and as the character soared in popularity this became the focal point of an elaborate promotional campaign that included officially licensed Kookie combs and Edd Byrnes's hit recording, "Kookie, Kookie, Lend Me Your Comb."

It may seem too simplistic to say that all Warner Bros. series followed a single basic formula for generating characters and stories, but the studio actively imposed this formula in order to rationalize and streamline the production process, making it possible to produce a high volume of episodes as efficiently as possible. Orr constantly reminded producers that the screenplay was not only the first cog in a smoothly orchestrated system of production but also the key to controlling costs and production schedules. It was the producer's duty to cut production costs at the scriptwriting stage—by cutting down on the number of characters in the script to eliminate unnecessary actors and extras, by excising superfluous scenes that didn't directly advance the plot, or by removing scenes that required the cast and crew to move from stage to stage. Above all, the shooting script had to make it possible to film the production in no more than six days. "The shows shot in seven days are no better than those shot in five or six," Orr argued. "In fact, a seventh day suggests that somebody does not know what they are doing. Tailor and retailor scripts to fit a six-day schedule." With so many episodes in production, the shooting script also needed to guarantee that the program would fit precisely into a network time slot after editing. A particular problem involved episodes that came in at radically different lengths during the first cut— anywhere from 1,200 feet short to 500 feet long—when network time slots demanded that each episode's running time be precisely one hour including commercials. This caused delays in the editing department as editors waited for producers to film additional footage. Orr warned his producers, "The cost of additional scenes plus the delays caused by holding these shows up are expenses we cannot afford. The producer is responsible for establishing the timing of the script. You must analyze the proportion of dialogue and action scenes, consider the shooting habits of the director, and come up with scripts that should be at least 300 feet over in a first cut. Establishing lengths of shows is such a basic element of producing that I hope it will never be necessary to mention it again."[60]

With the increase in studio activity during 1959, production on an episode had to begin at least eight weeks before the broadcast date in order to be completed by airtime. The production process often slowed because eight series—some of which were shooting multiple episodes simultaneously—shared the same backlot and a limited number of soundstages. Directors hired on short-term contracts were assigned to individual episodes and were responsible primarily for shooting the script in the prescribed amount of time.

Jules Schermer, the producer of *Lawman*, complained that the pace of production meant that most directors hired by the studio simply charged through scripts without regard for characterization or any of the script's other subtleties. Regardless of how long a writer might sweat over a script—and it was never very long—directors had a responsibility to dispatch the script in a few days. "Most directors don't even take the trouble to understand the script or to understand what they are doing," he explained. "They're more concerned with meeting a schedule than getting values out of a script." From Schermer's perspective, the success of a TV drama depended on establishing a particular tone. A television episode, he explained, "is basically only an incident built up with characterization. If a director plays the characterization wrong . . . the total effect of the teleplay is destroyed." Too often, rushed directors played scenes too broadly, giving the entire episode the appearance of cliché or caricature.[61]

Still, the directors themselves were not to blame for a system that forced them to work so hastily. Directors were constantly reminded to use no more than two or three takes on any given shot and to provide enough coverage through the standard alternation of medium shots and close-ups to ensure that there would be no need for reshooting once editors completed a rough cut. In order to keep the studio running smoothly, directors were not allowed to shoot retakes or additional scenes without Orr's approval.[62]

Once principal photography was completed, the footage was sent to the editing department, where editors delivered the first cut of the episode in eight days and a final cut in two weeks. There was a strict protocol to the editing process in which each episode passed through no more than four cuts. To prevent delays, no one except Orr was allowed to view the episode before the completion of the first cut. The episode's director and the producer of the series viewed the first cut and suggested changes. If the director had moved on to shoot another episode, as was frequently the case, the producers were ordered to "bypass the director's prerogative" and make the first cut by themselves. The producer alone viewed the second cut and suggested any further changes. Finally, Orr watched the third cut with the producer and negotiated any changes for the fourth and final version. While in the editing department, music and any additional sound effects were added to the final cut. After conforming the negative to the final cut and integrating network commercials, this version was sent to the lab for prints.[63]

Through close management supervision of an intricately organized production process, Warner Bros. Television was able to achieve an astonishing level of productivity without exorbitant expense. From the perspective of Jack Warner, William Orr, and other Warner Bros. executives, Warner Bros. Television was a smashing success by 1959. Because of the studio's determination to control residuals, Warner Bros. owned 100 percent of each series that it produced—something that no other telefilm producer could claim. Not a single writer, producer, or star was able to nibble away at the studio's profits, because Warner Bros. had successfully secured series authorship rights and had revived the studio era's exclusive long-term contracts. These contracts enabled Warner Bros. to lay claim to a stable of young actors unmatched in Hollywood.[64] The studio used this advantage to integrate TV and movie production more completely than any other studio, shuttling its TV actors into feature films throughout the late 1950s and early 1960s. For the most part these were formulaic, moderately budgeted features such as *Yellowstone Kelly* (1959) with Clint Walker, John Russell, and Edd Byrnes, or *Gold of the Seven Saints* (1961) with Walker and Roger Moore. James Garner appeared in *Sayonara, Darby's Rangers, Up Periscope,* and *Cash McCall* (1960). Efrem Zimbalist, Jr., acted in films like *The Violent Road* (1958), *Home Before Dark* (1958), and *The Crowded Sky* (1960).

By producing seven and a half hours of network programming each week, Warner Bros. took full advantage of a major studio's production capacity. In 1958 the entire studio grossed $70 million; in 1959 the television division alone grossed $30 million. These earnings seemed like the merest hint of the future profits to follow once the studio began capitalizing more completely on markets other than network prime time. While Warner Bros. still had not entered domestic syndication by 1959, it had begun to distribute television programming overseas.[65] After discovering a lucrative crossover market with Edd Byrnes's hit record "Kookie, Kookie, Lend Me Your Comb," Warner Bros. also planned to continue the cross-promotion between its

TV and music divisions. *77 Sunset Strip* was already a showcase for jazz groups signed to the Warner Bros. label, especially the Kenny Ortega Trio, which often performed in Dino's lounge. Along with Byrnes, TV stars Clint Walker, Roger Smith, Dorothy Provine, and Connie Stevens released records, and the record division tried to convince other stars, such as James Garner, to work with a voice coach in preparation for the transition to recording.[66] The cross-promotion of Warner Bros. TV series continued through a wide array of licensed merchandise that included books (a dictionary of Kookie's distinctive argot, *Maverick's Guide to Poker*), comic books, toys, board games, lunch boxes, and countless other items.

At the beginning of the 1950s, the future for Warner Bros. Pictures had appeared dismal. By the end of the decade, however, Warner Bros. was functioning at a level of productivity unimaginable even

By the end of the 1950s, the Warner Bros. studio was booming with activity. In this enthusiastic publicity still, Warner Bros. executives pose with the studio's contract performers. A smiling Jack Warner stands at the center, arm in arm with Angie Dickenson (*left*) and Natalie Wood (*right*). TV production chief William T. Orr stands next to Dickenson, and his second-in-command, Hugh Benson, is beside Wood.
(Courtesy of Bison Archives © Warner Bros.)

during the studio era, and television was the key to its revival. Though Jack Warner still cautioned that "motion pictures come first" in Hollywood, he also admitted that "television has been a very healthy influence on the motion picture industry."[67] By integrating production for television and movies, Warner Bros. discovered a way not only to survive but to thrive in the new Hollywood. With the studio functioning at full capacity and network license fees pouring in, Warner Bros. executives seemed confident that they had mastered television.

Eagerly anticipating the future, they commissioned a report to study the impact of the growing demand for TV production. Based on an expected 40 to 50 percent increase in production for the 1960–1961 season, this report estimated that studio facilities soon would be taxed beyond reasonable limits and recommended that Warner Bros. either lease rental space at another studio or acquire additional space by building or purchasing new facilities.[68] This projection was based, of course, on the assumption that the demand for Warner Bros. programs would continue to escalate at the same feverish rate. Studio chief William Orr exhibited this confidence when he led a *TV Guide* reporter on a tour of the bustling studio in October 1959. Describing his fast-rising company as the telefilm industry's "Cadillac" producer, Orr seemed certain that its phenomenal four-year growth was a matter of destiny, a portent of greater triumphs to come.[69] There was no reason even to consider the alternative scenario—that Warner Bros. Television may have reached the height of its success before the 1950s had even ended.

·X·
The Pathology of
Mass
Production

When Hollywood's major studios debuted in prime time during 1955, many observers in the entertainment industry worried that the studios would dominate television production as easily as they had controlled motion pictures. By 1960 that fear seemed at least premature, if not entirely unwarranted. Only Warner Bros. and Columbia's Screen Gems subsidiary actually prevailed in television; no other major studio found a foothold before 1960. By the end of the 1950s, in fact, the strongest companies in telefilm production were not the established movie studios that had hoped to colonize the new market, but entrepreneurial independent producers who achieved success entirely within the television industry. Although rankings in telefilm production changed with each new season's network orders, the list of major producers remained fairly stable during the late 1950s. For the 1959–1960 season, according to *Telefilm* magazine,[1] the major telefilm companies were:

Studio	Network Programs	Production Budget
Warner Bros.	10	$30 million
Revue	13	$24 million
Four Star	10	$11.5 million
Desilu	4	$10.5 million
Screen Gems	6	$ 8.5 million

The first thing to notice about this list is the absence of major motion picture studios. After years as the industry leader in television investment, Paramount made little effort to compete in television production during the 1950s. Paramount's long-term plans for television had been disrupted by the divorce of its theater chain, which, as United Paramount Theaters, merged with the ABC-TV network, and by its ill-fated investment in DuMont Laboratories and the DuMont Network, which ceased broadcasting in 1955. Paramount rented studio facilities to TV producers and engaged in some local production through its Los Angeles TV station, KTLA, but generally the studio hedged its bets on production while holding out hope that its system of pay-per-view television would find acceptance as an alternative to network broadcasting.[2]

Twentieth Century–Fox continued to develop series ideas after producing *The Twentieth Century–Fox Hour* (1955–1957) and *My Friend Flicka* (1956–1957), but the studio reluctantly disappeared from prime time after failing to sell any new programs during 1957 and 1958. Studio president Spyros Skouras pledged to rebuild the TV division in 1958 by allocating $15 million for new TV production and by hiring a new production chief, Martin Manulis, who had been producer of the anthology drama series *Playhouse 90* (1956–1961). Manulis was able to sell three programs for the 1959–1960 season—*The Many Loves of Dobie Gillis* (1959–1963), *Adventures in Paradise* (1959–1962), and *Five Fingers* (1959–1960)—but he lasted only one year at the helm. His replacement, Peter Leavethes, came from the Young and Rubicam advertising agency and assumed control over Fox's entire television business.[3]

The turnover at Fox during this period was matched by confusion at MGM. Following its first halfhearted season in television, MGM tried to develop several TV series based on past feature films, but the studio's television management changed nearly every year, as one vice president after another came and went. Without steady leadership, MGM produced only two prime-time series, *The Thin Man* (1957–1959) and *Northwest Passage* (1958–1959). Seeking stability during early 1959, MGM dissolved its television division, placing television production under the direct command of production chief Sol Siegel. In this new configuration, MGM-TV produced seven self-financed pilots, including adaptations of *The Asphalt Jungle* (1950) and *Father of the Bride* (1950). In spite of this ambitious effort, however, MGM hit bottom when none of its pilots found a buyer and the studio lost over $400,000. By the end of 1959, MGM had hired yet another new production chief. George Shupert assumed the position by announcing that MGM in the future would stop producing speculative pilots and would accept outside financing "to minimize risks and to gain the creative advice of potential buyers."[4]

The second thing to notice about the list of top telefilm producers is that Warner Bros., while standing atop the list, really shared few characteristics with the others, who had worked their way up through the television industry. The success of Warner Bros. Television was based on an astonishingly narrow definition of the television business. In essence, Warner Bros. produced a single type of product (the hour-long drama) for a single market (the ABC network), using a single method of financing (full studio ownership) and a single mode of production (strict managerial control of personnel under exclusive contracts). In contrast, the other companies explored the benefits of diversification. They produced programs in a wide variety of formats and genres, licensing them to major advertisers, local stations, and all three networks. These companies also entertained numerous financing and production strategies, particularly by inviting co-production deals with independent producers and performers. Finally, they shared one crucial characteristic that Warner Bros. lacked: Each of them had diversified beyond production, investing in other areas of the television industry, including program distribution.

Satisfied with its status as ABC's chief supplier—though this contradicted every lesson from the studio era—Warner Bros. was the least visionary of telefilm's top producers and the most vulnerable to changing conditions in the television industry. Consequently, the 1959–1960 season represented the apotheosis of Warner Bros. Television, the best that Warner Bros. could achieve using a management philosophy and a mode of production that looked backward toward the studio era. Built upon high-volume mass production, low wages for long-term contracts, and rigid studio management, the late-1950s success of Warner Bros. Television was a fragile edifice, as illusory as the New Orleans and Honolulu sets constructed on its Burbank soundstages. Warner Bros. might have succeeded in reviving a mode of production from the studio era had other telefilm producers adopted its perspective on the television business—as the major studios had informally collaborated to enforce the studio system. But by 1960 Warner Bros. was the only TV producer with any interest in returning to the studio system.

While the major movie studios failed to take over television production in the late 1950s, the telefilm industry nevertheless came to be dominated by a few large companies. By 1959, 80 percent of network prime-time programming was produced in Hollywood. At least twenty-five different telefilm producers supplied the networks, but the five leading producers accounted for more than 40 percent of Hollywood's output.[5] Fierce competition in the market for TV programming spurred this trend toward concentration.

By the late 1950s, the number of TV stations had stabilized, while the stockpile of programs continued to grow. As local stations began filling more hours with Hollywood feature films and off-network reruns, the demand for first-run syndicated programs virtually disappeared. In this radically tightened market, networks and stations also demanded higher-quality programs produced on larger budgets. In 1955, the average thirty-nine-episode half-hour series could be made on a $1 million budget; by 1958 the cost had doubled. As a result, the most competitive studios were those backed by extensive financial resources and well-established sales divisions. Assessing these developments in 1959, John Mitchell, vice president for sales at Screen Gems, argued that within five years the telefilm industry would be reduced to five or six companies. The telefilm company of the future, he explained, would have to be a producer-distributor active in many facets of the television industry "to have a cushion against all contingencies." The activities of a viable telefilm company would have to include producing studio-owned programs, packaging and producing programs for outside producers, making commercials and industrial films, selling first-run programs to networks and local stations, and distributing both feature films and off-network reruns in domestic and international markets.[6]

Under these conditions, telefilm companies scrambled to consolidate production and distribution—whether through mergers or by expansion. "It's felt that telefilmeries are following the development of the motion picture industry, which started with many companies, but shook down to a comparative handful," *Variety* noted. "Only a distribution organization with a large sales force and an insured production supply can assume a commanding position. The middle-size companies will go by the wayside. There will always be some small companies around, but their impact on the business will be as limited as their size."[7] Large, integrated studios had a number of advantages over independent companies. With an efficiently organized system for high-volume production, a large company could guarantee a steady flow of consistent programming, while spreading the expense of production across a number of series. A bigger bankroll also enabled large companies to sustain short-term losses, to take financial risks, to finance more-expensive programs, and to absorb the cost of speculative pilot production. In fact, the cost of pilot production had become the most substantial barrier faced by new companies entering the field. Formerly, an article in *Telefilm* magazine explained, "it was common practice for a producer to make a cheap pilot, hire a press agent, and christen himself John Doe Productions. But as an increasing number of these one-man companies crashed along with their pilots, fewer producers want to run the risk."[8]

The most significant difference between integrated studios and independent producers, however, involved the studio's ability to distribute its own programs in syndication. "Syndication," reporter Leon Morse observed, "places a net underneath the risky program production business." Though most producers still recouped only 80 percent of production costs (before adding studio overhead) from the first-run network broadcast, residual profits from the syndication of a half-hour series could run as high as $1.5 million for one season's episodes and might surpass $2.5 million for a one-hour series.[9] By syndicating its own library of filmed programs, a larger studio could generate a substantial cash reserve to meet the expense of new production.

The growing dominance of diversified telefilm companies was signaled most obviously by the fact that Desilu, Four Star, Revue, and Screen Gems all became publicly held corporations within the three-year period 1958–1961. By diversifying into many forms of television production and distribution, four companies that began as producers of a single television series in the early 1950s achieved a status among Hollywood's most prosperous studios by the end of the decade. Each of these studios developed a number of economic arrangements for financing TV production, not only filming their wholly owned series but also participating in joint ventures with independent producers, providing below-the-line production services for a fee, or simply leasing studio space and equipment.[10]

Desilu and Four Star rose the fastest in the field of telefilm production, because both of them literally began with a single property— Desilu's *I Love Lucy* and Four Star's *Four Star Playhouse*. As subsidiaries of established companies, Revue and Screen Gems were supported by their respective parents, the MCA talent agency and Columbia Pictures. Industry reporter Edwin H. James described the difference between the truly independent TV producers like Desilu and Four Star and those that spun off of other companies. The subsidiaries, he noted, "have been supported through lean seasons by the strength of their associated businesses. . . . For the independents, survival has required the possession of resourcefulness as a substitute for resources. Most of the independents that have lasted through the past few years started with one asset, a star or a television series that turned into a hit. The trick has been to create still other assets from the first one before its value declined."[11]

Desilu obviously capitalized on its first asset, *I Love Lucy*, which earned over $1 million a year from reruns by the mid-1950s. From this foundation, Desilu branched out into several types of production, a process of expansion that began with an investment of $5,000 in 1951 and saw the studio staff grow from twelve to eight hundred in just six years. Desilu produced series for the networks and for syndication under several types of financial arrangements: wholly owned series (*I Love Lucy, December Bride*), co-productions in which Desilu shared profits with producers or performers (*Sheriff of Cochise, The Texan*), and series which it filmed for other producers using Desilu's facilities, equipment, and staff, but without making a capital investment (*The Danny Thomas Show, The Life and Legend of Wyatt Earp*). In October 1956, Desilu sold the rights to *I Love Lucy* to CBS for $4.3 million. With the help of this windfall profit, Desilu purchased RKO's three studio facilities in January 1958 for $6.15 million. In acquiring the property of a major studio that had employed Desi Arnaz and Lucille Ball during the studio era, Desilu served as the clearest symbol of television's new influence in Hollywood. Yet Desilu was also the studio most vulnerable to the transitory conditions of the TV industry. Because Desilu never diversified beyond production, the studio's profits depended almost solely on its ability to convince networks or sponsors to purchase its programs. Desilu branched out into hour-long episodic dramas for the first time with the 1959 premiere of *The Untouchables* (1959–1963), for instance, but by 1961 that was the only Desilu series on the air.[12]

The rise of Four Star Productions was even more improbable than that of Desilu, because *Four Star Playhouse*, the company's initial asset, was never a top-rated series. An anthology series, *Four Star Playhouse* never generated the kind of loyalty that sent *I Love Lucy* into the commercial stratosphere. But Four Star possessed a unique asset in its relationship with the William Morris talent agency. Between 1952 and 1956, Four Star was a minor company with only one or two series on the air and an annual gross income of less than $2 million. In 1956, however, Four Star leapt to the top of the telefilm industry by acquiring an interest in Official Films, the distribution company that syndicated *Four Star Playhouse*, and by forming a close relationship with the William Morris agency. In the postwar years, the William Morris agency and MCA battled as the most powerful talent agencies in Hollywood. As the television market began to show promise, MCA formed Revue Productions, in order to make and sell programs using MCA clients. Instead of creating its own production company, William Morris forged an informal alliance with Four Star, directing its clients to the production company and marketing the company's series to sponsors and networks. Capitalizing on this privileged relationship, Four Star began to specialize in anthology series and Westerns. In the next few years, Four Star evolved from a small studio with a single network series to a corporation that supplied ten network series and held combined assets valued at $10 million.[13]

With the declining influence of sponsors in program production,

Dick Powell, Charles Boyer, and David Niven, cofounders of
Four Star Productions.
(Courtesy of Photofest © Four Star Productions)

Four Star president Dick Powell was able to lure Tom McDermott away from his position as vice president in charge of television at Benton and Bowles advertising agency in 1959. Based on years of production experience at the advertising agency, McDermott planned to make Four Star an attractive company for a new breed of writer-producers emerging in the late 1950s, such as Blake Edwards, Aaron Spelling, Sam Peckinpah, and the team of Richard Levinson and William Link. Rather than simply assign a producer from the ranks of studio management to oversee a series, Powell and McDermott hoped to allow writers to develop and supervise their own series. Consequently, Four Star signed writers to term contracts but offered them a share of the profits on any series that they developed—even if the idea for the series was provided by the company. This was a potentially lucrative arrangement for writers, since Four Star often used episodes from its anthology series as pilots for new series. Aaron Spelling, for instance, scripted the pilot for his first series, *Johnny*

Ringo (1959–1960), as an episode of the Western anthology *Zane Grey Theater* (1957–1959). In addition to writers, Four Star also signed profit-participation deals with its stars, giving actors an incentive to work at the studio. Approaching the end of the 1950s, Four Star was the fastest rising company in telefilm production—with ten series in prime time during 1959–1960 and twelve in 1960–1961.[14]

Revue Productions, the MCA talent agency's TV production subsidiary, remained at or near the top of the production charts throughout the mid- to late 1950s. Revue was formed in 1952, when Karl Kramer, an MCA vice president, suggested that the agency create a program to showcase its clients. There was one obstacle: Because it was a conflict of interest for talent agencies to act as producers, Screen Actors Guild policy prohibited agencies from engaging in production. Occasionally, the guild would grant waivers to this policy on an individual, case-by-case basis, but in 1952 the SAG board of directors, which included guild president Ronald Reagan and his wife, Nancy—both MCA clients—granted a unique blanket waiver to MCA, allowing the agency to act as a TV producer without requesting individual waivers for each production. This decision gave MCA an obvious advantage in telefilm production, which the agency quickly exploited by also branching out into distribution, first purchasing the rights to reruns of *Dragnet* in 1953, then acquiring United Television Programs, a syndicator with sixteen properties, in 1954.[15]

Supported by distribution income, Revue expanded so rapidly that gross revenues from television exceeded those of the talent agency by 1954—when MCA grossed $9 million from television and $6 million from commissions. The series that Revue produced during this period generally were star vehicles showcasing established radio and movie industry performers (or, in the case of Alfred Hitchcock, a "star director") who were in the process of making the transition to television. Though not all Revue series featured MCA talent, the majority of the production company's stars were MCA clients (Jack Benny, Lee Marvin, Ozzie and Harriet Nelson, Ronald Reagan) whom the agency set up in series production based on 50–50 profit partnerships. SAG rules wouldn't allow the agency to take more than a 10 percent commission for the series, but the economics of studio production and distribution allowed the agency to shave off additional income through overhead charges, rental fees, crew salaries, fees charged for the first-run sale to sponsors or a network, and distribution fees applied during syndication—all of which preceded any calculation of profits. If a series aired for three years in prime time and generated at least one hundred episodes, MCA's gross revenue after syndication would be around $7 million and the actor's 50 percent share would be around

MCA's Revue Productions coproduced several TV series with MCA clients, such as director Alfred Hitchcock, who became a celebrity as a result of his role as the wryly macabre host of the TV series *Alfred Hitchcock Presents.* (Courtesy of Wisconsin Center for Film and Theater Research © Revue Productions)

$1.8 million—which was not really exploitative when compared with the amount that an actor would have earned through salary alone.[16]

With these profits, MCA grew at a remarkable rate, so quickly in fact that it became the target of Justice Department antitrust investigations beginning in 1957. In that year, Revue's production budget of $25 million represented one-quarter of all television production in Hollywood. MCA branched out into the syndication of feature films in 1958 by purchasing TV rights to Paramount's film library. In 1959, MCA cemented its new status as the industry's production leader by purchasing the Universal Studios lot—the physical property and facilities—from Decca Records, Universal's parent company, paying $11.35 million in cash and later renting production space back to Universal for $1 million a year. By 1959, MCA's annual gross income had grown to $58 million—with $9 million from commissions, $3 million from studio rentals, and $46 million from television production and distribution.[17]

Columbia Pictures may have been a second-rank studio during much of the studio era, but its TV subsidiary, Screen Gems, became the model for success in the telefilm industry by promoting a policy of constant diversification. Screen Gems produced the commercials and TV series that initially drew the studio into television, but it also branched out into virtually every aspect of the television industry. Beginning with its first prime-time hit, *Father Knows Best*, Screen Gems established a reputation as a studio that welcomed partnerships with independent producers, who learned that it was much easier to use the facilities of a major studio than to rent space and equipment at a smaller studio. These producers also discovered the value of being represented by a large studio's sales and distribution force. The success of this approach can be seen in the case of Herbert Leonard, one of the most prolific independent producers at Screen Gems during the 1950s. Using the studio's financing and facilities, Leonard produced 445 episodes of such series as *The Adventures of Rin Tin Tin*, *Tales of the 77th Bengal Lancers* (1956–1957), *Circus Boy* (1956–1958), *Rescue 8* (1958–1959), and *Naked City* (1958–1963). By 1959 these productions had earned $22 million in syndication. With only a minimal personal financial risk, Leonard's share of this syndication income was $3.5 million. Because of such lucrative deals, Screen Gems led the industry in co-production partnerships, producing series with twelve different independent producers in 1958 alone.[18] With so many independent producers inhabiting the lot, the studio's production schedule was Hollywood's most diverse. During the 1950s, Screen Gems series included children's adventures like *Rin Tin Tin* and *Circus Boy*, sitcoms like *Father Knows Best* and *The Donna*

Father Knows Best was the first hit series for Columbia's Screen Gems TV
subsidiary. Pictured are Elinor Donahue, Lauren Chapin,
Robert Young, Jane Wyatt, and Billy Gray.
(Courtesy of Wisconsin Center for Film and Theater Research © Screen Gems)

Reed Show (1958–1966), police series like *Naked City* and *Manhunt*
(1959–1961), and prestige anthology dramas like *Playhouse 90* and
Alcoa/Goodyear Theatre (1958–1960).

While building its production schedule, Screen Gems also founded
a syndication division in 1953 and soon became the largest television
distributor in the world. Screen Gems syndicated its own first-run
series and off-network reruns, while also purchasing reruns from independent producers, such as its 1958 acquisition of *The George Burns
and Gracie Allen Show* (1950–1958), for $6 million. In 1956, Screen
Gems began distributing feature films to television, beginning with
104 Columbia features, then, in 1957, acquiring 600 features from Universal. By 1959, Screen Gems controlled a library of over 900 feature
films. In 1959, Screen Gems purchased a television commercial production company—Elliot, Unger and Elliot—and diversified into television ownership by acquiring its first television station, KCPX-TV in
Salt Lake City. "If you want to survive," Screen Gem's president
Ralph Cohn explained at the time, "you must have not one root, but

many roots in the TV soil. And the broader you sink the roots, the better equipped you are to survive."[19]

Diversification was the key to growth for the other telefilm companies, but Warner Bros. executives were so keenly focused on the short-term benefits of network television and the need to control both the production process and the ownership of the studio's products that they failed to recognize just how shallowly they had planted the studio's roots in television. With its decision to produce solely for ABC and its reluctance to diversify beyond production, Warner Bros. was ill-prepared for new or unexpected circumstances. Consequently, after reaching a peak in 1959, the studio declined so rapidly that within four years it had only a single series in prime time. There were many reasons for this fall from grace, but all of them can be traced to the conservative corporate policies that produced such a shortsighted approach to television. The studio's success in television masked a pathological undercurrent, in which the very elements that enabled Warner Bros. Television to reach the top of the telefilm industry ultimately prompted its downfall. Following the logic of mass production to the most absurd extremes, Warner Bros. television policies backfired in three specific areas: the studio's high-volume production of television series, its treatment of contract employees, and its exclusive relationship with ABC.

For a production company like Warner Bros., which hadn't diversified into other areas of the television industry, the only way to make a profit in television was to produce a high volume of programming as inexpensively as possible. Because production levels far exceeded anything imagined during the studio era, the defining characteristic of television production at Warner Bros. was its frantic pace, a constraint which took absolute precedence over everything else. Hounded by the network's adamant weekly deadlines, Warner Bros. Television was not so much engaged in the production of individual stories as in manufacturing a single, unbroken ribbon of programming that had to wind its way through the studio machinery without snarling or breaking at any point. The only way to orchestrate such a high level of production was to imagine it as being all of a piece, to streamline the production process by reducing the differences among episodes and series, to diminish the chance that any unpredictable element might slow or halt the pace of production. The streamlining of production made it possible to achieve the technical feat of turning out the equivalent of a feature film each day. But, whereas studio production had always struck a delicate balance between the need for

As production levels rose, Western heroes crowded the backlot at Warner Bros. studio. Pictured are Will Hutchins, Peter Brown (*Lawman*), Jack Kelly, Ty Hardin (*Bronco*), James Garner, Wayde Preston, and John Russell (*Lawman*). Clint Walker is absent from this photo because of his contract dispute with the studio. (Courtesy of Wisconsin Center for Film and Theater Research © Warner Bros.)

standardization and the need for differentiation, production at Warner Bros. Television displayed an ill-conceived willingness to sacrifice the distinctiveness of individual narratives in order to meet production quotas. It sometimes seemed that studio executives wanted to test the tolerance of audiences, to see how far the studio could go in standardizing its products before it alienated viewers.

As the volume of production increased, the studio made many decisions that streamlined production while blurring the distinctions between series. By limiting the range of difference among programs and by shooting entirely at the studio, Warner Bros. was able to rationalize series production so that crew members from the studio's many production departments could move from series to series without spending precious time orienting themselves to the peculiarities of a particular narrative. Within both the Western and the detective genres, the individual series shared costumes and sets, including the studio's fairly limited backlot locations. These practices helped to produce a remarkably uniform visual style among Warner Bros. series. When the demands of production began to overwhelm the editing department, William Orr decided that the studio couldn't afford the time to complete four cuts of each episode; in order to speed the editing process, episodes were to go through only two cuts unless extenuating circumstances demanded otherwise.[20] Obviously, such a pace offered little opportunity for refinement and placed pressure on the editors to resort to the crudest and most easily standardized editing patterns. With more series in production, it also became increasingly difficult for the casting department to avoid circulating the same supporting actors from series to series. Some producers worried about the frequency with which one detective series went on the air with a villain who had recently appeared on one of the other series.[21]

The detective series posed a particular problem since they relied on a very specific sense of place (Hollywood, Hawaii, New Orleans, Miami) yet couldn't afford to leave the studio lot—which was fast becoming the most overexposed piece of real estate in the country. The studio transported a minimal crew to Hawaii to shoot stock footage before beginning production on *Hawaiian Eye*; otherwise, all of the series established the requisite local flavor by relying on stock footage from the studio library. A typical complaint came from producer Charles Hoffman. "*Bourbon Street Beat* is rapidly losing the feeling of its locale," he said. "The exteriors of Louisiana bayou country look exactly like what they are: our hot dry, Burbank back lot. The decaying plantations are all the stage 18 set with very minor redressing. . . . Today's dailies have a ludicrous contrast between a storm-bound plantation (on stage) and exteriors of swampland (stock footage)." The Western series were also constrained by the studio backlot's single Western street. "Is there any possibility of placing a tree or a well or some such pieces in the center of our street, so that it will look different from show to show?" Orr once asked the studio production manager. Relying on a limited supply of stock footage and one crowded backlot, Warner Bros. series not only shared a striking visual resemblance but even recycled many of the same shots. At one point, the editing department requested that new stock footage be shot. "We've used what stock is available until it is embarrassing to put it in shows," they reported.[22]

By minimizing the difference among series, Warner Bros. also streamlined the activity of writers, bringing predictability to a stage of the production process that had the greatest potential for disrupting the smooth flow of production. At the height of production in 1960, the story department reported that Warner Bros. hired twenty-seven writers regularly. Because of the formulaic nature of the writing, virtually all of these writers were comfortable moving between the Western and detective series; few were identified with a single series.[23] Writer-producers Richard Levinson and William Link, who arrived in Hollywood during the summer of 1959, have described what it was like to write for a TV series produced at a major studio like Warner Bros. "Most of the shows of the time, particularly in the area of dramatic series, required little more from a writer than a knack for coming up with 'springboards,' or story premises, and a rough sense of structure," they recalled. "Writers were tailors, cutting bolts of cloth to a rigid set of specifications. They would be provided with an existing group of characters and a format, and any flexibility within these parameters was severely limited. The key words were 'jeopardy' and 'conflict,' and the emphasis was almost totally on plot."[24] Writers had only a marginal involvement with a series, since they were usually hired on a free-lance basis and seldom came in contact with anyone other than the story editor and the producer. Writers might be permitted to visit the set, but more often they received form postcards, alerting them that an episode based on their script was scheduled for an upcoming broadcast.

Major studios often had been described as assembly lines, but the analogy was never more appropriate than during the late 1950s at Warner Bros. Television, where the series truly seemed to consist of interchangeable parts. In an article describing the Screen Gems studio, industry reporter Richard Gehman contrasted the diversity of production at Screen Gems with the monotony of an unnamed studio, which was clearly Warner Bros. "At one of the other film factories," he described, "the stars of all the series all look like all the stars of all the series. The young heroes are consistently handsome and consistently vapid of expression. A resourceful producer could pluck one of them out of one series like a general playing *Kriegspiel* with lead soldiers, and set him down in another series. The actor would never know the difference. Neither, alas, would the audience. At that particular production company, there is no such thing as a shortage of fresh material. By using the names of the characters and the setting of one series' episodes, the producer can get himself a serviceable (if, perhaps, not fine) episode for another show."[25]

This description of production at Warner Bros. might seem like a paranoid fantasy of Hollywood's ability to degrade cultural production—if it weren't so accurate. After the studio successfully replaced

The handsome young cast of *Hawaiian Eye* (Anthony Eisley, Connie Stevens, Robert Conrad, and Poncie Ponce) bears a striking resemblance to . . .

Cheyenne with *Bronco* and discovered that audiences still tuned in, there developed a sense that the young contract actors were inter-changeable, that they were simply components to be inserted in one series or another, depending upon production schedules. When *Bourbon Street Beat* was canceled, for instance, Warner Bros. simply shuttled one star, Richard Long, to *77 Sunset Strip*, and transported supporting actor Van Williams to *Surfside Six*.

. . . the handsome young cast of *Surfside Six* (Troy Donahue, Lee Patterson, Diane McBain, and Van Williams).
(Both photos courtesy of Photofest © Warner Bros.)

Even the scripts at Warner Bros. were literally interchangeable. The narrative strategies for the various series were so similar that Warner Bros. management didn't even slow production during a six-month strike by the Writers Guild in 1960. Instead, management simply transposed existing scripts from one series to another, assigning the screenplay credit to the pseudonymous "W. Hermanos" (a joking Spanish-language version of "Warner Bros."). By changing locales and character names, Western scripts became private-eye stories and vice versa. The studio recycled so many scripts that story editor James Barnett was able to joke, "You are indeed an optimist if you think Warner Bros. has any suitable story material left for adaptation after four months of no writers. Soon, we'll be digging into old Bugs Bunny storyboards for source material—and now that I think of it, there might well be a *Maverick* or two in them."[26]

Amused studio executives found satisfaction in this ruse because it proved that audiences would accept anything the studio produced, no matter what compromises were made for the sake of production quotas. In the flow of narratives that rushed past TV viewers, it didn't seem to matter whether a story had appeared in a previous incarnation. Studio executives took pride in their ability to manage such a high volume of production, but they never seemed to question whether the level of production had become self-defeating, particularly as Warner Bros. series dissolved into an increasingly uniform product.

As a result of Warner Bros. Television's conception of mass production, performers and personnel also were treated as interchangeable components—which meant, of course, that the studio attempted to keep labor costs as low as possible. As a matter of policy, Warner Bros. not only avoided profit participation but also trailed many of the other major telefilm producers in salaries for producers, writers, and actors. This effort to keep a tight rein on costs made sense from a short-term perspective, but it subverted any possibility for inspiring a loyal and committed creative community at the studio. On the contrary, Warner Bros. Television became a place to leave on the way to a more lucrative deal in the television industry.

Writers were the first to flee Warner Bros. Unlike the producers and actors who were bound by term contracts, writers were hired on a free-lance basis. When the studio's wages were no longer competitive with those being offered elsewhere in the industry, writers simply drifted away. By the late 1950s, story editors warned that the studio no longer could afford the industry's best writers. "At the amount of money we intend to pay," Jack Emanuel explained, "in no instance can I hope to get established and proven teleplay writers. . . . We will have to consider novice talent or equally questionable has-beens." With Warner Bros. trailing other studios by as much as $3,000 per script in 1959, James Barnett warned Orr that Warner Bros. was having trouble hiring even its "former reliable stand-bys." Later, when Orr asked each producer to provide the names of six writers they'd like to hire but couldn't afford, the story department compiled a list of *fifty* writers who had once written for Warner Bros. but whose prices were now beyond its range.[27] The studio's reluctance to make competitive deals for writers undermined its ability to build a production company with lasting viability.

Thanks to the studio's penurious economic policies and its heavy production schedule, the overburdened Warner Bros. actors were a disgruntled and rebellious lot. In a sense, this was in keeping with the Warner Bros. tradition. During the studio era, Warner Bros. had been the site of a series of revolts by alienated actors protesting treatment by a studio that was notorious for consigning its actors to an extremely limited range of roles and for refusing to renegotiate contracts that had been signed by actors early in their careers. Bette Davis, Olivia de Havilland, Humphrey Bogart, and James Cagney all attempted to escape their Warner Bros. contracts at one time or another.[28] In the long run, the dissatisfaction of the studio's TV actors was particularly harmful, because Warner Bros. series were distinguished—if they were distinguished at all—by actors' performances and their unique personalities. With minimal production values, repetitive scripts, and routinized direction and editing, the Warner Bros. series depended on performers to provide nuances that otherwise were absent. This was particularly true of *77 Sunset Strip* and its progeny, which attempted to mimic Roy Huggins's wry humor without the benefit of Huggins-produced scripts.

The television actors were numbed by the repetition of the scripts and by the dreary, taxing routine of production. Even after returning from his yearlong holdout, Clint Walker hated working in Warner Bros. series, complaining to the press that he felt "like a caged animal" pacing back and forth in a zoo. "A TV series is a dead-end street," he lamented. "You work the same set, with the same actors, and with the same limited budgets. And you grind out twenty shows a year. Pretty soon you don't know which picture you're in and you don't care." In private, Walker was even more critical of the studio, admitting that he awoke each morning physically ill from the dread of working on *Cheyenne*. Even when Warner Bros. assigned Walker to feature films, the movies were inexpensive quickies. Walker begged for at least one opportunity to work on a more "important" movie, but the studio wouldn't oblige.[29]

Other Warner Bros. stars echoed Walker's disenchantment. Will Hutchins admitted hoping that *Sugarfoot* would be canceled. *Sugarfoot*'s episodes, he complained, are "pretty much the same after you've seen a handful. . . . They're moneymakers for the studio, the stations, and the actors, but there's a kind of empty feeling when you're through." James Garner expressed the resentment felt by most of the contract performers at the studio. "I feel like a slab of meat hanging there," he said. "Every once in a while they cut off a piece."[30]

Jack Warner had nothing but scorn for actors whose complaints were growing in frequency. In his mind their grumbling simply represented "the chickens coming home to roost" after the studio's "folly" of capitulating to Walker's demands for a higher salary and a reduced production schedule. "Naturally they want to get out of TV because the work is not easy," Warner said. "They want to get into features where they can have an easier occupation."[31] The conflicts between management and actors grew as Warner Bros. actors observed other performers reaping the rewards of profit-participation deals, while they were among the few actors in Hollywood still locked into exclusive contracts.

After a series of individual confrontations in which actors like Walker, Wayde Preston, and Edd Byrnes walked off their sets, the actors banded together in November 1959 to ask the Screen Actors Guild to crack down on Warner Bros. about the deteriorating conditions that had developed at the studio because of the hectic pace of production. The actors claimed that the studio routinely ignored rules requiring rest periods, meals, and payment for overtime. In the press, the actors also complained that exclusive, long-term contracts were an outdated form of servitude that kept them from realizing the rewards of TV stardom. As a result of the complaints, Warner Bros. executives agreed to be more diligent in meeting SAG guidelines, but otherwise they ignored the actors' grumbling. SAG therefore announced that it would seek to limit the studio's power over actors by prohibiting "combination" contracts that enabled studios to assign actors to both TV and films at the studio's discretion.[32]

Warner Bros.'s unsympathetic attitude toward its performers ultimately backfired when in 1960 James Garner, the studio's biggest star, filed a lawsuit to escape his contract. The situation that provided Garner with a means of escape arose because of the studio's arrogance during the 1960 writers' strike. After completing production on the season's episodes of *Maverick* in March 1960, the studio tried to save money by suspending Garner and Jack Kelly, invoking the standard force majeure clause in their contracts, which gave the studio the right to stop payment when extraordinary circumstances disrupted production. Warner Bros. claimed that the strike made it impossible to continue production on the series because the studio had exhausted its supply of scripts. In truth, the studio had no trouble working around the strike until the studio decided that the strike could be invoked for the sake of expediency in avoiding payments to actors. Garner sued for breach of contract and the studio countered with its own lawsuit.

While awaiting the trial, Garner refused to return for the 1960–1961 season. Warner Bros. simply replaced him with Roger Moore, who arrived as the Maverick brothers' British cousin, Beau. Studio executives held their breath, hoping that fans wouldn't revolt against this cynical contrivance. Though a similar tactic had worked two years earlier on *Cheyenne*, many suspected that James Garner would not be so easily replaceable. Two weeks after the season debut, the publicity department reported optimistically that only 161 letters protesting

Garner's absence had arrived. But plummeting ratings told a different story, one that threatened the studio's entire system of production. Garner's stardom had transcended the undifferentiated flow of series production; he was no interchangeable cog in the studio assembly line.

Retaining Garner became such a high priority that Jack Warner dispatched Steve Trilling, his right-hand man, to handle the delicate negotiations, which soon involved not only Warner Bros. but also Kaiser and ABC. Kaiser believed that Garner was so crucial to *Maverick*'s success that its representatives offered him half of the company's one-third share in the series, retroactive to the first episode. Warner Bros. broke all precedent by offering to raise Garner's salary from its existing terms of $1,750 per week with a $15,000 bonus for each feature film to $5,000 per episode—with his commitment reduced to thirteen episodes a season—and a $100,000 bonus per feature. Under this contract, Garner would continue in *Maverick* for two more seasons and then would work exclusively in features. Though this was the most lucrative TV contract ever offered at Warner Bros., Garner turned it down because he was adamantly opposed to any deal that involved either series television or an exclusive contract. Garner argued that he already had demonstrated his value as a movie star and that his career might be "dead" if he subjected himself to television's grueling pace for two more years.[33] Garner's ability to walk away from such an offer suggests just how badly actors wanted to escape TV production at Warner Bros.

Since Garner refused to return to the studio, the case proceeded to trial as scheduled in December 1960. Garner's lawyer called Jack Warner himself to the stand and, during cross-examination, Warner revealed the duplicity behind the attempt to suspend Garner when he acknowledged that the studio hadn't suffered much during the writers' strike because of the decision to recycle scripts. Following this testimony, the court ruled in Garner's favor, announcing that the studio's breach of conduct in falsely declaring a force majeure suspension had terminated its exclusive contract with the actor.[34] Warner Bros. executives had subverted their own interests, losing their single most valuable actor and the most obvious fruits of their talent development program. The studio kept *Maverick* alive in Garner's absence by hastily adding a previously unmentioned member of the Maverick family, younger brother Brent (Robert Colbert), and the series limped through one last season before being canceled.

At practically the same moment that Warner Bros. lost its most important TV actor, the studio also allowed its most important producer, Roy Huggins, to slip away. Because producers were signed to the same sort of exclusive contracts as actors, they too began to chafe at the restrictions placed on them by the studio administration—especially since Warner Bros. was the only studio that refused to share residual profits. The practice of inserting a level of management control into every decision about program development meant that responsibility for the creation of Warner Bros. series—and series ownership—rested solely with the institution, not with individuals. As the producer who guided *Cheyenne* through its first-season transformation, who created *Colt .45,* who created and produced *Maverick,* and who created and produced the pilot for *77 Sunset Strip,* Roy Huggins was directly linked to the studio's three most popular series. Despite having played such an important role at the studio, however, he had no right to share profits from the series.

Though Huggins was not entirely responsible for the studio's rise to prominence—particularly since he had nothing further to do with *77 Sunset Strip* after its creation—he was the most gifted, and perhaps indispensable, producer at Warner Bros. Whereas most of the studio's producers were efficient managers who supervised productions and kept things running smoothly, Huggins was a creative producer, more a writer than a supervisor. *Maverick* was the most distinctive Warner Bros. series because it bore the mark of his irreverent vision, imposed both by a core creative team that shared his perspective and by his own diligence in generating story ideas and constantly rewriting the scripts once they were submitted. After two years of producing *Maverick,* Huggins yearned to escape the grind and to have more freedom than his TV contract allowed.

Huggins asked to leave *Maverick* and to begin working in feature films. During the summer of 1959, Warner Bros. obliged by taking Huggins off of *Maverick* and replacing him with Coles Trapnell. Huggins now had responsibility for creating the studio's new Exploitation Film Division, a unit expected to produce low-budget films using the actors, writers, and directors who had been developed by Warner Bros. Television. Under this agreement, Huggins began preparations for his first feature at Warner Bros., *The Savage Streets,* a story of political intrigue starring Efrem Zimbalist, Jr., and Jack Kelly. Just as production was about to begin, however, Zimbalist's TV costar Roger Smith suffered a serious accident that prevented him from working on *77 Sunset Strip.* To avoid delaying the production schedule for the series, Zimbalist was recalled by the television division, and the movie was postponed indefinitely. Rather than allow Huggins simply to wait out the delay, the studio tried to reassign him to television production. Television, particularly at Warner Bros., Huggins told the press, "is no place for a compulsive perfectionist like myself."[35]

Placing Huggins temporarily under suspension, Warner Bros. warned other production companies not to approach him during the contract dispute. But the die was cast. Huggins went on to produce the Warner Bros. feature film, retitled *A Fever in the Blood* (1961), but he also convinced the studio to release him from his exclusive

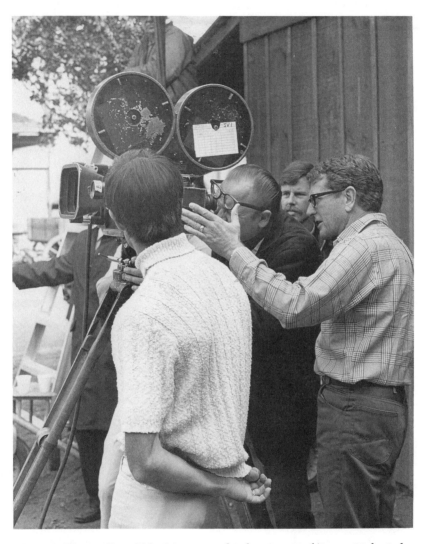

By 1960 Warner Bros. Television started to lose many of its most talented employees, including producer Roy Huggins (*far right*), who left to take over television production at Twentieth Century–Fox.
(Courtesy of Roy Huggins, personal collection)

contract. Once freed, Huggins immediately fielded offers not only to produce but also to supervise TV production at Twentieth Century–Fox and MGM. In October 1960, Huggins became vice president in charge of all television production at Twentieth Century–Fox.[36]

In a single season, 1959–1960, Warner Bros. Television reached the peak of its success in television, producing seven and a half hours of programming, and yet the studio also drove away two of its most valuable employees—Roy Huggins and James Garner, the men responsible for *Maverick,* the only Warner Bros. TV series ever to win an Emmy Award. In holding the line on studio-era exclusive contracts, Warner Bros. was temporarily rewarded with success in television production, but studio executives seemed not to care that the fastest-rising companies also offered less-restrictive contracts. Any actor, producer, or writer able to leave Warner Bros. could find a much more lucrative deal through independent production or through the higher wages and profit participation available at other studios. Inevitably, Warner Bros. suffered a depletion of its most talented personnel. This unwillingness to adapt to the economic practices of its competitors reflected Warner Bros.'s larger failure to diversify beyond its most immediate concern with supplying ABC's production orders.

Like the other major studios, Warner Bros. had been slow to enter television production because of its reluctance to create a product that it didn't distribute. Warner Bros. had attempted to form its own TV network during the late 1940s precisely because it feared allowing the existing TV networks to monopolize the channels of distribution. Yet when Warner Bros. finally began to produce for television, studio executives allowed themselves to become locked into an exclusive source of distribution—ABC-TV. In fact, after entering television, Warner Bros. only once negotiated with another network. In early 1959, the studio met with NBC to discuss two half-hour series, but when ABC's huge production order for fall 1959 filled the studio to capacity, Warner Bros. broke off negotiations.[37] Bound exclusively to ABC, Warner Bros. was both subject to the network's decisions and tied to its fortunes in the industry.

ABC achieved remarkable success in the ratings during the late 1950s, and Warner Bros. played a significant role in the network's rise. By programming hour-long dramas produced in Hollywood, ABC not only caught up with NBC and CBS but, in 1960, surpassed them in the Nielsen ratings for the twenty-four largest markets. During this period, ABC joined the other networks in ridding its schedule of sponsor-produced programming. By shifting almost entirely to hour-long programs, the networks drove sponsorship costs beyond the reach of single sponsors. As Howard Barnes, director of programs at CBS, explained, "The risk of sponsoring a program that fails to make the grade at those prices is too great. So the advertiser prefers to play it safe by spreading his TV appropriation over a number of different shows just as the prudent investor spreads his investment capital among a number of stocks rather than plunging it all on a single company." By the 1960–1961 season, *The Rifleman* was the only sponsor-controlled program remaining on ABC's schedule.[38]

With sponsors displaced from program production and local stations losing interest in first-run syndication because of the ready supply of feature films and off-network reruns, the three networks became just about the only buyers of television programming. Just as the major studios had feared, the networks gained almost exclusive control of the channels of distribution. With that power, ABC and the other networks began asking for a proprietary interest in the programs that they broadcast, arguing that they should receive 10 percent to 50 percent of residual profits—including syndication, merchandising, and foreign distribution—as compensation for the risk of financing pilots. By 1960, the networks had profit-participation agreements for the majority of the programs in their schedules. ABC, of course, shared in the residual profits for all Warner Bros. series after 1956.[39]

By relying on an exclusive relationship with ABC, Warner Bros. essentially gave the network control over its production schedule. After Goldenson and Treyz assumed control of ABC, the network developed a programming philosophy based on exploiting any proven hit by attempting to repeat its success. This was a fairly conservative programming strategy, built upon a belief in following formulas that had proved successful rather than searching for future hits through novel program forms. A clear example of this philosophy was ABC's attempt to capitalize on the success of *77 Sunset Strip* by ordering two more series that were almost identical to it. ABC's programming strategy became so narrowly focused that, of the thirty-three series in its 1959–1960 prime-time schedule, twelve were Westerns and seven were crime series.

These rigid programming strategies took their toll on ABC's relationship with its first important Hollywood producer, Walt Disney. As the Western vogue swept prime time, ABC became so committed to capitalizing on the genre's popularity that the network pressured Disney into transforming *Disneyland* into an omnibus Western series. Disney actually took pride in having introduced television's Western craze with his adaptation of the life of Davy Crockett, and he willingly created *Zorro* (1957–1959), his third series for the network. But Disney was unhappy when ABC pressured him to devote the majority of *Disneyland*'s episodes to limited-run Western series modeled after Davy Crockett. In 1957–1958, Disney produced one Western series, the eight-episode "Saga of Andy Burnett." Because of pressure from the network, he added two more Western series during the following season, "The Nine Lives of Elfego Baca" and "Tales of Texas John Slaughter." During the next two seasons, eighteen of *Disneyland*'s twenty-six annual episodes were devoted to Western series like "The Swamp Fox" and "Daniel Boone."

As a result, Disney himself railed against ABC's conservative approach to programming. "I gave ABC their first full-hour Western series with my Davy Crockett shows," he recalled, "and soon the network was flooded with other Westerns. They made so much money for ABC that before long I found myself in a straightjacket. I no longer had the freedom . . . I enjoyed in those first three years. They kept insisting I do more and more Westerns. . . . I found myself competing with *Maverick, Wyatt Earp,* and every other Western myth. When I came up with a fresh idea in another field, the network executives would say no. . . . One of their rejects was *The Shaggy Dog.* We made a theater movie out of it and grossed $9 million." Disney became so disgruntled about the terms of his exclusive contract with ABC that he filed suit to break the contract in 1959. Although the suit failed, the relationship between Disney and ABC turned so unpleasant that in 1960 Disney purchased ABC's Disneyland stock for $7.5 million. When his seven-year contract expired after the 1960–1961 season, he moved his flagship series to NBC.[40]

Warner Bros. recognized that the sustained life of a television producer depended as much upon creating and selling new series as upon actual production. Consequently, the television division proposed many different kinds of series to ABC, but ABC chose primarily to finance pilots for Westerns and crime series. Story editor James Barnett expressed the studio's growing exasperation over ABC's reluctance to branch out into other genres in a piece of doggerel that concluded: "I think that I shall never see/A format new for ABC."[41] For the 1960–1961 season, ABC ordered six and a half hours of programming from Warner Bros., a decline of one hour from the previous year's peak order. ABC canceled *The Alaskans* and *Bourbon Street Beat,* replacing them with two new Warner Bros. series: *Surfside Six,* which simply transposed *Bourbon Street Beat* into a new Sunbelt locale with an even younger team of detectives, and *The Roaring '20s* (1960–1962), a period series that ABC hoped would strike the same chord as its latest hit series, *The Untouchables.* In addition, the studio collapsed

Cheyenne, Sugarfoot, and *Bronco* into a single alternating series titled *The Cheyenne Show*.

Warner Bros. still produced a sizable amount of programming in 1960–1961, but its audiences were diminishing, and the aura of success that had enveloped the company during the previous season was fading. In 1959–1960, *77 Sunset Strip, Lawman, Cheyenne,* and *Maverick* all had been top-twenty series; by the following year, only *77 Sunset Strip* even squeezed into the top twenty-five. It was an ominous sign, therefore, when ABC merely renewed the existing Warner Bros. series for the 1961–1962 season, without placing any new orders. The trade press speculated that ABC retained the Warner Bros. series only to maintain its relationship with the studio; otherwise, it would have canceled most of them.[42] When no Warner Bros. series cracked the top twenty-five during the 1961–1962 season, ABC ordered only four hours in 1962–1963: *Cheyenne* (only thirteen episodes), *77 Sunset Strip, Hawaiian Eye,* and a new combat series, *The Gallant Men* (1962–1963). By the 1963–1964 season, only *77 Sunset Strip* survived.

The Warner Bros. series weren't the only ABC series to collapse in the ratings. After peaking in fall 1960, ABC's overall ratings went into a tailspin as the situation comedy genre experienced a periodic renaissance, propelling the sitcom-laden CBS back to the top. Overloaded with its narrowly defined schedule of aging action-adventure series, ABC fell back into third place and remained there for more than a decade. ABC executives later admitted that their big mistake had been in holding on to Warner Bros. series "too long beyond their useful run." In 1965, ABC programming chief Tom Moore recalled, "All of the shows began to look alike. *77 Sunset Strip* looked like *Surfside 6, Surfside 6* like *Hawaiian Eye.* We wore out our source of supply."[43] Warner Bros. hitched a ride to the top of the television industry with ABC, but, having established no relationships with the other networks, it also rode with ABC all the way back to the bottom.

Warner Bros. television policy consisted primarily of supplying ABC's orders for new product, and ABC's programming philosophy depended mainly on repeating successful formulas. These equally conservative policies meshed in such a way that both companies discovered themselves stalled at a dead end by 1960. Warner Bros. had never planned for the possibility that ABC might one day fall back into third place. For Warner Bros. executives, the business of television during the late 1950s meant only one thing: producing prime-time series for ABC. Considering everything that these executives knew about the importance of distribution, it is surprising that the studio made itself vulnerable by becoming so dependent on a single type of product and a single distributor. The other studios at the top of the telefilm industry by this time—Screen Gems, Revue, Desilu, and Four Star—were not as vulnerable because they possessed a much broader conception of television—in terms of program formats and genres, production financing, and diverse means of distribution.

Although each of the telefilm studios was involved primarily in producing series television for the networks, they demonstrated a range of strategies for organizing television production and for profiting from the medium. In their drive to diversify, however, they shared a common conception of the television industry as something distinctly different from the Hollywood studio system. Whether adopting profit-sharing incentives to attract the best talent or forming distribution divisions to capitalize on residual profits, these film companies saw television as an emergent industry, not as a reincarnation of the movie business. Warner Bros. briefly surged past these rising telefilm companies, but it did so without making a similar effort to put down roots in television. As the organic metaphor implied, long-term viability in the television industry depended on a more lasting commitment to television than Warner Bros. was capable of imagining before 1960. At Warner Bros., television looked like the resurrection of the B movie—an adequate, though not very glamorous, way to pay the bills while making more expensive and prestigious movies. Warner Bros. seemed incapable of recognizing the full range of activities that constituted the television industry because Jack Warner and the other studio executives still thought of movies as the nation's predominant cultural commodity. "That's the trouble with Jack Warner," Clint Walker said. "He has been in this business too long."[44]

There were signs of trouble at Warner Bros. Television by 1960, but at the time these seemed like temporary setbacks, not cause for alarm. In fact, during March 1961 Jack Warner appointed William Orr, the production chief for Warner Bros. Television, to take command of all production at Warner Bros.—including both television and movies. It was a triumphant moment for Orr and for the entire television division. In 1955 Jack Warner had disparaged television by announcing that Warner Bros. had decided to produce television series only to exploit an opportunity to publicize feature films. Just five years later, Warner felt comfortable turning over feature-film production to a man whose sole experience as a producer had been acquired in television. By assuming responsibility for all production at Warner Bros., Orr became the first television executive to take charge of feature-film production at a major studio. This transition, made in the confidence that

Warner Bros. Television would continue to prosper, marked the complete integration of motion picture and television production at Warner Bros. In his first public statements following the promotion, Orr announced that his administration would continue to concentrate on achieving higher earnings from fewer movies, while also working more actively to integrate movie and television production. To take advantage of the union between the two divisions, Orr planned to produce a feature film that would showcase all of the TV stars under contract at the studio.[45]

Although Orr's promotion represented the symbolic triumph of television at Warner Bros., it occurred at almost the same time that the studio's television division collapsed. By 1962 it was becoming clear that the studio's original plan for television was no longer working. While the industry trade press speculated that ABC would cancel nearly all of the Warner Bros. series, the studio quietly laid off 25 percent of the television staff—the first sign of retrenchment in the division's six-year history.

Watching the studio's prime-time fortunes dwindle away, Jack Warner charged Orr with the task of redesigning the studio's television operation. For the first time, Warner placed "no limits" on Orr's authority to develop new programs or to restructure the studio's television policies. Orr and his staff decided to implement a series of reforms intended to bring the studio in line with the other major telefilm producers. Stressing that the studio would be guided by a spirit of "imaginative exploration," Jack Warner announced that Warner Bros. would no longer be bound by allegiance to particular program formats, production methods, financial practices, or networks. In March 1962, the studio declared that it was eager to sign deals with any of the networks, and that it welcomed co-production deals with independent producers.[46]

The first independent producer to set up shop at Warner Bros. was Jack Webb, who arrived in March 1962 to produce *General Electric True Theater* (1962–1963), an anthology series based on actual incidents.[47] Though known primarily as an independent TV producer of *Dragnet* and a few short-lived series like *Noah's Ark* (1956–1957) and *The D.A.'s Man* (1959), Webb also had established strong ties with Warner Bros. as an independent movie producer. During the 1950s, the studio had financed several feature films that Webb produced and directed through his Mark VII Productions: *Dragnet* (1954), *Pete Kelly's Blues* (1955), *The D.I.* (1957), *-30-* (1959). By consistently traveling between television and movies, Webb was Hollywood's most aggressive independent producer in attempting to link the media.

The studio brought another newcomer onto the lot when it hired

ABC vice president Oliver Treyz after he was fired by the network in March 1962. As ABC's network vice president since 1956, Treyz had guided its expansion, but he was also held responsible by chairman Leonard Goldenson when ABC slid back into third place after 1960. With the Kennedy administration FCC scrutinizing network television and a Senate subcommittee investigating TV violence, ABC not only was falling in the ratings but also was suffering a public relations disaster as ABC and its Treyz-era programming practices—particularly its reliance on Hollywood-produced action-adventure series—came under attack for a variety of cultural crimes, from destroying television's Golden Age to defiling the nation's impressionable youths. Although Goldenson denied accusations that he held Treyz responsible for the public relations crisis, he fired the network vice president in March 1962 after Treyz had attempted unsuccessfully to defend the network at a series of public hearings.[48]

Warner Bros. hired Oliver Treyz in May 1962 to assist in an expansion program intended to return the studio to its competitive standing in television. The expansion took place on a number of fronts, including diversifying into syndication. During the same month in which Treyz started work, for instance, the studio founded a syndication division and began distributing its own programs for the first time—earning more than $7 million during the first year of operation.[49] In the midst of this expansion, Treyz was given the title of vice president and worldwide sales manager, but his duties were fairly vague. Although the studio announced that he would spearhead the drive to expand its overseas sales, he was also given responsibility for strengthening the ties between Warner Bros., advertising agencies, and the networks. Treyz immediately took charge of the studio's ambitious program development campaign, which was given the name "Operation Seven Hours"—an attempt to return to the glory days of 1959, when Warner Bros. supplied more than seven hours of prime-time programming.[50] In spite of this initiative, Warner Bros. succeeded in selling only two new series to ABC: *The Gallant Men*, a World War II combat series, and *The Dakotas*, a Western series ordered as a midseason replacement for *Cheyenne*.

It is quite possible that Warner Bros. hired Treyz with the intention of giving him command over Warner Bros. Television in the near future. Such a scenario might explain why Treyz left the studio as abruptly as he arrived once Jack Warner announced in February 1963 that he had convinced Jack Webb to oversee all production at Warner Bros. Television. With William Orr shifting solely to feature films, Webb arrived in the administrative offices promising to introduce a "new concept in television production" at Warner Bros. Indeed,

Webb made an immediate mark on the company. First, he announced that the exclusive relationship with ABC had ended forever. "It will be healthier," he declared, "to deal with all three networks." Second, he announced that Warner Bros. would begin to sign participation deals in order to attract outside producers, but also to lure big-name stars to the studio. After years of developing its own stars from young, inexpensive performers, Warner Bros., declared Webb, would pursue veteran performers by sharing series ownership with them. Former Warner Bros. contract employee Bette Davis became the first actor to sign a co-production deal when she and writer-producer Fay Kanin agreed to develop a dramatic series. Webb also signed co-production deals with George Burns for a situation comedy, *Wendy and Me* (1964–1965), and with Jeffrey Hunter for a Western, *Temple Houston* (1963–1964).[51]

In spite of his plans for reforming production at Warner Bros., Webb was ineffective in marketing Warner Bros. series. He sold *Temple Houston* to NBC, but otherwise succeeded only in convincing ABC to renew *77 Sunset Strip*, the last series remaining from the studio's peak years. If one thing can be said about Webb as a television producer, it is that he possessed a distinctive style and an unwavering vision of the crime genre. Nowhere was this more evident than in his treatment of *77 Sunset Strip*, the one studio series that he inherited. It is ironic that Webb was given control of a series that had been created in reaction to the TV crime genre as it had developed under the influence of *Dragnet*. By its very existence, *77 Sunset Strip* mocked *Dragnet*'s puritanical tone and its shrill allegiance to the moral clarity of the law. As though in retribution for its irreverence, Webb purged *77 Sunset Strip* by injecting it with his own grave preoccupations.

Shortly after taking over the television division, Webb signed his occasional collaborator William Conrad to produce, and sometimes direct, episodes of *77 Sunset Strip*. In collaboration, Webb and Conrad gutted the Warner Bros. formula and rebuilt the series from the ground up. Webb dismissed all of the actors except Efrem Zimbalist, Jr., and stripped away the hip milieu of Sunset Boulevard by transporting Stuart Bailey to an anonymous office building in downtown Los Angeles. Webb and Conrad launched the new *77 Sunset Strip* with an ambitious, five-part episode that was broadcast over a series of weeks. Featuring a huge cast of guest stars (including Richard Conte, Peter Lorre, Herbert Marshall, Burgess Meredith, Ed Wynn, and Tony Bennett), the multi-part narrative tracked Stuart Bailey through an intricately plotted conspiracy that led him across Europe and the Middle East in search of art treasures stolen during World War II. The episode was marketed as a unique new form of television narrative—an ongoing, epic TV episode that anticipated the later development of the mini-series. On the one hand, Webb's transformation of *77 Sunset Strip* demonstrated that Warner Bros. series didn't have to be governed by the banal uniformity imposed upon them during the Orr administration. On the other hand, under Webb's guidance what once had been among the brightest series on TV quickly settled into a routine of grim, emotionless professionalism. Stuart Bailey, television's very model of the sophisticated, sardonic playboy, metamorphosed into a tense film noir functionary, stranded alone in a shadowy world of conspiracy and paranoia.

Webb's intervention couldn't revive the flagging series, and it lasted only until the end of the season. With the additional cancellation of *Temple Houston*, Jack Webb's first year at the helm of Warner Bros. Television was viewed as a dismal failure. At the time he took over the studio, Webb informed Jack Warner that it would take two to three years to implement the changes that he envisioned for reviving Warner Bros. Television. Warner had signed Webb to a three-year contract, but he didn't wait to see the results of Webb's initiatives. In December 1963—just ten months after hiring Webb—Jack Warner fired him.[52]

Promising another "complete reevaluation of all TV operations," Warner assigned William Orr to return to television in December 1963.[53] During the next few years, Orr and his staff struggled to stabilize Warner Bros. Television, but the studio simply never recovered from the free-fall of the early 1960s. Situation comedies had come to dominate prime time once again, and Warner Bros. had very little experience in the genre. With the exception of *Room for One More*, a midseason replacement in 1963, Warner Bros. didn't produce a situation comedy until its 1964 co-production of *Wendy and Me* with George Burns. In 1965, the studio sold three other sitcoms—*Hank* (1965–1966), *Mr. Roberts,* and *F Troop* (1965–1967). A broad parody of the Western genre that had taken Warner Bros. to the top of the telefilm industry, *F Troop* lasted two seasons; the others were canceled after a single season. The only successful series launched at Warner Bros. after 1959 also premiered in 1965, but it wasn't even a Warner Bros. production. With Warner Bros. providing only the financing and studio facilities, independent producer Quinn Martin possessed complete creative control over his new series, *The F.B.I.,* which aired on ABC for nine seasons (1965–1974).

By the mid-1960s, even William Orr, the man who had guided Warner Bros. Television for a decade, was no longer safe in the midst of the tumult. As Jack Warner reduced his presence at the studio during the mid-1960s, Benjamin Kalmenson, head of the company's New

York offices, assumed a much stronger role in studio leadership. Kalmenson had never been a fervent supporter of television, and his support grew even more tentative when Warner Bros. Television settled into a pattern of failure. Revenue from the television division had reached its peak in 1962, when TV accounted for 43 percent of the studio's gross revenue, nearly equaling the motion picture division's share of 45 percent. By 1965, however, the income from television accounted for only 21 percent of the company's gross revenue. Despairing that television had become a lost cause, Kalmenson fired Orr and his staff without warning in fall 1965, replacing him with Robert Lewine, ABC's original West Coast executive at the time of the studio's debut in 1955. As Lewine gradually learned, Kalmenson hired him to serve merely as caretaker for a division being allowed to wither away. "There is no question but that they were disenchanted with television, even before I arrived at the studio," he later recalled.[54] Given very few resources to develop series, Lewine failed to launch any new productions.

In spite of the efforts to bring new blood into the studio, to adopt independent production, and to reach out to networks other than ABC, Warner Bros. Television slowly disintegrated during the 1960s, collapsing under the weight of an organization top-heavy in production. Had Warner Bros. seized the opportunity to diversify during the late 1950s, its television division might have been able to withstand the fall of ABC. But because of the studio's consistently conservative approach to television, Warner Bros. Television had nothing to fall back on except production. Studio executives didn't develop a long-range plan for television until it was too late. They failed to bring to television the most obvious economic lesson of the motion picture industry—the necessity of controlling distribution. Warner Bros. had attempted to acquire broadcast channels from the 1920s to the 1950s, but once expelled from the security of the studio system, its executives ignored long-term rewards from television in favor of the more immediate income that could be channeled into the production of expensive features. When Warner Bros. Television crumbled during the 1960s, any hopes of perpetuating the Hollywood studio system were buried in the debris.

·XI·
Epilogue

The New Holly-
wood began to take shape as soon as the major studios—those with
the greatest investment in the Old Hollywood of the studio system—forged a relationship between movies and television during the
1950s. Diversifying into television seemed adventuresome to the major studios in 1955, but less than a decade later those same studios
had come to depend for their very existence on the income provided
by television. At the same time, the networks and local stations
leaned heavily on Hollywood in order to satisfy their endless need
for programming. By the 1960s, anyone flipping on a TV set likely
would encounter a product from Hollywood, either a television series
or a feature film. This simple fact had enormous consequences for the
studios that once had formed the Hollywood studio system.

During the 1950s, the television networks and their advertisers
looked to major Hollywood producers to supply the glamour and
spectacle of Hollywood movies. David O. Selznick's production of
Light's Diamond Jubilee was the most ambitious attempt to create an
electronic analog for the epic Hollywood movies that Selznick, among
others, had contributed to the studio era. But Selznick's extravaganza
inspired few imitators, because it was both too costly and too un-
wieldy to serve as a model for Hollywood production within the economic structure and broadcast schedules of network television. By
signing production agreements with the major studios in 1955, the
networks tried again to import Hollywood production values into
television. Constrained by the limited budgets and frantic pace of series production, however, the Hollywood studios were incapable of
reproducing the spectacle of their movies. Instead, the technical efficiency of Hollywood production made studios like Warner Bros. more
valuable as suppliers of the episodic series that filled the bulk of
prime time.

The networks still alternated between programming regularly scheduled series, designed to encourage routine viewing, and unique events capable of capturing nationwide attention. In 1960, however, it became possible for Hollywood to serve both functions. For the first time, feature films made in Hollywood after 1948 became available to television, once the Screen Actors Guild reached a collective-bargaining agreement that guaranteed royalties for its members. Now the studios were able to supply both episodic telefilm series and recent feature films. The networks quickly recognized that the most efficient and predictable method for delivering Hollywood spectacle to the small screen was simply to broadcast recent feature films once they had completed their runs in the theaters.

NBC introduced Hollywood features to prime time in September 1961 with the premiere of *NBC's Saturday Night at the Movies*. Once the floodgates opened, Hollywood movies became an increasingly important component in prime-time schedules. At the same time, of course, television became a crucial secondary market for the movie industry. By 1965 the average price for network rights to a feature film reached $400,000; within three years that figure had doubled. The networks publicized the broadcast premiere of recent studio releases as national events, touting them as a departure from the everyday routine of regularly scheduled series. Indeed, the debut broadcasts for the most-celebrated movies often resembled the 1950s TV spectacular. In 1966, for instance, ABC paid Columbia $2 million for the rights to *The Bridge on the River Kwai* (1957), a movie that epitomized the big-budget independent productions of the blockbuster era. Sponsored solely by the Ford Motor Company in order to promote its new product line, the broadcast attracted 60 million television viewers, overwhelming the regularly scheduled programs on the other networks.[1]

Network television, as a market for episodic series, theatrical features, and—beginning in 1965—made-for-TV movies, represented not just a welcome source of additional income but an essential reason for the continued viability of movie studios. TV license fees for feature films rose so rapidly that the studios soon became targets for takeover bids by firms that coveted their film libraries. During November 1966 Warner Bros. received a buy-out offer from Seven Arts Productions, a rising television distributor. Shareholders for both companies approved the $32 million sale in June 1967. After the purchase, Warner Bros. Pictures, a studio with four decades of experience in the movie industry, existed only as a name on the masthead of the new corporation, Warner Bros.–Seven Arts.

Television's effect on Hollywood can be measured by the radically different trajectories that brought together Warner Bros., a venerable Hollywood studio that had barely diversified in television beyond producing for network prime time, and Seven Arts, a Canadian-based upstart that expanded rapidly from a foundation in television distribution. Just as the major studios had anticipated, the companies that prospered in television were those that controlled distribution. By distributing feature films and TV series, for instance, Columbia's Screen Gems grew steadily into the 1960s. By producing through Revue Studios and distributing feature films and TV series, MCA expanded so rapidly that the onetime talent agency was able to purchase Decca Records and its movie-studio subsidiary, Universal Pictures, in 1962.

Seven Arts didn't even enter the television business until 1960, when Eliot Hyman and Ray Stark joined with Canadian promoter Louis Chesler to acquire and distribute feature films for television. Warner Bros. and Seven Arts came together for the first time that year when studio executives awarded Chesler the television rights to 122 post-1948 Warner Bros. features for a price of $11 million and a share of profits. The distributor soon acquired another 215 features from Universal and nearly 500 from Twentieth Century–Fox. By 1966 Seven Arts controlled the rights to more than 3,000 feature films, short subjects, and cartoons. Fueled by the steadily rising prices for feature films on television, Seven Arts used its position in North American television distribution as the base from which to diversify into foreign distribution, station ownership, and joint-venture financing of movie and television production. In order to sustain the company's growth, Seven Arts then decided to diversify into the production of its own movies and TV series—and for that reason it purchased Warner Bros.[2]

In contrast, Warner Bros. Television deteriorated during the 1960s, having failed to expand much beyond production. The studio's TV division existed only tenuously after William Orr's dismissal in 1965 and disappeared altogether following the merger, when Seven Arts fired studio production chief Robert Lewine and installed its own executives at the helm of a new organization, Warner Bros.–Seven Arts Television. This new organization immediately pursued a range of interests that hadn't been imagined at the original Warner Bros. Television. The head of the new TV division, Don Klauber, held the title of executive vice president for video operations and supervised five different departments: network sales, foreign sales, domestic syndication sales, production, and broadcast stations.[3]

This new television division accomplished little, however, because Warner Bros.–Seven Arts became a candidate for takeover almost as soon as it came into existence, a victim of the late-1960s wave of conglomerate acquisition in the movie industry. In 1966, for instance, Paramount was purchased by Gulf and Western, which then acquired Desilu, a merger that enabled Paramount to compete in television production for the first time. United Artists was purchased by Transamerica in 1967, and MGM became the property of real estate mogul Kirk Kerkorian in 1969. During July 1969, Kinney National Services, a conglomerate with interests in funeral homes, parking lots, construction, and rental cars, purchased Warner Bros.–Seven Arts in order to add a Hollywood studio to its list of "leisure" industry acquisitions. Headed by Kinney's Steven Ross, this new conglomerate was named Warner Communications. Warner Bros. Television became simply one component in the conglomerate's leisure division, which soon included interests in a talent agency, book and comic book publishing, magazine distribution, the music industry, and cable television.[4]

The gulf that separated Warner Bros. Pictures, a movie studio founded in the 1920s, from Warner Communications, a leisure subsidiary of Kinney National Services, seems immense, but it is a gulf spanned by Hollywood's ongoing efforts to define the relationship between movies and television over the course of little more than a decade. In 1959, Warner Bros. believed that elements of the studio system could be sustained indefinitely with the help of television. Ten years later, not only had all traces of the studio system disappeared but television's demand for programming made the studios more valuable for their film libraries—the lasting legacy of the studio era—than for their decades of experience in motion picture production.

From an economic standpoint, the steady income provided by television production and the windfall profits from the sale of feature-film libraries helped to create the New Hollywood because it provided a secure underpinning for the industry's boom-or-bust philosophy, its elusive quest for blockbuster hits. From a cultural perspective, television's endless recycling of movies from the studio era, and its rearticulation of those movies in new television series, helped to form the peculiar historical consciousness that inspires the New Hollywood, the retrospective aesthetic of filmmakers as disparate as Robert Altman and Steven Spielberg. As the informal archive of the American cinema, television established the historical distance from which it was possible even to conceive of an "Old Hollywood," to fashion an image of the studio system as a lost epoch in American culture.[5]

The Hollywood studio system may have collapsed during the 1950s, moviegoing may have ceased to be a matter of habit for most Americans, but the Old Hollywood of the studio era did not simply disappear, left in ruins by the Vesuvian eruption of network television. Instead, the movie industry gradually came to terms with television. Though most of the major studios that had sustained the studio system were absorbed into media conglomerates, Hollywood itself was reinvented, entwined more deeply than ever with the national culture as television transported a never-ending stream of movies and TV series directly into the nation's homes. The thread of continuity that runs through the transition from the Old Hollywood of the studio era to the New Hollywood of the conglomerate era is contained in the impulse to integrate movies and television, the impulse by which Hollywood arrived in the American home, borne across the threshold by television's evanescent beam.

Notes

1. INTRODUCTION: HOLLYWOOD IN THE HOME

1. Robert Ardrey, "Hollywood: The Toll of the Frenzied Forties," *The Reporter*, 21 March 1957, p. 30.

2. David O. Selznick to John Hay Whitney, 7 August 1958, Selznick Collection. All Selznick-related sources are found in this collection.

3. William T. Orr, personal interview, 28 October 1986, Los Angeles; Roy Huggins, personal interview, 25 May 1991, Los Angeles. Other studios established similar rules. A 1949 memo at MGM reportedly prohibited mention of the word "television" in that studio's feature films. See "Hollywood in a Television Boom," *Broadcasting*, 26 October 1959, p. 88. For a discussion of this debate, see Milton MacKaye, "The Big Brawl: Hollywood versus Television," *Saturday Evening Post*, 19 January 1952, pp. 17–18; 26 January 1952, p. 30; 2 February 1952, p. 30; Warner Bros. Pictures, Inc., *Annual Report*, 1947–1953.

4. See William Lafferty, "'No Attempt at Artiness, Profundity, or Significance': *Fireside Theater* and the Rise of Filmed Television Programming," *Cinema Journal* 27, no. 1 (Fall 1987): 23–46.

5. "The Week in Review," *Time*, 8 November 1954, p. 95.

6. Leon Morse, "TV Film: The Battle for Power," *Television*, May 1959, pp. 47–49; "Six Major Studios Turning Out 37% of Webs Telepix," *Variety*, 1 July 1959, p. 36.

7. "WB's $30,000,000 TV Income," *Variety*, 24 June 1959, p. 77; Warner Bros. Pictures, Inc., *Annual Report*, 1957; "Warner Likes TV, Not Actors," *Variety*, 17 June 1959, p. 5.

8. For a discussion of this period in the film industry, see Tino Balio, ed., *The American Film Industry*, pp. 401–438; Janet Staiger, "Individualism versus Collectivism," *Screen* 24, nos. 4–5 (July–August 1983): 68–79.

9. Lawrence L. Murray, "Complacency, Competition, Cooperation: The Film Industry Responds to the Challenge of Television," *Journal of Popular Film* 6, no. 1 (1977): 47–68.

10. Todd Gitlin, "Down the Tubes," in Mark Crispin Miller, ed., *Seeing through Movies*, pp. 19, 48. Other articles in this anthology continue the argument that commercial television is either directly or indirectly responsible

for a catalog of artistic and ideological offenses committed by the contemporary American cinema.

11. Michele Hilmes, *Hollywood and Broadcasting: From Radio to Cable*; William Boddy, *Fifties Television: The Industry and Its Critics*; Tino Balio, ed., *Hollywood in the Age of Television*. See also such early influential articles as Edward Buscombe, "Thinking It Differently: Television and the Film Industry," *Quarterly Review of Film Studies* 9, no. 3 (Summer 1984): 196–203; Douglas Gomery, "Failed Opportunities: The Integration of the Motion Picture and TV Industries," *Quarterly Review of Film Studies* 9, no. 3 (Summer 1984): 219–228; Richard B. Jewell, "Hollywood and Radio: Competition and Partnership in the '30s," *Historical Journal of Film, Radio, and Television* 4, no. 2 (1984): 125–141; and Robert Vianello, "The Rise of the Telefilm and the Networks' Hegemony over the Motion Picture Industry," *Quarterly Review of Film Studies* 9, no. 3 (Summer 1984): 204–218.

12. Carolyn Marvin, *When Old Technologies Were New: Thinking about Electric Communication in the Late Nineteenth Century*, p. 8.

13. Robert C. Allen addresses this aspect of traditional broadcasting history in *Speaking of Soap Operas*, p. 96.

14. De Mille, always one of the industry's great showmen, relished the seeming ubiquity of a nationally broadcast program: "I liked the big [ratings] numbers but what the Lux program meant to me cannot be measured by any numbers. It meant families in Maine and Kansas and Idaho finishing the dishes or the schoolwork or the evening chores in time to gather around their radios. It meant the shut-ins, the invalid, the blind, the very young, and the very old who had no other taste of the theater. It meant people, not in the masses, but individuals, who did me the honor of inviting me into their homes." De Mille's exposure, including his signature statement, "This is Cecil B. De Mille saying good night to you from Hollywood," transformed his name into a trademark tantamount to the notion of the movie producer and helped to popularize the concept of authorship in the movie industry (Cecil B. De Mille, *The Autobiography of Cecil B. De Mille*, p. 347). For a more extensive description of the Lux program, see Bernard Lucich, "*The Lux Radio Theatre*," in Lawrence W. Lichty and Malachi C. Topping, eds., *American Broadcasting: A Sourcebook on the History of Radio and Television*, pp. 391–394; and Hilmes, *Hollywood and Broadcasting*, pp. 78–115. For De Mille's earnings, see Douglas Gomery, *The Hollywood Studio System*, p. 42. For a thorough discussion of the entire era of Hollywood's involvement in radio, see Hilmes, *Hollywood and Broadcasting*, pp. 26–77.

15. Gomery, *The Hollywood Studio System*, pp. 42–44. For a discussion of Paramount's early ties to the broadcasting industry, see Jonathon Buchsbaum, "Zukor Buys Protection: The Paramount Stock Purchase of 1929," *Cine-Tracts* 2 (Summer/Fall 1979): 49–62. For a discussion of Paramount's subsequent investments in television, see Timothy R. White, "Hollywood's Attempt at Appropriating Television: The Case of Paramount Pictures," in Balio, *Hollywood in the Age of Television*, pp. 145–164, and Timothy R. White, "Hollywood's Attempt to Appropriate Television: The Case of Paramount Pictures" (Ph.D. dissertation, University of Wisconsin-Madison, 1990).

16. Colin MacCabe, "The Discursive and the Ideological in Film: Notes on the Conditions of Political Intervention," *Screen* 19, no. 4 (Winter 1978–1979): 37–38.

17. Representations of TV sets in 1950s movies often continued this critique by depicting TV viewing as a sign of social pathology. *All That Heaven Allows* (1955) contains a scene in which the emotional abandonment of the Jane Wyman character by her grown children is captured in the striking image of her face reflected back by the indifferent TV screen that her children have given her as a gift. Television viewing signifies the disintegration of traditional family and community relations in such movies as *Rebel without a Cause* (1955) and *Bigger Than Life* (1956). In these films, TV viewing isolates family members from one another and obscures the larger social conflicts that threaten the viability of the family.

18. Theodor W. Adorno, "Television and the Patterns of Mass Culture," in Bernard Rosenberg and David Manning White, eds., *Mass Culture: The Popular Arts in America*, pp. 474–475.

19. Charles Eckert, "The Carole Lombard in Macy's Window," *Quarterly Review of Film Studies* 3, no. 1 (Winter 1978): 4. See also Stuart Ewen, *Captains of Consciousness: Advertising and the Social Roots of Consumer Culture*, p. 73.

20. As Mary Ann Doane has argued, "The film frame functions, in this context, not as a 'window on the world' as in the Bazinian formulation, but as a quite specific kind of window—a shop window" (Mary Ann Doane, *The Desire to Desire: The Woman's Film of the 1940s*, p. 24). Jane Gaines inverts the metaphor to analyze the relationships among shop windows, motion pictures, and consumer culture. See "The Queen Christina Tie-Ups: Convergence of Show Window and Screen," *Quarterly Review of Film & Video* 11, no. 1 (1989): 35–60. Mark Crispin Miller mistakenly sees product placements as a recent phenomenon and uses this insight to argue that the encroachment of TV's values on the cinema is both symptom and cause of the decline of the American cinema in the 1980s. See Mark Crispin Miller, "End of Story," in Mark Crispin Miller, ed., *Seeing through Movies*, pp. 186–246.

21. Laura Mulvey, "Melodrama In and Out of the Home," in Colin MacCabe, ed., *High Theory/Low Culture: Analyzing Popular Television and Film*, p. 98; Nick Browne, "The Political Economy of the Television (Super) Text," in Horace Newcomb, ed., *Television: The Critical View*, p. 597.

22. For a more extensive discussion of television's contested meanings in relation to notions of home and family in the 1950s, see Lynn Spigel, *Make Room for TV: Television and the Family Ideal in Postwar America*.

23. Thomas F. Brady, "New Hollywood Enterprise," *New York Times*, 9 January 1949, sec. 2, p. 5.

24. Buscombe, "Thinking It Differently," p. 201.

2. THWARTED AMBITIONS IN THE STUDIO ERA

1. For a thorough discussion of the *Paramount* decision—its history and its impact on the movie industry—see Michael Conant, *Antitrust in the Motion Picture Industry: Economic and Legal Analysis*. For a discussion of the relations between studios and exhibitors during the early years of television, see Wil-

liam Boddy, *Fifties Television: The Industry and Its Critics*, pp. 69, 135; Robert Vianello, "The Rise of the Telefilm and the Networks' Hegemony over the Motion Picture Industry," *Quarterly Review of Film Studies* 9, no. 3 (Summer 1984): 215.

2. Michele Hilmes, *Hollywood and Broadcasting: From Radio to Cable*, p. 8.

3. Ernest Borneman, "Rebellion in Hollywood: A Study of Motion Picture Finance," *Harper's*, October 1946, p. 338.

4. This overview of the studio system relies on Douglas Gomery, *The Hollywood Studio System*, pp. 1–25; and Mae D. Huettig, "Economic Control of the Motion Picture Industry," in Tino Balio, ed., *The American Film Industry*, pp. 285–310.

5. Gomery, *The Hollywood Studio System*, p. 14.

6. Ibid., p. 24.

7. Quoted in Hilmes, *Hollywood and Broadcasting*, pp. 34–35.

8. This account is taken from Douglas Gomery, "The Coming of Sound: Technological Change in the American Film Industry," in Balio, *The American Film Industry*, p. 236; Gomery, *Hollywood Studio System*, pp. 103–109; Hilmes, *Hollywood and Broadcasting*, pp. 33–36.

9. For a more detailed discussion of the CBS-Paramount and RCA-RKO relationships, see Jonathon Buchsbaum, "Zukor Buys Protection: The Paramount Stock Purchase of 1929," *Cine-Tracts* 2 (Summer/Fall 1979): 49–62; Gomery, *Hollywood Studio System*, pp. 124–132; Hilmes, *Hollywood and Broadcasting*, pp. 36–46.

10. Gomery, *Hollywood Studio System*, pp. 109–110; "Warner Bros. Go Heavily into Radio Field," *Variety*, 25 June 1930, pp. 1, 28. Quoted in David Alan Larson, "Integration and Attempted Integration between the Motion Picture and Television Industries through 1956" (Ph.D. dissertation, Ohio University, 1979), pp. 24–25.

11. "Warner Seeking MBS Interest But Rejection of Offer Is Seen," *Broadcasting*, 1 May 1936, p. 8.

12. Richard B. Jewell, "Hollywood and Radio: Competition and Partnership in the 1930s," *Historical Journal of Film, Radio, and Television*, 4, no. 2 (1984): 126. For a more detailed account of this period, see Hilmes, *Hollywood and Broadcasting*, pp. 53–74.

13. Jewell, "Hollywood and Radio," p. 137; Frank Buxton and Bill Owen, *The Big Broadcast, 1920–1950*, pp. 31, 85; Hilmes, *Hollywood and Broadcasting*, p. 69.

14. Charles Eckert, "The Carole Lombard in Macy's Window," *Quarterly Review of Film Studies* 3, no. 1 (Winter 1978): 19.

15. For examples of the enthusiasm sparked by innovations in TV technology during the 1930s, see J. Fred MacDonald, *One Nation under Television: The Rise and Decline of Network TV*, pp. 9–13.

16. "Film Industry Advised to Grab Television," *Broadcasting*, 15 June 1937, p. 7. Quoted in Larson, "Integration," p. 31. For more on the movie industry's consideration of television during the 1930s, see Eric Smoodin, "Motion Pictures and Television, 1930–1945: A Pre-History of Relations between the

Two Media," *Journal of the University Film and Video Association* 34, no. 3 (Summer 1982): 3–8.

17. Warner Bros. Pictures, General Television Files, 1930–1936; Lawrence Bergreen, *Look Now, Pay Later: The Rise of Network Broadcasting*, p. 121.

18. Tino Balio, *United Artists: The Company Built by the Stars*, pp. 136–138.

19. "Television Is Ready," *Hollywood Reporter*, 28 November 1934, p. 1. This article is contained in Selznick's files.

20. Ronald Haver, *David O. Selznick's Hollywood*, p. 176; John Wharton to David O. Selznick, 9 September 1936.

21. John Wharton to David O. Selznick, 26 May 1936; John Wharton, "Memorandum on the TV Situation," n.d. [c. October 1936]; David O. Selznick to John Wharton, 1 June 1936.

22. David O. Selznick to John Wharton, 15 October 1936.

23. John Wharton to David O. Selznick, 24 November 1937.

24. David O. Selznick to John Hay Whitney, 17 November 1937; David O. Selznick to John Wharton, 24 November 1937.

25. See Douglas Gomery, "Failed Opportunities: The Integration of the Motion Picture and TV Industries," *Quarterly Review of Film Studies* 9, no. 3 (Summer 1984): 219–228; Hilmes, *Hollywood and Broadcasting*, pp. 116–137.

26. For a full discussion of Paramount's interests in television, see Timothy R. White, "Hollywood's Attempt at Appropriating Television: The Case of Paramount Pictures," in Tino Balio, ed., *Hollywood in the Age of Television*, pp. 145–164.

27. "Hollywood Digs In," *Business Week*, 24 March 1945, pp. 94–95; Larson, "Integration," pp. 59, 73–74; Gomery, "Failed Opportunities," pp. 221, 225; Thomas F. Brady, "Warners to Make Television Films," *New York Times*, 4 January 1949, p. 21; "Suit against Warner Holds Up Radio Deal," *New York Times*, 18 February 1949, p. 37. Actually, Harry Warner's daughter Doris, the wife of director Mervyn LeRoy, became the first Warner actively to pursue the integration of the film industry and television when, during 1944, she became a majority shareholder in the New York–based Cine-Television Studios, a company founded to produce filmed "experimental television programs."

28. Dennis J. Dombkowski, "Film and Television: An Analytical History of Economic and Creative Integration," p. 36; Larson, "Integration," pp. 74, 166; Gomery, "Failed Opportunities," p. 221.

29. For a more detailed account of these conditions, see Douglas Gomery, "The Coming of Television and the 'Lost' Motion Picture Audience," *Journal of Film and Video* 38 (Summer 1985): 5–11; and Thomas H. Guback, "Hollywood's International Market," in Balio, *The American Film Industry*, pp. 470–475.

30. Warner Bros. Pictures, Inc., *Annual Reports*.

31. Thomas F. Brady, "Hollywood Studio in Contract Field," *New York Times*, 22 November 1948, p. 29.

32. Rudy Behlmer, *Inside Warner Bros. (1935–1951)*, pp. 308–309.

33. Janet Staiger, "Individualism versus Collectivism," *Screen* 24, nos. 4–5 (July–August 1983): 73–78.

34. Thomas F. Brady, "New Hollywood Enterprise," *New York Times*, 9 January 1949, sec. 2, p. 5.

35. "Suit against Warners Holds Up Radio Deal," p. 37; Boddy, *Fifties Television*, pp. 50–52; Gomery, "Failed Opportunities," p. 227; Hilmes, *Hollywood and Broadcasting*, p. 130.

36. Marcus Cohn to Stanley P. Friedman, 9 April 1949; "Warners Wants Out on Chi TV, But Assures FCC on Coast Aspirations," *Variety*, 11 May 1949, p. 26; "FCC Okays WINS, KLAC-TV Sales, Approves Other Transfers," *Variety*, 30 December 1953, p. 33; Warner Bros. Pictures, Inc., *Annual Report*, 1951–1953.

37. Thomas F. Brady, "Filmland Strategy," *New York Times*, 9 July 1950, sec. 2, p. 5.

38. "Bring Costs Down to 'Realistic' Level, Jack Warner Sez in Economy Moves," *Variety*, 24 April 1951, p. 5; Thomas F. Brady, "Hollywood Upset," *New York Times*, 6 May 1951, sec. 2, p. 5.

39. The most thorough discussion of the rise of independent production in Hollywood during the 1950s can be found in Tino Balio, *United Artists: The Company That Changed the Film Industry*.

40. "Fidelity's 10 Pix Via WB Opens Door to Other Indie Releases," *Variety*, 2 May 1951, p. 3.

41. "That WB-RCA Rumor Again," *Variety*, 25 April 1951, p. 5.

42. Abel Green, "Lurie Group Buying Warners," *Variety*, 2 May 1951, p. 1; Thomas M. Pryor, "Warners Cancels Movie Sale Deal," *New York Times*, 11 May 1951, p. 33; Brady, "Hollywood Upset," p. 5; "Warners for Sale," *Newsweek*, 14 May 1951, p. 80; "The Brother Act Retires," *Time*, 14 May 1951, p. 103.

43. "Warners for Sale," p. 80.

44. "WB Deal as Industry Hypo," *Variety*, 9 May 1951, p. 3; Abel Green, "Lurie Huddling with Warner Bros. As Deal Proceeds on Several Fronts," *Variety*, 9 May 1951, p. 3; "The Brother Act Retires," pp. 101–103.

45. Pryor, "Warners Cancels Movie Sale Deal," p. 33; "Personal Indemnification for Six Years of Warners Key to Scuttled Lurie Deal," *Variety*, 1 May 1951, p. 3.

46. U.S. Senate Select Committee on Small Business, *Motion Picture Trade Practices—1956*, 336; Thomas M. Pryor, "Big Wage Slashes Seen at Warners," *New York Times*, 9 April 1953, p. 34; "Warners Will Resume Filming," *Los Angeles Times*, 10 July 1953, p. 34; "Dependence of WB on 'Outsiders' Clear from Analysis of Annual Report," *Variety*, 23 December 1953, p. 3.

47. "No Warners Films on Video, Jack L. Tells Sales Chiefs," *Los Angeles Daily News*, 14 July 1950, p. 27.

3. ESCAPE FROM THE STUDIO SYSTEM: INDEPENDENT PRODUCERS AND TELEVISION

1. Samuel Goldwyn, "Hollywood in the Television Age," *New York Times Magazine*, 13 February 1949, p. 15. See also Samuel Goldwyn, "Television's Challenge to the Movies," *New York Times Magazine*, 25 March 1950, p. 17.

2. In 1940 he briefly considered a plan to join forces with an established

company, either CBS, NBC, or an advertising agency. During November 1943 he met with a representative of the N. W. Ayer and Son advertising agency who made preliminary inquiries for his client, General Electric. In April 1946 CBS president William Paley informed Selznick that the J. Walter Thompson advertising agency had lined up a sponsor for a Selznick-produced TV program and that this sponsor was willing to pay $4,000 a week for the production, even though the television audience for any program was still so limited that it barely justified supporting a series of that price. Selznick considered producing a program featuring his younger contract performers until aides convinced him that any program would cost more than $4,000 a week to produce. See David O. Selznick to Ray Klune, 14 April 1940; G. M. Lewander to David O. Selznick, 17 November 1943; David O. Selznick to Daniel O'Shea, 18 January 1944; David O. Selznick to Ted Wick, 22 March 1946; Ted Wick to David O. Selznick, 26 March 1946; David O. Selznick to Charles Glett, 16 April 1946.

3. Thomas Schatz, *The Genius of the System: Hollywood Filmmaking in the Studio Era*, p. 292.

4. Ronald Haver, *David O. Selznick's Hollywood*, pp. 386–387. Aside from the costs of distribution, promotion, and company overhead, each of these two films cost more than $4 million to produce. With the additional expense of interest on loans borrowed for the productions, Selznick estimated his losses for the two films at $12 million.

5. David O. Selznick to Harriett Flagg, 5 October 1943.

6. David O. Selznick to Harriett Flagg, 18 February 1944. Among other things, Selznick demanded a budget that could finance "the costliest program ever put on radio," a coveted slot on one of the networks' Sunday evening schedules, time to test-market his program on small local stations, and complete creative authority. "If they want us they will have to meet my terms," he said. "I have never spared the horses as far as pictures are concerned, and I don't intend to do anything but the very top programs if I ever go into radio." See David O. Selznick to Harriett Flagg, 5 October 1943.

7. David O. Selznick to E. L. Scanlon, 8 April 1948.

8. For examples of press speculation on the casting of Scarlett O'Hara, see Haver, *David O. Selznick's Hollywood*, pp. 243, 259–262. Selznick's discussion of actresses demonstrates the extent to which he believed that he created them as stars. This is most clearly evident in the case of Joan Fontaine. See Schatz, *Genius of the System*, pp. 324–325.

9. See Richard Dyer, *Heavenly Bodies: Film Stars and Society*, pp. 1–18; Richard DeCordova, *Picture Personalities: The Emergence of the Star System in America*.

10. David O. Selznick to Argyle Nelson, 9 April 1948; N. R. London to Cecil Barker, 15 April 1948.

11. David O. Selznick to Paul McNamara and Daniel O'Shea, 30 April 1948.

12. David O. Selznick to Argyle Nelson, 19 May 1948.

13. Earl Beaman to David O. Selznick, 7 November 1950; "Selznick Television Corporation Will Begin Production on Experimental TV Shows Within

Next 60 Days," Press Release, n.d. [c. July 1948]; David O. Selznick to Sidney M. Stortz, 15 June 1948. The subjects for potential series ranged from the banal to the esoteric, but none of them appeared even remotely like the sub ject for a motion picture. Among the ideas were series based on: the forty-eight states; the National Audubon Society; a 7:30 A.M. calisthenics class; a nonsectarian round table in which Catholic, Protestant, and Jewish leaders would discuss the issues of the day; a ballet classroom; a women's health clinic; the Metropolitan Opera; the Folies Bergère; series based on the lives of Eisenhower, Mussolini, and Gandhi; an "aerial study of every coastal and in-dustrial city in the United States." See Staff to David O. Selznick, 20 April 1948.

14. Arthur Fellows and Cecil Barker to David O. Selznick, 10 May 1948.

15. David O. Selznick to Cecil Barker, 21 June 1948.

16. Jerry Fairbanks, "New Low-Cost TV Film Technique," *Television*, November 1949, pp. 23, 28; Jerry Fairbanks, "Multiple-Camera Techniques for Making Films," *American Cinematographer*, July 1950, pp. 238, 244.

17. Mary Gannon, "Hollywood and Television Try New Financial Patterns," *Television*, November 1948, p. 32.

18. "Film for '52," *Newsweek*, 11 August 1952, p. 54.

19. See J. Fred MacDonald, *Who Shot the Sheriff? The Rise and Fall of the TV Western*, pp. 20–24.

20. Much of this information is taken from "The Men Who Make and Sell TV Film," *Television*, July 1953, pp. 19–21. See also Barbara Moore, "The Cisco Kid and Friends: The Syndication of Television Series from 1948 to 1952," *Journal of Popular Film and Television* 8 (Spring 1980): 26–33.

21. "Hollywood Can Grind Out Film Fare for TV," *Business Week*, 24 November 1951, pp. 122–126.

22. Frederick Kugel, "The Economics of Film," *Television*, July 1951, p. 13.

23. William Lafferty, "'No Attempt at Artiness, Profundity, or Significance': *Fireside Theater* and the Rise of Filmed Television Programming," *Cinema Journal* 27, no. 1 (Fall 1987): 23–46. For a discussion of *Fireside Theater* from the period, see also Brewster Morgan, "To Film or Not to Film," *Television*, March 1950, pp. 21–23.

24. Kugel, "Economics of Film," p. 12; "10 Examples of What's Done with Film," *Sponsor*, 10 March 1952, p. 105.

25. Gannon, "Hollywood and Television," pp. 18, 32; "TV and Film: Marriage of Necessity," *Business Week*, 15 August 1953, p. 108; "TV Film: $60 Mil Business in '54," *Sponsor*, 25 January 1954, pp. 52–53.

26. Douglas Gomery, *The Hollywood Studio System*, pp. 148, 157.

27. "The Feature Is the Commercial," *Broadcasting*, 13 January 1958, p. 46.

28. Gomery, *Hollywood Studio System*, p. 158.

29. "The Major Movie Makers Awaken to Television Lure," *Broadcasting*, 25 April 1955, p. 28; William Boddy, "The Studios Move into Prime Time: Hollywood and the Television Industry in the 1950s," *Cinema Journal* 24, no. 4 (Summer 1985): 27; "Hollywood Learns How to Live with TV," *Business Week*, 9 August 1952, p. 47; "Telefilm Industry's Story Famine Laid at Doorstep of Pic Majors," *Variety*, 11 March 1953, p. 22. When the major studios signed

television production deals in 1955, Universal contemplated making another attempt at series production, but ultimately rejected the idea, claiming that the studio didn't have the capacity in talent or facilities to meet expanded production demands, and that it was sufficiently exploiting its feature films on television without the added expense of a series. The television company was reassigned from United World to the parent company in 1956. By 1958 it had produced more than 5,000 commercials for fifty different advertisers, adding $3 million yearly to studio gross revenues. See "Al Duff's Point of View on TV: Universal Can't Divide Loyalty," *Variety*, 8 June 1955, p. 4; "The Feature Is the Commercial," p. 46.

30. "Screen Gems Has New Iron in Fire," *Broadcasting*, 13 April 1958, p. 76.

31. Albert R. Kroeger, "Steady As She Goes—Upward," *Television*, December 1965, p. 52; "Screen Gems Has New Iron," p. 76.

32. Art Woodstone, "SG: The Upswing of an Upstart," *Variety*, 15 April 1959, p. 112.

33. Ibid.; "Ford Pact for Col-Produced Pix May Cue Swing of Studios into TV," *Variety*, 11 June 1953, p. 21; Thomas M. Pryor, "Hollywood Canvas," *New York Times*, 15 June 1952, sec. 2, p. 5.

34. "Screen Gems Has New Iron," p. 76.

35. Fred Kugel, "TV Film: $100,000,000 a Year Industry," *Television*, July 1952, p. 17; "The Movie Makers Look for Gold on the TV Screen," *Business Week*, 23 April 1955, pp. 154–156; "The Selling Is Furious But the Pricing Lacks System," *Sponsor*, 10 March 1952, pp. 90–93; Dave Glickman, "Film in the Future," *Broadcasting*, 10 September 1951, p. 48.

36. "The Men Who Make and Sell TV Film," p. 21; "Who's Who in TV," *Television*, July 1955, p. 50.

37. Desilu Productions, Inc., "American Stock Exchange Listing," Application No. 3156, 5 March 1959.

38. "Hollywood Learns How to Live with TV," p. 47. Joel McCrea originally was intended to be the fourth of the company's four stars.

39. Kugel, "TV Film," p. 17.

40. "Jack Webb's Dragnet," *TV Guide*, 10 April 1953, pp. 5–7. In an interview, costar Ben Alexander claimed that Webb didn't force his actors to speak in a rapid-fire monotone—it just seemed that way. "The editing makes it sound monotonous," Alexander explained. See Val Adams, "Friday's Man Smith," *New York Times*, 17 January 1954, p. 36.

41. Frank Rasky, "Film Programming," *Television*, July 1952, p. 22. For descriptions of this shooting strategy by Freund and Arnaz, see also Bart Andrews, *The "I Love Lucy" Book*, and Desi Arnaz, *A Book*. For a more detailed account of Desilu's growth and impact on television production, see Thomas Schatz, "Desilu, *I Love Lucy*, and the Rise of Network TV," in Robert J. Thompson and Gary Burns, eds., *Making Television: Authorship and the Production Process*, pp. 117–136.

42. Jack Gould, "A Plea for Live TV," *New York Times*, 7 December 1952, sec. 2, p. 17. Quoted in William Boddy, *Fifties Television: The Industry and Its Critics*, p. 74.

4. THE SPONSOR'S MEDIUM: *LIGHT'S DIAMOND JUBILEE* AND THE CAMPAIGN FOR THE PEACEFUL ATOM

1. Michele Hilmes, *Hollywood and Broadcasting: From Radio to Cable*, pp. 80–81.

2. Critical histories of the American cinema during the 1950s often assume this "reflectionist" reading of the era's movies. See Peter Biskind, *Seeing Is Believing: How Hollywood Taught Us to Stop Worrying and Love the Fifties*, and Nora Sayre, *Running Time: The Films of the Cold War*.

3. Jules Backman, *The Economics of the Electrical Machinery Industry*, pp. 9, 34–35; Edwin H. Lewis, *Marketing Electrical Apparatus and Supplies*, p. 3.

4. See *American Magazine*, October 1954, 4.

5. Richard Randolph and Scott Ridley, *Power Struggle: The Hundred-Year War over Electricity*, p. xi. For another useful history of the electric industry and the political debate surrounding it, see Thomas P. Hughes, *Networks of Power: Electrification in Western Society, 1880–1930*.

6. The electric industry's first promotional campaigns were organized during the early 1920s by Samuel Insull and the National Electric Light Association (NELA), the industry's first trade organization. Modeled after propaganda techniques originated in World War I bond drives, these campaigns, according to Richard Randolph and Scott Ridley, were "launched by a network coordinated by NELA and backed with funds that were unmatched in the history of American industry. The purpose was virtually to reshape how the public conceived of electricity and the private companies that delivered it." The industry purchased newspaper and magazine advertisements, distributed press releases, and spent enormous sums printing and distributing to schoolchildren instructional pamphlets with titles like "Ohm Queen" and "Aladdins of Industry." Matthew Sloan, public relations director for this early campaign, expressed the industry's cultural ambitions when he claimed that he regretted only that it was "perhaps impossible to make our public relations work stretch from the cradle to the grave" (see Randolph and Ridley, *Power Struggle*, p. 48). David E. Nye provides a detailed description of electric industry advertising and public relations during this era in his study of the use of photography at General Electric. See his *Image Worlds: Corporate Identities at General Electric, 1890–1939*.

7. The Federal Trade Commission compiled an eighty-four-volume study of abuses by the electric industry's first trade organization, the National Electric Light Association. Ernest Gruening describes this action and the industry's early attempts to shape public opinion about the value of electricity in *The Public Pays: A Study of Power Propaganda*.

8. Randolph and Ridley, *Power Struggle*, pp. 51, 97.

9. Edwin Vennard, "This I Believe," *Edison Electric Institute Bulletin*, June 1957, p. 215. Similar anti-communist rhetoric was used by General Electric and Westinghouse to justify attempts to break the industry's unions. See David Caute, *The Great Fear: The Anti-Communist Purge under Truman and Eisenhower*, pp. 376–391.

10. "Electric Industry Celebrates 75th Anniversary," *New York Times*, 2 June 1954, p. 47; Charles E. Wilson, "The Meaning of Light's Diamond Jubilee,"

Edison Electric Institute Bulletin, June 1954, pp. 187, 192; D. C. Luce, "Report on Light's Diamond Jubilee," *Edison Electric Institute Bulletin,* December 1954, p. 401.

11. Daniel Ford, *The Cult of the Atom: The Secret Papers of the Atomic Energy Commission,* p. 41; Randolph and Ridley, *Power Struggle,* p. 87.

12. Quoted in Randolph and Ridley, *Power Struggle,* p. 96.

13. Ford, *Cult of the Atom,* p. 49; Peter Pringle and James Spigelman, *The Nuclear Barons,* pp. 86, 101–102.

14. Pringle and Spigelman, *Nuclear Barons,* pp. 40–41; Stephen Hilgartner, Richard C. Bell, and Rory O'Connor, *Nukespeak: Nuclear Language, Visions, and Mindset,* p. 38.

15. Pringle and Spigelman, *Nuclear Barons,* p. 122; Ford, *Cult of the Atom,* p. 49.

16. For instance, Light's Golden Jubilee in 1929 also celebrated Edison in order to legitimize the electric industry. In the midst of Justice Department investigations into electric industry abuses, the industry hired Edward Bernays, the era's leading public relations expert, to orchestrate a national celebration on the fiftieth anniversary of Edison's invention. As a result of Bernays's publicity campaign, the U.S. government issued a "Light's Golden Jubilee" stamp, composer George M. Cohan wrote a commissioned song, "Edison—Miracle Man," and the celebration climaxed with a testimonial banquet broadcast over the CBS and NBC radio networks, attended by prominent government, industrial, and financial leaders, including Henry Ford, President Herbert Hoover, and Edison himself. "You recognize [Edison] can be made a myth," Bernays claimed, "so you start myth-building." See Edward Bernays, *Biography of an Idea: Memoirs of a Public Relations Counsel,* pp. 444–460. For further discussion of the electric industry's invocation of Edison as a mythic patriarch, see Wyn Wachhorst, *Thomas Alva Edison: An American Myth.*

17. Wilson, "The Meaning of Light's Diamond Jubilee," p. 188.

18. Thomas Richards, *The Commodity Culture of Victorian England: Advertising and Spectacle, 1851–1914,* pp. 3, 19, 39.

19. Robert W. Rydell, *All the World's a Fair: Visions of Empire at American International Expositions, 1876–1916,* pp. 4–5.

20. Carolyn Marvin, *When Old Technologies Were New: Thinking about Electric Communication in the Late Nineteenth Century,* p. 175.

21. Carolyn Marvin, "Dazzling the Multitude: Imagining the Electric Light as a Communications Medium," in Joseph J. Corn, ed., *Imagining Tomorrow: History, Technology, and the American Future,* p. 204.

22. Folke T. Kihlstedt, "Utopia Realized: The World's Fairs of the 1930s," in Corn, *Imagining Tomorrow,* p. 97.

23. Brian Horrigan, "The Home of Tomorrow," in Corn, *Imagining Tomorrow,* p. 154; Warren J. Susman, *Culture as History: The Transformation of American Society in the Twentieth Century,* p. 224.

24. Quoted in Kihlstedt, "Utopia Realized," p. 110.

25. Ibid.

26. Wilson, "The Meaning of Light's Diamond Jubilee," p. 192.

27. Marvin, *When Old Technologies Were New*, p. 189.

28. See Daniel Boorstin, *The Image: A Guide to Pseudo-Events in America*.

29. Daniel Dayan and Elihu Katz, "Performing Media Events," in James Curran, Anthony Smith, and Pauline Wingate, eds., *Impacts and Influences: Essays on Media Power in the Twentieth Century*, p. 182.

30. David Cardiff and Paddy Scannell, "Broadcasting and National Unity," in Curran, Smith, and Wingate, *Impacts and Influences*, pp. 157, 162.

31. Dayan and Katz, "Performing Media Events," p. 174.

32. Ibid., p. 194.

33. "Spectaculars Force TV into New Fields," *Business Week*, 8 October 1955, p. 31; Erik Barnouw, *Tube of Plenty: The Evolution of American Television*, p. 190; Herman Land, "The Spectaculars: An Interim Report," *Sponsor*, 15 November 1954, p. 29.

34. There is very little scholarly discussion of special programming during the radio era, but information is available through the writing of collectors and radio enthusiasts. For example, see Thomas A. DeLong, "Specials on the Radio Airwaves," *Sperdvac Radiogram*, July 1992, pp. 7–14.

35. See Nick Browne, "The Political Economy of the Television (Super) Text," in Horace Newcomb, ed., *Television: The Critical View*, pp. 588–589.

36. Thomas Whiteside, "The Communicator," Part 2: "What about the Gratitude Factor?" *The New Yorker*, 23 October 1954, p. 59.

37. "Spectacular NBC," *Newsweek*, 31 May 1954, p. 71; "NBC-TV Will Burst into Color This Fall," *Business Week*, 21 August 1954, p. 41; "TV Is Going More Spectacular," *Business Week*, 20 August 1955, pp. 66–72; "Spectaculars Force TV into New Fields," p. 32. For a detailed list of NBC and CBS spectaculars during 1954–1956, including comparative ratings, see "Fact Sheet: The Spectaculars," *Television*, February 1956, p. 30.

38. Whiteside, "The Communicator," p. 67.

39. Vance Kepley, Jr., "The Weaver Years at NBC," *Wide Angle* 12, no. 2 (April 1990): 57. By reducing the cost of sponsorship, NBC opened the television market to a wider range of advertisers. CBS sold advertising time to 95 companies during the 1953–1954 season, but NBC had 165 clients. Only 2 CBS sponsors had advertising budgets under $100,000, but NBC had 18 sponsors with budgets under that figure. See "NBC-TV Will Burst into Color," p. 42.

40. "TV: The Coming Showdown," *Fortune*, September 1954, p. 164; George Rosen, "Rodgers and Hammerstein B'way-to-TV Cavalcade a Case of $750,000 Disenchanted Evening," *Variety*, 31 March 1954, p. 31.

41. "One-shots: Do They Pay?" *Sponsor*, 3 May 1954, pp. 110–111.

42. "The Spectaculars," *Television*, 26 February 1956, p. 29.

43. The Light's Diamond Jubilee *Plan Book* and *Fact Book* are found in the Selznick Archives. Unless otherwise noted, all accounts of plans for local Diamond Jubilee activities are taken from these sources.

44. "What the Chairmen Say," *Edison Electric Institute Bulletin*, August 1954, p. 272.

45. "Atlantic City Set for Festive Year," *New York Times*, 3 January 1954, p. 59; "What the Companies Are Doing," *Edison Electric Institute Bulletin*, Au-

gust 1954, pp. 276–286; "More on What the Companies Are Doing," *Edison Electric Institute Bulletin*, September 1954, pp. 308–310; "Report on Light's Diamond Jubilee," *Edison Electric Institute Bulletin*, December 1954, pp. 401–403; "Still More on What the Companies Did on Light's Diamond Jubilee," *Edison Electric Institute Bulletin*, December 1954, pp. 405–414.

46. "Report on Light's Diamond Jubilee," pp. 401–403.

47. Dayan and Katz, "Performing Media Events," p. 187.

48. "The Royal Hotfoot for Video's Haloed Heads," *Variety*, 9 January 1946, p. 119. Quoted in Judine Mayerle, "The Development of the Television Variety Show as a Major Program Genre at the National Broadcasting Company, 1946–1956," p. 60; J. Fred MacDonald, *One Nation under Television: The Rise and Decline of Network TV*, p. 51.

49. See Lynn Spigel, *Make Room for TV: Television and the Family Ideal in Postwar America*, pp. 47–48.

50. "An Atomic Open House," *Life*, 5 May 1952, pp. 37–38. Interestingly, while the test itself was considered a huge success, the TV coverage at this early stage in the medium's technical development was criticized because the image wavered and jiggled. *Variety*'s headline read, "A-Bomb in TV Fluff Fizzles Fission Vision."

51. "It Better Be Good," *Newsweek*, 9 May 1955, pp. 84–85.

52. Susan Sontag, *Against Interpretation*, pp. 212–213; Paul Boyer, *By the Bomb's Early Light: American Thought and Culture at the Dawn of the Atomic Age*, p. 14.

53. "Mouse at Yucca Flats," *Newsweek*, 16 May 1955, p. 63.

54. "This is the worst thing I've ever heard of. Selling the presidency like cereal," Eisenhower once complained. See David Halberstam, *The Powers That Be*, pp. 323–331.

55. "The President Is Watching Too," *TV Guide*, 12 February 1955, p. 5; "The President on Television," *TV Guide*, 7 May 1954, p. 5; "The Producer and the President," *TV Guide*, 30 October 1954, pp. 4–7. For further discussion of Robert Montgomery's influence in the Eisenhower administration, see Craig Allen, "Robert Montgomery Presents: Hollywood Debut in the Eisenhower White House," *Journal of Broadcasting and Electronic Media* 35, no. 4 (Fall 1991): 431–448.

56. "President to Open Atom Site Today," *New York Times*, 6 September 1954, p. 26; William G. Weart, "President Starts Atom Plant Work," *New York Times*, 7 September 1954, p. 1; "A Wand Wave, a New Era," *Life*, 20 September 1954, pp. 141–142; "An Historic Step Forward," *Edison Electric Institute Bulletin*, September 1954, p. 307.

57. Ronald Haver, *David O. Selznick's Hollywood*, p. 311.

5. DAVID O. SELZNICK AND THE MAKING OF *LIGHT'S DIAMOND JUBILEE*

1. Thomas A. Pryor, "David O. Selznick Discusses His TV Debut," *New York Times*, 24 October 1954, sec. 10, p. 13.

2. David O. Selznick to Frank Davis, 4 March 1954.

3. Thomas Schatz, *The Genius of the System: Hollywood Filmmaking in the Studio Era*, pp. 178–179.

4. Schatz, *Genius of the System*, p. 179.

5. Ibid., p. 407.

6. Janet Staiger, "Individualism Versus Collectivism," *Screen* 24, nos. 4–5 (October 1983): 68–79. An issue of *The Velvet Light Trap* includes a number of excellent case studies of independent producers in Hollywood during this period. See *The Velvet Light Trap* 22 (1986), especially Kevin Hagopian, "Declaration of Independence: A History of Cagney Productions," pp. 16–32; Matthew Bernstein, "Fritz Lang, Incorporated," pp. 33–52; Tino Balio, "When Is an Independent Producer Independent?: The Case of United Artists after 1948," pp. 53–64.

7. David O. Selznick, File Memo, 10 April 1954.

8. David O. Selznick and N. W. Ayer and Son, *Light's Diamond Jubilee* Production Agreement, 8 March 1954.

9. David O. Selznick to Frank Davis, 4 March 1954 and 19 July 1954; Charles Miller to David O. Selznick, 3 March 1954.

10. Production Agreement; David O. Selznick to Frank Davis, 15 March 1954.

11. Production Agreement; James Hanna to David O. Selznick, 5 May 1954.

12. David O. Selznick to Frank Davis, 13 March 1954.

13. David O. Selznick to Frank Davis, 29 March 1954.

14. David O. Selznick to Frank Davis, 17 March 1954.

15. David O. Selznick to Frank Davis, 6 April 1954.

16. David O. Selznick to Frank Davis, 9 April 1954; 15 April 1954.

17. Selznick also decided to educate himself about television since he wasn't a regular viewer. He asked John Crosby to send him a list of the best TV programs of the past few years. Crosby sent a list of thirteen anthology drama episodes from such series as *Philco Playhouse, Studio One, Danger,* and *U.S. Steel Hour.* Selznick immediately ordered kinescopes of these episodes. See David O. Selznick to Frank Davis, 14 April 1954 and 20 April 1954.

18. As a favor to Selznick, Hecht agreed to write *Light's Diamond Jubilee* for just $10,000. On *Notorious,* his last credited screenplay for Selznick, Hecht had received $5,000 per week. See Schatz, *Genius of the System,* p. 393.

19. David O. Selznick to Frank Davis, 15 March 1954, 18 March 1954, 29 May 1954; David O. Selznick to Earl Beaman, 11 June 1954; Ben Hecht, Contract, *Light's Diamond Jubilee,* 20 July 1954 and 18 September 1954.

20. Robert Cunniff, "Selznick Talks about Television," *Television,* February 1955, p. 62; Bob Thomas, "First $1 Mil Show in TV History," Associated Press Wire Service, 23 October 1954.

21. David O. Selznick to Charles Wilson, 6 August 1954.

22. David O. Selznick to Eddie Mannix, 7 September 1954.

23. Paul Boyer, *By the Bomb's Early Light: American Thought and Culture at the Dawn of the Atomic Age,* p. 109.

24. David O. Selznick to Charles Wilson, 28 June 1954.

25. David O. Selznick, "Entertainment Ideas," n.d. [c. May 1954].

26. William Phillipson to Lucille Sullivan, 18 August 1954.

27. David O. Selznick to Eddie Mannix, 7 September 1954; David O. Selznick to Dwight Van Meter, 20 July 1954.

28. David O. Selznick to Frank Davis, 1 July 1954 and 29 July 1954; Nancy Stern to David O. Selznick, 6 May 1954.

29. David O. Selznick to Frank Davis, 20 September 1954 and 21 September 1954.

30. David O. Selznick to Frank Davis, 29 July 1954; 30 July 1954; Shirley Hardin to Frank Davis, 29 July 1954; David O. Selznick to Bing Crosby, 3 August 1954.

31. David O. Selznick to Frank Davis, 29 July 1954.

32. David O. Selznick to Frank Davis, 11 March 1954 and 18 March 1954.

33. O'Shea would use the standard, though never formalized, channels for determining the acceptability of individuals in question. This involved checking with advertising agencies, examining network precedent, and reviewing the various lists of "subversives" compiled by such groups as the American Legion, Hollywood's ultraconservative Motion Picture Alliance for the Preservation of American Ideals, and those who made a profitable business by servicing the blacklist, groups like Aware, Inc., and American Business Consultants, publishers of *Counterattack* and *Red Channels*. See Erik Barnouw, *A History of Broadcasting in the United States,* vol. 3: *The Image Empire,* p. 280; Shirley Hardin to William Phillipson, 4 August 1954; Frank Davis to William Phillipson, 12 August 1954. For a more detailed account of blacklisting and clearance procedures, see Victor Navasky, *Naming Names,* and Larry Ceplair and Steven Englund, *The Inquisition in Hollywood: Politics in the Film Community, 1930–1960.*

34. Daniel O'Shea, File Memo, 27 August 1954; Frank Davis, File Memo, 14 September 1954; Frank Davis to William Phillipson, 17 August 1954, 27 August 1954, 17 September 1954, 27 September 1954; Frank Davis to Shirley Hardin, 3 August 1954.

35. David O. Selznick to William Phillipson, 6 September 1954.

36. At this point there was still one segment for Vidor to shoot, the adaptation of Ray Bradbury's "Powerhouse," which was to star Gary Cooper and Jennifer Jones, Selznick's wife. But when negotiations with Cooper stalled, the segment was pulled from the program, even though elaborate sets had been constructed. See William Phillipson to Earl Beaman, 7 September 1954; David O. Selznick to Betty Goldsmith, 8 September 1954; Daily Production Reports; William Phillipson to Screen Directors Guild, 5 October 1954; David O. Selznick to William Phillipson, 24 September 1954.

37. David O. Selznick to Furth Ullman and to Arthur Fellows, 9 October 1954.

38. David O. Selznick to Furth Ullman and to Arthur Fellows, 28 September 1954.

39. William Phillipson to Dwight Van Meter, 1 October 1954; David O. Selznick to William Phillipson, 28 September 1954.

40. David O. Selznick to William Phillipson, 6 October 1954.

41. Susan Sontag, *Against Interpretation,* p. 224.

42. John Steinbeck, *The Red Pony,* pp. 118–119.

43. James W. Carey, *Communication As Culture: Essays on Media and Society,* pp. 114–115.

44. Carolyn Marvin, *When Old Technologies Were New: Thinking about Electric Communication in the Late Nineteenth Century,* p. 232.

45. Carey, *Communication As Culture,* p. 129.

46. Luce, "Report on Light's Diamond Jubilee," p. 402.

47. John Crosby, "Let There Be Selznick," *New York Herald Tribune,* 27 October 1954; George Rosen, "Selznick 'Lamp' Discovers America in $1,000,000 Fusion of Talents," *Variety,* 27 October 1954, p. 28; Jack Gould, "Television in Review," *New York Times,* 25 October 1954, p. 36; "The Week in Review," *Time,* 8 November 1954, p. 95.

48. Matters were made worse by the fact that *Light's Diamond Jubilee* wouldn't deliver residual profits in syndication or foreign theatrical distribution. In order to sign talent and properties at costs low enough to bring the show in on budget, Selznick's staff had been able to acquire only the rights for a one-time broadcast of the program. It would now take a full-time staff and enormous sums of money to acquire clearances for subsequent rights from performers and crew. And yet there wasn't even much interest in the program. In the days immediately following the broadcast, Decca records had inquired about making an LP version. *Reader's Digest* had suggested devoting an entire issue to an adaptation of the program. Even a year after the broadcast, Selznick considered distributing the program theatrically, suggesting the domestic title *To America with Love* and the foreign title, *The Truth about America.* Yet none of these projects ever materialized. See Frank Davis to Major E. W. Maxson, 21 January 1955; William Phillipson to Arthur Jacobs, 29 October 1954; David O. Selznick to Frank Davis, 4 November 1955.

49. David O. Selznick to Earl Beaman, 22 November 1954; James Hanna to Charles Miller, 21 December 1954; Riley Jackson to William Phillipson, 1 December 1954; William Phillipson to David O. Selznick, 7 December 1954.

50. David O. Selznick to Earl Beaman, 3 January 1955.

51. Ibid.; David O. Selznick to Dwight Van Meter, n.d. [c. December 1954; written but not sent].

52. James Hanna to Charles Miller, 21 December 1954; David O. Selznick to Barry Brannen, 6 April 1956.

53. At the time, Selznick wanted to form a new production company, Selznick-NBC, in which he and the network would split the stock. Selznick would receive a long-term contract that would pay a salary plus expenses. The new company would purchase the TV rights to all past and future Selznick feature films. Selznick-NBC would produce a number of series, including one based upon stories from the Bible, as well as a series of TV specials. The source of working capital would be open to negotiation, but a line of credit would be extended by NBC's parent company, RCA. Two stages at NBC's Burbank studios would be reserved for Selznick. Finally, Selznick was to have sole authority on all production and executive matters. See David O. Selznick, File Memo, 6 August 1954.

54. David O. Selznick to Emanuel Sacks, 15 January 1955 [written but not sent].

55. David O. Selznick to Leonard Goldenson, 2 September 1955.

6. DISNEYLAND

1. For an account of the post-1952 boom in new television stations, television advertising revenue, and television set ownership, see J. Fred MacDonald, *One Nation under Television: The Rise and Decline of Network TV*, pp. 59–62.

2. Katherine Greene and Richard Greene, *The Man behind the Magic: The Story of Walt Disney*, p. 119; Frank Orme, "Disney: 'How Old Is a Child?'" *Television*, December 1954, p. 37; "Disney 'Not Yet Ready' for TV," *Variety*, 23 May 1951, p. 5; "Disney's 7-Year ABC-TV Deal," *Variety*, 21 February 1954, p. 41.

3. "The Wide World of Walt Disney," *Newsweek*, 31 December 1962, pp. 49–51; "The Mouse That Turned to Gold," *Business Week*, 9 July 1955, p. 74. The origins of Disney's character merchandising are described in "The Mighty Mouse," *Time*, 25 October 1948, pp. 96–98. For a more detailed discussion of the Disney corporation's use of character merchandising in relation to other TV producers of the early 1950s, see "He'll Double as a Top-Notch Salesman," *Business Week*, 21 March 1953, pp. 43–44.

4. John McDonald, "Now the Bankers Come to Disney," *Fortune*, May 1966, p. 141.

5. During its initial release, *Snow White* grossed $8 million and became the first movie to exceed $5 million at the box office. *Gone with the Wind* grossed more than $20 million in its first year of release. See Richard Schickel, *The Disney Version*, p. 229; Ronald Haver, *David O. Selznick's Hollywood*, p. 309.

6. Schickel, *The Disney Version*, p. 28.

7. McDonald, "Now the Bankers Come to Disney," pp. 141, 224; Schickel, *The Disney Version*, pp. 308–316; "Disney's Live-Action Profits," *Business Week*, 24 July 1965, p. 78.

8. Spencer Klan, "ABC-Paramount Moves In," *Fortune*, April 1957, pp. 134, 232. For more on the ABC-UPT merger, see Timothy R. White, "Hollywood on (Re)Trial: The American Broadcasting–United Paramount Merger Hearing," *Cinema Journal* 31, no. 3 (Spring 1992): 19–36.

9. William Boddy, *Fifties Television: The Industry and Its Critics*, p. 145.

10. "The abc of ABC," *Forbes*, 15 June 1959, p. 16.

11. By 1955, ABC had 84 affiliates and a live clearance rate of 58 percent, but these improved figures still left the network trailing CBS, which had 121 stations and 87 percent live clearance, and NBC, which had 104 stations and 90 percent live clearance. See Boddy, *Fifties Television*, pp. 42–57, 145.

12. By fall 1956, 63 percent of ABC programming was filmed, compared to 20 percent for CBS and 16 percent for NBC. See "Reflections on ABC's Climb to the Big Time," *Broadcasting*, 5 March 1956, p. 9.

13. Boddy, *Fifties Television*, p. 146.

14. "ABC's Unique 'Big 3' Status as a Propertyless Network," *Variety*, 27 July 1955, p. 20. NBC and CBS produced 50 percent of their programs by 1955; ABC produced only 14 percent.

15. Boddy, *Fifties Television*, p. 146.

16. "The Spectaculars: An Interim Report," *Sponsor*, 15 November 1954, p. 31; "Twenty-Five Years Wiser about Show Business, Goldenson Finds TV the Biggest Star," *Broadcasting*, 14 July 1958, p. 84.

17. Herman Land, "ABC: An Evaluation," *Television*, December 1957, p. 94.

18. Ibid., p. 93; "The abc of ABC," p. 17; "The TV Fan Who Runs a Network," *Sponsor*, 15 June 1957, p. 45. It should be noted that ABC did not possess demographic ratings that would have enabled the network to determine the success of its programming strategy.

19. "Peaches and Cream at ABC-TV," *Variety*, 16 June 1954, p. 25; "The abc of ABC," p. 17; Klan, "ABC-Paramount Moves In," p. 242; Albert R. Kroeger, "Miracle Worker of West 66th Street," *Television*, February 1961, p. 66; "Corporate Health, Gains in Radio-TV Theme of AB-UPT Stockholders Meeting," *Broadcasting*, 21 May 1956, p. 64; Frank Orme, "TV's Most Important Show," *Television*, June 1955, p. 32.

20. William Boddy, "The Studios Move into Prime Time: Hollywood and the Television Industry in the 1950s," *Cinema Journal* 24, no. 4 (Summer 1985): 31–32.

21. See Michele Hilmes, *Hollywood and Broadcasting: From Radio to Cable*, pp. 63–72, 78–112.

22. Walt also recognized that the Disney empire needed an identifiable author to crystallize the company's identity for the public, to "personify the product," as *Business Week* once noted. The naming of an author was an issue within the company as far back as the 1920s, when Walt convinced Roy to change the name of the company they had cofounded from Disney Brothers Productions to Walt Disney Productions. Consequently, as the studio expanded in 1953, Walt began to assume a more public persona, hosting the TV program and identifying himself with all things Disney, while diminishing Roy's identity. In 1953—against Roy's opposition—Walt formed Retlaw Enterprises (Walter spelled backwards), a private company that completely controlled merchandising rights to the name Walt Disney. In return for licensing the name to Walt Disney Productions, Retlaw received 5 percent of the income from all corporate merchandise. Since the Disney name was imprinted on everything associated with the company, Retlaw immediately generated enormous wealth for Walt. See John Taylor, *Storming the Magic Kingdom: Wall Street, the Raiders, and the Battle for Disney*, pp. 7, 10.

23. Schickel, *The Disney Version*, p. 20.

24. "Disneyland Repeats Getting Bigger Audiences Than First Time Around," *Variety*, 20 April 1955, p. 32. A complete filmography of Disney television programs through 1967 appears in Leonard Maltin, *The Disney Films*, pp. 321–326. For an examination of the Disneyland-inspired Davy Crockett phenomenon that swept through American culture beginning in 1954, see Margaret Jane King, "The Davy Crockett Craze: A Case Study in Popular Culture."

25. Orme, "How Old Is a Child?," pp. 37, 72.

26. Critics within both the movie and the television industries sarcastically referred to this episode as "The Long, Long Trailer." See "A Wonderful World: Growing Impact of the Disney Art," *Newsweek*, 18 April 1955, pp. 62–63.

27. Schickel, *The Disney Version*, p. 152; "Tinker Bell, Mary Poppins, Cold Cash," *Newsweek*, 12 July 1965, p. 74.

28. Neil Harris, *Humbug: The Art of P. T. Barnum*, p. 79.

29. Tim Brooks and Earle Marsh, *The Complete Directory to Prime Time Network TV Shows*, p. 1031. *Disneyland* remained among the top fifteen programs through 1957, and then fell from the top twenty until it shifted to NBC—and color broadcasts—in 1961.

30. Charles Sinclair, "Should Hollywood Get It for Free?" *Sponsor*, 8 August 1955, p. 102.

31. Maltin, *The Disney Films*, p. 315.

32. "Disney Parlays Romp Home," *Variety*, 30 November 1955, p. 3; "All-Time Top Grossing Films," *Variety*, 4 January 1956, p. 84. At the time, *20,000 Leagues under the Sea* was the nineteenth-highest-grossing film of all time.

33. "Disney Parlays Romp Home."

34. "The Wild Frontier," *Time*, 23 May 1955, p. 92. Unfortunately for Disney, the studio could not control licensing of Crockett products, because it did not possess exclusive rights to the name or character of Davy Crockett. Since the mid-nineteenth century companies had used the Crockett name on products from chewing tobacco to whiskey. The Disney studio never again made this mistake. See also "U.S. Again Subdued by Davy," *Life*, 25 April 1955, p. 27; "Mr. Crockett Is a Dead Shot As a Salesman," *New York Times*, 1 June 1955, p. 38.

35. Schickel, *The Disney Version*, p. 313.

36. "Father Goose," *Time*, 27 December 1954, p. 42; "Tinker Bell, Mary Poppins, Cold Cash," p. 74.

37. For an account of the opening ceremonies, see Bob Chandler, "Disneyland As 2-Headed Child of TV and Hollywood," *Variety*, 20 July 1955, p. 2. Chandler observes that the inauguration of Disneyland marked the "integration and interdependence of all phases of show biz."

38. Dean MacCannell, *The Tourist: A New Theory of the Leisure Class*, p. 159.

39. "How to Make a Buck," *Time*, 29 July 1957, p. 76.

40. Ibid.; Schickel, *The Disney Version*, p. 316.

41. Benjamin Kalmenson, Testimony, *United States v. 20th Century-Fox et al.*, 31 October 1955 (Warner Bros. Pictures Collection, Princeton).

42. Michele Hilmes describes the use of this strategy in the Hollywood-produced radio program, *Lux Radio Theatre*. See Hilmes, *Hollywood and Broadcasting*, pp. 108–110.

43. Max Horkheimer and Theodor W. Adorno, *Dialectic of Enlightenment*, p. 124.

7. ORIGINS OF WARNER BROS. TELEVISION

1. Jack L. Warner, Testimony, *United States v. 20th Century-Fox et al.*, 31 October 1955 (Warner Bros. Pictures Collection, Princeton). A 1955 report writ-

ten by the William Morris agency for MGM revealed a similar attitude motivating that studio's decision to produce for television. The report stated: "The return for MGM in entering television is not wholly the number of dollars which it will earn as a production firm, but the vital opportunity to use this greatest of all advertising media in the promotion of its theater releases." See David Alan Larson, "Integration and Attempted Integration between the Motion Picture and Television Industries through 1956," p. 236.

2. Freeman Lincoln, "The Comeback of the Movies," *Fortune*, February 1955, p. 127.

3. "A Turn for the Bigger," *Business Week*, 14 November 1953, p. 148; Lincoln, "Comeback of the Movies," p. 130.

4. "WB's 16 in 54 Will Cost As Much As 42 Previous Pix—Jack Warner," *Variety*, 6 January 1954, p. 3; "WB in Record Indie Financing," *The Hollywood Reporter*, 17 November 1954, p. 3; "Warner Talent Policy Pays Off," *The Hollywood Reporter*, 6 July 1954, p. 5; Warner Bros. Pictures, Inc., *Annual Report*, 1955.

5. "This Is Film's Cadillac Age," *Variety*, 9 February 1955, p. 3.

6. "Backlog Deal Timely Extra Coin for WB," *Variety*, 29 February 1956, p. 5; "Top Box-Office Pix Also Top Risks," *Variety*, 9 April 1958, p. 3; "Blockbuster Age Economics a Pain in Transition," *Variety*, 30 April 1958, p. 3; "Blockbuster's Fallout Risk," *Variety*, 7 May 1958, p. 3.

7. "Warners Steps Up Own Producing," *Variety*, 12 January 1955, p. 5.

8. Charles Sinclair, "Should Hollywood Get It for Free?" *Sponsor*, 8 August 1955, p. 32; "Mayer-Selznick Roast Schary-Metro," *Variety*, 17 February 1954, 1; Tim Brooks and Earle Marsh, *The Complete Directory to Prime Time Network TV Shows*, p. 923.

9. "WB Nixes Sullivan on 'Streetcar' Clips," *Variety*, 16 January 1952, p. 25; "Film's Cadillac Age," p. 3; "NBC Gives 90 Minutes to Universal for Celebration of Benny Goodman," *Variety*, 22 June 1955, p. 4; Sinclair, "Should Hollywood Get It for Free?" p. 104; "1955 Box-Office Champs," *Variety*, 22 June 1955, p. 4.

10. "Getting Them Back to the Movies," *Business Week*, 22 October 1955, p. 60; "Film's Cadillac Age," p. 3. By the mid-1950s the highest price paid by Warners for feature film rights to a Broadway play was $750,000 plus 50 percent of the net profits, which it paid for both *The Pajama Game* and *Damn Yankees*. See "Yankees to WB at 750G & 50%," *Variety*, 29 February 1956, p. 1.

11. "1954 Box-Office Champs," *Variety*, 5 January 1955, p. 59.

12. Jack L. Warner to Benjamin Kalmenson, 30 June 1954, 14 December 1954, 11 April 1955; Benjamin Kalmenson to Jack L. Warner, 1 July 1954, 14 December 1954, 1 March 1955; Ed Sullivan to Jack L. Warner, 15 July 1955; Jack L. Warner to Steve Trilling, 23 July 1955; Steve Trilling to Jack L. Warner, 9 March 1955, 18 August 1955, 3 September 1955; William T. Orr to Steve Trilling, 26 April 1955. See also "WB to Produce Eve Arden in 'Our Miss Brooks,'" *Variety*, 11 May 1953, p. 3; "Sullivan Biopic Off Warners Schedule," *Variety*, 18 January 1956, p. 3.

13. Thomas Pryor, "Hollywood Tie-Up," *New York Times*, 17 May 1955.

14. Kalmenson, Testimony, *United States v. 20th Century-Fox et al.*, 31 October 1955 (Warner Bros. Pictures Collection, Princeton).

15. Ibid.; Warner, Testimony.

16. Jack L. Warner to Benjamin Kalmenson, 15 December 1954; "All Studios Go TV in 2 Yrs.," *Variety*, 2 February 1955, p. 3; "Film's Cadillac Age," p. 3.

17. Jack L. Warner, Benjamin Kalmenson, and Robert Kintner, Joint Press Release, n.d. [c. 3 April 1955].

18. Ibid.

19. Ibid.

20. Steve Trilling to Jack L. Warner, 8 March 1955.

21. Unless otherwise indicated, all of the information pertaining to the contracts comes from the following sources: American Broadcasting Company and Sunset Productions, Inc., Preliminary Production Agreement, 8 March 1955; American Broadcasting Company and Warner Bros. Pictures, Inc., Contract for *Warner Bros. Presents*, 22 September 1955.

22. Warner, Testimony.

23. "*Warner Bros. Presents*," *Variety*, 28 September 1955, p. 38.

24. ABC Television Network, "*Warner Bros. Presents*" (Sales Brochure), n.d. [c. March 1955]. Unless otherwise indicated, all information pertaining to ABC's marketing of *Warner Bros. Presents* is taken from this document.

25. "$6 Mil Sale for WB Series," *Variety*, 6 April 1955, p. 25; "Monsanto Signs as 3rd Bankroller on WB Presents," *Variety*, 27 April 1955, p. 23.

26. Robert Kintner to Jack L. Warner, 6 April 1955.

27. U.S. Federal Communications Commission, Office of Network Study, *Second Interim Report: Network Program Procurement Practices*, p. 669.

28. Leonard Goldenson once claimed that Jack Warner's distaste for B movies was the major obstacle to overcome in negotiating with Warner Bros. over the first TV series. See Sterling Quinlan, *Inside ABC: The American Broadcasting Company's Rise to Power*, pp. 50–51.

29. Douglas Gomery, *The Hollywood Studio System*, pp. 112–115.

30. "Warner Bros.," *Fortune*, December 1937, pp. 110–113. Quoted in Rudy Behlmer, *Inside Warner Bros. (1935–1951)*, p. 62. See also the budgets for such Warners B films as *Trailin' West* (17 April 1936), *Midnight Court* (14 October 1936), *Bengal Tiger* (25 April 1936), and *The Case of the Caretaker's Cat* (25 June 1936). For a discussion of B-movie economics during the studio era, see Charles Flynn and Todd McCarthy, "The Economic Imperative: Why Was the B Movie Necessary?," in Charles Flynn and Todd McCarthy, eds., *Kings of the Bs: Working within the Hollywood System*, pp. 13–43.

31. Thomas F. Brady, "Hollywood Memos—B Pictures Quietly Revived at Warners," *New York Times*, 18 January 1948, p. 27. For a general discussion of these conditions, see Janet Staiger, "Individualism versus Collectivism," *Screen* 24, nos. 4–5 (July–August 1983): 70–71.

32. Brady, "Hollywood Memos," p. 27.

33. Herb Golden, "When's a 'B' Film Not a 'B'?" *Variety*, 4 February 1948, p. 7.

34. Leonard Maltin, *The Great Movie Shorts*, pp. 22–26.

35. Although the primary negotiations between ABC and Warner Bros. were conducted by Benjamin Kalmenson in New York, Jack Junior occasionally entered the negotiations, as during the meeting with NBC executives and a brief discussion with Procter and Gamble about the possibility of producing a half-hour series to air on NBC in fall 1955. See Jack M. Warner to Jack L. Warner, 15 March 1955.

36. Fred Hift, "Studios: 'Our TV Will Shine,' " *Variety*, 9 March 1955, p. 2.

37. F. E. Witt to All Departments, 3 May 1955; Sunset Productions, Inc. to Thomas MacGowan, n.d. [c. October 1956]; "Sunset Productions Formed as Warner TV Subsidiary," *Broadcasting*, 11 April 1955, p. 42.

38. David Bordwell, Janet Staiger, and Kristin Thompson, *The Classical Hollywood Cinema: Film Style and Mode of Production to 1960*, p. 330.

39. Ibid., pp. 320–322.

40. William T. Orr, Personal Interview, 28 October 1986, Los Angeles; William T. Orr, Deposition, *Richard Sanville v. Warner Bros. Pictures, Inc.*, 25 April 1957; Bryan Moore to Jack L. Warner, 17 May 1955; "Name Stevens to Warners TV Job," *Variety*, 20 April 1955, p. 32; Dwight Whitney, "The Producer Assembles His Product," *TV Guide*, 31 October 1959, p. 22.

41. Jack L. Warner to Gary Stevens, 15 April 1955, 8 July 1955; Orr, Deposition.

42. Moore to Warner, 17 May 1955; Finlay McDermid to Jack L. Warner, 8 April 1955.

43. Moore to Warner, 17 May 1955.

44. Moore to Warner, 17 May 1955; Richard L. Bare, Personal Interview, 28 October 1986, Los Angeles. For discussions of the producer's role in television, see Horace Newcomb and Robert Alley, *The Producer's Medium: Conversations with Creators of American TV*, and David Marc, *Demographic Vistas: Television in American Culture*.

45. Bryan Moore to Richard Pease, 21 June 1955; Bryan Moore to Richard Diggs, 13 May 1955; Moore to Warner, 17 May 1955.

46. See Janet Staiger's discussion of these issues in Bordwell, Staiger, and Thompson, *Classical Hollywood Cinema*, pp. 96–113.

47. Behlmer, *Inside Warner Bros.*, p. 62. Representing the distribution division, however, Harry Warner was not nearly as enthusiastic about the studio's use of remakes because that practice decreased the market value of the films. In a 1944 telegram to Jack Warner, he wrote, "The minute you announce a remake exhibitors get wise to it and it just makes it harder to sell. . . . In one breath you say you have built up an organization to produce great pictures and in a second breath you want to do things to make it harder for yourself, the selling organization, and everyone else by making pictures of remakes. You can't do this and succeed." See Behlmer, *Inside Warner Bros.*, pp. 241–242.

48. Richard Maltby, *Harmless Entertainment: Hollywood and the Ideology of Consensus*, p. 27; Behlmer, *Inside Warner Bros.*, pp. 88–89, 109.

49. David Harmon to Gary Stevens, n.d. [c. April 1955]; Bryan Moore, File Memo, 12 January 1962.

50. Bryan Moore, File Memo, 15 November 1961; Bryan Moore to Art Silver, 12 January 1959; Bryan Moore to R. J. Obringer, 1 January 1958.

51. Moore, File Memo, 15 November 1961; Milton Orman to Bryan Moore, 15 November 1961; Paul B. Stager to Bryan Moore, 2 February 1962.

52. Jack L. Warner to All Concerned, 30 June 1955; Jack L. Warner to Gary Cooper, 28 October 1955 and 15 November 1955; Art Silver to Jack L. Warner, 17 November 1955.

53. Oren Haglund to Gary Stevens, 31 May 1955; Weekly Summary of Picture Costs—TV, 26 May 1956.

54. Orr, Personal Interview, 28 October 1986, Los Angeles; Philip K. Scheuer, "Warners Frankly States That It's Making Films for TV," *Los Angeles Times*, 7 August 1955, p. 24; Jack L. Warner to Steve Trilling, 17 August 1955 and 18 August 1955; Steve Trilling to Jack L. Warner, 18 August 1955 and 20 August 1955; "Gary Stevens Denies Warners Axed Him," *Variety*, 7 September 1955, p. 35.

55. Jack L. Warner to William T. Orr, 28 August 1955; William T. Orr to Jack L. Warner, 26 August 1955.

56. Orr to Warner, 26 August 1955.

57. For an example of this criticism, see Sinclair, "Should Hollywood Get It for Free?" p. 102. Among independent producers, the most vocal critic of the major studios was Frederick Ziv. See "Movie Industry Blasted by Ziv," *Broadcasting*, 15 August 1955, pp. 44–48, and "Ziv in Blast at Pix Majors," *Variety*, 10 August 1955, p. 31.

58. "Problems of 20th's Vidpix Subsidiary," *Variety*, 6 July 1955, p. 3; "Zanuck Steps into 20th Tele Setup at Behest of GE," *Variety*, 24 August 1955, p. 26; Bob Chandler, "Majors' TV Woes Ain't Minor," *Variety*, 31 August 1955, p. 23; "20th's Flicka Stays in Can," *Variety*, 14 September 1955, p. 35.

59. "Metro Ends TV Holdout," *Variety*, 22 June 1955, p. 1; "Loew's Deal with ABC Net," *Variety*, 13 July 1955, p. 13; "Metro Format," *Variety*, 13 July 1955, p. 29; Chandler, "Majors' TV Woes," p. 23; "MGM TV First Intro'd by Schary," *Variety*, 31 August 1955, p. 15.

60. Kalmenson, Testimony (Warner Bros. Pictures Collection, Princeton).

8. NEGOTIATING THE TELEVISION TEXT: *WARNER BROS. PRESENTS*

1. Robert Kintner to Jack L. Warner, 12 September 1955; Jack L. Warner to Robert Kintner, 17 September 1955.

2. Kintner reported the negative reviews in New York and Los Angeles newspapers, but advised Warner to ignore them because ABC believed that unfavorable reviews had no significant effect on television audiences (Robert Kintner to Jack L. Warner, 14 September 1955 and 28 September 1955). For examples of the negative reaction, see "Review of *Warner Bros. Presents*," *Variety*, 21 September 1955, pp. 35–36; "Hollywood Stubs Its Toe," *TV Guide*, 7 December 1955, pp. 4–6; "Critics Rap Film-TV Offspring," *Sponsor*, 3 October 1955, p. 37.

3. Robert Kintner to Jack L. Warner, 23 September 1955.

4. Robert Kintner to Jack L. Warner, 28 September 1955.

5. Warner Bros. Pictures, Inc., and American Broadcasting Co., Contract, *Warner Bros. Presents,* 22 September 1955.

6. Benjamin Kalmenson, Testimony, *United States v. 20th Century-Fox et al.,* 31 October 1955 (Warner Bros. Pictures Collection, Princeton).

7. At the time, for example, ABC chairman Leonard Goldenson explained that his network would pursue an audience consisting primarily of "youthful families." See Herman Land, "ABC: An Evaluation," *Television,* December 1957, p. 94. John Fiske discusses the relations between television's modes of address and its modes of reception from a theoretical perspective in *Television Culture,* pp. 55–59, 72–77. A number of recent critics have argued that television spectatorship is characterized by distraction, rather than concentration. For instance, John Ellis contrasts the cinema spectator's "gaze" at the screen with the television spectator's "glance." As a result, television textual strategies are often designed to call the viewer's glance back to the TV screen, in Rick Altman's words, "to identify that which is worth looking at." See Rick Altman, "Television Sound," in Horace Newcomb, ed., *Television: The Critical View,* pp. 566–584; John Ellis, *Visible Fictions,* pp. 109–172.

8. Raymond Williams, *Television: Technology and Cultural Form,* pp. 86–96. For a discussion of the implications of segmentation and flow, see Fiske, *Television Culture,* pp. 99–105.

9. "The abc of ABC," *Forbes,* 15 June 1959, p. 16.

10. Robert Kintner to Jack L. Warner, 6 April 1955. The ABC programs that followed *Warner Bros. Presents* were *The Life and Legend of Wyatt Earp, Make Room for Daddy,* and *DuPont Cavalcade Theater.*

11. For examples of the antagonism between advertisers and the major studios, see "Majors TV Plan—New Faces; But Ad Accts Want Big Stars," *Variety,* 20 April 1955, p. 37; Charles Sinclair, "Should Hollywood Get It for Free?" *Sponsor,* 8 August 1955, p. 31.

12. Robert Kintner to Jack L. Warner, 14 September 1955, 16 September 1955, 21 September 1955; Edgar Monsanto Queeny to Robert Kintner, 14 September 1955; Robert Kintner to Edgar Monsanto Queeny, 20 September 1955; Robert Kintner to Jack L. Warner, 21 September 1955; M. F. Mahoney to Robert Kintner, 7 October 1955.

13. Milton Orman to Bryan Moore, 15 November 1961.

14. John Peyser to William T. Orr, 19 October 1955.

15. John J. Louis to Jack L. Warner, 31 October 1955; "Clouds Thicken over Film Makers' Part in TV Programming," *Advertising Age,* 31 October 1955, p. 16.

16. Jack L. Warner to Robert Kintner, 14 October 1955.

17. Robert Kintner to Jack L. Warner, 23 September 1955.

18. William T. Orr to Richard Diggs, Roy Huggins, Jerome Robinson, Ellis St. Joseph, 30 September 1955.

19. Ibid.

20. Robert Lewine to Monsanto, General Electric, Liggett and Myers, 27 September 1955.

21. J. English Smith to William T. Orr, 30 September 1955; J. English Smith to Robert Lewine, 27 September 1955.

22. Jack L. Warner to Robert Kintner, 28 September 1955.

23. Robert Kintner to Jack L. Warner, 20 September 1955; Jack L. Warner to Robert Kintner, 28 September 1955.

24. "The abc of ABC," p. 16; "ABC-TV in Laps of Pix Gods," *Variety*, 7 September 1955, p. 25; Richard Diggs to Robert Lewine, 6 October 1955.

25. "Gals Gang Up on Warner Bros. Presents," *Variety*, 28 September 1955, p. 31; Richard Diggs to Robert Lewine, 8 October 1955. At Diggs's insistence, Lewine commissioned the network's research department to conduct a study of the audience available during the time period and the performance of the various types of programming scheduled earlier than 9:00 P.M. Lewine returned a six-page report with statistics that refuted all of Warner's complaints. It concluded that the program was more important than the time slot in determining audience characteristics. "The program itself will determine the audience attracted," the report stated. Donald W. Coyle to Robert Lewine, 7 November 1955.

26. Art Silver to Jack L. Warner, 11 October 1955.

27. Jack L. Warner to Robert Kintner, 14 October 1955; Robert Kintner to Jack L. Warner, 18 October 1955.

28. For instance, when the major studios wanted to caricature TV, as in the 1954 film *Bigger Than Life*, the family television set emits only a raucous assault of stampedes, cavalry charges, and gunfire from these Westerns.

29. For further discussion of the movie Western in the context of 1950s Hollywood, see Christopher Anderson, "Jesse James, the Bourgeois Bandit: The Transformation of a Cultural Hero," *Cinema Journal* 26, no. 1 (Fall 1986): 43–64.

30. For instance, in an article titled "Can You Tell the Difference?," *TV Guide* offered readers a "scholarly survey" comparing adult and children's Westerns. See *TV Guide*, 21 September 1957, pp. 20–23. Film industry celebrities often joked about the differences. John Wayne once distinguished the classical Western from the "adult" Western by explaining that an adult Western was solved by talking the villain to death. Alfred Hitchcock observed that in the adult Western there seemed to be no more villains—"only good guys and neurotics." See Horace Newcomb, *TV: The Most Popular Art*, p. 62; "Hitchcock Steals Show As NBC-TV Close-Circuits Its 58–59 Lineup," *Variety*, 11 September 1957, p. 33.

31. J. Fred MacDonald, *Who Shot the Sheriff? The Rise and Fall of the Television Western*, p. 47. Throughout this critical history of TV Westerns, MacDonald unquestioningly uses the distinction between "adult" and "juvenile" Westerns as though these were natural categories, not cultural constructs. To see how this distinction is replicated in another recent work, see Gary A. Yoggy, "When Television Wore Six-Guns: Cowboy Heroes on TV," in Archie P. McDonald, ed., *Shooting Stars: Heroes and Heroines of Western Film*, pp. 218–257.

32. Of course, Wayne had a vested interest for offering his endorsement. Initially, *Gunsmoke* star James Arness was under contract to Wayne's movie production company.

33. Kintner, 21 and 23 September 1955; Jack L. Warner to Benjamin Kal-

menson, 21 September 1955; Robert Kintner to William M. Farrell, 27 September 1955.

34. Richard Diggs to Jack L. Warner, 28 September 1955; Richard Diggs to William T. Orr, 28 October 1955; Roy Huggins to [unnamed] Milliken, 31 October 1955.

35. "Review of Warner Bros. Presents—Cheyenne," *Variety*, 28 September 1955, p. 38 and 2 November 1955, p. 34.

36. This comparison is skewed slightly by the fact that the competition was relatively weak until 8:00 P.M.

37. Robert Kintner to Jack L. Warner, 18 October 1955 and 17 November 1955.

38. Robert Kintner to William T. Orr, 27 October 1955; Robert Kintner to Jack L. Warner, 17 November 1955; Ellis St. John to William T. Orr, 22 December 1955; Robert Lewine to Jack L. Warner, 14 December 1955.

39. Paul Stewart to Gary Stevens, 24 May 1955.

40. Warner Bros.–ABC, Contract.

41. Robert Kintner to Jack L. Warner, 17 November 1955; Bryan Moore to Stephen Karnot, 27 March 1962.

42. Richard Diggs to William T. Orr, 2 December 1955.

43. Robert Kintner to Jack L. Warner, 9 December 1955; "WB to Drop King's Row," *Variety*, 14 December 1955, p. 39; William T. Orr, Deposition, *Richard Sanville v. Warner Bros. Pictures, Inc.*, 25 April 1957.

44. Jack Warner to Robert Kintner, 14 October 1955. Kintner responded: "It is a cardinal rule of the business that unless the emergency is unbelievable, advertisers are not let out of commitments. In addition, in view of the ratings, we would have a difficult time replacing them" (Robert Kintner to Jack L. Warner, 18 October 1955).

45. "Metro Format Still Up in Air," *Variety*, 18 January 1956, p. 29; "Ingrid's 'Gaslight' for 'MGM Parade,'" *Variety*, 25 January 1956, p. 22; "Problems of 20th's Vidpix Subsidiary," *Variety*, 6 July 1955, p. 3; "Zanuck Steps into 20th Tele Setup at Behest of GE," *Variety*, 24 August 1955, p. 26; "Otto Lang Resigns 20th TV Subsid," *Variety*, 29 February 1956, p. 32. During this period, MGM also replaced executive producer Leslie Peterson with Leonard Spidelgass.

46. "Majors $2.875 Mil TV Rap," *Variety*, 1 February 1956, p. 37.

47. Robert Kintner to Jack L. Warner, 9 December 1955.

48. "Boston to Hollywood," *Time*, 21 May 1956, pp. 96–97.

9. REVIVING THE STUDIO SYSTEM AT WARNER BROS. TELEVISION

1. Robert Kintner to William T. Orr, 16 July 1956; "Cheseborough-Ponds Buys 'WB Presents,'" *Variety*, 8 August 1956, p. 23.

2. Richard Maltby, *Harmless Entertainment: Hollywood and the Ideology of Consensus*, pp. 49–50, 53.

3. "Big Warner Cash in Indie Films," *Variety*, 9 June 1954, p. 5; "Backlog Deal Timely Extra Coin for WB," *Variety*, 7 March 1956, p. 5; "Nearly All WB Net from 'Giant,'" *Variety*, 11 December 1957, p. 4.

4. "TV Shows Are a Gold Mine—But Hard to Dig," *Business Week,* 5 October 1957, p. 69.

5. Ibid., pp. 70, 74. For a discussion of the industry debate surrounding the rise of reruns, see William Boddy, *Fifties Television: The Industry and Its Critics,* p. 141; and Thomas Schatz, "Desilu, *I Love Lucy,* and the Rise of Network TV," in Robert J. Thompson and Gary Burns, eds., *Making Television: Authorship and the Production Process,* pp. 127–128.

6. "TV Shows Are a Gold Mine—But Hard to Dig," p. 74; "Official Absorbs 2 Four Star Cos.," *Broadcasting,* February 13, 1956, p. 41. For Reagan's account of the *General Electric Theater* deal, see Dan E. Moldea, *Dark Victory: Reagan, MCA, and the Mob,* pp. 167–201.

7. "ABC Dickering for Entire Pre-'48 WB Backlog," *Variety,* 1 February 1956, p. 1; "$15 Mil Profit in Warner Film Sale," *Broadcasting,* 27 August 1956, p. 69; Michele Hilmes, *Hollywood and Broadcasting: From Radio to Cable,* pp. 160–161.

8. Hilmes, *Hollywood and Broadcasting,* p. 160.

9. Leon Morse, "TV Film: The Battle for Power," *Television,* May 1959, p. 92.

10. "Boston to Hollywood," *Time,* 21 May 1956, pp. 96–97; "Warners Selling Studio Control," *New York Times,* 11 May 1956, p. 17; George Arnell, "Warners' 'Lock-Stock-&-Out,'" *Variety,* 2 May 1956, p. 1; George Arnell, "Events Move Fast at Warners," *Variety,* 9 May 1956, p. 3; "TV: Studio Meat, Exhibition Poison," *Variety,* 16 May 1953, p. 3; "Jerry Wald's Fabian Talks," *Variety,* 16 May 1956, p. 4.

11. "Bare Strife of Warner Clan," *Variety,* 30 May 1956, p. 3; "Jack L. Warner Heavily Loaded in WB Shares," *Variety,* 4 July 1956, p. 5; "Group Buys Control of Warner Bros.," *Broadcasting,* 16 July 1956, pp. 53–54; "A Bank's the Star," *Newsweek,* 23 July 1956, pp. 63–64.

12. "New Blood, New Bounce Make Hollywood Studios Hum," *Business Week,* 22 September 1956, pp. 106–116.

13. "AB-PT '55 Gain Up 74% from '54," *Variety,* 28 March 1956, p. 26; Herman Land, "ABC: An Evaluation," *Television,* December 1957, pp. 53, 86; "Goldenson Attempts Coup at ABC," *Broadcasting,* 15 October 1956, pp. 43–44; "Goldenson Gets His Way with ABC," *Broadcasting,* 22 October 1956, pp. 31–32.

14. "Treyz Getting Lots of Coin to Pour into ABC-TV Weak Spots," *Variety,* 7 November 1956, p. 25; Art Woodstone, "Guided by Clearance Problems, Goldenson Hews Close to Kintner Program Pattern," *Variety,* 12 December 1956, p. 36; "AB-PT Secures $60 Million Loan," *Broadcasting-Telecasting,* 24 December 1956, p. 58; Spencer Klan, "ABC-Paramount Moves In," *Fortune,* April 1957, pp. 132–134; "ABC-TV Ready to Pull Out the Stops," *Broadcasting,* 28 January 1957, pp. 27–28.

15. "Meeting with Robert Lewine," Warner Bros. File Memo, 24 October 1956; William T. Orr to Robert Lewine, 30 October 1956.

16. "The Major Studios Awaken to Television Lure," *Broadcasting,* 25 April 1955, p. 28; Script Progress Report, Sunset Productions, Inc., 14 May 1955;

Cedric Francis to Norman Moray, 8 September 1955; Daily Production Report, *Port of Call* TV Presentation, 11–12 January 1956; Cedric Francis to Jack M. Warner, 9 April 1956.

17. Cedric Francis to Norman Moray, 30 March 1956; Jack M. Warner to William T. Orr, 16 October 1956.

18. Cedric Francis to Norman Moray, 21 October 1955; Jack M. Warner to Cedric Francis, 4 April 1956; Cedric Francis to Jack M. Warner, 9 April 1956.

19. Cedric Francis to Thomas MacGowan, 20 December 1956, 16 January 1957; Thomas MacGowan to Cedric Francis, 12 February 1957 and 16 March 1957; Jack Emanuel to Bryan Moore, 14 April 1957; Analysis of Production #26903, "Warning of the Feather," n.d. [c. May 1957]; Bryan Moore to Cedric Francis, 4 February 1958.

20. Jack L. Warner to William T. Orr, 6 December 1956.

21. "WB/TV Forecasts $1 Million in TV Commercials First Year," *Broadcasting*, 15 July 1957, p. 49; "Warners Names TV Officials; Opens Ad, Film Accounts Offices," *Broadcasting*, 11 February 1957, p. 40; Certificate of Amendment of Certificate of Incorporation, Warner Bros. TV Commercial and Industrial Films, Inc., 4 April 1957 (Warner Bros. Pictures Collection, Princeton).

22. "Warner Bros. to Erect $1 Million TV Building," *Broadcasting*, 15 July 1957, p. 51.

23. Lynn Woolley, Robert W. Malsbary, and Robert G. Strange, Jr., *Warner Bros. Television: Every Show of the Fifties and Sixties Episode-by-Episode*, p. 210.

24. "ABC Bags Kaiser with $7 Million Sun. TV Billings," *Variety*, 3 July 1957, p. 23; "Weaver to 'Direct' Kaiser's TV Advertising," *Variety*, 17 July 1957, p. 21; "Maverick's Gotta Make It by Jan. 1 or Kaiser Vamps," *Variety*, 31 July 1957, p. 24; "Agreement for the Exploitation of Residual Rights in the Maverick Programs," 13 September 1957.

25. Roy Huggins to Bryan Moore, 13 February 1958.

26. Ibid.; Bob Johnson, "Code of the Westerns? Bah!" *TV Guide*, 1 August 1959, pp. 18–19.

27. Bryan Moore to William T. Orr, 9 December 1957; Bryan Moore to Jack Emanuel, 27 December 1957.

28. Roy Huggins to Bryan Moore, 13 February 1958.

29. William T. Orr to Steve Trilling, 20 December 1956.

30. Hugh Benson to William T. Orr, 19 April 1957.

31. William T. Orr to Robert Lewine, 30 October 1956.

32. William T. Orr to Jack L. Warner, 7 June 1957; William T. Orr to James Aubrey, 1 July 1957; Bryan Moore to William T. Orr, 1 October 1957; William T. Orr to Oliver Treyz and James Aubrey, 11 October 1957.

33. John P. Shanley, "Maverick's Creator—A Cynical Approach," *New York Times*, 5 April 1959, p. 15; Irv Broughton, *Producers on Producing: The Making of Film and Television*, p. 167.

34. "Happy Larceny," *Newsweek*, 19 January 1959, p. 82.

35. Marion Hargrove, "This Is a Television Cowboy?" *Life*, 19 January 1959, pp. 75–78.

36. "Maverick Pulls a Fastie," *Variety*, 2 October 1957, p. 27; "Maverick

Gives S & A a Hotfoot," *Variety*, 13 November 1957, p. 34; "Maverick Still Big ABC-TV Gun," *Variety*, 11 December 1957, p. 37; "Kaiser Just Crazy about TV," *Variety*, 25 June 1958, p. 25.

37. Bryan Moore to E. L. Depatie, 18 June 1956; Roy Huggins to William T. Orr, 3 February 1958; E. Henry Lewis to William T. Orr, 4 February 1958; William T. Orr to Bryan Moore, 13 March 1958.

38. Bryan Moore to Jack L. Warner, 5 September 1956.

39. William T. Orr, "The TV Stairway to Stardom," *Hollywood Reporter*, 24 November 1958.

40. William T. Orr to Steve Trilling, 20 March 1958.

41. C. F. Hendricks to William T. Orr, 17 May 1961.

42. "Ty Hardin Gallops In as Clint Walker Departs Cheyenne," *TV Guide*, 6 September 1958, pp. 24–26.

43. See Woolley, Malsbary, and Strange, *Warner Bros. Television*, pp. 208–210.

44. Bryan Moore to William T. Orr, 24 December 1959. For a complete list of network series in which ABC and CBS obtained a percentage of subsidiary rights during the period 1957–1968, see "Exhibit B: The Government's Case," *Variety*, 10 January 1990, p. 49.

45. William T. Orr to Benjamin Kalmenson, 28 February 1958.

46. Bryan Moore to William T. Orr, 7 October 1964.

47. Ibid.; Jack Emanuel to William T. Orr, 4 October 1957.

48. Roy Huggins to Jack Emanuel, 23 June 1958.

49. Bryan Moore to William T. Orr, 7 October 1964.

50. "Strategy for a Programming Battle," *Broadcasting*, 17 August 1959, p. 27; Albert R. Kroeger, "Miracle Worker of West 66th Street," *Television*, February 1961, p. 62; "The abc of ABC," *Forbes*, 15 June 1959, p. 15.

51. George Rosen, "WB-ABC: Love and Marriage," *Variety*, 14 January 1959, p. 33; Gene Arneel, "WB Policy: 12–14 a Year All Big," *Variety*, 12 November 1958, p. 4; Bob Chandler, "WB Shows the Way as Major Studios Embrace TV," *Variety*, 26 November 1958, p. 27; Warner Bros. Pictures, Inc., *Annual Report*, 1959; "JLW on WB's Outlook," *Variety*, 14 October 1959, p. 26; "TV Cited for WB Upsurge," *Variety*, 2 December 1959, p. 4.

52. J. Fred MacDonald, *Who Shot the Sheriff? The Rise and Fall of the Television Western*, p. 55.

53. "ABC-TV's 'Son of Sunset Strip,'" *Variety*, 8 April 1958, p. 26; "Showmen Don't Need a Pilot," *Variety*, 26 August 1959, p. 35; William T. Orr, Personal Interview, 28 October 1986, Los Angeles.

54. Charles F. Greenlaw to Hugh Benson, 9 February 1960; B. P. Meyer to William T. Orr, 20 July 1960; Dwight Whitney, "The Producer Assembles His Products," *TV Guide*, 31 October 1959, p. 21; Murray Horowitz, "WB's 'How High Is Up' Telepix Horizons as the 'Cadillac House' of Web Entries," *Variety*, 26 August 1959, p. 25.

55. "WB Announce Top Echelon TV Changes," *Broadcasting*, 20 February 1961, p. 136.

56. William T. Orr to All Producers, 17 July 1961.

57. Jack Emanuel to William Orr, 16 July 1957.

58. William T. Orr to All Producers, 25 June 1960.

59. For more on the development of the "continuity script" and its use as a blueprint for production in Hollywood, see Janet Staiger, "Blueprints for Feature Films: Hollywood's Continuity Scripts," in Tino Balio, ed., *The American Film Industry*, pp. 173–192.

60. William T. Orr to All Producers, 13 August 1958, 20 July 1959, 29 August 1960, 31 January 1961; James Moore to Jack Emanuel, 14 March 1959.

61. "Too Many Bad Directors Botching Up Good Scripts, Schermer Laments," *Variety*, 26 August 1959, p. 25.

62. William T. Orr to All Producers, 29 February 1959; William T. Orr to Andre De Toth, 9 October 1959.

63. William T. Orr to All Producers, 25 June 1960; William T. Orr to James Moore, 4 August 1958; James Moore to All Producers, 30 October 1958; Hugh Benson to All Producers, 18 August 1959.

64. Horowitz, "WB's 'How High Is Up,'" p. 25; "TV Cues Expansion of WB Contract Players," *Variety*, 8 April 1959, p. 30; Hy Hollinger, "New Faces—More Than Ever," *Variety*, 4 November 1959, p. 1.

65. Leon Morse, "TV Film: The Battle for Power," *Television*, May 1959, p. 92; "Warner Bros. TV Films at $30 Million Level," *Broadcasting*, 22 June 1959, p. 70; "WB: One Third of a Network," *Variety*, 6 May 1959, p. 27; "Int'l Note as WB Launches 3-Day Meet at Studio," *Variety*, 17 June 1959, p. 7. In June 1958 Warner Bros. sold the syndication rights to forty episodes of *Warner Bros. Presents* and *Conflict* that had been edited to fill half-hour time slots. This package did not include episodes of *Cheyenne*. See "NTA Acquires 40 Warner Films," *Broadcasting*, 23 June 1958, p. 44.

66. James B. Conkling to Karl Engeman, 7 July 1959.

67. "Warner Likes TV, Not Actors," *Variety*, 17 June 1959, p. 5.

68. Charles F. Greenlaw to Hugh Benson, 9 February 1960.

69. Whitney, "The Producer Assembles His Products," p. 22.

10. THE PATHOLOGY OF MASS PRODUCTION

1. "The Economics of Television Film Production," *Telefilm*, April 1960, 9. The discrepancy between the rankings in number of programs and production budgets is a result of the fact that the list does not distinguish between one-hour and half-hour programs.

2. See Timothy R. White, "Hollywood's Attempt at Appropriating Television: The Case of Paramount Pictures," in Tino Balio, ed., *Hollywood In the Age of Television*, pp. 145–163; and Timothy White, "Life after Divorce: The Corporate Strategy of Paramount Pictures Corporation in the 1950s," *Film History* 2 (1988): 99–119.

3. "TV Haunts 20th-Century Meet," *Broadcasting*, 26 May 1958, p. 62; "Twentieth Century–Fox in Turnabout," *Broadcasting*, 15 December 1958, p. 46; "Leavethes Exits Y & R for Top Job at 20th TV," *Variety*, 23 September 1959, p. 31.

4. Charles Barry, "The ABC's of Pilot-Making," *Variety*, 31 July 1957, p. 32;

"Metro's TV Aspirations," *Variety*, 2 October 1957, p. 28; "MGM Readies Heavy Film Barrage," *Broadcasting*, 19 January 1959, p. 82; "MGM-TV Shooting the Works for 60–61," *Variety*, 21 October 1959, p. 31.

5. "The Big Four," *Variety*, 28 January 1959, p. 25; "Hollywood in a Television Boom," *Broadcasting*, 26 November 1959, p. 90; "Six Major Studios Turning Out 37% of Web's Telepix," *Variety*, 1 July 1959, p. 31.

6. "Rich Getting Richer in TV Film Business," *Broadcasting*, 2 February 1959, pp. 39–40.

7. "The New Corporate Images," *Variety*, 4 February 1959, p. 31.

8. "Have Pilot Will Travel," *Telefilm*, November 1958, p. 7.

9. Leon Morse, "TV Film: The Battle for Power," *Television*, May 1959, p. 49; "The Economics of Television Film Production," p. 9.

10. Norris Willat, "Canned TV," *Barron's*, 24 July 1961, p. 5.

11. Edwin H. James, "The Boss Is His Brightest Star," *Television*, September 1962, p. 50.

12. "'Lucy' to Lucre: Arnaz Tells of Desilu's 6-yr Climb," *Broadcasting*, 24 December 1956, p. 46; Desilu Productions, Inc., American Stock Exchange Listing Application No. 3156, 5 March 1959.

13. "Powell's 4-Star Generalship," *Variety*, 11 February 1959, p. 29; John Bartlow Martin, "Television USA," Part 3: "The Master Planners," *Saturday Evening Post*, 4 November 1961, p. 37; "Wm. Morris's Favorite Client," *Variety*, 23 March 1960, p. 23; "Who Controls What in TV Film," *Broadcasting*, 17 October 1960, p. 34.

14. James, "The Boss Is His Biggest Star," pp. 50–65; Bob Chandler, "Ascendancy of Writer-Producers in Telefilm Area," *Variety*, 12 August 1959, p. 31; "4-Star's 'Salary Plus Participation' As Come-on for Creative Staffers," *Variety*, 23 September 1959, p. 25.

15. Edward T. Thompson, "There's No Show Business Like MCA's Show Business," *Fortune*, July 1960, pp. 160, 165; Dan E. Moldea, *Dark Victory: Reagan, MCA, and the Mob*, p. 5; David F. Prindle, *The Politics of Glamour: Ideology and Democracy in the Screen Actors Guild*, pp. 78–81.

16. Thompson, "There's No Show Business," pp. 115, 119.

17. Ibid., p. 115; Barton Hickman, "This Is MCA," *Television*, October 1957, p. 53; Morris Gehman, "The Hollywood Story," *Television*, September 1963, p. 36.

18. "SG at Peak with Pards," *Variety*, 20 August 1958, p. 30; "Case History of a TV Producer," *Variety*, 14 October 1959, p. 25.

19. "Screen Gems Has New Iron in Fire," *Broadcasting*, 14 April 1959, pp. 76–77; "Businessman Who Blends the World of TV and Movies," *Printer's Ink*, 1 May 1959, pp. 60–66; Bob Speilman, "Screen Gems: The Legacy of a Man," *Telefilm*, September 1959, pp. 18–26; Morse, "TV Film," p. 91.

20. Cedric Francis to James Moore, 3 March 1960; William T. Orr to All Producers, 6 February 1961.

21. Howie Horwitz to William T. Orr, 29 May 1959.

22. Charles Hoffman to William T. Orr, 30 June 1959; James Moore to Oren Haglund, 19 December 1959; William T. Orr to Oren Haglund, 1 August 1959.

23. James Barnett to Kent Williamson, 3 October 1960.

24. Richard Levinson and William Link, *Stay Tuned: An Inside Look at the Making of Prime-Time Television,* pp. 13–14.

25. Richard Gehman, "Inside the Walls of a Film Factory," pt. 2, *TV Guide,* 2 June 1962, p. 23.

26. James Moore to William T. Orr, 26 February 1960; James Barnett to Charles Sinclair, 16 May 1960.

27. Jack Emanuel to William T. Orr, 14 July 1959; James Barnett to William T. Orr, 18 November 1959; James Barnett to All Producers, 14 June 1961; Carl Stucke to Hugh Benson, 13 October 1961.

28. For accounts of many of these conflicts, see Thomas Schatz, *The Genius of the System: Hollywood Filmmaking in the Studio Era.*

29. "Walker Wins His War with Warners," *TV Guide,* 25 April 1959, p. 12; Dwight Whitney, "The Cowboy's Lament," *TV Guide,* 21 November 1959, pp. 17–19; Hugh Benson to Roy Obringer, 19 August 1960.

30. "Hutchins: 'You Get an Empty Feeling,'" *TV Guide,* 14 June 1961, pp. 14–15; "Unhappy People—with Spurs," *Newsweek,* 30 November 1959, p. 72.

31. Jack L. Warner to William T. Orr, 2 June 1960.

32. "SAG Cracks Down on WB Violation," *Variety,* 4 November 1959, p. 27; "Kookie Threatens to Walk Unless WB Ups His Ante," *Variety,* 18 November 1959, p. 31; "Unhappy People," pp. 71–72; Art Woodstone, "Television's Itchy Thesps," *Variety,* 14 June 1961, p. 34.

33. C. F. Hendricks to Jack L. Warner, 20 October 1960; Steve Trilling, File Notes, 10 November 1960.

34. *Warner Bros. Pictures, Inc. v. James Baumgarner,* District Court of Appeals of the State of California, Los Angeles, California, 27 November 1961; "Court to Release James Garner from Exclusive WB Pact," *Variety,* 14 December 1960, p. 35.

35. "Trapnell Vice Huggins as 'Maverick' Producer," *Variety,* 17 June 1959, p. 17; "WB Warns: 'Lay Off Roy Huggins,'" *Broadcasting,* 5 August 1959, p. 28.

36. "Sampling Vidfilm Wares," *Variety,* 11 January 1961, p. 23; Roy Huggins, Personal Interview, 25 May 1991, Los Angeles.

37. James Stabile to Benjamin Kalmenson, 16 February 1959, 31 March 1959.

38. "ABC Rise Ushers in New Three-Network Economy," *Variety,* 24 February 1960, p. 34; "Why the Rush to Hour-Long Shows?" *Broadcasting,* 17 April 1961, p. 108; "ABC-TV's 99% Control of Schedule," *Variety,* 16 March 1960, p. 25.

39. The figures were ABC, 58 percent; NBC, 60 percent; CBS, 69 percent. "The Swing to Network Control," *Broadcasting,* 16 May 1960, pp. 99–101; Murray Horowitz, "Webs Equity in Pix Shows," *Variety,* 19 April 1961, p. 31.

40. Disney is quoted in Leonard Maltin, *The Disney Films,* pp. 319–320; "Disney Eyeing Another Web?" *Variety,* 8 July 1959, p. 24; "ABC-TV, Disney Go to Court," *Broadcasting,* 6 July 1959, p. 76; John McDonald, "Now the Bankers Come to Disney," *Fortune,* May 1966, p. 226.

41. James Barnett to William T. Orr, 11 June 1962. Among the pilots that the network rejected were situation comedies like *Las Vegas Story* and *Room for One More* (which later ran for half a season in 1963), Westerns like *Billy the Kid* and *Doc Holliday*, and crime series like *House of Wax, Las Vegas File, Solitaire,* and *Public Enemy*.

42. "Webs Vidpix: Infant Mortality," *Variety*, 10 May 1961, p. 27.

43. Albert R. Kroeger, "New Dealer, New Hand for ABC-TV," *Television*, October 1963, p. 62; Deborah Haber, "The Studio That Came In from the Cold," *Television*, September 1965, p. 35.

44. Hugh Benson to Roy Obringer, 19 August 1960.

45. Jack L. Warner to Staff, 1 March 1961; "Orr in Gotham Reveals Rationale," *Variety*, 4 April 1961, p. 3; "WB Putting All Its Contracted TV Stars into a Feature Film," *Variety*, 8 November 1961, p. 23.

46. "Orr Gets Free Hand," *Broadcasting*, 12 March 1962, p. 10; "WB Now Invites All TV Comers," *Variety*, 7 March 1962, p. 13.

47. "New HQ for Webb," *Broadcasting*, 12 March 1962, p. 79.

48. Jack Gould, "TV: Discharge of Treyz," *New York Times*, 21 March 1962, p. 67; Leonard H. Goldenson, *Beating the Odds: The Untold Story behind the Rise of ABC*, pp. 172–180.

49. "Sales Hit $1.2 Million," *Broadcasting*, 25 March 1961, p. 52.

50. "Treyz Gets Post at Warner Bros.," *Broadcasting*, 2 April 1962, pp. 74–76; Oliver Treyz to Benjamin Kalmenson, 4 May 1962 and 15 May 1962; Oliver Treyz to Jack L. Warner, 5 June 1962.

51. "Treyz to Schick," *Broadcasting*, 25 March 1963, p. 5; Press Release, Warner Bros. Television, 20 February 1963; "Jack Webb Heads WB TV Prodn," *Variety*, 20 February 1963, p. 27; "Jack Webb to Head TV Production at Warners," *Broadcasting*, 25 February 1963, p. 54; "Warner Bros. Makes Big TV Plans," *Broadcasting*, 18 March 1963, p. 72; "Jack Webb Sets Up Participation Deals on WBTV Shows," *Variety*, 20 March 1963, p. 31.

52. "Major Casualties at Majors," *Variety*, 23 December 1963, p. 21; "Webb Sues Warner for Right to Work," *Broadcasting*, 6 January 1964, p. 61.

53. "Bill Orr's No. 2 Status," *Variety*, 18 December 1963, p. 21; "Orr Replaces Webb," *Broadcasting*, 23 December 1963, p. 10.

54. Notice of Special Meeting of Stockholders, Warner Bros. Pictures, Inc., 16 June 1967 (Warner Bros. Pictures Collection, Princeton); "Bob Lewine Gets Shut Out of W7," *Variety*, 22 November 1967, p. 24.

11. EPILOGUE

1. Tino Balio, ed., *The American Film Industry*, 435–436. See also William Lafferty, "Feature Films on Prime-Time Television," in Tino Balio, ed., *Hollywood in the Age of Television*, 235–256.

2. Ralph Tyler, "The Midas Touch in TV Film," *Television*, March 1966, pp. 45–57; Robert Gustafson, "'What's Happening to Our Pix Biz?' From Warner Bros. to Warner Communications, Inc.," in Tino Balio, ed., *The American Film Industry*, 576; Notice of Special Meeting of Stockholders, 16 June 1967.

3. "Kotler, Mitchell, and Hammer into Key Posts in W7's Television Setup," *Variety*, 29 November 1967, 24.

4. Gustafson, "'What's Happening,'" 576–578.

5. For suggestive discussions of television's archival function and the peculiar historical consciousness that it encourages, see James Naremore, "Authorship and the Cultural Politics of Film Criticism," *Film Quarterly* (Fall 1990): 17–18; and Jim Collins, "Television and Postmodernism," in Robert C. Allen, ed., *Channels of Discourse, Reassembled,* pp. 333–336.

Bibliography

ARCHIVES

Memoranda, production records, and business documents cited in this book are from the following collections:

David O. Selznick Collection, Harry Ransom Humanities Research Center, University of Texas at Austin.
Warner Bros. Pictures Collection, Department of Special Collections, Doheny Library, University of Southern California.
Warner Bros. Pictures Collection, Theatre Collection, Firestone Library, Princeton University.

Unless otherwise indicated, all Warner Bros. documents are from the collection at the University of Southern California. Documents from the collection at Princeton are identified in the notes. The chapter on *Disneyland* was based on secondary sources because the Disney organization refuses to provide access to its archives, which are generally open only to authors writing books that promote the Disney company and its products.

Television programs discussed in this book are from the Library of Congress collection or from private collections.

BOOKS, ARTICLES, AND DISSERTATIONS

The following newspapers, newsmagazines, and trade periodicals have published frequently on the film and broadcasting industries: *Advertising Age, American Cinematographer, Barron's, Broadcasting, Business Week, Forbes, Fortune, Hollywood Reporter, Life, New York Times, Newsweek, Printer's Ink, Sponsor, Telefilm, Television, Time, TV Guide, Variety*. For specific references from these publications, see the notes for each chapter.

Adorno, Theodor W. "Television and the Patterns of Mass Culture." In *Mass Culture: The Popular Arts in America,* edited by Bernard Rosenberg and David Manning White, pp. 474–488. New York: Free Press, 1957.
Allen, Craig. "Robert Montgomery Presents: Hollywood Debut in the Eisenhower White House." *Journal of Broadcasting and Electronic Media* 35, no. 4 (Fall 1991): 431–448.

Allen, Robert C. *Speaking of Soap Operas*. Chapel Hill: University of North Carolina Press, 1985.

Altman, Rick. "Television Sound." In *Television: The Critical View*. 4th ed., edited by Horace Newcomb, pp. 566–584. New York: Oxford University Press, 1987.

Anderson, Christopher. "Jesse James, the Bourgeois Bandit: The Transformation of a Cultural Hero." *Cinema Journal* 26, no. 1 (Fall 1986): 43–64.

Andrews, Bart. *The "I Love Lucy" Book*. New York: Doubleday, 1985.

Ardrey, Robert. "Hollywood: The Toll of the Frenzied Forties." *The Reporter*, 21 March 1957, pp. 29–33.

Arnaz, Desi. *A Book*. New York: William Morrow, 1976.

Backman, Jules. *The Economics of the Electrical Machinery Industry*. New York: New York University Press, 1962.

Balio, Tino. *United Artists: The Company Built by the Stars*. Madison: University of Wisconsin Press, 1976.

———. *United Artists: The Company That Changed the Film Industry*. Madison: University of Wisconsin Press, 1987.

———. "When Is an Independent Producer Independent?: The Case of United Artists after 1948." *The Velvet Light Trap* 22 (1986): 53–64.

———, ed. *The American Film Industry*. Rev. ed. Madison: University of Wisconsin Press, 1985.

———, ed. *Hollywood in the Age of Television*. Boston: Unwin Hyman, 1990.

Barnouw, Erik. *A History of Broadcasting in the United States*. Vol. 2, *The Golden Web*. New York: Oxford University Press, 1968.

———. *A History of Broadcasting in the United States*. Vol. 3, *The Image Empire*. New York: Oxford University Press, 1968.

———. *Tube of Plenty: The Evolution of American Television*. Rev. ed. New York: Oxford University Press, 1982.

Behlmer, Rudy. *Inside Warner Bros. (1935–1951)*. New York: Viking, 1985.

Bergreen, Lawrence. *Look Now, Pay Later: The Rise of Network Broadcasting*. New York: Mentor Books, 1980.

Bernays, Edward. *Biography of an Idea: Memoirs of a Public Relations Counsel*. New York: Simon and Schuster, 1965.

Bernstein, Matthew. "Fritz Lang, Incorporated." *The Velvet Light Trap* 22 (1986): 33–52.

Biskind, Peter. *Seeing Is Believing: How Hollywood Taught Us to Stop Worrying and Love the Fifties*. New York: Pantheon, 1983.

Boddy, William. *Fifties Television: The Industry and Its Critics*. Champaign: University of Illinois Press, 1990.

———. "The Studios Move into Prime Time: Hollywood and the Television Industry in the 1950s." *Cinema Journal* 24, no. 4 (Summer 1985): 23–37.

Boorstin, Daniel. *The Image: A Guide to Pseudo-Events in America*. New York: Harper and Row, 1964.

Bordwell, David, Janet Staiger, and Kristin Thompson. *The Classical Hollywood Cinema: Film Style and Mode of Production to 1960*. New York: Columbia University Press, 1985.

Borneman, Ernest. "Rebellion in Hollywood: A Study of Motion Picture Finance." *Harper's*, October 1946, pp. 337–343.

Boyer, Paul. *By the Bomb's Early Light: American Thought and Culture at the Dawn of the Atomic Age*. New York: Pantheon, 1985.

Brooks, Tim, and Earle Marsh. *The Complete Directory to Prime Time Network TV Shows*. 3d ed. New York: Ballantine Books, 1985.

Broughton, Irv. *Producers on Producing: The Making of Film and Television*. Jefferson, N.C.: McFarland, 1986.

Browne, Nick. "The Political Economy of the Television (Super) Text." In *Television: The Critical View*. 4th ed., edited by Horace Newcomb, pp. 585–599. New York: Oxford University Press, 1987.

Buchsbaum, Jonathon. "Zukor Buys Protection: The Paramount Stock Purchase of 1929." *Cine-Tracts* 2 (Summer/Fall 1979): 49–62.

Buscombe, Edward. "Thinking It Differently: Television and the Film Industry." *Quarterly Review of Film Studies* 9, no. 3 (Summer 1984): 196–203.

Buxton, Frank, and Bill Owen. *The Big Broadcast, 1920–1950*. Rev. ed. New York: Avon Books, 1972.

Cardiff, David, and Paddy Scannell. "Broadcasting and National Unity." In *Impacts and Influences: Essays on Media Power in the Twentieth Century*, edited by James Curran, Anthony Smith, and Pauline Wingate, pp. 157–173. London: Methuen, 1987.

Carey, James W. *Communication As Culture: Essays on Media and Society*. Boston: Unwin Hyman, 1989.

Caute, David. *The Great Fear: The Anti-Communist Purge under Truman and Eisenhower*. New York: Simon and Schuster, 1978.

Ceplair, Larry, and Steven Englund. *The Inquisition in Hollywood: Politics in the Film Community, 1930–1960*. New York: Anchor Press, 1980.

Collins, Jim. "Television and Postmodernism." In *Channels of Discourse, Reassembled*. 2d ed., edited by Robert C. Allen, pp. 327–353. Chapel Hill: University of North Carolina Press, 1992.

Conant, Michael. *Antitrust in the Motion Picture Industry: Economic and Legal Analysis*. Berkeley: University of California Press, 1960.

Dayan, Daniel, and Elihu Katz. "Performing Media Events." In *Impacts and Influences: Essays on Media Power in the Twentieth Century*, edited by James Curran, Anthony Smith, and Pauline Wingate, pp. 174–197. London: Methuen, 1987.

DeCordova, Richard. *Picture Personalities: The Emergence of the Star System in America*. Champagne: University of Illinois Press, 1990.

DeLong, Thomas A. "Specials on the Radio Airwaves." *Sperdvac Radiogram*, July 1992, pp. 7–14.

De Mille, Cecil B. *The Autobiography of Cecil B. De Mille*. Englewood Cliffs, N.J.: Prentice-Hall, 1959.

Doane, Mary Ann. *The Desire to Desire: The Woman's Film of the 1940s*. Bloomington: Indiana University Press, 1987.

Dombkowski, Dennis J. "Film and Television: An Analytical History of Economic and Creative Integration." Ph.D. dissertation, University of Illinois, 1982.

Dyer, Richard. *Heavenly Bodies: Film Stars and Society*. New York: St. Martin's Press, 1986.

Eckert, Charles. "The Carole Lombard in Macy's Window." *Quarterly Review of Film Studies* 3, no. 1 (Winter 1978): 1–21.

Ellis, John. *Visible Fictions*. London: Routledge and Kegan Paul, 1982.

Ewen, Stuart. *Captains of Consciousness: Advertising and the Social Roots of Consumer Culture*. New York: McGraw-Hill, 1976.

Fiske, John. *Television Culture*. New York: Routledge, 1987.

Flynn, Charles, and Todd McCarthy. "The Economic Imperative: Why Was the B Movie Necessary?" In *Kings of the Bs: Working within the Hollywood System*, edited by Charles Flynn and Todd McCarthy, pp. 13–43. New York: Dutton, 1975.

Ford, Daniel. *The Cult of the Atom: The Secret Papers of the Atomic Energy Commission*. New York: Simon and Schuster, 1982.

Gaines, Jane. "The Queen Christina Tie-Ups: Convergence of Show Window and Screen." *Quarterly Review of Film & Video* 11, no. 1 (1989): 35–60.

Gitlin, Todd. "Down the Tubes." In *Seeing through Movies*, edited by Mark Crispin Miller, pp. 14–48. New York: Pantheon, 1990.

Goldenson, Leonard H. *Beating the Odds: The Untold Story behind the Rise of ABC*. New York: Scribner's, 1991.

Gomery, Douglas. "The Coming of Sound: Technological Change in the American Film Industry." In *The American Film Industry*. Rev. ed., edited by Tino Balio, pp. 229–251. Madison: University of Wisconsin Press, 1985.

———. "The Coming of Television and the 'Lost' Motion Picture Audience." *Journal of Film and Video* 38 (Summer 1985): 5–11.

———. "Failed Opportunities: The Integration of the Motion Picture and TV Industries." *Quarterly Review of Film Studies* 9, no. 3 (Summer 1984): 219–228.

———. *The Hollywood Studio System*. New York: St. Martin's Press, 1986.

Greene, Katherine, and Richard Greene. *The Man behind the Magic: The Story of Walt Disney*. New York: Viking, 1991.

Gruening, Ernest. *The Public Pays: A Study of Power Propaganda*. New York: Vanguard Press, 1931.

Guback, Thomas H. "Hollywood's International Market." In *The American Film Industry*. Rev. ed., edited by Tino Balio, pp. 463–486. Madison: University of Wisconsin Press, 1985.

Gustafson, Robert. "'What's Happening to Our Pix Biz?' From Warner Bros. to Warner Communications, Inc." In *The American Film Industry*. Rev. ed., edited by Tino Balio, pp. 574–586. Madison: University of Wisconsin Press, 1985.

Hagopian, Kevin. "Declaration of Independence: A History of Cagney Productions." *The Velvet Light Trap* 22 (1986): 16–32.

Halberstam, David. *The Powers That Be*. New York: Dell, 1979.

Harris, Neil. *Humbug: The Art of P. T. Barnum*. Chicago: University of Chicago Press, 1973.

Haver, Ronald. *David O. Selznick's Hollywood*. New York: Bonanza Books, 1980.

Hilgartner, Stephen, Richard C. Bell, and Rory O'Connor. *Nukespeak: Nuclear Language, Visions, and Mindset.* San Francisco: Sierra Club Books, 1982.

Hilmes, Michele. *Hollywood and Broadcasting: From Radio to Cable.* Champaign: University of Illinois Press, 1990.

"An Historic Step Forward." *Edison Electric Institute Bulletin,* September 1954, pp. 307, 310.

Horkheimer, Max, and Theodor W. Adorno. *Dialectic of Enlightenment.* New York: Continuum, 1987.

Horrigan, Brian. "The Home of Tomorrow." In *Imagining Tomorrow: History, Technology, and the American Future,* edited by Joseph J. Corn, pp. 137–163. Cambridge: MIT Press, 1986.

Huettig, Mae D. "Economic Control of the Motion Picture Industry." In *The American Film Industry.* Rev. ed., edited by Tino Balio, pp. 285–310. Madison: University of Wisconsin Press, 1985.

Hughes, Thomas P. *Networks of Power: Electrification in Western Society, 1880–1930.* Baltimore: Johns Hopkins University Press, 1985.

Jewell, Richard B. "Hollywood and Radio: Competition and Partnership in the 1930s." *Historical Journal of Film, Radio, and Television* 4, no. 2 (1984): 125–141.

Kepley, Jr., Vance. "The Weaver Years at NBC." *Wide Angle* 12, no. 2 (April 1990): 46–63.

Kihlstedt, Folke T. "Utopia Realized: The World's Fairs of the 1930s." In *Imagining Tomorrow: History, Technology, and the American Future,* edited by Joseph J. Corn, pp. 97–118. Cambridge: MIT Press, 1986.

King, Margaret Jane. "The Davy Crockett Craze: A Case Study in Popular Culture." Ph.D. dissertation, University of Hawaii, 1976.

Lafferty, William. "Feature Films on Prime-Time Television." In *Hollywood in the Age of Television,* edited by Tino Balio, pp. 235–256. Boston: Unwin Hyman, 1990.

———. "'No Attempt at Artiness, Profundity, or Significance': *Fireside Theater* and the Rise of Filmed Television Programming." *Cinema Journal* 27, no. 1 (Fall 1987): 23–46.

Larson, David Alan. "Integration and Attempted Integration between the Motion Picture and Television Industries through 1956." Ph.D. dissertation, Ohio University, 1979.

Levinson, Richard, and William Link. *Stay Tuned: An Inside Look at the Making of Prime-Time Television.* New York: St. Martin's Press, 1981.

Lewis, Edwin H. *Marketing Electrical Apparatus and Supplies.* New York: McGraw-Hill, 1961.

Luce, D. C. "Report on Light's Diamond Jubilee." *Edison Electric Institute Bulletin,* December 1954, pp. 401–403.

Lucich, Bernard. "*The Lux Radio Theatre.*" In *American Broadcasting: A Sourcebook on the History of Radio and Television,* edited by Lawrence W. Lichty and Malachi C. Topping, pp. 391–394. New York: Hastings House, 1975.

MacCabe, Colin. "The Discursive and the Ideological in Film: Notes on the Conditions of Political Intervention." *Screen* 19, no. 4 (Winter 1978–1979): 29–43.

MacCannell, Dean. *The Tourist: A New Theory of the Leisure Class*. New York: Schocken Books, 1976.

MacDonald, J. Fred. *One Nation under Television: The Rise and Decline of Network TV*. New York: Pantheon, 1990.

———. *Who Shot the Sheriff? The Rise and Fall of the Television Western*. New York: Praeger, 1987.

MacKaye, Milton. "The Big Brawl: Hollywood versus Television." *Saturday Evening Post*. Part 1, 19 January 1952, pp. 17–19, 70–72; Part 2, 26 January 1952, pp. 30, 119–122; Part 3, 2 February 1952, pp. 30, 100–102.

Maltby, Richard. *Harmless Entertainment: Hollywood and the Ideology of Consensus*. Metuchen, N.J.: Scarecrow Press, 1983.

Maltin, Leonard. *The Disney Films*. 2d ed. New York: Crown Publishers, 1984.

———. *The Great Movie Shorts*. New York: Bonanza Books, 1972.

Marc, David. *Demographic Vistas: Television in American Culture*. Philadelphia: University of Pennsylvania Press, 1984.

Martin, John Bartlow. "Television USA." Part 1: "Wasteland or Wonderland?" *Saturday Evening Post*, 21 October 1961, pp. 19–25; Part 2: "Battle of the Big Three." *Saturday Evening Post*, 28 October 1961, pp. 56–58, 60–62; Part 3: "The Master Planners." *Saturday Evening Post*, 4 November 1961, pp. 34, 36–39.

Marvin, Carolyn. "Dazzling the Multitude: Imagining the Electric Light as a Communications Medium." In *Imagining Tomorrow: History, Technology, and the American Future*, edited by Joseph J. Corn, pp. 202–218. Cambridge: MIT Press, 1986.

———. *When Old Technologies Were New: Thinking about Electric Communication in the Late Nineteenth Century*. New York: Oxford University Press, 1988.

Mayerle, Judine. "The Development of the Television Variety Show as a Major Program Genre at the National Broadcasting Company, 1946–1956." Ph.D. dissertation, Northwestern University, 1983.

McDonald, Archie P. *Shooting Stars: Heroes and Heroines of Western Film*. Bloomington: Indiana University Press, 1987.

Miller, Mark Crispin. "End of Story." In *Seeing through Movies*, edited by Mark Crispin Miller, pp. 186–246. New York: Pantheon, 1990.

Moldea, Dan E. *Dark Victory: Reagan, MCA, and the Mob*. New York: Viking, 1986.

Moore, Barbara. "The Cisco Kid and Friends: The Syndication of Television Series from 1948 to 1952." *Journal of Popular Film and Television* 8 (Spring 1980): 26–33.

"More on What the Companies Are Doing." *Edison Electric Institute Bulletin*, September 1954, pp. 308–310.

Mulvey, Laura. "Melodrama In and Out of the Home." In *High Theory/Low Culture: Analyzing Popular Television and Film*, edited by Colin MacCabe, pp. 80–100. New York: St. Martin's Press, 1986.

Murray, Lawrence L. "Complacency, Competition, Cooperation: The Film Industry Responds to the Challenge of Television." *Journal of Popular Film* 6, no. 1 (1977): 47–68.

Naremore, James. "Authorship and the Cultural Politics of Film Criticism." *Film Quarterly* (Fall 1990): 14–23.

Navasky, Victor. *Naming Names*. New York: Viking Press, 1980.

Newcomb, Horace. *TV: The Most Popular Art*. New York: Anchor Books, 1974.

———, ed. *Television: The Critical View*. 4th ed. New York: Oxford University Press, 1987.

Newcomb, Horace, and Robert Alley. *The Producer's Medium: Conversations with Creators of American TV*. New York: Oxford University Press, 1983.

Nye, David E. *Image Worlds: Corporate Identities at General Electric, 1890–1939*. Cambridge: MIT Press, 1985.

Prindle, David F. *The Politics of Glamour: Ideology and Democracy in the Screen Actors Guild*. Madison: University of Wisconsin Press, 1988.

Pringle, Peter, and James Spigelman. *The Nuclear Barons*. New York: Holt, Rinehart and Winston, 1981.

Quinlan, Sterling. *Inside ABC: The American Broadcasting Company's Rise to Power*. New York: Hastings House, 1979.

Randolph, Richard, and Scott Ridley. *Power Struggle: The Hundred-Year War over Electricity*. New York: Harper and Row Publishers, 1986.

Richards, Thomas. *The Commodity Culture of Victorian England: Advertising and Spectacle, 1851–1914*. Stanford: Stanford University Press, 1990.

Rydell, Robert W. *All the World's a Fair: Visions of Empire at American International Expositions, 1876–1916*. Chicago: University of Chicago Press, 1984.

Sayre, Nora. *Running Time: The Films of the Cold War*. New York: Dial Press, 1982.

Schatz, Thomas. "Desilu, *I Love Lucy*, and the Rise of Network TV." In *Making Television: Authorship and the Production Process*, edited by Robert J. Thompson and Gary Burns, pp. 117–136. New York: Praeger, 1990.

———. *The Genius of the System: Hollywood Filmmaking in the Studio Era*. New York: Pantheon, 1989.

Schickel, Richard. *The Disney Version*. New York: Simon and Schuster, 1968.

Smoodin, Eric. "Motion Pictures and Television, 1930–1945: A Pre-History of Relations between the Two Media." *Journal of the University Film and Video Association* 34, no. 3 (Summer 1982): 3–8.

Sontag, Susan. *Against Interpretation*. New York: Dell Publishing, 1966.

Spigel, Lynn. *Make Room for TV: Television and the Family Ideal in Postwar America*. Chicago: University of Chicago Press, 1992.

Staiger, Janet. "Blueprints for Feature Films: Hollywood's Continuity Scripts." In *The American Film Industry*. Rev. ed., edited by Tino Balio, pp. 173–192. Madison: University of Wisconsin Press, 1985.

———. "Individualism versus Collectivism." *Screen* 24, nos. 4–5 (July–August 1983): 68–79.

Steinbeck, John. *The Red Pony*. New York: Viking Press, 1945.

"Still More on What the Companies Did on Light's Diamond Jubilee." *Edison Electric Institute Bulletin*, December 1954, pp. 405–414.

Susman, Warren J. *Culture as History: The Transformation of American Society in the Twentieth Century*. New York: Pantheon, 1984.

Taylor, John. *Storming the Magic Kingdom: Wall Street, the Raiders, and the Battle for Disney*. New York: Alfred A. Knopf, 1987.

Vennard, Edwin. "This I Believe." *Edison Electric Institute Bulletin*, June 1957, pp. 215–218, 224.

Vianello, Robert. "The Rise of the Telefilm and the Networks' Hegemony over the Motion Picture Industry." *Quarterly Review of Film Studies* 9, no. 3 (Summer 1984): 204–218.

Wachhorst, Wyn. *Thomas Alva Edison: An American Myth*. Cambridge: MIT Press, 1981.

"What the Chairmen Say." *Edison Electric Institute Bulletin*, August 1954, pp. 272–273.

"What the Companies Are Doing." *Edison Electric Institute Bulletin*, August 1954, pp. 276–286.

White, Timothy R. "Hollywood's Attempt at Appropriating Television: The Case of Paramount Pictures." In *Hollywood in the Age of Television*, edited by Tino Balio, pp. 145–163. Boston: Unwin Hyman, 1990.

———. "Hollywood's Attempt to Appropriate Television: The Case of Paramount Pictures." Ph.D. dissertation, University of Wisconsin-Madison, 1990.

———. "Hollywood on (Re)Trial: The American Broadcasting–United Paramount Merger Hearing." *Cinema Journal* 31, no. 3 (Spring 1992): 19–36.

———. "Life after Divorce: The Corporate Strategy of Paramount Pictures Corporation in the 1950s," *Film History* 2 (1988): 99–119.

Whiteside, Thomas. "The Communicator." Part 1: "Athens Starts Pouring In." *The New Yorker*, 16 October 1954, pp. 37–38; Part 2: "What about the Gratitude Factor?" *The New Yorker*, 23 October 1954, pp. 43–44, 57–69.

Williams, Raymond. *Television: Technology and Cultural Form*. New York: Schocken Books, 1974.

Wilson, Charles E. "The Meaning of Light's Diamond Jubilee." *Edison Electric Institute Bulletin*, June 1954, pp. 187–192.

Woolley, Lynn, Robert W. Malsbary, and Robert G. Strange, Jr. *Warner Bros. Television: Every Show of the Fifties and Sixties Episode-by-Episode*. Jefferson, N.C.: McFarland, 1985.

Yoggy, Gary A. "When Television Wore Six-Guns: Cowboy Heroes on TV." In *Shooting Stars: Heroes and Heroines of Western Film*, edited by Archie P. McDonald, pp. 218–257. Bloomington: Indiana University Press, 1987.

DOCUMENTS: GOVERNMENT, BUSINESS, AND LEGAL

Desilu Productions, Inc. "American Stock Exchange Listing." Application No. 3156, 5 March 1959.

U.S. Federal Communications Commission, Office of Network Study. *Second Interim Report: Network Program Procurement Practices*. Washington, D.C.: Government Printing Office, 1965.

U.S. Senate Select Committee on Small Business. *Motion Picture Trade Practices—1956*. Report of Senate Select Committee on Small Business. 84th Congress, 2d Session, 1956.

Warner Bros. Pictures, Inc. v. James Baumgarner. District Court of Appeals of the State of California. Los Angeles, California, 27 November 1961.

PERSONAL INTERVIEWS
Richard Bare, Personal Interview, Los Angeles, 28 October 1986.
Hugh Benson, Personal Interview, Los Angeles, 29 October 1986.
Roy Huggins, Personal Interview, Los Angeles, 25 May 1991.
William T. Orr, Personal Interview, Los Angeles, 28 October 1986.
Harry Tatleman, Personal Interview, Los Angeles, 29 October 1986.

Index